A Latin Reader for Colleges

A Latin Reader
for Colleges

Harry L. Levy

THE UNIVERSITY OF CHICAGO PRESS

Chicago & London

The University of Chicago Press, Chicago 60637
The University of Chicago Press, Ltd., London

International Standard Book Number: 0-226-47601-4
Library of Congress Catalog Card Number: 62-18119

⊚ The paper used in this publication meets the minimum
requirements of the American National Standard for
Information Sciences—Permanence of Paper for Printed
Library Materials, ANSI Z39.48—1984.

PREFACE

THIS book is the outgrowth of several years' experience with the third semester of elementary Latin at Hunter College of the City of New York. In this course, reading material similar to, and in considerable part identical with, that presented here has been found not only to be instructive and interesting in itself, but also to serve as a very satisfactory bridge between the beginner's book and the Orations of Cicero.

The passages to be read consist of selections from Aulus Gellius, Nepos, Caesar, and Phaedrus (see pages 193-194). The selections from Gellius have been rather freely adapted. The other selections are presented with little change, save for the conversion of several passages in Selection 59 from indirect to direct discourse, as noted in the footnote to page 193. The selections and adaptations are based on the Teubner texts of the four authors.

The notes are, it is believed, suited to the abilities of students of college grade; no attempt has been made to over-simplify the problems involved. On the historical side, the notes are perhaps somewhat fuller than is customary; if, however, they succeed in clothing with some degree of reality the persons, places, and institutions mentioned in the text, the author feels that the space devoted to them will be fully justified.

Grammatical constructions which the student is presumed to have studied previously are reviewed in the numbered sections of the Grammatical Outline, pages 161-183, with examples taken from, or based upon, the text. Where classes have not learned certain of these constructions, it will be well to assign the appropriate section before the first appearance of the construction in the text.

New grammatical constructions are explained in the notes,

v

and merely referred to in the Grammatical Outline, rather than
vice versa. The author believes that, in a reading course, the
best method of implanting a new construction in a student's
mind is to discuss it in connection with, and as far as possible
in terms of, the passage in which it is first met, and to make
several subsequent references to that passage.

The author is greatly indebted to Nall's *Stories from Aulus
Gellius* (London, Macmillan, 1902), a book which, in conjunction with a mimeographed supplement prepared by the present
author, has been in use at Hunter College for several years. In
connection with Book I of the *Noctēs Atticae*, the edition of
Hornsby (Dublin, Hodges, Figgis and Co., 1936) has been
helpful. In preparing the notes on the passages from Caesar,
the editions of Meusel (Berlin, Weidmann, 1913) and of Holmes
(Oxford, Clarendon Press, 1914) were of assistance. Considerable use was made of Hale and Buck's *Latin Grammar* (Boston,
Ginn, 1903), which was followed both in the matter of quanti-
ties and in the matter of the assimilation of prefixes. The
etymologies given in the vocabulary are based on Ernout and
Meillet's *Dictionnaire Étymologique de la Langue Latine* (Paris,
Klincksieck, 1932). Though the author feels a certain doubt
concerning some of the theories there advanced, he deemed it
best to follow a standard work consistently.

The author wishes to make grateful acknowledgment to
Professor Clinton W. Keyes of Columbia University, who read
the manuscript in its early stages and offered much valuable
advice and encouragement; to Professor Casper J. Kraemer, Jr.,
of New York University, the publishers' Classical Editor, and
to Professor E. Adelaide Hahn, Chairman of the Department of
Classics at Hunter College, both of whom read the entire manuscript with minute care, and gave it the benefit of their thorough
scholarship; and to Dr. Meriwether Stuart of the Department
of Classics at Hunter College, who assisted materially in check-
ing the quantity-marks of the Latin text.

H.L.L.

TABLE OF CONTENTS

INTRODUCTION

SELECTIONS FOR READING

I. AULUS GELLIUS

II. CORNELIUS NEPOS

A Latin Reader for Colleges

INTRODUCTION

I. Aulus Gellius

THE FIRST fifty selections in this book are adaptations of passages from the *Noctēs Atticae* of Aulus Gellius.

Of the life of Aulus Gellius we know very little; we have no exact indication of his birthplace or of the dates of his birth and death. From certain statements in the *Noctēs Atticae*, it 5 is considered probable that he was born about 125 A. D.; and his literary activity does not seem to have continued beyond the year 165. If he was not born at Rome, he certainly came to that city very early in life; there he studied "grammar"[1] and rhetoric[2] under some of the most celebrated teachers of the 10 age. He seems to have chosen law for his profession; for some time he served as judge in the lower civil courts. At an undetermined point in his career he spent at least a year in Athens, where he devoted himself to philosophy, a study upon which he had probably spent some time in Rome. Of his later life, 15 nothing is known save that he had several children, to whom he dedicated his *Noctēs Atticae*.

From the meager indications referred to above, one thing is clear: Gellius' literary activity fell largely, if not entirely, within the reigns of Antoninus Pius (138–161 A.D.) and of Marcus 20 Aurelius (161–180 A.D.). At that time, says Gibbon,[3] ". . . the empire of Rome comprehended the fairest part of the earth, and the most civilized portion of mankind. The frontiers of

---

[1] By this term the Romans denoted a study of language and literature, corresponding roughly to that given in our high schools; incidental instruction in history, geography, and mythology was given. Additional subjects, such as geometry and music, were sometimes studied.

[2] See Note 25 24*b*, page 106.

[3] Gibbon, Edward, *The History of the Decline and Fall of the Roman Empire*, Chapter I, first paragraph.

that extensive monarchy were guarded by ancient renown and disciplined valor. . . . The peaceful inhabitants enjoyed . . . the advantages of wealth and luxury." Though the Roman legions might be called to battle on distant frontiers, within 5 the Empire men enjoyed a period of profound peace such as Europe has not known since that time. It was, however, a peace which was ordered from above, and regulated by the all-powerful will of the Emperor. Such a condition allows the leisure but does not provide the stimulation for original literary 10 productions of genius. Latin literature thrived best in times of stress; most of its great works were produced in the tumult of the Punic Wars and during the conquest of the East, in the social upheavals of the Gracchan period, in the struggles between Marius and Sulla, in the death throes of the Re- 15 public and the birth pains of the Empire. Even before the time we are discussing, the productive literary genius of the Romans, with rare exceptions, had worn itself out; literary men turned their faces back upon the past and studied the masterpieces of a more virile age.

20 At the time of which we speak, the pendulum had swung so far back that men read the pioneer productions of Cato and Ennius rather than the polished masterpieces of Cicero and Vergil; but, at any rate, they studied and commented upon the works of their great predecessors instead of producing new 25 works of current inspiration.

Aulus Gellius was typical of the age in which he lived. The *Noctēs Atticae*, his only extant work, and probably the only one he ever wrote, is the fruit of extensive reading rather than of original thought. The book derives its somewhat fanciful title 30 from the fact that it was begun during the long winter evenings of Gellius' stay at Athens. It was his habit, as he read, to ·make notes and excerpts on matters which he considered of interest. When he had a large number of these on hand, he assembled them, together with certain anecdotes from his own 35 experience, and made of the whole a miscellany of the type which was popular at the time. He tells us expressly that he made no attempt to introduce an ordered plan into the work;

the notes in the completed book follow the fortuitous arrangement into which they fell as he collected them.

There is the widest possible variety of subject matter. Notes on history, science, law, literature, grammar, and philosophy; quotations from ancient authors, anecdotes about famous men 5 of the past or of Gellius' own day—all these are crowded helter-skelter into the twenty "books"[4] which compose the *Noctēs Atticae.*

Gellius' manner of writing is also characteristic of the age in which he lived; it is by no means a model of Latin prose style. 10 The terseness and vigor of an earlier day had given way to the wordiness and repetition which are symptomatic of weakness. The *Noctēs Atticae* will never be read as great literature; the interest of the work is almost wholly in its content.

For the purposes of this reader, passages which seemed of 15 interest to modern students were selected.. These were then adapted by removing unimportant details or needless obscurities, by condensing Gellius' prolixity, and occasionally by rewriting so as to bring the language into conformity with the standards of the Latin which the student will meet in his later 20 studies. On the whole, however, the student will derive from these selections a fairly accurate idea of Gellius' work.[5]

II. Cornelius Nepos

Selections 51 to 57 are chosen, and slightly adapted, from the works of Cornelius Nepos,[6] a biographer and minor historian of the first century B.C. The dates of his birth and 25 death are unknown, but he is believed to have lived from about 100 B.C. to about 25 B.C. He was born in Northern Italy, but seems to have spent much of his life in Rome. He took

---

[4] The ancients used the term "book" for an amount of writing which could conveniently fit on the pages of one papyrus roll, or "volume"; the term corresponds roughly to a rather long chapter of a modern work.

[5] Only one passage (Selection 42) is presented exactly as it has come down to us in the manuscripts; in several others, the changes are so slight as to be negligible.

[6] His *praenōmen* (see page 8) is unknown.

no part in political affairs, but was on friendly terms with
Cicero, as well as with the poet Catullus.

The works of Nepos included love poems, an outline of world
history called *Chronica*, the *Exempla*,[7] biographies of Cato the
5 Censor and of Cicero, and the *Dē Virīs Illūstribus* (*Lives of
Famous Men*). All of these have perished except the last, of
which portions survive. Our selections are taken from a section of the *Dē Virīs Illūstribus* called "Dē Excellentibus Ducibus
Exterārum Gentium" ("Eminent Generals of Foreign Na-
10 tions").

III. Julius Caesar

Selections 58 and 59 are taken from the works of Julius
Caesar, one of the most important figures in Roman history.
C. Julius Caesar was born in 100 B.C. of an ancient and
noble family. In his political career, however, he attached
15 himself to the democratic or "popular" party; with this he remained until he outgrew the need for partisan support.

Caesar began his public career in 68 B.C. as *Quaestor*, that
is, Financial Secretary, to the Governor of Further Spain, who
entrusted him in addition with certain judicial duties. In 65
20 he was *Aedile*, or Commissioner of Public Works, Markets, and
Games; during this year his lavish expenditures from his own
purse endeared him to the populace. He served as *Praetor*, or
Judge, in 62, and spent the following year in Further Spain,
this time as *Propraetor*, or Governor. Upon his return to Rome,
25 he associated himself with Pompey, the leading military hero,
and Crassus, the richest man in Rome, in a coalition for mutual
advancement. This triple alliance of political sagacity, military prestige, and enormous wealth, later known as the First
Triumvirate, proceeded to crush all opposition and to take
30 complete control of the Roman governmental machinery.

Caesar was elected to the consulship[8] for the year 59. In

---

[7] See Note **29** 18, page 111.
[8] See Note **13** 1c, pages 79–80, third paragraph.

addition to putting into effect the legislative program of the
Triumvirate, Caesar secured for himself the governorship for
five years (subsequently extended) of a group of territories
which included the provinces of Cisalpine Gaul[9] and of Transalpine Gaul. The latter consisted merely of the southeastern 5
part of what is now France; it comprised the coastal district
from the Pyrenees to the Alps, and was bounded on the north
by Lake Geneva and the Rhone, whence the frontier ran along
the Cevennes Mountains and the Tarn down into the center of
the Pyrenees. Using the Province of Transalpine Gaul as his 10
base of operations, Caesar availed himself of one pretext after
another to carry on a series of campaigns, which by 51 B.C.
made him the master of all Gaul[10] and head of a large army
entirely devoted to his interests.

This achievement was most momentous for the future of 15
Europe: it was Caesar's conquest of Gaul which determined
that the boundary between the Latin and the Germanic peoples
was to be the River Rhine, and not the Pyrenees and the Alps.
It seems hardly likely that any subsequent Roman general, even
if he possessed the ability, could have mustered the re- 20
sources or have found the time to effect a permanent subjugation of the Gallic territory, which was then being threatened
and would soon have been overwhelmed by Germanic invasions.

Caesar's growth in power had of course aroused the jealousy of
Pompey (Crassus had died in 53 B.C.), who now allied himself 25
with the Senate, which was bitterly hostile to Caesar. The
better part of 51 and 50 were taken up with a dispute as to the
continuance of Caesar's governmental career. Finally the Senate and Pompey manoeuvred Caesar into a position in which
he had either to place himself at the mercy of his enemies or 30
maintain his position by force of arms. Caesar chose the latter
course, and in January, 49, crossed the Rubicon, which separated Cisalpine Gaul from Italy proper, at the head of an insurgent army. The Civil War between Caesar and the Sena-

---

[9] See Note **64** 36*a*, page 149.
[10] See Note **45** 2, page 133.   The region is there referred to by its Latin
name, *Gallia*.

torial-Pompeian, or Republican, forces lasted over three years.
In August, 48, Caesar defeated Pompey at Pharsalus in Thessaly; he then marched east, spending some time in conquest
but more in dalliance with Cleopatra. On his return to the
5 West, he vigorously attacked the remaining Republican forces,
all but a small group of which he crushed at the Battle of
Thapsus, in Northern Africa, April, 46 B.C.

Caesar had held the dictatorship in 49 and again in 48–47;
in the year 46 he was made dictator for ten years, and later
10 for life. As the supreme head of the Roman state, he set about
reconstituting it on an autocratic and military basis. On the
eve of his departure for the East to win a strategic eastern
boundary for the Empire, Caesar was murdered (March 15,
44 B.C.) by a group of Senators who believed that by assassi-
15 nating Caesar they could restore the Roman Republic. As a
matter of fact, they plunged the Roman world into another
period of civil strife, from which there emerged, as sole ruler of
the Empire, Caesar's adopted son and heir, his grand-nephew
Octavius, later called Augustus.

20   Caesar's contribution to literature was not inconsiderable;
besides his orations and collected letters, there were youthful
love poems and other verse, a treatise on astronomy, one on
grammar,[11] an invective against Cato,[12] and a collection of
witticisms. All these, however, have perished. Caesar's pres-
25 ent-day reputation as a man of letters rests on his *Commentaries
on the Gallic War* and his *Commentaries on the Civil War*.

The ostensible purpose of the *Commentaries on the Gallic War*,
in seven books, was to provide source material for later his-
torians; their real aim, however, was to persuade Caesar's con-
30 temporaries that his conquest of Gaul was the inevitable result
of his prudent and patriotic handling of problems which beset
him as Governor of the Roman province of Transalpine Gaul.
Similar in character and aim are the *Commentaries on the Civil
War*, in which Caesar attempts, with greater justification, to
35 show how it became necessary for him to conquer if he was to

---

[11] See Note 20 8, page 96.
[12] See Note 36 3*b*, page 121.

survive, and how he accomplished his victory with as little shedding of Roman blood as possible.

Selection 58 is composed of passages from the *Commentaries on the Gallic War* in which Caesar digresses from his military narrative to discuss the manners and customs of the Gauls and 5 the Germans, with both of whom his campaigns brought him into contact. These accounts are among our most important sources for the study of the very early history of two major European nations.

Selection 59 consists of the latter half of Book I of the *Com-* 10 *mentaries on the Gallic War*.[13] It describes Caesar's conflict—first diplomatic, then military—with the German chieftain Ariovistus, who had established himself as overlord of several Gallic states. Ariovistus' contemptuous rejection of Caesar's diplomatic advances, his attempted treachery, and his final de- 15 feat and expulsion from Gaul form one of the most vivid episodes in Caesar's Gallic campaigns.

IV. Phaedrus

The last group of selections is composed of thirty of Phaedrus' *Fābulae Aesōpiae* (*Fables Based on Aesop*).

Phaedrus was a native of Pieria, a mountainous district of 20 Thrace, and the fabled home of the Muses. He is believed to have been born about 15 B.C. and to have come to Italy as a boy. For a time he was a slave in the household of the Emperor Augustus or his successor Tiberius, but he was later given his freedom, probably as a reward for his literary attainments. 25

Phaedrus' literary activities were, so far as we know, restricted to the composition of fables in verse. Most of these are based on the collection which circulated under the name of Aesop,[14] but others are either original or based on other sources; some deal with contemporary themes. The first two books, 30

---

[13] This selection has been adapted for the purposes of this reader by the conversion of several speeches from indirect to direct discourse. A list of the passages so changed will be found on page 193, footnote 8.

[14] See Note 30 20a, page 113.

from which most of our selections are taken, seem to have been published during the reign of Tiberius (14–37 A.D.); three books were later added at different times. The collection has come down to us in a mutilated form, with many fables missing.

5   It is an interesting reflection on the dangers of literary composition during the Empire that even the production of beast fables was not without peril. Certain of Phaedrus' fables (probably our Selections 61, 62, and 65) were interpreted as a slur upon Sejanus, the corrupt and powerful minister of Tibe-
10 rius, and the author was punished with some severity.

No further details of Phaedrus' life are known, but he seems to have lived to an advanced age.

The fables of Phaedrus exercised considerable influence upon the French fabulist Jean de La Fontaine (1621–1695). La
15 Fontaine handled most of the themes which appear in our selections; for the purpose of comparison, parallel references are given in the notes.

V. The Roman Name

The typical name of the male Roman citizen consisted of three parts, *praenōmen, nōmen,* and *cognōmen:* for example,
20 Marcus Tullius Cicero.

1. The *praenōmen* (*forename*), corresponds to our given name. The total number of Roman *praenōmina* is comparatively small; in the first century B.C. only eighteen were in common use, and of these most families, by the force of tradi-
25 tion, restricted themselves to but three or four. It was customary to abbreviate them when they were used as part of the full name. The fifteen most common *praenōmina* are listed below, each followed by its conventional abbreviation:

Aulus (A.)	Lucius (L.)	Servius (Ser.)
Decimus (D.)	Manius (M')	Sextus (Sex.)
Gaius (C.[15])	Marcus (M.)	Spurius (S.)
Gnaeus (Cn.[15])	Publius (P.)	Tiberius (Ti.)
Kaeso (K.)	Quintus (Q.)	Titus (T.)

30

[15] See Note 13 1c, page 79, first paragraph.

For convenience, every abbreviation of this sort which occurs in the selections is listed in its proper place in the Vocabulary (pages 195 to 264), and is followed by the full form of the name.

2. The *nōmen* (*name*) is also called *nōmen gentīle* (*gentile name*), because it denotes the *gēns*, or *clan*, to which the Roman 5 belonged. For example, Tullius, the *nōmen* of M. Tullius Cicero, shows that he belonged to the *gēns Tullia*, the *Tullian clan*. The *nōmina gentīlia* regularly end in *-ius*.

3. The *cognōmen* (*surname*) shows to which family or branch of the *gēns* a citizen belonged. Thus the orator's *cognōmen*, 10 Cicero, shows that he belonged to the branch of that name which formed part of the Tullian clan.

The triple name just described was most common. Some Romans, however, like A. Gellius, lacked a *cognōmen*, while others had two or more. Additional *cognōmina* are usually due 15 to one or more of the following circumstances:

(*a*) The branch designated by the *cognōmen* described above was sometimes further subdivided: the name P. *Cornēlius Scīpiō Nāsīca* shows that its bearer belonged to the subdivision called *Nāsīca* of the branch *Scīpiō* of the Cornelian *gēns*. 20

(*b*) A victorious general was sometimes given a surname expressive of his victory; thus P. *Cornēlius Scīpiō Āfricānus* was given his additional *cognōmen* in honor of his victory at Zama in Africa.

(*c*) When one Roman citizen adopted another, the adopted 25 son took his new father's entire name, with an additional surname formed by changing the ending *-us* of his former *nōmen* to *-ānus*. Thus L. *Aemilius Paulus*, adopted by P. *Cornēlius Scīpiō*, became P. *Cornēlius Scīpiō Aemiliānus*.

VI. Methods of Study

The suggestions embodied in Sections 1 to 9 below may prove 30 helpful in the preparation of assignments.

1. If your assignment covers more than about ten lines, divide it into passages of convenient length, ordinarily of not more than ten lines each.

2. Read the first passage through *in Latin*. Do not stop at 5 this time to look up words which you do not know, but make every effort to grasp the thought of the passage as it appears in Latin. In the early stages of your work, the results of this step are apt to be discouragingly slight. Do not on that account neglect this procedure! The goal at which you are aim- 10 ing is to be able to read Latin at first sight; as you progress, you will find yourself comprehending more and more at this first reading.

3. Now reread the first sentence, or as far as the first semi-colon, without stopping to look up words which you do not 15 know. Try to make use of any information which you may have gleaned from your reading of the rest of the passage. Strive to grasp the *structure* of the sentence as a whole in the original word order, even if you are not familiar with some of the words.

20 4. Work out the meaning of the first sentence, using vo-cabulary, notes, grammar, and any other legitimate aid. Follow the word order of the Latin as closely as possible; do not skip around the sentence!

5. When you have fully grasped the meaning of the first 25 sentence, reread it (it should now make sense to you *in Latin*) and continue reading right on through the next sentence without stopping.

6. Work out the meaning of the second sentence as you were directed to do for the first sentence in Section 4 above, 30 then reread it (see Section 5), and so on through the whole passage.

7. When you have worked through the whole passage, re-read it from beginning to end, following the sense *in the Latin*.

If you cannot do this, repeat the procedure described in Sections 2 to 6 above until you can.

8. After rereading the first passage, continue right on through the second. Repeat the procedure described in Sections 2 to 7, and continue until the assignment is finished. 5

9. If your assignment calls for translation, some time may be necessary to phrase in idiomatic English the thought of the passage which you have read. This is a separate process and should not be confused with the task of understanding the Latin itself. Generally speaking, comprehension should pre- 10 cede translation.

The practice of writing translations is not recommended as a general rule. If the student finds it impossible to remain familiar with a passage for a reasonable length of time without recourse to a written translation, it is probably a symptom of 15 insufficient preparation.

An effort has been made in the Notes (pages 79 to 160) to give the student all the historical background necessary for the comprehension of the selections to be read. From the nature of the case, however, the treatment is somewhat uneven, and 20 the student is strongly advised to familiarize himself with the main outlines of Greek and Roman history. For this purpose the following books are recommended:

Botsford, George W., *Hellenic History*, New York, The Macmillan Company, 1922. 25

Boak, Arthur E. R., *A History of Rome to 565 A.D.* (revised edition), New York, The Macmillan Company, 1929.

Frank, Tenney, *A History of Rome*, New York, Henry Holt and Company, 1923.

Other books which will be of assistance in connection with 30 topics mentioned in the selections and Notes are:

Dimsdale, Marcus S., *A History of Latin Literature*, London, William Heinemann, 1915.

Duff, J. Wight, *A Literary History of Rome from the Origins to the*

Close of the Golden Age, London, T. Fisher Unwin Ltd., 1910.

—————, *A Literary History of Rome in the Silver Age*, London, T. Fisher Unwin Ltd., 1927.

Mackail, J. W., *Latin Literature*, New York, Charles Scribners' Sons, 1895.

Abbott, Frank Frost, *A History and Description of Roman Political Institutions* (third edition), Boston, Ginn and Company, 1911.

Johnston, Harold W., *The Private Life of the Romans* (revised by Johnston, Mary), Chicago, Scott, Foresman and Company, 1932.

SELECTIONS FOR READING

I. AULUS GELLIUS

1. Fabricius and the Samnite Gold

Lēgātī ā Samnītibus ad C. Fabricium Luscīnum, imperātōrem
populī Rōmānī, vēnērunt, et, memorātīs multīs magnīsque
rēbus, quās bene ac benevolē post redditam pācem Samnītibus
fēcerat, obtulērunt dōnō grandem pecūniam, ōrāvēruntque ut
acciperet ūterēturque. "Quae facimus," inquiunt, "quod multa 5
ad splendōrem domūs atque vīctūs dēfierī vidēmus." Tum
Fabricius manūs ab auribus ad oculōs et īnfrā deinceps ad nārēs
et ad ōs et ad gulam atque inde ad ventrem dēdūxit, et lēgātīs
ita respondit: "Dum hīs omnibus membrīs, quae attigī, imperāre
possum, numquam quicquam mihi deerit; proptereā hanc pe- 10
cūniam, quā nihil mihi est ūsus, ā vōbīs, quibus eam sciō ūsuī
esse, nōn accipiō."

2. Hannibal's Jest

In librīs veterum memoriārum scrīptum est Hannibalem
Carthāginiēnsem apud rēgem Antiochum facētissimē cavillātum
esse. Ea cavillātiō huiuscemodī fuit. Ostendēbat eī Antiochus 15
in campō cōpiās ingentīs, quās bellum populō Rōmānō factūrus
comparāverat, convertēbatque exercitum īnsignibus argenteīs
et aureīs micantem; indūcēbat etiam currūs cum falcibus, et
elephantōs cum turribus, equitātumque frēnīs, ephippiīs, monīlibus, phalerīs praefulgentem. Atque ibi rēx Hannibalem aspi- 20
cit et, "Putāsne," inquit, "satis esse Rōmānīs haec omnia?"
Tum Poenus, ēlūdēns ignāviam mīlitum eius pretiōsē armātōrum, "Satis, plānē satis esse crēdō Rōmānīs haec omnia, etiam
sī avārissimī sunt."

3. The Death of Milo

Milō Crotōniēnsis, āthlēta inlūstris, exitum habuit ē vītā miserandum et mīrandum. Cum, iam nātū grandis, artem āthlēticam dēsīsset, iterque faceret forte sōlus in locīs Ītaliae silvestribus, quercum vīdit proximē viam rīmīs in parte mediā 5 hiantem. Tum experīrī, crēdō, etiam tunc volēns, an ūllae sibi reliquae vīrēs adessent, immissīs in cavernās arboris digitīs, dīdūcere et rescindere quercum cōnātus est. Ac mediam quidem partem dīscidit dīvellitque; quercus autem in duās dīducta partīs, cum ille, quasi perfectō negōtiō, manūs laxāsset, cessante 10 vī rediit in nātūram, manibusque eius retentīs inclūsīsque dīlacerandum hominem ferīs praebuit.

4. A Hoax: The Story of Papirius Praetextatus

Mōs anteā senātōribus Rōmae fuit in cūriam cum praetextātīs fīliīs introīre. Tum, cum in senātū rēs maior quaepiam cōnsultāta eaque in diem posterum prōlāta est, placuit ut eam 15 rem nē quis ēnūntiāret, priusquam dēcrēta esset. Māter Papīriī puerī, quī cum parente suō in cūriā fuerat, percontāta est fīlium, quidnam in senātū patrēs ēgissent. Puer respondit id dīcī nōn licēre. Mulier fit audiendī cupidior; silentium puerī animum eius ad inquīrendum stimulat: quaerit igitur ācrius 20 violentiusque. Tum puer, mātre urgente, lepidī atque fēstīvī mendāciī cōnsilium capit. Āctum in senātū dīxit, utrum vidērētur ūtilius exque rē pūblicā esse, ūnusne ut duās uxōrēs habēret, an ut ūna duōbus nūpta esset.

5. The Result of the Hoax

Hoc illa ubi audīvit, domō trepidāns ēgreditur, ad cēterās 25 mātrōnās sē adfert. Venit ad senātum postrīdiē mātrum familiās caterva; lacrimantēs atque obsecrantēs ōrant, ut ūna potius duōbus nūpta fieret, quam ut ūnī duae. Senātōrēs, ingredientēs in cūriam, quid illa mulierum īnsānia et quid sibi postulātiō

istaec vellet mīrābantur. Puer Papīrius, in mediam cūriam
prōgressus, quid māter audīre īnstitisset, quid ipse mātrī dīxisset, dēnārrat. Senātus fidem atque ingenium puerī laudat;
cōnsultum facit, utī posthāc puerī cum patribus in cūriam nē
introeant, praeter illum ūnum Papīrium; atque puerō posteā 5
cognōmen honōris grātiā datum "Praetextātus" ob tacendī
loquendīque in aetāte praetextae prūdentiam.

6. Virgil and His Poems

Dīcēbat P. Vergilius parere sē versūs mōre ursīnō. "Namque
ut illa bēstia," inquit, "fētum ēdit īnfōrmem, lambendōque
posteā cōnformat et fingit, sīc ingeniī quoque meī partūs re- 10
centēs rudī sunt faciē et imperfectā, sed deinceps tractandō
colendōque reddō iīs ōris et vultūs līneāmenta." Itaque ubi,
morbō oppressus, adventāre mortem vīdit, petīvit ā suīs amī-
cissimīs impēnsē, ut Aenēida, quam nōndum satis ēlīmāvisset,
combūrerent. 15

7. Menander and Philemon

Menander ā Philēmone, nēquāquam parī scrīptōre, in certāminibus cōmoediārum ambitū grātiāque saepenumerō vincēbātur. Eī cum forte factus esset obviam Menander, "Quaesō,"
inquit, "Philēmō, bonā veniā dīc mihi: cum mē vincis, nōnne
ērubēscis?" 20

8. Socrates and His Wife

Xanthippē, Sōcratis philosophī uxor, mōrōsa admodum fuisse
fertur et lītigiōsa, īrīsque muliebribus per diem perque noctem
scatēbat. Quam rem Alcibiadēs dēmīrātus interrogāvit Sōcratēn, quaenam ratiō esset cur mulierem tam acerbam domō
nōn exigeret. "Quoniam," inquit Sōcratēs, "cum illam domī 25
tālem perpetior, īnsuēscō et exerceor, ut cēterōrum quoque forīs
petulantiam et iniūriam facilius feram."

9. Socrates' Powers of Concentration; His Temperance

Id quoque accēpimus Sōcratēn facere īnsuēvisse: stāre solitus Sōcratēs dīcitur per diem perque noctem ā lūcis ortū ad alterum sōlem orientem immōbilis, īsdem in vestīgiīs, et ōre atque oculīs eundem in locum dīrēctīs, cōgitāns, tamquam quōdam sēcessū 5 mentis atque animī factō ā corpore.

Temperantiā quoque fuisse eum tantā trāditum est, ut omnia ferē vītae suae tempora valītūdine integrā vīxerit. In illā etiam pestilentiā, quae in bellī Peloponnēnsiacī prīncipiīs Athēniēn-sium cīvitātem dēpopulāta est, is parcendī moderandīque ra-10 tiōnibus dīcitur salūtem corporis retinuisse.

10. Alexander and Bucephalas

Equus Alexandrī rēgis et capite et nōmine 'Būcephalās' fuit. Ēmptum Charēs scrīpsit talentīs tredecim et rēgī Philippō dō-nātum; hoc autem aeris nostrī summa est sēstertia trecenta duodecim. Hic equus ubi ōrnātus erat armātusque ad proeli-15 um, haud umquam īnscendī sēsē ab aliō nisi ab rēge passus est. Cum īnsidēns in eō Alexander bellō Indicō facinora faceret fortia, in hostium cuneum, nōn satis sibi prōvidēns, immīsit. Coniectīs undique in Alexandrum tēlīs, vulneribus altīs in cer-vīce atque in latere equus perfossus est. Moribundus tamen 20 ac prope iam exsanguis ē mediīs hostibus rēgem magnō cursū rettulit, atque ubi eum extrā tēla extulerat, īlicō concidit, et, dominī iam superstitis sēcūrus, quasi cum sēnsūs hūmānī sōlāciō animam exspīrāvit. Tum rēx Alexander, partā eius bellī vic-tōriā, oppidum in īsdem locīs condidit idque ob equī honōrēs 25 'Būcephalon' appellāvit.

11. Alcibiades and the Pipes

Alcibiadēs Athēniēnsis, cum apud avunculum Periclēn puer artibus ac disciplīnīs līberālibus ērudīrētur, et arcessī Periclēs

Antigenidam tībīcinem iussisset, ut eum canere tībiīs, quod
honestissimum tum vidēbātur, docēret, trāditās sibi tībiās, cum
ad ōs adhibuisset īnflāssetque, commōtus ōris dēfōrmitāte abiēcit īnfrēgitque. Ea rēs cum percrēbuisset, omnium tum Athēniēnsium cōnsēnsū disciplīna tībiīs canendī dēsita est. 5

12. Tarquin and the Sibylline Books

In antīquīs annālibus memoria dē librīs Sibyllīnīs haec prōdita
est: Anus hospita atque incognita ad Tarquinium Superbum
rēgem adiit novem librōs ferēns, quōs esse dīcēbat dīvīna ōrā-
cula: eōs sē velle vēndere. Tarquinius pretium percontātus
est. Mulier nimium atque immēnsum poposcit; rēx, quasi anus 10
aetāte dēsiperet, dērīsit. Tum illa foculum cōram cum ignī
appōnit, trīs librōs ex novem deūrit, et, ecquid reliquōs sex
eōdem pretiō emere vellet, rēgem interrogāvit. Sed enim Tarquinius id multō rīsit magis, dīxitque anum iam procul dubiō
dēlīrāre. Mulier ibīdem statim trīs aliōs librōs exussit, atque 15
id ipsum dēnuō placidē rogat, ut trīs reliquōs eōdem illō pretiō
emat. Tarquinius ōre iam sēriō atque attentiōre animō fit, eam
cōnstantiam cōnfīdentiamque nōn contemnendam intellegit,
librōs trīs reliquōs mercātur nihilō minōre pretiō, quam quod
erat petītum prō omnibus. Sed ea mulier, tunc ā Tarquiniō 20
dīgressa, posteā nusquam locī vīsa est. Librī trēs, in sacrārium
conditī, "Sibyllīnī" appellātī; ad eōs quasi ad ōrāculum quīndecimvirī adeunt, cum dī immortalēs pūblicē cōnsulendī sunt.

13. Scipio Africanus Impeached

Cum M. Naevius tribūnus plēbis accūsāret Scīpiōnem Āfricānum ad populum, dīceretque accēpisse eum ā rēge Antiochō 25
pecūniam, ut condiciōnibus mollibus pāx cum eō populī Rōmānī
nōmine fieret, et quaedam item alia crīminī daret indigna tālī
virō, tum Scīpiō, pauca praefātus quae dignitās vītae suae atque
glōria postulābat, "Memoriā," inquit, "Quirītēs, repetō diem
esse hodiernum, quō Hannibalem Poenum, imperiō vestrō ini- 30
mīcissimum, magnō proeliō vīcī in terrā Āfricā, pācemque et

victōriam vōbīs peperī praeclāram. Nē igitur sīmus adversum
deōs ingrātī, et, cēnseō, relinquāmus nebulōnem hunc, eāmus
hinc prōtinus Iovī Optimō Maximō grātulātum." Id cum
dīxisset, āvertit et īre ad Capitōlium coepit. Tum cōntiō ūni-
5 versa, quae ad sententiam dē Scīpiōne ferendam convēnerat,
relictō tribūnō Scīpiōnem in Capitōlium comitāta atque inde
ad aedēs eius cum laetitiā et grātulātiōne sollemnī prōsecūta est.

14. Scipio Africanus: Another Impeachment

Item aliud est factum eius praeclārum. Petīliī quīdam, tribūnī plēbis, ā M., ut aiunt, Catōne, inimīcō Scīpiōnis, compa-
10 rātī in eum atque immissī, dēsīderābant in senātū, ut pecūniae
Antiochīnae praedaeque in eō bellō captae ratiōnem redderet;
fuerat enim L. Scīpiōnī Asiāticō, frātrī suō, imperātōrī in eā
prōvinciā lēgātus. Ibi Scīpiō exsurgit, et, prōlātō ē sinū togae
librō, ratiōnēs in eō scrīptās esse dīxit omnis pecūniae omnisque
15 praedae; inlātum, ut palam recitārētur et ad aerārium dēferrētur. "Sed enim id iam nōn faciam," inquit, "nec mē ipse adfi-
ciam contumēliā"; eumque librum statim cōram suīs manibus
dīscidit, aegrē passus, quod, cui salūs imperiī ac reī pūblicae
accepta referrī dēbēret, ab eō ratiō praedae poscerētur.

15. Scipio Africanus and the Gods

20 P. Scīpiō Āfricānus, quī Hannibalem et Carthāginiēnsēs in
Āfricā bellō Poenicō secundō vīcit, vir esse virtūtis dīvīnae
crēditus est. Id etiam dīcere haud piget, quod iī, quī dē vītā
et rēbus Āfricānī scrīpsērunt, litterīs mandāvērunt. Solitus est
noctis extrēmō in Capitōlium ventitāre ac iubēre aperīrī cellam
25 Iovis, atque ibi sōlus diū dēmorārī, quasi cōnsultāns dē rē pūblicā cum Iove. Aeditumī eius templī saepe dēmīrātī sunt
quod in eum sōlum id temporis in Capitōlium ingredientem
canēs, semper in aliōs saevientēs, neque lātrārent neque incurrerent.
30 Hās vulgī dē Scīpiōne opīniōnēs cōnfirmāre atque approbāre
vidēbantur dicta factaque eius plēraque admīranda. Ex quibus

est ūnum huiuscemodī. Adsidēbat oppugnābatque oppidum
in Hispāniā situm, moenibus dēfēnsōribusque validum et mūnī-
tum, rē etiam cibāriā cōpiōsum, nūllaque eius capiendī spēs erat.
Quōdam diē iūs in castrīs sedēns dīcēbat, atque ex eō locō id
oppidum procul vīsēbātur. Tum ē mīlitibus, quī in iūre apud 5
eum stābant, interrogāvit quispiam ex mōre, in quem diem locumque vadimōnium prōmittī iubēret, et Scīpiō, manum ad
ipsam oppidī, quod obsidēbātur, arcem prōtendēns, "Perendiē,"
inquit, "sēsē sistant illō in locō." Atque ita factum: diē tertiō,
in quem vadārī iusserat, oppidum captum est, eōdemque eō diē 10
in arce eius oppidī iūs dīxit.

16. Strange Legal Ethics

Lacedaemonius Chīlō, vir ex illō inclutō numerō sapientium,
in vītae suae postrēmō, cum iam mors adventāret, apud cir-
cumstantīs amīcōs sīc locūtus est: "Nihil," inquit, "in aetāte
longā commissum est ā mē, cuius memoria mihi aegritūdinī est, 15
nisi illud profectō ūnum: Super amīcī capite iūdex cum duōbus
aliīs fuī. Ita lēx fuit, utī eum hominem condemnārī necesse
esset. Aut amīcō igitur caput perdendum aut adhibenda fraus
lēgī fuit. Multa cum animō meō ad cāsum tam ancipitem me-
dendum cōnsultāvī. Vīsum est id, quod fēcī, tolerātū facilius 20
esse, quam alia. Ipse tacitus ad condemnandum sententiam
tulī; iīs qui simul iūdicābant, ut absolverent persuāsī. Sīc mihi
et iūdicis et amīcī officium in rē tantā salvum fuit. Hanc capiō
ex eō factō molestiam, quod rēctēne an perperam fēcerim nōndum mihi plānē liquet." 25

17. Favorinus on Obsolete Language

Favōrīnus philosophus adulēscentī, veterum verbōrum cupidissimō, et plērāsque vōcēs nimis prīscās et ignōtās in cotīdiānīs
sermōnibus exprōmentī, "Curius," inquit, "et Fabricius et Coruncānius, antīquissimī virī, et hīs antīquiōrēs Horātiī illī trige-
minī, plānē ac dīlūcidē cum suīs locūtī sunt, neque Auruncōrum 30
aut Sicānōrum aut Pelasgōrum, quī prīmī coluisse Ītaliam dī-

cuntur, sed aetātis suae verbīs ūsī sunt; tū autem, proinde quasi
cum mātre Euandrī nunc loquāre, sermōne abhinc multīs annīs
iam dēsitō ūteris, quod scīre atque intellegere nēminem vīs,
quae dīcās. Nōnne, homō inepte, ut quod vīs abundē cōnse-
5 quāris, tacēs? Sed antīquitātem tibi placēre ais, quod honesta
et bona et sōbria et modesta sit. Vīve ergō mōribus praeteritīs,
loquere verbīs praesentibus; atque id, quod ā C. Caesare, excellentis ingeniī ac prūdentiae virō, in prīmō Dē Analogiā librō
scrīptum est, habē semper in memoriā atque in pectore, ut
10 tamquam scopulum, sīc fugiās inaudītum atque īnsolēns
verbum."

18. Torquatus and the Gaul: The Challenge

T. Mānlius summō locō nātus est. Eī Mānliō cognōmen
factum est Torquātus. Causam cognōminis fuisse accēpimus
torquem ex aurō factam, quam ex hoste, quem occīderat, dē-
15 tractam induit. Verba Q. Claudiī, quibus pugna illa dēpicta
est, adscrīpsī: "Gallus quīdam nūdus praeter scūtum et gladiōs
duōs, torque atque armillīs decorātus, prōcessit, quī et vīribus
et magnitūdine et adulēscentiā, simulque virtūte, cēterīs praestābat. Is, maximē proeliō commōtō, atque utrīsque summō
20 studiō pugnantibus, manū significāre coepit utrīsque, quiēscerent. Extemplō silentiō factō, vōce maximā conclāmat, sī quis
sēcum dēpugnāre vellet, utī prōdīret. Nēmō audēbat propter
magnitūdinem atque immānem faciem. Deinde Gallus inrīdēre
coepit atque linguam exsertāre. Doluit T. Mānlius, tantum
25 flāgitium cīvitātī accidere, ē tantō exercitū nēminem prōdīre.
Is īlicō prōcessit, neque passus est virtūtem Rōmānam turpiter
spoliārī. Scūtō pedestrī et gladiō Hispānicō cīnctus contrā
Gallum cōnstitit."

19. Torquatus and the Gaul: The Battle

"Metū magnō ea congressiō in ipsō ponte, utrōque exercitū
30 īnspectante, facta est. Ita, ut dīxī, cōnstitērunt: Gallus suā

disciplīnā, scūtō prōiectō, cūnctābundus; Mānlius, animō magis
quam arte cōnfīsus, scūtō scūtum percussit atque statum Gallī
conturbāvit.   Dum sē Gallus iterum eōdem pactō cōnstituere
studet, Mānlius iterum scūtō scūtum percutit atque dē locō
hominem iterum dēiēcit; eō pactō eī sub Gallicum gladium suc- 5
cessit atque Hispānicō pectus hausit; deinde continuō umerum
dextrum incīdit neque recessit usquam, dōnec subvertit. Ubi
eum ēvertit, caput praecīdit, torquem dētrāxit, eamque sangui-
nulentam sibi in collum impōnit.   Quō ex factō ipse posterīque
eius Torquātī sunt cognōmināti."   10
     Ab hōc T. Mānliō, cuius hanc pugnam Quadrīgārius dēscrīp-
sit, imperia et aspera et immītia 'Mānliāna' dicta sunt, quoniam posteā, bellō adversum Latīnōs cum esset cōnsul, fīlium
suum secūrī percussit, quī, speculātum ab eō missus, pugnā
interdictā, hostem, ā quō prōvocātus erat, occīderat.   15

20. Valerius Corvinus: The Origin of His Name

     Cōpiae Gallōrum ingentēs agrum Pomptīnum īnsēderant,
īnstruēbanturque aciēs ā cōnsulibus, dē vī ac multitūdine hostium satis agentibus.   Dux intereā Gallōrum, vāstā et arduā
prōcēritāte, armīsque aurō praefulgentibus, manū tēlum vibrāns
incēdēbat; perque contemptum et superbiam circumspiciēns 20
dēspiciēnsque omnia, venīre iubet et congredī, sī quis pugnāre
sēcum ex omnī Rōmānō exercitū audēret.   Tum Valerius adulēscēns, tribūnus mīlitāris, cēterīs inter metum pudōremque
ambiguīs, cum ā cōnsulibus impetrāsset, ut in Gallum tam
immāniter adrogantem pugnāre sēsē permitterent, prōgreditur 25
intrepidē modestēque obviam; et congrediuntur, et cōnsistunt,
et cōnserēbantur iam manūs.   Atque ibi vīs quaedam dīvīna
fit: corvus repente imprōvīsus advolat et super galeam tribūnī
īnsistit; atque inde in adversāriī ōs atque oculōs pugnāre incipit:
unguibus manum laniābat, et prōspectum ālīs arcēbat, atque, 30
ubi satis saevierat, revolābat in galeam tribūnī.   Sīc tribūnus,
spectante utrōque exercitū, et suā virtūte nīxus, et operā corvī
adiūtus, ducem hostium vīcit interfēcitque, atque ob hanc cau-

sam cognōmen habuit Corvīnum. Id factum est annīs quadringentīs quīnque post Rōmam conditam.
  Statuam Corvīnō illī dīvus Augustus in forō suō statuendam
cūrāvit. In eius statuae capite corvī simulācrum est, reī pug-
5 naeque, quam dīximus, monimentum.

21. Pyrrhus and Fabricius

  Cum Pyrrhus rēx in Ītaliā esset et ūnam atque alteram
pugnās prōsperē pugnāsset, satisque agerent Rōmānī, et plēraque Ītalia ad rēgem dēscīvisset, tum Ambraciēnsis quīdam,
Tīmocharēs, rēgis Pyrrhī amīcus, ad C. Fabricium cōnsulem
10 fūrtim vēnit ac praemium petīvit, et, sī dē praemiō convenīret,
prōmīsit sē rēgem venēnīs necātūrum esse; idque facile esse
factū dīxit, quoniam fīlius suus pōcula in convīviō rēgī ministrāret. Eam rem Fabricius ad senātum scrīpsit. Senātus ad
rēgem lēgātōs mīsit mandāvitque, ut dē Tīmochare nihil prō-
15 derent, sed monērent utī rēx cautius ageret atque ā proximōrum
īnsidiīs salūtem tūtārētur. Hoc, ita ut dīximus, in Valeriī Antiātis Historiā scrīptum est. Quadrīgārius autem in librō tertiō
nōn Tīmocharem, sed Nīciam adīsse ad cōnsulem scrīpsit, neque
lēgātōs ā senātū missōs, sed ā cōnsulibus; et Pyrrhum populō
20 Rōmānō laudēs atque grātiās scrīpsisse, captīvōsque omnēs,
quōs tum habuit, vestīvisse et reddidisse.

22. Androclus and the Lion: Scene in the Circus

  In circō maximō vēnātiō amplissima populō dabātur. Multae
ibi saevientēs ferae, sed praeter alia omnia leō corpore vāstō,
terrificōque fremitū et sonōrō, animōs oculōsque omnium in
25 sēsē converterat. Intrōductus erat inter complūrīs cēterōs ad
pugnam bēstiārum datōs servus virī cōnsulāris; eī servō Androclus nōmen fuit. Hunc ille leō ubi vīdit procul, repente quasi
admīrāns stetit ac deinde sēnsim atque placidē, tamquam familiāris, ad hominem accēdit. Tum caudam mōre adūlantium
30 canum clēmenter et blandē movet, hominisque sē corporī adiun-
git, crūraque eius et manūs, prope iam exanimātī metū, linguā

lēniter dēmulcet. Homō Androclus inter illa tam atrōcis ferae
blandimenta āmissum animum recuperat, paulātim oculōs ad
contuendum leōnem refert. Tum, quasi mutuā recognitiōne
factā, laetōs et grātulantēs vidērēs hominem et leōnem.

23. Androclus and the Lion: The Slave's Story

Haec tam mīra rēs maximōs populī clāmōrēs excitat. Arces- 5
situr ā Caesare Androclus, quaeriturque causa, cūr illī atrōcissi-
mus leō ūnī pepercisset. Ibi Androclus rem mīrificam nārrat
atque admīrandam. "Cum prōvinciam," inquit, "Āfricam
prōcōnsulārī imperiō meus dominus obtinēret, ego ibi inīquīs
eius et cotīdiānīs verberibus ad fugam sum coāctus, et, ut mihi 10
ā dominō, terrae illīus praeside, tūtiōrēs latebrae forent, in cam-
pōrum et harēnārum sōlitūdinēs concessī; ac, sī dēfuisset cibus,
cōnsilium fuit mortem aliquō pactō quaerere. Tum diē mediō,
sōle flagrante, specum quendam nanctus remōtum latēbrōsum-
que, in eum mē recondō. Neque multō post ad eundem specum 15
vēnit hic leō, dēbilī ūnō et cruentō pede, gemitūs ēdēns et mur-
mura propter dolōrem cruciātumque vulneris. Atque illīc
prīmō quidem cōnspectū advenientis leōnis territus et pavefac-
tus sum, sed postquam intrōgressus leō videt mē procul dēlitēs-
centem, mītis et mānsuētus accessit, et sublātum pedem osten- 20
dere mihi et porrigere quasi opis petendae grātiā vīsus est. Ibi
ego stirpem ingentem, in vestīgiō pedis eius haerentem, revellī,
saniemque vulnere intimō expressī, et, sine magnā iam formī-
dine, siccāvī penitus atque dētersī cruōrem. Illā tunc meā
operā levātus, pede in manibus meīs positō, recubuit et quiēvit. 25

24. Androclus and the Lion: The Slave's Story (Contd.)

Ex eō diē triennium tōtum ego et leō in eōdem specū eōdemque vīctū vīximus. Nam ferārum, quas vēnābātur, membra
opīmiōra ad specum mihi ferēbat, quās ego, ignis cōpiam nōn
habēns, merīdiānō sōle torrēns edēbam. Sed ubi mē vītae illīus
ferīnae iam pertaesum est, leōne in vēnātum profectō, relīquī 30
specum, et, viam fermē trīduī permēnsus, ā mīlitibus vīsus

apprehēnsusque sum et ad dominum ex Āfricā Rōmam dēductus. Is mē statim reī capitālis damnandum dandumque ad bēstiās cūrāvit. Intellegō autem hunc quoque leōnem, mē tunc sēparātō, captum, grātiam mihi nunc beneficiī et medicīnae 5 referre." Haec dīxit Androclus; atque ubi ea omnia, scrīpta circumlātaque tabulā, populō dēclārāta sunt, cūnctīs petentibus dīmissus est Androclus et poenā solūtus, leōque eī suffrāgiīs populī dōnātus. Posteā Androclus et leō lōrō tenuī revīnctus urbe tōtā circum tabernās eunt; dōnātur aere Androclus, flōri-10 bus spargitur leō, omnēsque ubīque obviī exclāmant, "Hic est leō hospes hominis, hic est homō medicus leōnis."

25. The Actor Polus

Histriō in terrā Graeciā fuit fāmā celebrī, quī gestūs et vōcis clāritūdine et venustāte cēterīs praestābat; nōmen fuisse aiunt Polum. Is Polus ūnicē amātum fīlium morte āmīsit. Mortem 15 eius ubi satis lūxit, rediit ad quaestum artis. Eō tempore Athēnīs Ēlectram Sophoclis āctūrus gestāre urnam quasi cum Orestī ossibus dēbēbat. Ita compositum fābulae argūmentum est, ut velutī frātris reliquiās ferēns Ēlectra complōret interitum eius exīstimātum. Polus igitur, lūgubrī habitū Ēlectrae indū-20 tus, ossa atque urnam ē sepulcrō tulit fīliī, et, quasi Orestī amplexus, opplēvit omnia nōn simulācrīs, sed lūctū et lāmentīs vērīs et spīrantibus. Itaque cum agī fābula vidērētur, dolor āctus est.

26. Demosthenes and the Milesians

Lēgātī Mīlētō auxiliī petendī grātiā vēnērunt Athēnās. Tum 25 quī prō sēsē verba facerent advocāvērunt; advocātī, utī erat mandātum, verba prō Mīlēsiīs ad populum fēcērunt; Dēmosthenēs autem Mīlēsiōrum postulātīs ācriter respondit: neque Mīlēsiōs auxiliō dignōs neque ex rē pūblicā id esse contendit. Rēs in posterum diem prōlāta est. Lēgātī ad Dēmosthenēn 30 vēnērunt, magnōque opere ōrāvērunt, utī contrā nē dīceret. Is pecūniam petīvit, et quantam petīverat abstulit. Postrīdiē

cum rēs agī dēnuō coepta esset, Dēmosthenēs lānā multā collum
circumvolūtus ad populum prōdiit, et dīxit sē *synanchēn* patī;
eō contrā Mīlēsiōs loquī nōn quīre.   Tum ē populō ūnus exclā-
mat nōn *synanchēn*, quod Dēmosthenēs paterētur, sed *argyranchēn* esse.   5
Ipse etiam Dēmosthenēs nōn id posteā cēlāvit; quīn etiam
glōriae hoc sibi adsignāvit.   Nam cum interrogāsset Aristodēmum, āctōrem fābulārum, quantum mercēdis, utī ageret, accēpisset, et Aristodēmus, "Talentum," respondisset, "At ego
plūs," inquit, "accēpī, ut tacērem."   10

27. Cicero's House on the Palatine

Cicerō cum emere vellet in Palātiō domum et pecūniam in
praesēns nōn habēret, ā P. Sullā, quī tum reus erat, mūtua
sēstertium vīciēns tacita accēpit.   Ea rēs tamen, priusquam
emeret, prōdita est et in vulgus exīvit, obiectumque eī est, quod
pecūniam domūs emendae causā ā reō accēpisset.   Tum Cicerō, 15
inopīnātā opprobrātiōne permōtus, accēpisse sē negāvit, ac domum quoque sē ēmptūrum negāvit, atque, "Adeō," inquit,
"vērum sit accēpisse mē pecūniam, sī domum ēmerō."   Sed
cum posteā ēmisset, et hoc mendācium in senātū eī ab amīcīs
obicerētur, rīsit satis atque inter rīdendum, "ἀκοινονόητοι,"[1] 20
inquit, "hominēs estis, sī ignōrātis prūdentis et cautī patris
familiās esse, quod emere velit, ēmptūrum sēsē negāre propter
competītōrēs ēmptiōnis."

28. Fires at Rome: A Remedy

Dēclāmāverat Antōnius Iūliānus rhētor fēlīcissimē; nōs autem
familiārēs eius circumfūsī undique eum prōsequēbāmur do- 25
mum, cum inde subeuntēs montem Cispium cōnspicimus īnsulam quandam, multīs arduīsque tabulātīs ēditam, occupātam
ignī, et propinqua iam omnia flagrāre vāstō incendiō.   Tum
quispiam ibi ex comitibus Iūliānī, "Magnī," inquit, "reditūs

---

[1] akoinonóētoi.

urbānōrum praediōrum, sed perīcula sunt longē maxima. Sī
quid autem posset remediī esse, ut nē tam adsiduē domūs Rōmae ardērent, vēnum hercle dedissem rēs rūsticās et urbicās
ēmissem." Atque illī Iūliānus, "Sī annālem," inquit, "ūndēvī-
5 cēnsimum Q. Claudiī lēgissēs, optimī et sincērissimī scrīptōris,
docuisset tē profectō Archelāus, rēgis Mithridātī praefectus,
quō remediō ignem dēfenderēs. In eō enim librō scrīptum
invēnī, cum oppugnāret L. Sulla in terrā Atticā Pīraeum, et
contrā Archelāus ex eō oppidō prōpugnāret, turrim ligneam
10 dēfendendī grātiā strūctam, cum ex omnī latere circumdata ignī
esset, ardēre nōn quīsse, quod alūmine ab Archelāō oblita esset."

29. Arion and the Dolphin: The Robbery

Vetus et nōbilis Ariōn fidicen fuit. Is locō et oppidō Mēthymnaeus, terrā atque īnsulā omnī Lesbius fuit. Eum Ariō-
nem rēx Corinthī Periander amīcum habuit artis grātiā. Is
15 inde ā rēge proficīscitur ut terrās inclutās Siciliam atque Ītaliam
vīseret. Ubi eō vēnit, aurēs omnium mentēsque in utrīusque
terrae urbibus dēlectāvit; et posteā, grandem pecūniam adeptus,
Corinthum īnstituit redīre. Navem igitur et nautās, ut nōtiō-
rēs amīciōrēsque sibi, Corinthiōs dēlēgit. Sed eī Corinthiī,
20 homine acceptō, navīque in altum prōvectā, praedae pecūniae-
que cupidī, cōnsilium cēpērunt dē necandō Ariōne. Tum ille,
perniciē intellēctā, pecūniam cēteraque sua eīs dedit; vītam
modo sibi ut parcerent, ōrāvit. Nautae precum eius hārum
miseritī sunt hāctenus, ut eī necem per vim suīs manibus nōn
25 adferrent; sed imperāvērunt, ut iam statim cōram dēsilīret praeceps in mare. Homō ibi territus, spē omnī vītae perditā, id
ūnum posteā ōrāvit, ut, priusquam mortem oppeteret, induere
permitterent sua sibi omnia vestīmenta et fidēs capere et canere
carmen. Ferōs et immānēs nautās studium tamen audiendī
30 subit; quod ōrāverat, impetrat. Atque ibi mox dē mōre cīnctus,
amictus, ōrnātus, stānsque in summā puppī, carmen, quod
'orthium' dīcitur, vōce sublātissimā cantāvit. Ad postrēma
cantūs cum fidibus ōrnātūque omnī, sīcut stābat canēbatque,
iēcit sēsē procul in prōfundum.

30. Arion and the Dolphin: The Rescue

Nautae, haudquāquam dubitantēs quīn perīsset, cursum quem facere coeperant tenuērunt. Sed novum et mīrum et pium facīnus contigit. Delphīnus repente inter undās adnāvit, fluitantīque sēsē hominī subdidit, et, dorsō super flūctūs ēditō, vectāvit; incolumīque eum corpore et ōrnātū Taenarum in ter- 5 ram Lacōnicam dēvexit. Tum Arīōn prōrsus ex eō locō Corinthum petīvit, tālemque Periandrō rēgī, quālis delphīnō vectus erat, inopīnantī sēsē obtulit, eīque rem, sīcutī acciderat, nārrāvit. Rēx istaec parum crēdidit; Arīōnem, quasi falleret, custōdīrī iussit; nautās inquīsītōs, ablēgātō Arīōne, dissimulanter 10 interrogāvit, ecquid audīssent in hīs locīs, unde vēnissent, dē Arīōne. Dīxērunt hominem, cum inde īrent, in terrā Italiā fuisse, eumque illīc flōrēre. Tum inter haec eōrum verba Arīōn cum fidibus et vestīmentīs, cum quibus sē in salum dēiēcerat, exstitit; nautae, stupefactī convictīque, īre īnfitiās nōn quīvē- 15 runt. Eam fābulam dīcunt Lesbiī et Corinthiī, atque est fābulae argūmentum, quod simulācra duo aēnea ad Taenarum vīsuntur, delphīnus vehēns et homō īnsidēns.

31. Mithridates

Mithridātēs ille, Pontī rēx, remediōrum adsiduō ūsū ā clandestīnīs epulārum īnsidiīs cavēbat; quīn etiam ūltrō, ostentandī 20 grātiā, venēnum rapidum et vēlōx saepenumerō hausit, atque id tamen sine noxā fuit. Quāmobrem posteā, cum proeliō victus in ūltima rēgnī refūgisset et morī dēcrēvisset, venēna violentissima festīnandae necis causā frūstrā expertus, suō sē ipse gladiō trānsēgit. 25

Q. Ennius tria corda habēre sēsē dīcēbat, quod loquī Graecē et Oscē et Latīnē scīret; Mithridātēs autem quīnque et vīgintī gentium, quās sub diciōne habuit, linguās sciēbat, cumque eārum omnium gentium virīs haud umquam per interpretem conlocūtus est, sed ut quemque appellāvit, prōinde linguā et ōrā- 30 tiōne ipsīus, nōn minus scītē, quam sī gentīlis eius esset, locūtus est.

32. Protagoras and His Pupil

Euāthlus, adulēscēns dīves, ēloquentiae discendae causārum-
que ōrandārum cupidus fuit.   Is in disciplīnam Prōtagorae sēsē
dedit, datūrumque sē promīsit mercēdem grandem pecūniam,
quantam Prōtagorās petīverat; dīmidiumque eius dedit iam
5 tunc statim, priusquam disceret, pepigitque, ut reliquum dīmidium daret, quō prīmō diē causam apud iūdicēs ōrāsset et vīcis-
set.   Posteā, cum diū audītor Prōtagorae fuisset, causās tamen
nōn reciperet, tempusque iam longum trānscurreret, et facere
id vidērētur, nē reliquum mercēdis daret, capit cōnsilium Prōta-
10 gorās, ut tum exīstimābat, astūtum: petere īnstitit ex pactō
mercēdem, lītem cum Euāthlō contestātur.
   Et cum ad iūdicēs vēnissent, tum Prōtagorās sīc exōrsus est:
"Disce," inquit, "stultissime adulēscēns, utrōque modō fore utī
reddās quod petō, sīve contrā tē prōnūntiātum erit sīve prō tē.
15 Nam sī contrā tē līs data erit, mercēs mihi ex sententiā dēbēbitur, quia ego vīcerō; sīn vērō secundum tē iūdicātum erit, mercēs
mihi ex pactō dēbēbitur, quia tū vīceris."
   Ad ea respondit Euāthlus: "Disce tū quoque, magister sapien-
tissime, utrōque modō fore utī nōn reddam quod petis, sīve
20 contrā mē prōnūntiātum erit sīve prō mē.   Nam sī iūdicēs prō
causā meā sēnserint, nihil tibi ex sententiā dēbēbitur, quia ego
vīcerō; sīn contrā mē prōnūntiāverint, nihil tibi ex pactō dēbēbitur, quia nōn vīcerō."
   Tum iūdicēs, inexplicābile hoc esse ratī, rem iniūdicātam re-
25 līquērunt, caüsamque in diem longissimam distulērunt.   Sīc ab
adulēscente discipulō magister ēloquentiae inclutus suō ipse
argūmentō cōnfūtātus est.

33.   Roman Respect for an Oath

Post proelium Cannēnse Hannibal, Carthāginiēnsium imperātor, ex captīvīs nostrīs ēlēctōs decem Rōmam mīsit, mandā-
30 vitque eīs pactusque est ut, sī populō Rōmānō vidērētur, permūtātiō fieret captīvōrum, et prō hīs, quōs alterī plūrēs acciperent,
darent argentī pondō lībram et sēlībram.   Hoc, priusquam pro-

ficīscerentur, iūsiūrandum eōs adēgit: reditūrōs sē esse in castra.
Poenica, sī Rōmānī captīvōs nōn permūtārent.

Veniunt Rōmam decem captīvī. Mandātum Poenī imperātōris in senātū expōnunt. Permūtātiō senātuī nōn placet. Pa-
rentēs, cognātī, adfīnēsque captīvōrum amplexī eōs postlīminiō 5
in patriam redīsse dīcēbant, statumque eōrum integrum incolu-
memque esse, ac, nē ad hostēs redīre vellent, ōrābant. Tum
octō ex hīs postlīminium iūstum nōn esse sibi respondērunt,
quoniam iūreiūrandō vīnctī essent, statimque, utī iūrātī erant,
ad Hannibalem profectī sunt. Duo reliquī Rōmae mānsērunt 10
solūtōsque sē esse ac līberātōs religiōne dīcēbant, quoniam, cum
ēgressī castra hostium essent, commentīciō cōnsiliō regressī
eōdem essent tamquam ob aliquam fortuītam causam, atque
rūrsum iniūrātī abīssent. Haec eōrum fraudulenta calliditās
tam esse turpis existimāta est ut contemptī vulgō sint, cēnsō- 15
rēsque eōs posteā omnibus ignōminiīs adfēcerint, quoniam, quod
factūrōs sē iūrāverant, nōn fēcissent.

Cornēlius autem Nepōs in librō Exemplōrum quīntō id quoque
litterīs mandāvit: multīs in senātū placuisse, ut hī, quī redīre
nōllent, datīs custōdibus ad Hannibalem dēdūcerentur; sed eam 20
sententiam numerō plūrium, quibus id nōn vidērētur, superā-
tam; eōs tamen, quī ad Hannibalem nōn redīssent, usque adeō
invīsōs fuisse, ut taedium vītae cēperint necemque sibi cōnscī-
verint.

34. Sertorius and the Doe

Sertōrius, vir ācer ēgregiusque dux, et ūtendī et regendī exerci- 25
tūs perītus fuit. Is in temporibus difficillimīs et mentiēbātur
mīlitibus, si mendācium proderat, et litterās compositās prō
vērīs legēbat, et somnium simulābat, et falsās religiōnēs cōnferē-
bat, sī quid istae rēs eum apud mīlitum animōs adiuvābant.
Illud Sertōriī nōbile est: Cerva alba eximiae pulchritūdinis et 30
vīvācissimae celeritātis ā Lūsitānō eī quōdam dōnō data est.
Hanc sibi oblātam dīvīnitus et īnstīnctam Diānae nūmine conloquī sēcum monēreque et docēre quae ūtilia factū essent, omnibus
persuāsit; ac, sī quid dūrius vidēbātur, quod mīlitibus faciendum

erat, ā cervā sēsē monitum praedicābat. Id cum dīxerat, ūni-
versī, tamquam sī deō, libentēs eī pārēbant.   Ea cerva quōdam
diē, cum incursiō esset hostium nūntiāta, fēstīnātiōne et tumultū
cōnsternāta in fugam sē prōripuit atque in palūde proximā
5 dēlituit, et posteā requīsīta perīsse crēdita est.

35.   Sertorius and the Doe (*Contd.*)

Neque multīs diēbus post, inventam esse cervam Sertōriō
nūntiātur.   Tum eum, quī nūntiāverat, iussit tacēre, ac, nē cui
palam dīceret, interminātus est; praecipitque, ut eam posterō
diē repente in eum locum, in quō ipse cum amīcīs esset, immitte-
10 ret.   Admissīs deinde amīcīs postrīdiē, vīdisse sē in quiēte ait
cervam, quae perīsset, ad sē revertī, et, ut prius consuērat, quod
opus esset factō, praedīcere; tum hominī signum dat, cerva
ēmissa in cubiculum Sertōriī intrōrūpit, clāmor factus et orta
admīrātiō est.
15   Eaque hominum barbarōrum crēdulitās Sertōriō in magnīs
rēbus magnō ūsuī fuit.   Memoria prōdita est ex hīs nātiōnibus,
quae cum Sertōriō faciēbant, cum multīs proeliīs superātus esset,
nēminem umquam ab eō dēscīvisse, quamquam id genus hominum esset mōbilissimum.

36.   Aesop's Fable of the Lark and the Reapers

20   Aesōpus ille fābulārum scrīptor haud immeritō sapiēns exīsti-
mātus est, quoniam, quae ūtilia monitū suāsūque erant, nōn
sevērē neque imperiōsē praecēpit, ut philosophīs mōs est, sed,
fēstīvōs apologōs commentus, rēs salūbrēs in mentēs animōsque
hominum cum audiendī quādam inlecebrā intrōdūxit.   Velut
25 haec eius fābula dē parvae avis nīdulō lepidē et iūcundē monet
spem fīdūciamque rērum, quās efficere quis possit, haud umquam in aliō, sed in sēmet ipsō habendam.   "Avis," inquit,
"est parva, nōmen est cassita.   Habitat in segetibus id fermē
temporis ut appetat messis pullīs iam iam plūmantibus.   Cassita
30 quaedam nīdum in sēmentēs forte congesserat tempestīviōrēs;

proptereā, frūmentīs flāvēscentibus, pullī etiam tunc implūmēs
erant.　Dum igitur ipsa īret cibum pullīs quaesītum, monet eōs,
ut, sī quid ibi reī novae fieret dicerēturve, animadverterent,
idque sibi, ubi redīsset, nūntiārent."

37.　The Lark and the Reapers (Contd.)

"Dominus posteā segetum illārum fīlium adulēscentem vocat 5
et, 'Vidēsne,' inquit, 'haec mātūruisse et manūs iam postulāre?
Idcircō crās, ubi prīmum dīlūcēscit, fac amīcōs eās et rogēs,
veniant operamque mūtuam dent et in hāc messī nōs adiuvent.'
Haec ubi ille dīxit, discessit.　Atque ubi redit cassita, pullī
tremibundī circumstrepere ōrāreque mātrem, ut iam statim 10
properet inque alium locum sēsē asportet: 'Nam dominus,'
inquiunt, 'mīsit, quī amīcōs roget, utī lūce oriente veniant et
metant.'　Māter iubet eōs ōtiōsō animō esse: 'Sī enim dominus,'
inquit, 'messim ad amīcōs reicit, crās seges nōn metētur, neque
necesse est hodiē mē vōs auferre.'　Diē posterō māter in pābu- 15
lum volat.　Dominus quōs rogāverat opperītur.　Sōl fervit, et
fit nihil; it diēs, et amīcī nūllī eunt.　Tum ille rūrsum fīliō,
'Amīcī istī,' inquit, 'cessatōrēs sunt.　Quīn potius īmus et cognātōs adfīnēsque nostrōs ōrāmus, ut adsint crās ad metendum?' "

38.　The Lark and the Reapers (Concld.)

"Itidem hoc pullī pavefactī mātrī nūntiant.　Māter hortā- 20
tur, ut tum quoque sine metū ac sine cūrā sint; cognātōs adfīnēsque nūllōs fermē tam facilēs esse ait, ut ad labōrem capessen-
dum nihil cūnctentur et statim dictō oboediant: 'Vōs modo,'
inquit, 'advertite, sī modo quid dēnuō dīcētur.'　Aliā lūce ortā,
avis in pāstum profecta est.　Cognātī et adfīnēs operam, quam 25
dare rogātī sunt, neglēxērunt.　Ad postrēmum igitur dominus
fīliō, 'Valeant,' inquit, 'amīcī cum propinquīs.　Adferēs prīmā
lūce falcēs duās: ūnam egomet mihi et tū tibi capiēs alteram, et
frūmentum nōsmet ipsī manibus nostrīs crās metēmus.'　Id ubi
ex pullīs dīxisse dominum māter audīvit, 'Tempus,' inquit, 'est 30
cēdendī et abeundī; fīet nunc dubiō procul quod futūrum dīxit.

In ipsō enim iam vertitur cuius rēs est, non in aliō, unde peti-
tur.' Atque ita cassita ē nīdō migrāvit, seges ā dominō dēmessa
est." Hunc Aesōpī apologum Q. Ennius in Satirīs scītē admodum et venustē versibus quadrātīs composuit. Quōrum duo
5 postrēmī hī sunt, quōs habēre in corde atque in memoriā operae
pretium esse hercle putō:

Hóc erit tibi árgūmentum sémper in prōmptú situm
né quid exspectés amīcōs, quód tūte agere póssīes.

39. Metellus on Marriage

Multīs et ērudītīs virīs audientibus legēbātur ōrātiō Metellī
10 Numidicī, gravis ac disertī virī, quam in cēnsūrā dīxit ad populum dē dūcendīs uxōribus, cum eum ad mātrimōnia capessenda
hortārētur. In eā ōrātiōne ita scrīptum est: "Sī sine uxōre
vīvere possēmus, Quirītēs, omnī eā molestiā carērēmus; sed
quoniam ita nātūra trādidit, ut nec cum illīs satis commodē,
15 nec sine illīs ūllō modō vīvī possit, salūtī perpetuae potius quam
brevī voluptātī cōnsulendum est." Vidēbātur quibusdam
Q. Metellum cēnsōrem, cui cōnsilium esset ad uxōrēs dūcendās
populum hortārī, nōn oportuisse dē molestiā incommodīsque
perpetuīs reī uxōriae cōnfitērī; T. autem Castricius rēctē atque
20 dignē Metellum esse locūtum exīstimābat. "Aliter," inquit,
"cēnsor loquī dēbet, aliter rhētor. Rhētorī concessum est sen-
tentiīs ūtī falsīs, audācibus, versūtīs, dum modo vērī similēs
sint; sed enim Metellum, sānctum virum, illā gravitāte et fidē
praeditum, cum tantā honōrum atque vītae dignitāte apud
25 populum Rōmānum loquentem, nihil decuit aliud dīcere, quam
quod vērum esse sibi atque omnibus vidēbātur, praesertim cum
dē eā rē dīceret, quae cotīdiānā intellegentiā et commūnī vītae
ūsū comprehenderētur. Dē molestiā igitur cūnctīs hominibus
nōtissimā cōnfessus, tum dēnique facile, quod fuit rērum vali-
30 dissimum et vērissimum, eīs persuāsit cīvitātem salvam esse
sine mātrimōniōrum frequentiā nōn posse."

40. The Pythagorean Curriculum

Ōrdō atque ratiō Pȳthagorae recipiendī īnstituendīque discipulōs huiuscemodī fuisse trāditur: Iam ā prīncipiō adulēscentēs,
quī sēsē ad discendum obtulerant, ἐφυσιογνωμόνει.[2] Id verbum significat mōrēs nātūrāsque hominum coniectūrā quādam
dē ōris et vultūs ingeniō dēque totīus corporis habitū cognōscere. 5
Tum quī, explōrātus ab eō, idōneus inventus erat, recipī in
disciplīnam statim iubēbat et tempus certum tacēre: nōn omnēs
idem, sed aliōs aliud tempus prō aestimātō captū sollertiae.
Is autem, qui tacēbat, quae dīcēbantur ab aliīs audiēbat, neque
percontārī, sī parum intellēxerat, neque commentārī, quae 10
audierat, fās erat; sed nōn minus quisquam tacuit quam biennium: hī appellābantur intrā tempus tacendī audiendīque
ἀκουστικοί.[3] Ubi autem rēs didicerant rērum omnium difficilli-
mās, tacēre audīreque, atque esse iam coeperant silentiō ērudītī,
tum verba facere et quaerere, quaeque audierant scrībere, et 15
quae ipsī opīnābantur exprōmere poterant; hī dīcēbantur in eō
tempore μαθηματικοί,[4] ab hīs scīlicet artibus, quās iam discere
atque meditārī coeperant: quoniam geōmetriam, gnōmonicam,
mūsicam cēterāsque item disciplīnas altiōrēs μαθήματα[5] veterēs
Graecī appellābant. Exinde, hīs scientiae studiīs ōrnātī, ad 20
perspicienda mundī opera et prīncipia nātūrae prōcēdēbant, ac
tunc dēnique nōminābantur φυσικοί.[6] Sed id quoque nōn
praetereundum est, quod omnēs, simul atque ā Pȳthagorā in
cohortem illam disciplīnārum receptī erant, in medium dabant
quod quisque pecūniae habēbat. 25

41. Roman Military Discipline

P. Crassus Mūciānus cum in cōnsulātū obtinēret Asiam prōvinciam et adsidēre oppugnāreque Leucās parāret, opusque esset

---

[2] ephysiognōmónei.
[3] akoustikof.
[4] mathēmatikof
[5] mathḗmata.
[6] physikof.

firmā atque longā trabe, quā arietem faceret, quō mūrōs eius
oppidī quateret, scrīpsit ad architectona Mȳlasēnsium, sociōrum
amīcōrumque populī Rōmānī, ut ex mālīs duōbus, quōs apud
eōs vīdisset, uter maior esset, eum mittendum cūrāret. Tum
5 architectōn, cum comperīsset quamobrem mālum dēsīderāret,
nōn, utī iussus erat, maiōrem, sed, quem esse magis idōneum
aptiōremque faciendō arietī faciliōremque portātū exīstimabat,
minōrem mīsit. Crassus eum vocārī iussit, et, cum interrogāsset, cūr nōn, quem iusserat, mīsisset, causīs ratiōnibusque
10 quas dictitābat sprētīs, vestīmenta dētrahī iussit virgīsque multum cecīdit, corrumpī atque dissolvī omnem auctōritātem imperātōris ratus, sī quis ad id, quod facere iussus est, nōn obsequiō
dēbitō, sed cōnsiliō nōn dēsīderātō respondeat.

42. Epitaphs of Three Roman Poets

Trium poētārum inlūstrium epigrammata, Cn. Naeviī, Plautī,
15 M. Pācuviī, quae ipsī fēcērunt et incīdenda sepulcrō suō relīquē-
runt, nōbilitātis eōrum grātiā et venustātis scrībenda in hīs
commentāriīs esse dūxī.

Epigramma Naeviī plēnum superbiae Campānae, quod testimōnium esse iūstum potuisset, nisi ab ipsō dictum esset:

20   Immortālēs mortālēs sī foret fās flēre
    flērent dīvae Camēnae Naevium poētam.
    Itaque postquam est Orchī trāditus thēsaurō
    oblītī sunt Rōmae loquier linguā Latīnā.

Epigramma Plautī, quod dubitāssēmus, an Plautī foret, nisi
25 ā M. Varrōne positum esset in librō Dē Poētīs prīmō:

    Postquam est mortem aptus Plautus, Cōmoedia lūget,
    scaena est dēsertā, dein Rīsus, Lūdus, Iocusque,
    et Numerī innumerī simul omnēs conlacrimārunt.

Epigramma Pācuviī verēcundissimum et pūrissimum dignum-
30 que eius ēlegantissimā gravitāte:

Aduléscēns, tam etsī próperās, hoc tē sáxulum
rogat út sē aspiciās, deínde quod scrīptúm est legās:
hīc súnt poētae Pácuvī Mārcī sita
ossa.   Hóc volēbam néscius nē essēs.   Valē!

43. Deaths Caused by Overwhelming Joy

Diagorās Rhodius trīs fīliōs adulēscentēs habuit, ūnum pugi- 5
lem, alterum pancratiastēn, tertium luctātōrem.   Eōs omnēs
vīdit vincere corōnārīque Olympiae eōdem diē, et, cum ibi eum
trēs adulēscentēs amplexī, corōnīs suīs in capite patris positīs,
suāviārentur, cum populus flōrēs undique in eum iaceret, ibīdem
in stadiō, īnspectante populō, in ōsculīs atque in manibus fīliō- 10
rum animam exspīrāvit.

Praetereā in nostrīs annālibus scrīptum legimus, quō tempore
apud Cannās exercitus populī Rōmānī caesus est, anum mātrem,
nūntiō dē morte fīliī allātō, lūctū atque maerōre adfectam esse;
sed is nūntius nōn vērus fuit, atque is adulēscēns nōn multō post 15
ex eā pugnā in urbem redit; anus, repente fīliō vīsō, cōpiā atque
quasi ruīnā incidentis inopīnātī gaudiī oppressa exanimātaque
est.

44. Fabricius and Rufinus

Fabrícius Luscīnus magnā glōriā vir magnīsque rēbus gestīs
fuit.   P. Cornēlius Rūfīnus manū quidem strēnuus, et bellātor 20
bonus, mīlitārisque disciplīnae perītus admodum fuit, sed fūrāx
homō et avāritiā ācrī erat.   Hunc Fabricius nōn probābat,
neque amīcō ūtēbātur, ōditque eum propter mōrēs.   Sed cum
in temporibus difficillimīs cōnsulēs creandī forent, et is Rūfīnus
peteret cōnsulātum, competītōrēsque eius essent imbellēs quī- 25
dam et futtilēs, summā ope adnīxus est Fabricius, utī Rūfīnō
cōnsulātus dēferrētur.   Eam rem plērīsque admīrantibus, quod
hominem avārum, cui esset inimīcissimus, creārī cōnsulem vellet, "Cīvis," inquit, "potius mē compīlet, quam hostis vēndat!"
Hunc Rūfīnum posteā bis cōnsulātū et dictātūrā functum 30

cēnsor Fabricius senātū mōvit ob lūxuriae notam, quod decem
pondō lībrās argentī factī habēret.

45. An Ancient Filibuster

C. Caesar cōnsul M. Catōnem sententiam rogāvit. Catō
rem, quae cōnsulēbātur, quoniam nōn ē rē pūblicā vidēbātur,
5 perficī nōlēbat. Eius reī dūcendae grātiā longā ōrātiōne ūtēbātur, eximēbatque dīcendō diem. Erat enim iūs senātōrī, ut
sententiam rogātus dīceret ante quicquid dē aliā rē vellet et
quoad vellet. Caesar cōnsul viātōrem vocāvit eumque, cum
fīnem nōn faceret, prēndī loquentem et in carcerem dūcī iussit.
10 Senātus cōnsurrēxit et prōsequēbātur Catōnem in carcerem.
Hāc invidiā factā, Caesar dēstitit et mittī Catōnem iussit.

46. Protagoras and Democritus

Prōtagoram, virum in studiīs doctrīnārum ēgregium, cuius
nōmen Platō librō suō illī inclutō īnscrīpsit, adulēscentem aiunt
vīctūs quaerendī grātiā baiulum fuisse. Is dē proximō fundō
15 Abdēra in oppidum, cuius cīvis fuit, caudicēs lignī plūrimōs,
fūniculō brevī circumdatōs, portābat. Tum forte Dēmocritus,
cīvitātis eiusdem cīvis, homō ante aliōs virtūtis et philosophiae
grātiā venerandus, cum ēgrederētur extrā urbem, videt eum,
cum illō onere tam impedītō, facile atque expedītē incēdentem;
20 et prope accēdit, et iūnctūram lignī scītē perītēque factam cōnsī-
derat, petitque, ut paululum adquiēscat. Quod ubi Prōtagorās,
ut erat petītum, fēcit, atque Dēmocritus acervum illum et quasi
orbem caudicum, brevī vinculō comprehēnsum, ratiōne quasi
geōmetricā librārī continērīque animadvertit, interrogāvit, quis
25 id lignum ita composuisset; et cum ille id ā sē compositum
dīxisset, dēsīderāvit ut solveret, ac dēnuō in modum eundem
conlocāret. At postquam ille solvit et similiter composuit, tum
Dēmocritus animī aciem sollertiamque hominis nōn doctī dēmīrātus, "Mī adulēscēns," inquit, "cum ingenium bene faciendī
30 habeās, sunt maiōra meliōraque, quae facere mēcum potes";

abdūxitque eum statim, sēcumque habuit, et philosophiam eum
docuit; effēcitque ut fieret quantus posteā fuit.

47. How Croesus' Son Found His Voice

Fīlius Croesī rēgis, cum iam fārī per aetātem posset, īnfāns
erat, et, cum iam multum adolēvisset, item nihil fārī quībat.
Mūtus igitur diū habitus est. Cum in patrem eius, bellō magnō 5
victum, et urbe in quā erat captā, hostis, gladiō dēductō, eum
rēgem esse ignōrāns, invāderet, dīdūxit adulēscēns ōs, clāmāre
nītēns; eōque nīsū, atque impetū spīritūs, vitium nōdumque
linguae rūpit, plānēque ēlocūtus est, clāmāns in hostem, nē rēx
Croesus occiderētur. Tum et hostis gladium redūxit, et rēx 10
vītā dōnātus est, et adulēscēns loquī prōrsum deinceps coepit.

48. A Devoted Pupil of Socrates

Philosophus Taurus, vir disciplīnā Platōnicā celeber, cum
aliīs bonīs multīs salūbribusque exemplīs iuvenēs hortābātur ad
philosophiam capessendam, tum maximē hāc rē eōrum animōs
excitābat, quam dīcēbat Euclīdem Sōcraticum factitāvisse. 15
"Dēcrētō," inquit, "suō Athēniēnsēs cāverant, ut, quī Megarōrum cīvis esset, sī intulisse Athēnās pedem inventus esset, ut
ea rēs eī hominī capitālis esset; tantō Athēniēnsēs," inquit,
"odiō flagrābant fīnitimōrum hominum Megarēnsium. Tum
Euclīdēs, quī Megarēnsis erat, quīque ante id dēcrētum et esse 20
Athēnīs et audīre Sōcratēn cōnsuēverat, postquam id dēcrētum
sānxērunt, sub noctem, cum advesperāsceret, tunicā longā mu-
liebrī indūtus et palliō versicolōre amictus et caput rīcā vēlātus,
domō suā Megarīs Athēnās ad Sōcratēn commeābat, ut, vel
noctis aliquō tempore, cōnsiliōrum sermōnumque eius fieret 25
particeps; rūrsusque sub lūcem mīlia passuum paulō amplius
vīgintī, eādem veste illā tēctus, redībat. At nunc," inquit,
"vidēre possumus philosophōs ultrō currere, ut doceant, ad forēs
iuvenum dīvitum, eōsque ibi sedēre atque opperīrī ad merīdiem,
donec discipulī nocturnum omne vīnum ēdormiant."   30

49. Ancient Public Libraries

Librōs Athēnīs disciplīnārum līberālium pūblicē ad legendum
praebendōs prīmus cūrāsse dīcitur Pīsistratus tyrannus. Deinceps studiōsius accūrātiusque ipsī Athēniēnsēs auxērunt; sed
omnem illam posteā librōrum cōpiam Xerxēs, Athēnārum potī-
5 tus, urbe ipsā praeter arcem incēnsā, abstulit asportāvitque in
Persās. Eōs porrō librōs ūniversōs, multīs post annīs, Seleucus
rēx, quī Nīcānōr appellātus est, referendōs Athēnās cūrāvit.
Ingēns posteā numerus librōrum in Aegyptō ab Ptolemaeīs
rēgibus cōnfectus est ad mīlia fermē volūmina septingenta: sed
10 ea omnia bellō Alexandrīnō, dum dīripitur ea cīvitās, ā mīlitibus
auxiliāriīs forte incēnsa sunt.

50. Alexander and Aristotle

Philippus, terrae Macedoniae rēx, cum in omnī ferē tempore
negōtiīs bellī victōriīsque exercitus esset, ā līberālī tamen Mūsā
et ā studiīs hūmānitātis numquam āfuit. Feruntur adeō librī
15 epistulārum eius, munditiae et venustātis et prūdentiae plēnā-
rum; velut sunt illae litterae, quibus Aristotelī philosophō nā-
tum esse sibi Alexandrum nūntiāvit.

Ea epistula exscrībenda esse vīsa est ad commonendōs paren-
tum animōs. Expōnenda est igitur ad hanc fermē sententiam:

20   Philippus Aristotelī Salūtem Dīcit

Fīlium mihi genitum scītō. Quā dē causā equidem
dīs habeō grātiam; nōn proinde quia nātus est, quam
prō eō, quod nāscī contigit temporibus vītae tuae.
Spērō enim fore ut, ēductus ērudītusque ā tē, dignus
25 exsistat et nōbīs et rērum nostrārum susceptiōne.

II. CORNELIUS NEPOS

51. Themistocles and the Walls of Athens

Magnus bellō Persicō Themistoclēs fuit neque minor in pāce. Cum enim Phalēricō portū neque magnō ncque bonō Athēniēn- sēs ūterentur, huius cōnsiliō triplex Pīraeī portus cōnstitūtus est iīsque moenibus circumdatus ut ipsam urbem dignitāte aequiperāret, ūtilitāte superāret. Īdem mūrōs Athēniēnsium 5 restituit praecipuō suō perīculō. Namque Lacedaemoniī cau- sam idōneam nactī propter barbarōrum excursiōnes, quā negā- rent oportēre extrā Peloponnēsum ūllam urbem mūrōs habēre, nē essent loca mūnīta, quae hostēs possīderent, Athēniēnsēs aedificantēs prōhibēre sunt cōnātī. Hoc longē aliō spectābat 10 atque vidērī volēbant. Athēniēnsēs enim duābus victōriīs, Marathōniā et Salamīniā, tantam glōriam apud omnēs gentēs erant cōnsecūtī, ut intellegerent Lacedaemoniī de prīncipātū sibi cum iīs certāmen fore. Quārē eōs quam īnfirmissimōs esse volēbant. Postquam autem audiērunt mūrōs struī, lēgātōs 15 Athēnās mīsērunt, quī id fierī vetārent. Hīs praesentibus dēsiē- runt ac sē dē eā rē lēgātōs ad eōs missūrōs dīxērunt. Hanc lēgātiōnem suscēpit Themistoclēs et sōlus prīmō profectus est; reliquī lēgātī ut tum exīrent, cum satis altī tuendō mūrī exstrūctī vidērentur, praecēpit; interim omnēs, servī atque līberī, opus 20 facerent, neque ūllī locō parcerent, sīve sacer sīve prīvātus esset sīve pūblicus, et undique, quod idōneum ad mūniendum putā- rent, congererent. Quō factum est ut Athēniēnsium mūrī ex sacellīs sepulcrīsque cōnstārent.

Themistoclēs autem, ut Lacedaemonem vēnit, adīre ad ma- 25 gistrātūs nōluit, et dedit operam ut quam longissimē tempus dūceret, causam interpōnēns sē collēgās exspectāre. Cum Lacedaemoniī quererentur opus nihilō minus fierī, eumque in eā rē cōnārī fallere, interim reliquī lēgātī sunt cōnsecūtī. Ā

quibus cum audīsset nōn multum superesse mūnītiōnis, ad ephorōs Lacedaemoniōrum accessit, penes quōs summum erat imperium, atque apud eōs contendit falsa iīs esse dēlāta; quārē
aequum esse illōs virōs bonōs nōbilēsque mittere, qui rem explō-
5 rārent; intereā sē obsidem retinērent. Gestus est eī mōs,
trēsque lēgātī, functī summīs honōribus, Athēnās missī sunt.
Cum hīs collēgās suōs Themistoclēs iussit proficiscī, iīsque praedīxit, ut nē prius Lacedaemoniōrum lēgātōs dīmitterent quam
ipse esset remissus. Hōs postquam Athēnās pervēnisse ratus
10 est, ad magistrātūs senātumque Lacedaemoniōrum adiit et apud
eōs līberrimē prōfessus est: Athēniēnsēs suō cōnsiliō, quod commūnī iūre gentium facere possent, deōs pūblicōs, suōsque patriōs, ac penātēs, quō facilius ab hoste possent dēfendere, mūrīs
saepsisse; neque, in eō, quod inūtile esset Graeciae fēcisse. Nam
15 illōrum urbem prōpugnāculum oppositum esse barbarīs, apud
quam iam bis cōpiās rēgias fēcisse naufragium. Lacedaemoniōs
autem male et iniūstē facere, quī id potius intuērentur, quod
ipsōrum dominātiōnī, quam quod ūniversae Graeciae ūtile esset.
Quārē, sī suōs lēgātōs recipere vellent, quōs Athēnās mīserant,
20 sē remitterent, cum aliter illōs numquam in patriam essent
receptūrī.

52. The Ostracism of Aristides

Aristīdēs, Lȳsimachī fīlius, Athēniēnsis, aequālis ferē fuit
Themistoclī atque cum eō dē prīncipātū contendit: namque
obtrectārunt inter sē. In hīs autem cognitum est, quantō ante-
25 stāret ēloquentia innocentiae. Quamquam enim adeō excellē-
bat Aristīdēs abstinentiā, ut ūnus post hominum memoriam
cognōmine Iūstus sit appellātus, tamen ā Themistocle conlabe-
factus testulā illā exsiliō decem annōrum multātus est. Quī
quidem cum intellegeret reprimī concitātam multitūdinem nōn
30 posse, cēdēnsque animadvertisset quendam scrībentem, ut
patriā pellerētur, quaesīsse ab eō dīcitur, quārē id faceret, aut
quid Aristīdēs commīsisset, cūr tantā poenā dignus dūcerētur.
Cui ille respondit sē ignōrāre Aristīdēn, sed sibi nōn placēre,
quod tam cupidē labōrāsset, ut praeter cēterōs Iūstus appellārē-

tur. Hic decem annōrum lēgitimam poenam nōn pertulit.
Nam postquam Xerxēs in Graeciam dēscendit, populī scītō in
patriam restitūtus est.

53. Lysander's Self-Accusation

Lȳsander Lacedaemonius cum, praefectus classis, in bellō
multa crūdēliter avārēque fēcisset, dēque iīs rēbus suspicārētur 5
ad cīvēs suōs esse perlātum, petiit ā Pharnabāzō ut ad ephorōs
sibi testimōnium daret, quantā sānctitāte bellum gessisset so-
ciōsque tractāsset, dēque eā rē accūrātē scrīberet: magnam
enim eius auctōritātem in eā rē futūram. Huic ille līberāliter
pollicētur; librum grandem verbīs multīs cōnscrīpsit, in quibus 10
summīs eum effert laudibus. Quem cum hic lēgisset probāsset-
que, dum signātur, alterum parī magnitūdine, et tantā similitū-
dine ut discernī nōn posset, signātum subiēcit, in quō accūrā-
tissimē eius avāritiam perfidiamque accūsārat. Lȳsander domum cum redīsset, postquam dē suīs rēbus gestīs apud maxi- 15
mum magistrātum quae voluerat dīxerat, testimōniī locō librum
ā Pharnabāzō datum trādidit. Hunc, summōtō Lȳsandrō cum
ephorī cognōssent, ipsī legendum dedērunt. Ita ille imprūdēns
ipse suus fuit accūsātor.

54. Epaminondas of Thebes

Epamīnōndam Thēbānum fuisse patientem, suōrumque iniū- 20
riās ferentem cīvium, quod sē patriae īrāscī nefās esse dūceret,
haec sunt testimōnia. Cum eum propter invidiam cīvēs suī
praeficere exercituī nōluissent, duxque esset dēlēctus bellī imperītus, cuius errōre rēs eō esset dēducta, ut omnēs dē salūte
pertimēscerent, quod locōrum angustiīs clausī ab hostibus obsi- 25
dēbantur, dēsīderārī coepta est Epamīnōndae dīligentia: erat
enim ibi, prīvātus, numerō mīlitis. Ā quō cum peterent opem,
nūllam adhibuit memoriam contumēliae, et exercitum obsidiōne
līberātum domum redūxit incolumem. Nec vērō hoc semel
fēcit, sed saepius; maximē autem fuit inlūstre, cum in Pelopon- 30
nēsum exercitum dūxisset adversus Lacedaemoniōs, habēretque

collēgās duōs, quōrum alter erat Pelopidās, vir fortis ac strēnuus.
Hī cum, crīminibus adversāriōrum, omnēs in invidiam vēnissent,
ob eamque rem imperium iīs esset abrogātum, atque in eōrum
locum aliī praetōrēs successissent, Epamīnōndās populī scītō
5 nōn pāruit, idemque ut facerent persuāsit collēgīs; et bellum,
quod suscēperat, gessit. Namque animadvertēbat, nisi id fēcisset, tōtum exercitum propter praetōrum imprūdentiam īnscī-
tiamque bellī peritūrum. Lēx erat Thēbīs, quae morte multā-
bat, sī quis imperium diūtius retinuisset, quam lēge praefīnītum
10 foret. Hanc Epamīnōndās cum reī pūblicae cōnservandae
causā lātam vidēret, ad perniciem cīvitātis cōnferrī nōluit, et
quattuor mēnsibus diūtius, quam populus iusserat, gessit imperium.

Postquam domum reditum est, collēgae eius hōc crīmine
15 accūsābantur. Quibus ille permīsit, ut omnem causam in sē
trānsferrent, suāque operā factum contenderent, ut lēgī nōn
oboedīrent. Quā dēfēnsiōne illīs perīculō līberātīs, nēmō Epamīnōndam respōnsūrum putābat, quod quid dīceret nōn habēret.
At ille in iūdicium vēnit; nihil eōrum negāvit, quae adversāriī
20 crīminī dabant, omniaque quae collēgae dīxerant cōnfessus est;
neque recūsāvit quōminus lēgis poenam subīret, sed ūnum ab
iīs petīvit, ut in sepulcrō suō īnscrīberent: "Epamīnōndās ā
Thēbānīs morte multātus est, quod eōs coēgit apud Leuctra
superāre Lacedaemoniōs, quōs ante sē imperātōrem nēmō
25 Boeōtōrum ausus sit aspicere in aciē, quodque ūnō proeliō nōn
sōlum Thēbās ab interitū retrāxit, sed etiam ūniversam Graeciam in lībertātem vindicāvit, eōque rēs utrōrumque perdūxit,
ut Thēbānī Spartam oppugnārent, Lacedaemoniī satis habērent,
sī salvī esse possent; neque prius bellāre dēstitit, quam, Messēnē
30 restitūtā, urbem eōrum obsidiōne clausit." Haec cum dīxisset,
rīsus omnium cum hilaritāte coortus est, neque quisquam iūdex
ausus est dē eō ferre suffrāgium. Sīc ā iūdiciō capitis maximā
discessit glōriā.

55. Hannibal's Oath

Hannibal velut hērēditāte relictum odium paternum ergā
35 Rōmānōs sīc cōnservāvit, ut prius animam quam id dēposuerit,

quī quidem, cum patriā pulsus esset et aliēnārum opum indigēret, numquam dēstiterit animō bellāre cum Rōmānīs.   Nam ut
omittam Philippum, quem absēns hostem reddidit Rōmānīs,
omnium iīs temporibus potentissimus rēx Antiochus fuit.   Hunc
tantā cupiditāte incendit bellandī, ut ūsque ā rubrō marī arma 5
cōnātus sit īnferre Ītaliae.   Ad quem cum lēgātī vēnissent Rōmānī, quī dē eius voluntāte explōrārent, darentque operam
cōnsiliīs clandestīnīs ut Hannibalem in suspiciōnem rēgī addūcerent, tamquam ab ipsīs corruptus alia atque anteā sentīret,
neque id frūstrā fēcissent idque Hannibal comperisset, sēque ab 10
interiōribus cōnsiliīs sēgregārī vīdisset, tempore datō adiit ad
rēgem, eīque cum multa dē fidē suā et odiō in Rōmānōs comme-
morāsset, hoc adiūnxit: "Pater meus," inquit, "Hamilcar, pue-
rulō mē, utpote nōn amplius novem annōs nātō, in Hispāniam
imperātor proficīscēns Carthāgine Iovī Optimō Maximō hostiās 15
immolāvit.   Quae dīvīna rēs dum cōnficiēbātur, quaesīvit ā mē
vellemne sēcum in castra proficīscī.   Id cum libenter accēpissem
atque ab eō petere coepissem nē dubitāret dūcere, tum ille,
'Faciam,' inquit, 'sī mihi fidem quam postulō dederis.'   Simul
mē ad āram addūxit, apud quam sacrificāre īnstituerat, eamque, 20
cēterīs remōtīs, tenentem iūrāre iussit numquam mē in amīcitiā
cum Rōmānīs fore.   Id ego iūsiūrandum patrī datum usque ad
hanc aetātem ita cōnservāvī, ut nēminī dubium esse dēbeat,
quīn reliquō tempore eādem mente sim futūrus.   Quārē sī quid
amīcē dē Rōmānīs cōgitābis, nōn imprūdenter fēceris, sī mē 25
cēlāris; cum quidem bellum parābis, tē ipsum frūstrāberis, sī
nōn mē in eō prīncipem posueris."

56.   Hannibal and the Cretans

Antiochō fugātō verēns Hannibal nē dederētur, quod sine
dubiō accidisset, sī suī fēcisset potestātem, Crētam ad Gortȳniōs
vēnit, ut ibi, quō sē cōnferret, cōnsīderāret.   Vīdit autem vir 30
omnium callidissimus in magnō sē fore perīculō, nisi quid prō-
vīdisset, propter avāritiam Crētēnsium: magnam enim sēcum
pecūniam portābat, dē quā sciēbat exīsse fāmam.   Itaque capit
tāle cōnsilium: amphorās complūrēs complet plumbō, summās

operit aurō et argentō; hās, praesentibus prīncipibus, dēpōnit
in templō Diānae, simulāns sē suās fortūnās illōrum fideī crēdere. Hīs in errōrem inductīs, statuās aēneās, quās sēcum
portābat, omnī suā pecūniā complet, eāsque in prōpatulō domī
5 abicit. Gortȳniī templum magnā cūrā custōdiunt, nōn tam ā
cēterīs quam ab Hannibale, nē ille, īnscientibus iīs, tolleret sua
sēcumque dūceret.

57. Hannibal's Death

Accidit cāsū ut lēgātī Prūsiae Rōmae apud T. Quīntium Flāminīnum cōnsulārem cēnārent, atque ibi, dē Hannibale men-
10 tiōne factā, ex iīs ūnus dīceret eum in Prūsiae rēgnō esse. Id
posterō diē Flāminīnus senātuī dētulit. Patrēs cōnscrīptī, quī
Hannibale vīvō numquam sē sine īnsidiīs futūrōs exīstimārent,
lēgātōs in Bīthȳniam mīsērunt, in iīs Flāminīnum, quī ab rēge
peterent nē inimīcissimum suum sēcum habēret, sibique dēderet.
15 Hīs Prūsiās negāre ausus nōn est; illud recūsāvit, nē id ā sē
fierī postulārent, quod adversus iūs hospitiī esset; ipsī, sī possent,
comprehenderent; locum, ubi esset, facile eōs inventūrōs. Hannibal enim ūnō locō sē tenēbat, in castellō quod eī ā rēge datum
erat mūnerī, idque sīc aedificārat, ut in omnibus partibus aedi-
20 ficiī exitūs habēret, scīlicet verēns nē ūsū venīret, quod accidit.
Hūc cum lēgātī Rōmānōrum vēnissent ac multitūdine domum
eius circumdedissent, puer ab ianuā prōspiciēns Hannibalī dīxit
plūrēs, praeter cōnsuētūdinem, armātos appārēre. Quī imperāvit eī, ut omnēs forēs aedificiī circumīret ac properē sibi
25 nūntiāret, num eōdem modō undique obsidērētur. Puer cum
celeriter quid vīdisset renūntiāsset, omnēsque exitūs occupātōs
ostendisset, sēnsit id nōn fortuītō factum, sed sē petī, neque sibi
diūtius vītam esse retinendam. Quam nē aliēnō arbitriō dī-
mitteret, memor prīstinārum virtūtum, venēnum, quod semper
30 sēcum habēre cōnsuērat, sūmpsit.

III. JULIUS CAESAR

58. Caesar on the Gauls and the Germans

Quoniam ad hunc locum perventum est, nōn aliēnum esse vidētur dē Galliae Germāniaeque mōribus, et quō differant hae nātiōnēs inter sē, prōpōnere. In Galliā, nōn sōlum in omnibus cīvitātibus atque in omnibus pāgīs partibusque, sed paene etiam in singulīs domibus, factiōnēs sunt, eārumque factiōnum sunt 5 prīncipēs quī summam auctōritātem eōrum iūdiciō habēre exīstimantur, quōrum ad arbitrium iūdiciumque summa omnium rērum cōnsiliōrumque redeat. Idque eius reī causā antīquitus īnstitūtum vidētur, nē quis ex plēbe contrā potentiōrem auxiliī egēret. Suōs enim quisque opprimī et circumvenīrī nōn patitur, 10 neque, aliter sī faciat, ūllam inter suōs habeat auctōritātem. Haec eadem ratiō est in summā tōtīus Galliae; namque omnēs cīvitātēs dīvīsae sunt in duās partēs.

In omnī Galliā eōrum hominum quī aliquō sunt numerō atque honōre, genera sunt duo. Nam plēbēs paene servōrum habētur 15 locō, quae nihil audet per sē, nūllō adhibētur cōnsiliō. Plērīque, cum aut aere aliēnō aut magnitūdine tribūtōrum aut iniūriā potentiōrum premuntur, sēsē in servitūtem dicant. Nōbilibus in hōs eadem omnia sunt iūra quae dominīs in servōs. Sed dē hīs duōbus generibus alterum est druidum, alterum equitum. 20 Illī rēbus dīvīnīs intersunt, sacrificia pūblica ac prīvāta prōcūrant, religiōnēs interpretantur. Ad hōs magnus adulēscentium numerus disciplīnae causā concurrit; magnōque hī sunt apud eōs honōre. Nam ferē dē omnibus contrōversiīs pūblicīs prīvātīsque cōnstituunt, et, sī quod est facinus admissum, sī caedēs 25 facta, sī dē hērēditāte, dē fīnibus contrōversia est, īdem dēcernunt, praemia poenāsque cōnstituunt. Sī quī aut prīvātus aut populus eōrum dēcrētō nōn stetit, sacrificiīs interdīcunt. Haec poena apud eōs est gravissima. Quibus ita est interdictum, hī

numerō impiōrum ac scelerātōrum habentur, hīs omnēs dēcēdunt, aditum eōrum sermōnemque dēfugiunt, nē quid ex contā-
giōne incommodī accipiant, neque hīs petentibus iūs redditur,
neque honōs ūllus commūnicātur. Hīs autem omnibus druidi-
5 bus praeest ūnus, qui summam inter eōs habet auctōritātem.
Hōc mortuō, aut sī quī ex reliquīs excellit dignitāte, succēdit,
aut sī sunt plūrēs parēs, suffrāgiō druidum, nōnnumquam etiam
armīs, dē prīncipātū contendunt. Hī certō annī tempore in
fīnibus Carnūtum, quae regiō tōtīus Galliae media habētur,
10 cōnsīdunt in locō cōnsecrātō. Hūc omnēs undique quī contrō-
versiās habent conveniunt, eōrumque dēcrētīs iūdiciīsque pā-
rent. Disciplīna in Britanniā reperta atque inde in Galliam
trānslāta exīstimātur, et nunc, quī dīligentius eam rem cognōscere volunt, plērumque illō discendī causā proficīscuntur.
15 Druidēs ā bellō abesse consuērunt, neque tribūta ūnā cum
reliquīs pendunt. Tantīs excitātī praemiīs, et suā sponte multī
in disciplīnam conveniunt, et ā parentibus propinquīsque mit-
tuntur. Magnum ibi numerum versuum ēdiscere dīcuntur.
Itaque annōs nōnnūllī vīcēnōs in disciplīnā permanent. Neque
20 fās esse exīstimant ea litterīs mandāre, cum in reliquīs ferē rēbus, pūblicīs prīvātīsque ratiōnibus, Graecīs ūtantur litterīs. Id
mihi duābus dē causīs īnstituisse videntur, quod neque in vulgum disciplīnam ēfferrī velint, neque eōs quī discunt, litterīs
cōnfīsōs, minus memoriae studēre, quod ferē plērīsque accidit,
25 ut, praesidiō litterārum, dīligentiam in perdiscendō ac memoriam remittant. In prīmīs hoc volunt persuādēre: nōn interīre
animās, sed ab aliīs post mortem transīre ad aliōs, atque hōc
maximē ad virtūtem excitārī putant, metū mortis neglēctō.
Multa praetereā dē sīderibus atque eōrum mōtū, dē mundī ac
30 terrārum magnitūdine, dē rērum nātūrā, dē deōrum immortālium vī ac potestāte disputant et iuventūtī trādunt.
Alterum genus est equitum. Hī, cum est ūsus, atque aliquod
bellum incidit (quod ante Caesaris adventum ferē quotannīs
accidere solēbat, utī aut ipsī iniūriās īnferrent aut inlātās prō-
35 pulsārent), omnēs in bellō versantur, atque eōrum ut quisque
est genere cōpiīsque amplissimus, ita plūrimōs circum sē ambac-

tōs clientēsque habet. Hanc ūnam grātiam potentiamque
nōvērunt.

Nātiō est omnis Gallōrum admodum dēdita religiōnibus, atque ob eam causam, quī sunt adfectī graviōribus morbīs, quīque in proeliīs perīculīsque versantur, aut prō victimīs hominēs 5
immolant, aut sē immolātūrōs vovent, administrīsque ad ea
sacrificia druidibus ūtuntur, quod prō vītā hominis nisi hominis
vīta reddātur, nōn posse deōrum immortālium nūmen plācārī
arbitrantur; pūblicēque eiusdem generis habent īnstitūta sacrificia. Aliī immānī magnitūdine simulācra habent, quōrum con- 10
texta vīminibus membra vīvīs hominibus complent; quibus
succēnsīs, circumventī flammā exanimantur hominēs. Supplicia eōrum quī in fūrtō aut latrōciniō aut aliquā noxiā sint com-
prehēnsī, grātiōra dīs immortālibus esse arbitrantur. Sed cum
eius generis cōpia dēficit, etiam ad innocentium supplicia dē- 15
scendunt.

Deōrum maximē Mercurium colunt. Huius sunt plūrima
simulācra, hunc omnium inventōrem artium ferunt, hunc viā-
rum atque itinerum ducem, hunc ad quaestūs pecūniae mercā-
tūrāsque habēre vim maximam arbitrantur. Post hunc Apolli- 20
nem et Mārtem et Iovem et Minervam. Dē hīs eandem ferē
quam reliquae gentēs habent opīniōnem: Apollinem morbōs
dēpellere, Minervam operum atque artificiōrum initia trādere,
Iovem imperium caelestium tenēre, Martem bella regere. Huic,
cum proeliō dīmicāre cōnstituērunt, ea quae bellō cēperint, plē- 25
rumque dēvovent; cum superāvērunt, animālia capta immolant,
reliquās rēs in ūnum locum cōnferunt. Multīs in cīvitātibus
hārum rērum exstrūctōs cumulōs locīs cōnsecrātīs cōnspicārī
licet; neque saepe accidit ut neglēctā quispiam religiōne aut
capta apud sē occultāre, aut posita tollere, audēret; gravissi- 30
mumque eī reī supplicium cum cruciatū cōnstitūtum est.

Gallī sē omnēs ab Dīte patre prōgnātōs praedicant, idque ab
druidibus prōditum dīcunt. Ob eam causam spatia omnis
temporis nōn numerō diērum, sed noctium fīniunt; diēs nātālēs
et mēnsum et annōrum initia sīc observant ut noctem diēs subse- 35
quātur. In reliquīs vītae īnstitūtīs hōc ferē ab reliquīs differunt,

quod suōs līberōs, nisi cum adolēvērunt ut mūnus mīlitiae sustinēre possint, palam ad sē adīre nōn patiuntur, fīliumque puerīlī
aetāte in pūblicō in cōnspectū patris adsistere turpe dūcunt.
Virī, quantās pecūniās ab uxōribus dōtis nōmine accēpērunt,
5 tantās ex suīs bonīs, aestimātiōne factā, cum dōtibus commūni-
cant. Huius omnis pecūniae coniūnctim ratiō habētur frūctūs-
que servantur; uter eōrum vītā superāvit, ad eum pars utrīusque cum frūctibus superiōrum temporum pervenit. Virī in
uxōrēs, sīcutī in līberōs, vītae necisque habent potestātem; et
10 cum pater familiae inlūstriōre locō nātus dēcessit, eius propinquī
conveniunt, et dē morte sī rēs in suspiciōnem vēnit, dē uxōribus
in servīlem modum quaestiōnem habent, et, sī compertum est,
ignī atque omnibus tormentīs excruciātās interficiunt. Fūnera
sunt prō cultū Gallōrum magnifica et sūmptuōsa; omniaque
15 quae vīvīs cordī fuisse arbitrantur in ignem īnferunt, etiam animālia; ac paulō suprā hanc memoriam servī et clientēs quōs ab
iīs dīlēctōs esse cōnstābat, iūstīs fūnebribus cōnfectīs, ūnā
cremābantur.
Quae cīvitātēs commodius suam rem pūblicam administrāre
20 exīstimantur, habent lēgibus sānctum, sī quis quid dē rē pūblicā
ā fīnitimīs rūmōre ac fāmā accēperit, utī ad magistrātum dē-
ferat nēve cum quō aliō commūnicet, quod saepe hominēs teme-
rāriōs atque imperītōs falsīs rūmōribus terrērī et ad facinus
impellī et dē summīs rēbus cōnsilium capere cognitum est.
25 Magistrātūs quae vīsa sunt occultant, quaeque esse ex ūsū
iūdicāvērunt, multitūdinī prōdunt. Dē rē pūblicā nisi per
concilium loquī nōn concēditur.
Germānī multum ab hāc cōnsuētūdine differunt. Nam neque
druidēs habent quī rēbus dīvīnīs praesint, neque sacrificiīs stu-
30 dent. Deōrum numerō eōs sōlōs dūcunt quōs cernunt et quōrum apertē opibus iuvantur, Sōlem et Vulcānum et Lūnam; reliquōs nē fāmā quidem accēpērunt. Vīta omnis in vēnātiōnibus
atque in studiīs reī mīlitāris cōnsistit; ā parvīs labōrī ac dūritiae
student.
35　Agrī cultūrae nōn student, maiorque pars eōrum vīctūs in
lacte cāseō carne cōnsistit. Neque quisquam agrī modum certum aut fīnēs habet propriōs, sed magistrātūs ac prīncipēs in

annōs singulōs gentibus cognātiōnibusque hominum, quīque ūnā
coiērunt, quantum et quō locō vīsum est agrī attribuunt, atque
annō post aliō trānsīre cōgunt.   Eius reī multās adferunt causās:
nē adsiduā cōnsuētūdine captī studium bellī gerendī agrī cultūrā
commūtent; nē lātōs fīnēs parāre studeant, potentiōrēsque hu- 5
miliōrēs possessiōnibus expellant; nē accūrātius ad frīgora atque
aestūs vītandōs aedificent; nē qua oriātur pecūniae cupiditās,
quā ex rē factiōnēs dissēnsiōnēsque nāscuntur; ut animī aequitāte plēbem contineant, cum suās quisque opēs cum potentissi-
mīs aequārī videat.   10
   Cīvitātibus maxima laus est quam lātissimē circum sē, vās-
tātīs fīnibus, sōlitūdinēs habēre.   Hoc proprium virtūtis exīstimant, expulsōs agrīs fīnitimōs cēdere, neque quemquam prope
sē audēre cōnsistere.   Simul hōc sē fore tūtiōrēs arbitrantur,
repentīnae incursiōnis timōre sublātō.   Cum bellum cīvitās aut 15
inlātum dēfendit, aut īnfert, magistrātūs quī eī bellō praesint et
vītae necisque habeant potestātem dēliguntur.   In pāce nūllus
est commūnis magistrātus, sed prīncipēs regiōnum atque pāgō-
rum inter suōs iūs dīcunt contrōversiāsque minuunt.   Latrō-
cinia nūllam habent īnfāmiam quae extrā fīnēs cuiusque cīvitā- 20
tis fiunt, atque ea iuventūtis exercendae ac dēsidiae minuendae
causā fierī praedicant.   Atque ubi quis ex prīncipibus in conciliō
dīxit sē ducem fore, quī sequī velint profiteantur, cōnsurgunt iī
quī et causam et hominem probant, suumque auxilium pollicen-
tur atque ā multitūdine conlaudantur; quī ex hīs secūtī nōn 25
sunt, in dēsertōrum ac prōditōrum numerō dūcuntur, omniumque hīs rērum posteā fidēs dērogātur.   Hospitem violāre fās
nōn putant; quī quācumque dē causā ad eōs vēnērunt, ab iniūriā
prohibent sānctōsque habent, hīsque omnium domūs patent
vīctusque commūnicātur.   30
   Suēbōrum gēns est longē maxima et bellicōsissima Germānōrum omnium.   Hī centum pāgōs habēre dīcuntur, ex quibus
quotannīs singula mīlia armātōrum bellandī causā suīs ex fīnibus
ēdūcunt.   Reliquī, quī domī mānsērunt, sē atque illōs alunt.
Hī rūrsus invicem annō post in armīs sunt, illī domī remanent. 35
Sīc neque agrī cultūra nec ratiō atque ūsus bellī intermittitur.
Neque multum frūmentō, sed maximam partem lacte atque

pecore vīvunt, ut suprā dēmōnstrāvimus, multumque sunt in
vēnātiōnibus. Quae rēs et cibī genere et cotīdiānā exercitātiōne
et lībertāte vītae, quod ā puerīs nūllō officiō aut disciplīnā adsuēfactī nihil omnīnō contrā voluntātem faciunt, et vīrēs alit et
5 immānī corporum magnitūdine hominēs efficit. Atque in eam
sē cōnsūetūdinem addūxērunt, ut locīs frīgidissimīs neque vestītūs praeter pellēs habeant quicquam, quārum propter exiguitā-
tem magna est corporis pars aperta, et laventur in flūminibus.
Mercātōribus est aditus magis eō ut quae bellō cēperint qui-
10 bus vēndant habeant, quam quō ūllam rem ad sē importārī dēsī-
derent. Quīn etiam iūmentīs, quibus maximē Gallī dēlectantur
quaeque impēnsō parant pretiō, Germānī importātīs nōn ūtuntur, sed quae sunt apud eōs nāta, parva atque dēfōrmia, haec
cotīdiānā exercitātiōne summī ut sint labōris efficiunt. Eques-
15 tribus proeliīs saepe ex equīs dēsiliunt ac pedibus proeliantur,
equōsque eōdem remanēre vestīgiō adsuēfaciunt, ad quōs sē
celeriter cum ūsus est recipiunt. Neque eōrum mōribus turpius
quicquam aut inertius habētur quam ephippiīs ūtī. Itaque ad
quemvīs numerum ephippiātōrum equitum quamvīs paucī adīre
20 audent. Vīnum ad sē omnīnō importārī nōn patiuntur, quod
eā rē ad labōrem ferendum remollēscere hominēs atque effemi-
nārī arbitrantur.
Ac fuit anteā tempus cum Germānōs Gallī virtūte superārent,
ultrō bella īnferrent, propter hominum multitūdinem agrīque
25 inopiam trāns Rhēnum colōniās mitterent. Itaque ea quae
fertilissima Germāniae sunt loca circum Hercyniam silvam,
quam Eratosthenī et quibusdàm Graecīs fāmā nōtam esse videō,
quam illī Orcyniam appellant, Volcae Tectosagēs occupāvērunt
atque ibi cōnsēdērunt; quae gēns ad hoc tempus hīs sēdibus sēsē
30 continet summamque habet iūstitiae et bellicae laudis opīniōnem. Nunc quoniam in eādem inopiā egestāte patientiā, quā
ante, Germānī permanent, eōdem vīctū et cultū corporis ūtuntur, Gallīs autem prōvinciārum prōpinquitās et trānsmarīnārum
rērum nōtitia multa ad cōpiam atque ūsus largītur, paulātim
35 adsuēfactī superārī, multīsque victī proeliīs, nē sē quidem ipsī
cum illīs virtūte comparant.

59. Caesar and Ariovistus

Bellō Helvctiōrum cōnfectō, tōtīus ferē Galliae lēgātī, prīncipēs cīvitātum, ad Caesarem grātulātum convēnērunt: intellegere sēsē, tametsī prō veteribus Helvetiōrum iniūriīs populī
Rōmānī ab hīs poenās bellō repetīsset, tamen eam rem nōn
minus ex ūsū terrae Galliae quam populī Rōmānī accidisse, 5
proptereā quod eō cōnsiliō, flōrentissimīs rēbus, domōs suās
Helvetiī relīquissent, utī tōtī Galliae bellum īnferrent imperiōque
potīrentur, locumque domiciliō ex magnā cōpiā dēligerent quem
ex omnī Galliā opportūnissimum ac frūctuōsissimum iūdicāssent,
reliquāsque cīvitātēs stīpendiāriās habērent. Petīvērunt utī 10
sibi concilium tōtīus Galliae in diem certam indīcere idque
Caesaris voluntāte facere licēret: sēsē habēre quāsdam rēs quās
ex commūnī cōnsēnsū ab eō petere vellent. Eā rē permissā,
diem conciliō cōnstituērunt, et iūreiūrandō nē quis ēnūntiāret,
nisi quibus commūnī cōnsiliō mandātum esset, inter sē sānxē- 15
runt.

Eō conciliō dīmissō, īdem prīncipēs cīvitātum quī ante fuerant
ad Caesarem revertērunt, petiēruntque utī sibi sēcrētō in occultō
dē suā omniumque salūte cum eō agere licēret. Eā rē impe-
trātā, sēsē omnēs flentēs Caesarī ad pedēs prōiēcērunt: "Nōn 20
minus," inquiunt, "id contendimus et labōrāmus, nē ea quae
dīxerimus ēnūntientur, quam utī ea quae volumus impetrēmus,
proptereā quod sī ēnūntiātum erit, summum in cruciātum nōs
ventūrōs vidēmus."

Locūtus est prō hīs Dīviciācus Aeduus: "Galliae tōtīus," in- 25
quit, "factiōnēs sunt duae: hārum alterīus prīncipātum tenent
Aeduī, alterīus Arvernī. Hī cum tantopere dē potentātū inter
sē multōs annōs contenderent, factum est utī ab Arvernīs Sēquanīsque Germānī mercēde arcesserentur. Hōrum prīmō circiter mīlia XV Rhēnum trānsiērunt; posteāquam agrōs et cul- 30
tum et cōpiās Gallōrum hominēs ferī ac barbarī adamāvērunt,
trāductī sunt plūrēs; nunc sunt in Galliā ad centum et vīgintī
mīlium numerum.

"Cum hīs Aeduī eōrumque clientēs semel atque iterum armīs
contendērunt; magnam calamitātem pulsī accēpērunt: omnem
nōbilitātem, omnem senātum, omnem equitātum āmīsērunt.
Quibus proeliīs calamitātibusque frāctī, quī et suā virtūte et
5 populī Rōmānī hospitiō atque amīcitiā plūrimum ante in Galliā
potuerant, coāctī sunt Sēquanīs obsidēs dare nōbilissimōs cīvitātis, et iūreiūrandō cīvitātem obstringere, sēsē neque obsidēs
repetītūros neque auxilium ā populō Rōmānō implōrātūrōs,
neque recūsātūrōs quōminus perpetuō sub illōrum diciōne atque
10 imperiō essent. Ūnus ego sum ex omnī cīvitāte Aeduorum quī
addūcī nōn potuī ut iūrārem aut līberōs meōs obsidēs darem.
Ob eam rem ex cīvitāte prōfūgī et Rōmam ad senātum vēnī
auxilium postulātum, quod sōlus neque iūreiūrandō neque obsidibus tenēbar.

15   "Sed peius victōribus Sēquanīs quam Aeduīs victīs accidit,
proptereā quod Ariovistus, rēx Germānōrum, in eōrum fīnibus
cōnsēdit, tertiamque partem agrī Sēquanī — quī est optimus
tōtīus Galliae — occupāvit, et nunc dē alterā parte tertiā Sēquanōs dēcēdere iubet, proptereā quod paucīs mēnsibus ante
20 Harūdum mīlia hominum XXIIII ad eum vēnērunt, quibus locus
ac sēdēs parārentur. Paucīs annīs omnēs ex Galliae fīnibus
pellēmur, atque omnēs Germānī Rhēnum trānsībunt: neque
enim cōnferendus est Gallicus cum Germānōrum agrō, neque
haec cōnsuētūdō vīctūs cum illā comparanda.

25   "Ariovistus autem, ut semel Gallōrum cōpiās proeliō vīcit
(quod proelium factum est ad Magetobrigam), superbē et crūdēliter imperat; obsidēs nōbilissimī cuiusque līberōs poscit, et
in eōs omnia exempla cruciātūsque ēdit, sī qua rēs nōn ad nūtum
aut ad voluntātem eius facta est. Homō est barbarus īrācundus
30 temerārius: nōn possumus eius imperia diūtius sustinēre.

"Nisi quid in tē populōque Rōmānō erit auxiliī, omnibus
Gallīs idem est faciendum quod Helvetiī fēcērunt, ut domō
ēmigrēmus, aliud domicilium, aliās sēdēs remōtās ā Germānīs
petāmus, fortūnamque, quaecumque accidet, experiāmur. Haec
35 sī ēnūntiāta Ariovistō erunt, nōn dubitō quīn dē omnibus obsidibus, quī apud eum sunt, gravissimum supplicium sūmat. Tū,
Caesar, vel auctōritāte tuā atque exercitūs recentī victōriā, vel

nōmine populī Rōmānī, dēterrēre potes nē maior multitūdō
Germānōrum Rhēnum trādūcātur; Galliamque omnem ab Ariovistī iniūriā potes dēfendere."
Hāc ōrātiōne ab Diviciācō habitā, omnēs quī aderant magnō
flētū auxilium ā Caesare petere coepērunt. Animadvertit 5
Caesar ūnōs ex omnibus Sēquanōs nihil eārum rērum facere
quās cēterī facerent, sed trīstēs capite dēmissō terram intuērī.
Eius reī quae causa esset mīrātus, ex ipsīs quaesiit. Nihil Sēquanī respondēre, sed in eādem trīstitiā tacitī permanēre.
Cum ab hīs saepius quaereret neque ūllam omnīnō vōcem 10
exprimere posset, īdem Dīviciācus Aeduus respondit: "Hōc est
miserior," inquit, "et gravior fortūna Sēquanōrum quam reli-
quōrum, quod sōlī nē in occultō quidem querī neque auxilium
implōrāre audent, absentisque Ariovistī crūdēlitātem, velut sī
cōram adsit, horrent, proptereā quod reliquīs tamen fugae facul- 15
tās datur, Sēquanīs vērō, quī intrā fīnēs suōs Ariovistum recēperint, quōrum oppida omnia in potestāte eius sint, omnēs
cruciātūs sunt perferendī."
Hīs rēbus cognitīs, Caesar Gallōrum animōs verbīs cōnfirmāvit, pollicitusque est sibi eam rem cūrae futūram; magnam sē 20
habēre spem et beneficiō suō et auctōritāte adductum Ariovistum fīnem iniūriīs factūrum. Hāc ōrātiōne habitā, concilium
dīmīsit.
Et secundum ea multae rēs eum hortābantur quārē sibi eam
rem cōgitandam et suscipiendam putāret, in prīmīs quod Ae- 25
duōs, frātres cōnsanguineōsque populī Rōmānī saepenumerō ā
senatū appellātōs, in servitūte atque diciōne vidēbat Germānōrum tenērī, eōrumque obsidēs esse apud Ariovistum ac Sēquanōs
intellegēbat; quod in tantō imperiō populī Rōmānī turpissimum
sibi et reī pūblicae esse arbitrābātur. 30
Paulātim autem Germānōs cōnsuēscere Rhēnum trānsīre et
in Galliam magnam eōrum multitūdinem venīre populō Rōmānō
perīculōsum vidēbat, neque sibi hominēs ferōs ac barbarōs temperātūrōs exīstimābat quīn, cum omnem Galliam occupāvissent,
ut ante Cimbrī Teutonīque fēcissent, in prōvinciam exīrent, 35
atque inde in Ītaliam contenderent, praesertim cum Sēquanōs
ā prōvinciā nostrā Rhodanus dīvideret; quibus rēbus quam

mātūrrimē occurrendum putābat. Ipse autem Ariovistus tan-
tōs sibi spīritūs, tantam adrogantiam sūmpserat ut ferendus
nōn vidērētur.

Quamobrem placuit eī ut ad Ariovistum lēgātōs mitteret quī
5 ab eō postulārent utī aliquem locum medium utrīusque conloquiō dēligeret: velle sē dē rē pūblicā et summīs utrīusque rēbus
cum eō agere. Eī lēgātiōnī Ariovistus ita respondit: "Sī quid
mihi ā Caesare opus esset, ego ad eum vēnissem; sī quid ille mē
vult, illum ad mē venīre oportet. Praetereā," inquit, "neque
10 sine exercitū in eās partēs Galliae venīre audeō quās Caesar
possidet, neque exercitum sine magnō commeātū atque mōlī-
mentō in ūnum locum contrahere possum. Mihi autem mīrum
vidētur quid in meā Galliā, quam bellō vīcī, aut Caesarī aut
omnīnō populō Rōmānō negōtiī sit."

15 Hīs respōnsīs ad Caesarem relātīs, iterum ad eum Caesar
lēgātōs cum hīs mandātīs mittit: quoniam tantō suō populīque
Rōmānī beneficiō adfectus, cum in cōnsulātū suō rēx atque
amīcus ab senātū appellātus esset, hanc sibi populōque Rōmānō
grātiam referret, ut in conloquium venīre invitātus gravārētur,
20 neque dē commūnī rē dīcendum sibi et cognōscendum putāret,
haec esse quae ab eō postulāret: prīmum, nē quam multitūdinem
hominum amplius trāns Rhēnum in Galliam trādūceret; deinde,
obsidēs quōs habēret ab Aeduīs redderet, Sēquanīsque permitte-
ret ut quōs illī habērent voluntāte eius reddere illīs licēret; nēve
25 Aeduōs iniūriā lacesseret nēve hīs sociīsque eōrum bellum īn-
ferret. Sī id ita fēcisset, sibi populōque Rōmānō perpetuam
grātiam atque amīcitiam cum eō futūram; sī nōn impetrāret,
sēsē — quoniam M. Messālā M. Pīsōne cōnsulibus senātus
cēnsuisset utī quīcumque Galliam prōvinciam obtinēret, quod
30 commodō reī pūblicae facere posset, Aeduōs cēterōsque amīcōs
populī Rōmānī dēfenderet — sē Aeduōrum iniūriās nōn neglēctūrum.

Ad haec Ariovistus ita respondit: "Iūs est bellī ut quī vīcērunt
iīs quōs vīcērunt quemadmodum volunt imperent; item populus
35 Rōmānus victīs nōn ad alterīus praescrīptum, sed ad suum arbitrium imperāre cōnsuēvit. Sī ego populō Rōmānō nōn prae-

scrībō quemadmodum suō iūre ūtātur, nōn oportet mē ā populō
Rōmānō in meō iūre impedīrī.

"Aeduī mihi, quoniam bellī fortūnam temptāverant et armīs
congressī ac superātī erant, stīpendiāriī factī sunt. Magnam
Caesar iniūriam facit quī suō adventū vectīgālia mihi dēteriōra 5
faciat. Aeduīs obsidēs nōn reddam; neque hīs neque eōrum
sociīs iniūriā bellum īnferam, sī in eō manēbunt quod convēnit,
stīpendiumque quotannīs pendent; sī id nōn fēcerint, longē hīs
frāternum nōmen populī Rōmānī aberit. Quod mihi Caesar
dēnūntiat sē Aeduōrum iniūriās nōn neglēctūrum, nēmō mēcum 10
sine suā perniciē contendit. Cum volet, congrediātur! Intelle-
get quid invictī Germānī, exercitātissimī in armīs, quī inter
annōs XIIII tēctum nōn subiērunt, virtūte possint."

Haec eōdem tempore Caesarī mandāta referēbantur, et lēgātī
ab Aeduīs et ā Trēverīs veniēbant: Aeduī questum quod Ha- 15
rūdēs, quī nuper in Galliam trānsportātī essent, fīnēs eōrum
populārentur: sēsē nē obsidibus quidem datīs pācem Ariovistī
redimere potuisse; Trēverī autem, pāgōs centum Suēbōrum ad
rīpās Rhēnī cōnsēdisse quī Rhēnum trānsīre cōnārentur; hīs
praeesse Nasuam et Cimberium frātrēs. Quibus rēbus Caesar 20
vehementer commōtus mātūrandum sibi exīstimāvit, nē, sī nova
manus Suēbōrum cum veteribus cōpiīs Ariovistī sē coniūnxisset,
minus facile resistī posset. Itaque, rē frūmentāriā quam celerrimē potuit comparātā, magnīs itineribus ad Ariovistum
contendit. 25

Cum trīduī viam prōcessisset, nūntiātum est eī Ariovistum
cum suīs omnibus cōpiīs ad occupandum Vesontiōnem, quod est
oppidum maximum Sēquanōrum, contendere, trīduīque viam ā
suīs fīnibus prōcessisse. Id nē accideret magnopere sibi prae-
cavendum Caesar exīstimābat. Namque omnium rērum quae 30
ad bellum ūsuī erant summa erat in eō oppidō facultās, idque
nātūrā locī sīc mūniēbātur, ut magnam ad dūcendum bellum
daret facultātem, proptereā quod flūmen Dūbis, ut circinō circumductum, paene tōtum oppidum cingit; reliquum spatium,
quod est nōn amplius pedum sēscentōrum, quā flūmen inter- 35
mittit, mōns continet magnā altitūdine, ita ut rādicēs eius

montis ex utrāque parte rīpae flūminis contingant. Hunc
mūrus circumdatus arcem efficit et cum oppidō coniungit. Hūc
Caesar magnīs nocturnīs diurnīsque itineribus contendit, occu-
pātōque oppidō, ibi praesidium conlocat.

5 Dum paucōs diēs ad Vesontiōnem reī frūmentāriae commeā-
tūsque causā morātur, ex percontātiōne nostrōrum vōcibusque
Gallōrum ac mercātōrum, quī ingentī magnitūdine corporum
Germānōs, incrēdibilī virtūte atque exercitātiōne in armīs esse
praedicābant,— saepenumerō sēsē cum hīs congressōs nē vul-
10 tum quidem atque aciem oculōrum dīcēbant ferre potuisse,—
tantus subitō timor omnem exercitum occupāvit, ut nōn medioc-
riter omnium mentēs animōsque perturbāret.

Hic prīmum ortus est ā tribūnīs mīlitum, praefectīs, reliquīs-
que quī, ex urbe amīcitiae causā Caesarem secūtī, nōn magnum
15 in rē mīlitārī ūsum habēbant. Quōrum alius aliā causā inlātā,
quam sibi ad proficīscendum necessāriam esse dīceret, petēbat
ut eius voluntāte discēdere licēret; nōnnullī pudōre adductī, ut
timōris suspiciōnem vītārent, remanēbant. Hī neque vultum
fingere neque interdum lacrimās tenēre poterant; abditī in taber-
20 nāculīs aut suum fātum querēbantur aut cum familiāribus suīs
commūne perīculum miserābantur. Vulgō tōtīs castrīs testā-
menta obsignābantur.

Hōrum vōcibus ac timōre paulātim etiam iī quī magnum in
castrīs ūsum habēbant, mīlitēs centuriōnēsque, quīque equitātuī
25 praeerant, perturbābantur. Quī sē ex hīs minus timidōs exīsti-
mārī volēbant, nōn sē hostem verērī, sed angustiās itineris et
magnitūdinem silvārum quae intercēderent inter ipsōs atque
Ariovistum, aut rem frūmentāriam ut satis commodē supportārī
posset, timēre dīcēbant. Nōnnullī etiam Caesarī nūntiābant,
30 cum castra movērī ac signa ferrī iussisset, nōn fore dictō audientēs mīlitēs neque propter timōrem signa lātūrōs.

Haec cum animadvertisset, convocātō cōnsiliō, omniumque
ōrdinum ad id cōnsilium adhibitīs centuriōnibus, vehementer
eōs incūsāvit: prīmum, quod aut quam in partem aut quō cōn-
35 siliō dūcerentur sibi quaerendum aut cōgitandum putārent.
"Ariovistus," inquit, "mē cōnsule cupidissimē populī Rōmānī
amīcitiam appetīvit; cur hunc tam temerē quisquam ab officiō

discessūrum iūdicet? Mihi quidem persuādētur, cognitīs meīs
postulātīs atque aequitāte condiciōnum perspectā, eum neque
meam neque populī Rōmānī grātiam repudiātūrum. Quod sī,
furōre atque āmentiā impulsus, bellum intulerit, quid tandem
verēminī? Aut cur dē vestrā virtūte aut dē meā dīligentiā 5
dēspērātis? Factum est eius hostis perīculum patrum nostrōrum mcmoriā, cum, Cimbrīs ct Tcutonīs ā C. Mariō pulsīs, nōn
minōrem laudem exercitus quam ipse imperātor meritus vidēbātur; factum est etiam nūper in Ītaliā servīlī tumultū, quōs
tamen aliquid ūsus ac disciplīna quam ā nōbīs accēperant suble- 10
vābant. Ex quō iūdicārī potest quantum habeat in sē bonī
cōnstantia: proptereā quod, quōs aliquamdiū inermēs sine causā
timuistis, hōs posteā armātōs ac victōrēs superāvistis.

"Dēnique hī sunt īdem quibuscum saepenumerō Helvetiī congressī nōn sōlum in suīs, sed etiam in illōrum fīnibus plērumque 15
superāvērunt, quī tamen parēs esse nostrō exercituī nōn potuē-
runt. Sī quōs adversum proelium et fuga Gallōrum commovet,
hī, sī quaerent, reperīre poterunt, diūturnitāte bellī dēfatigātīs
Gallīs, Ariovistum, cum multōs mēnsēs castrīs sē ac palūdibus
tenuisset, neque suī potestātem fēcisset, dēspērantēs iam dē 20
pugnā et dīspersōs subitō adortum, magis ratiōne et cōnsiliō
quam virtūte vīcisse. Cui ratiōnī contrā hominēs barbarōs
atque imperītōs locus fuit, hāc nē ipse quidem spērat nostrōs
exercitūs capī posse.

"Quī suum timōrem in reī frūmentāriae simulātiōnem angus- 25
tiāsque itineris cōnferunt, faciunt adroganter, cum aut dē
officiō imperātōris dēspērāre aut praescrībere videantur. Haec
mihi sunt cūrae; frūmentum Sēquanī Leucī Lingonēs subminis-
trant, iamque sunt in agrīs frūmenta mātūra; dē itinere, ipsī
brevī tempore iūdicābitis. 30

"Quod nōn fore dictō audientēs neque signa lātūrī dīciminī,
nihil eā rē commoveor; sciō enim quibuscumque exercitus dictō
audiēns nōn fuerit, aut male rē gestā fortūnam dēfuisse aut
aliquō facinore compertō avāritiam esse convictam. Mea inno-
centia perpetuā vītā, fēlīcitās Helvetiōrum bellō est perspecta. 35

"Itaque quod in longiōrem diem conlātūrus fuī, repraesentā-
bō, et proximā nocte dē quārtā vigiliā castra movēbō, ut quam

prīmum intellegere possim utrum apud vōs pudor atque officium
an timor plūs valeat. Quod sī practereā nēmō sequētur, tamen
cum sōlā decimā legiōne ībō, dē quā nōn dubitō, mihique ea
praetōria cohors erit." Huic legiōnī Caesar et indulserat praeci-
5 puē et propter virtūtem cōnfīdēbat maximē.

Hāc ōrātiōne habitā, mīrum in modum conversae sunt omnium mentēs, summaque alacritās et cupiditās bellī gerendī inlāta
est; prīncepsque decima legiō per tribūnōs mīlitum eī grātiās
ēgit, quod dē sē optimum iūdicium fēcisset, sēque esse ad bellum
10 gerendum parātissimam cōnfirmāvit. Deinde reliquae legiōnēs
cum tribūnīs mīlitum et primōrum ōrdinum centuriōnibus ēgērunt, utī per eōs Caesarī satis facerent: sē neque umquam
dubitāsse neque timuisse neque dē summā bellī suum iūdicium,
sed imperātōris esse exīstimāvisse.

15 Eōrum satisfactiōne acceptā, et itinere exquīsītō per Dīviciā-
cum, quod ex Gallīs eī maximam fidem habēbat, ut mīlium
amplius quīnquāgintā circuitū locīs apertīs exercitum dūceret,
dē quartā vigiliā, ut dīxerat, profectus est. Septimō diē, cum
iter nōn intermitteret, ab explōrātōribus certior factus est
20 Ariovistī cōpiās ā nostrīs mīlia passuum quattuor et vīgintī
abesse.

Cognitō Caesaris adventū, Ariovistus lēgātōs ad eum mittit:
quod anteā dē conloquiō postulāsset, id per sē fierī licēre, quoniam propius accessisset, sēque id sine perīculō facere posse
25 exīstimāret. Nōn respuit condiciōnem Caesar, iamque eum ad
sānitātem revertī arbitrābātur, cum id quod anteā petentī
dēnegāsset ultrō pollicērētur; magnamque in spem veniēbat prō
suīs tantīs populīque Rōmānī in eum beneficiīs, cognitīs suīs
postulātīs, fore utī pertināciā dēsisteret. Diēs conloquiō dictus
30 est ex eō diē quīntus.

Interim saepe ultrō citrōque cum lēgātī inter eōs mitterentur,
Ariovistus postulāvit nē quem peditem ad conloquium Caesar
addūceret: vererī sē nē per īnsidiās ab eō circumvenīrētur; uterque cum equitātū venīret; aliā ratiōne sēsē nōn esse ventūrum.
35 Caesar, quod neque conloquium, interpositā causā, tollī volēbat,
neque salūtem suam Gallōrum equitātuī committere audēbat,
commodissimum esse statuit, omnibus equīs Gallīs equitibus

dētractīs, legiōnāriōs eō mīlitēs legiōnis decimae, cui quam
maximē cōnfīdēbat, impōnere, ut praesidium quam amīcissi-
mum, sī quid opus factō esset, habēret.   Quod cum fieret, nōn
inrīdiculē quīdam ex mīlitibus decimae legiōnis dīxit plūs quam
pollicitus esset Caesarem facere: pollicitum sē in cohortis prae- 5
tōriae locō decimam legiōnem habitūrum, ad equum rescrībere.
Plānitiēs erat magna, et in eā tumulus terrēnus satis grandis.
Hic locus aequum ferē spatium ā castrīs utrīusque aberat.   Eō,
ut erat dictum, ad conloquium vēnērunt.   Legiōnem Caesar
quam equīs dēvexerat passibus ducentīs ab eō tumulō cōnstituit; 10
item equitēs Ariovistī parī intervāllō cōnstitērunt.   Ariovistus
ex equīs ut conloquerentur et praeter sē dēnōs ad conloquium
addūcerent postulāvit.

Ubi eō ventum est, Caesar initiō ōrātiōnis sua senātūsque in
eum beneficia commemorāvit, quod rēx appellātus esset ā 15
senātū, quod amīcus, quod mūnera amplissimē missa; quam
rem et paucīs contigisse et prō magnīs hominum officiīs cōnsuēsse
tribuī docēbat; illum, cum neque aditum neque causam postu-
landī iūstam habēret, beneficiō ac līberālitāte suā ac senātūs ea
praemia cōnsecūtum.   20
Docēbat etiam quam veterēs quamque iūstae causae necessitūdinis ipsīs cum Aeduīs intercēderent, quae senātūs consulta,
quotiēns, quamque honōrifica, in eōs facta essent, ut omnī
tempore tōtīus Galliae prīncipātum Aeduī tenuissent, prius
etiam quam nostram amīcitiam appetīssent.   Populī Rōmānī 25
hanc esse cōnsuētūdinem, ut sociōs atque amīcōs nōn modo suī
nihil dēperdere, sed grātiā dignitāte honōre auctiōrēs velit esse;
quod vērō ad amīcitiam populī Rōmānī attulissent, id iīs ēripī
quis patī posset?   Postulāvit deinde eadem quae lēgātīs in
mandātīs dederat: nē aut Aeduīs aut eōrum sociīs bellum īn- 30
ferret; obsidēs redderet; si nūllam partem Germānōrum domum
remittere posset, at nē quōs amplius Rhēnum trānsīre paterētur.

Ariovistus ad postulāta Caesaris pauca respondit, dē suīs
virtūtibus multa praedicāvit: "Trānsiī Rhēnum," inquit, "nōn
meā sponte, sed rogātus et arcessītus ā Gallīs; nōn sine magnā 35
spē magnīsque praemiīs domum propinquōsque relīquī; sēdēs
habeō in Galliā ab ipsīs concessās, obsidēs ipsōrum voluntāte

datōs; stīpendium capiō iūre bellī quod victōres victīs impōnere
cōnsuērunt. Nōn ego Gallīs, sed Gallī mihi bellum intulērunt;
omnēs Galliae cīvitātēs ad mē oppugandum vēnērunt, ac contrā
mē castra habuērunt; eae omnēs cōpiae ūnō ā mē proeliō pulsae
5 ac superātae sunt. Sī iterum experīrī volunt, parātus sum dē-
certāre; sī pāce ūtī volunt, inīquum est dē stīpendiō recūsāre,
quod suā voluntāte ad hoc tempus pependērunt.

"Amīcitiam populī Rōmānī mihi ōrnāmentō et praesidiō, nōn
dētrīmentō esse oportet, eamque hāc spē petīvī. Sī per popu-
10 lum Rōmānum stīpendium remittētur et dēditīciī subtrahentur,
nōn minus libenter recūsābō populī Rōmānī amīcitiam quam
appetīvī. Quod multitūdinem Germānōrum in Galliam trādūcō,
id meī mūniendī, nōn Galliae oppugnandae causā faciō. Eius
reī testimōnium est quod, nisi rogātus, nōn vēnī, et quod bellum
15 nōn intulī, sed dēfendī.

"Prius in Galliam vēnī quam populus Rōmānus. Numquam
ante hoc tempus exercitus populī Rōmānī Galliae fīnēs ingressus
est. Quid tibi vīs cūr in meās possessiōnēs vēnerīs? Prōvincia
mea haec est Gallia, sīcut illa vestra. Ut mihi concēdī nōn
20 oportēret sī in vestrōs fīnēs impetum facerem, sīc item vōs estis
inīquī quod in meō iūre mē interpellātis.

"Quod ā senātū frātrēs populī Rōmānī Aeduōs appellātōs
dīcis, nōn tam barbarus neque tam imperītus sum rērum ut nōn
sciam neque bellō Allobrogum proximō Aeduōs Rōmānīs auxi-
25 lium tulisse, neque ipsōs in hīs contentiōnibus quās Aeduī mēcum et cum Sēquanīs habuērunt auxiliō populī Rōmānī ūsōs
esse. Dēbeō suspicārī simulātā tē amīcitiā, quem exercitum in
Galliā habēs, meī opprimendī causā habēre. Nisi dēcēdēs atque
exercitum dēdūcēs ex hīs regiōnibus, ego tē nōn prō amīcō, sed
30 prō hoste habēbō.

"Quod sī tē interfēcerō, multīs nōbilibus prīncipibusque populī
Rōmānī grātum faciam,— id ab ipsīs per eōrum nūntiōs compertum habeō,— quōrum omnium grātiam atque amīcitiam tuā
morte redimere possum. Quod sī dēcesseris et līberam posses-
35 siōnem Galliae mihi trādideris, magnō tē praemiō remūnerābor,
et quaecumque bella gerī volēs, sine ūllō tuō labōre et perīculō
cōnficiam."

Multa ā Caesare in eam sententiam aicta sunt quārē negōtiō
dēsistere nōn posset: "Neque mea," inquit, "neque populī Rōmānī cōnsuētūdō patitur utī optimē meritōs sociōs dēseram;
neque iūdicō Galliam potius esse tuam quam populī Rōmānī.
Bellō superātī sunt Arvernī et Rutēnī ā Q. Fabiō Maximō, qui- 5
bus populus Rōmānus ignōvit, neque in prōvinciam redēgit,
neque stīpendium imposuit. Quod sī antīquissimum quodque
tempus spectārī oportet, populī Rōmānī iūstissimum est in
Galliā imperium; si iūdicium senātūs observārī oportet, lībera
dēbet esse Gallia, quam bellō victam suīs lēgibus ūtī voluit." 10
Dum haec in conloquiō geruntur, Caesarī nūntiātum est
equitēs Ariovistī propius tumulum accēdere et ad nostrōs ade-
quitāre, lapidēs tēlaque in nostrōs conicere. Caesar loquendī
fīnem fēcit, sēque ad suōs recēpit, suīsque imperāvit nē quod
omnīnō tēlum in hostēs reicerent. Nam etsī sine ūllō perīculō 15
legiōnis dēlēctae cum equitātū proelium fore vidēbat, tamen
committendum nōn putābat ut, pulsīs hostibus, dīcī posset eōs
ab sē per fidem in conloquiō circumventōs.
Posteāquam in vulgus mīlitum ēlatum est quā adrogantiā in
conloquiō Ariovistus ūsus omnī Galliā Rōmānīs interdīxisset, 20
impetumque in nostrōs eius equitēs fēcissent, eaque rēs conloquium ut dīrēmisset, multō maior alacritās studiumque pugnandī maius exercituī iniectum est.
Bīduō post Ariovistus ad Caesarem lēgātōs mittit: velle sē dē
iīs rēbus quae inter eōs agī coeptae neque perfectae essent, agere 25
cum eō; utī aut iterum conloquiō diem cōnstitueret, aut, sī id
minus vellet, ex suīs lēgātum aliquem ad sē mitteret. Conlo-
quendī Caesarī causa vīsa nōn est, et eō magis quod prīdiē eius
diēī Germānī retinērī nōn potuerant quīn tēla in nostrōs conice-
rent. Lēgātum ex suīs sēsē magnō cum perīculō ad eum missū- 30
rum et hominibus ferīs obiectūrum exīstimābat.
Commodissimum vīsum est C. Valerium Procillum, C. Valeriī
Caburī fīlium, summā virtūte et hūmānitāte adulēscentem,
cuius pater ā C. Valeriō Flaccō cīvitāte dōnātus erat, et propter
fidem et propter linguae Gallicae scientiam, quā multā iam 35
Ariovistus longinquā cōnsuētūdine ūtēbātur, et quod in eō
peccandī Germānīs causa nōn esset, ad eum mittere, et ūnā

M. Maecium, qui hospitiō Ariovistī ūtēbātur. Hīs mandāvit
ut quae dīceret Ariovistus cognōscerent et ad sē referrent.
Quōs cum apud sē in castrīs Ariovistus cōnspexisset, exercitū suō
praesente conclāmāvit, "Quid ad mē venītis? An speculandī
5 causā?" Cōnantēs dīcere prohibuit et in catēnās coniēcit.
Eōdem diē castra prōmōvit et mīlibus passuum sex ā Caesaris
castrīs sub monte cōnsēdit. Postrīdiē eius diēī praeter castra
Caesaris suās cōpiās trādūxit et mīlibus passuum duōbus ultrā
eum castra fēcit, eō cōnsiliō, utī frūmentō commeātūque quī ex
10 Sēquanīs et Aeduīs supportārētur Caesarem interclūderet. Ex
eō diē diēs continuōs quīnque Caesar prō castrīs suās cōpiās
prōdūxit et aciem īnstrūctam habuit, ut, sī vellet Ariovistus
proeliō contendere, eī potestās nōn deesset. Ariovistus hīs
omnibus diēbus exercitum castrīs continuit, equestrī proeliō
15 cotīdiē contendit.

Genus hoc erat pugnae quō sē Germānī exercuerant: equitum
mīlia erant sex, totidem numerō peditēs vēlōcissimī ac fortissimī,
quōs ex omnī cōpiā singulī singulōs suae salūtis causā dēlēgerant;
cum hīs in proeliīs versābantur, ad hōs sē equitēs recipiēbant;
20 hī, sī quid erat dūrius, concurrēbant; sī quī, graviōre vulnere
acceptō, equō dēciderat, circumsistēbant; sī quō erat longius
prōdeundum aut celerius recipiendum, tanta erat hōrum exercitātiōne celeritās, ut iubīs sublevātī equōrum cursum adae-
quārent.

25   Ubi eum castrīs sē tenēre Caesar intellēxit, nē diūtius commeātū prohibērētur, ultrā eum locum quō in locō Germānī
cōnsēderant, circiter passūs sēscentōs ab hīs castrīs, idōneum
locum dēlēgit, aciēque triplicī īnstrūctā, ad eum locum vēnit.
Prīmam et secundam aciem in armīs esse, tertiam castra mūnīre
30 iussit. Is locus ab hoste circiter passūs sēscentōs, utī dictum
est, aberat.

Eō circiter hominum numerō sēdecim mīlia expedīta cum
omnī equitātū Ariovistus mīsit, quae cōpiae nostrōs terrērent et
mūnītiōne prohibērent. Nihilō sētius Caesar, ut ante cōnstitue-
35 rat, duās aciēs hostem prōpulsāre, tertiam opus perficere iussit.
Mūnītīs castrīs, duās ibi legiōnēs relīquit et partem auxiliōrum,
quattuor reliquās legiōnēs in castra maiōra redūxit.

Proximō diē, īnstitūtō suō, Caesar ex castrīs utrīsque cōpiās
suās ēdūxit, paulumque ā maiōribus castrīs prōgressus, aciem
īnstrūxit, hostibusque pugnandī potestātem fēcit. Ubi nē tum
quidem eōs prōdīre intellēxit, circiter merīdiem exercitum in
castra redūxit. Tum dēmum Ariovistus partem suārum cōpiā- 5
rum quae castra minōra oppugnāret mīsit. Ācriter utrimque
usque ad vesperum pugnātum est.
Sōlis occāsū suās cōpiās Ariovistus, multīs et inlātīs et accep-
tīs vulneribus, in castra redūxit. Cum ex captīvīs quaereret
Caesar, quamobrem Ariovistus proeliō nōn dēcertāret, hanc 10
reperiēbat causam, quod apud Germānōs ea cōnsuētūdō esset
ut mātrēs familiae eōrum sortibus vāticinātiōnibusque dēclārā-
rent, utrum proelium committī ex ūsū esset necne; eās ita dīcere:
nōn esse fās Germānōs superāre, sī ante novam lūnam proeliō
contendissent.   15
Postrīdiē eius diēī Caesar praesidiō utrīsque castrīs quod satis
esse vīsum est relīquit, ālāriōs omnēs in cōnspectū hostium prō
castrīs minōribus cōnstituit, quod minus multitūdine mīlitum
legiōnāriōrum prō hostium numerō valēbat, ut ad speciem
ālāriīs ūterētur; ipse, triplicī īnstrūctā aciē, ūsque ad castra 20
hostium accessit.
Tum dēmum necessāriō Germānī suās cōpiās castrīs ēdūxē-
runt, generātimque cōnstituērunt paribus intervāllīs Harūdēs
Marcomannōs Tribocōs Vangionēs Nemētēs Eudusiōs Suēbōs,
omnemque aciem suam raedīs et carrīs circumdedērunt, nē qua 25
spēs in fugā relinquerētur. Eō mulierēs imposuērunt, quae ad
proelium proficīscentēs passīs manibus flentēs implōrābant, nē
sē in servitūtem Rōmānīs trāderent.
Caesar singulīs legiōnibus singulōs lēgātōs et quaestōrem prae-
fēcit, uti eōs testēs suae quisque virtūtis habēret; ipse ab dextrō 30
cornū, quod eam partem minimē firmam hostium esse animad-
verterat, proelium commīsit. Ita nostrī ācriter in hostēs, signō
datō, impetum fēcērunt, itaque hostēs repente celeriterque prō-
currērunt, ut spatium pīla in hostēs coniciendī nōn darētur.
Relictīs pīlīs, comminus gladiīs pugnātum est. At Germānī, 35
celeriter ex cōnsuētūdine suā phalange factā, impetūs gladiōrum
excēpērunt. Repertī sunt complūrēs nostrī quī in phalangem

īnsilīrent et scūta manibus revellerent et dēsuper vulnerārent.
Cum hostium aciēs ā sinistrō cornū pulsa atque in fugam
coniecta esset, ā dextrō cornū vehementer multitūdine suōrum
nostram aciem premēbant. Id cum animadvertisset P. Crassus
5 adulēscēns, quī equitātuī praeerat, quod expedītior erat quam iī
quī inter aciem versābantur, tertiam aciem labōrantibus nostrīs
subsidiō mīsit.

Ita proelium restitūtum est, atque omnēs hostēs terga vertē-
runt, nec prius fugere destitērunt quam ad flūmen Rhēnum,
10 mīlia passuum ex eō locō circiter quīnquāgintā, pervēnērunt.
Ibi perpaucī aut vīribus cōnfīsī trānāre contendērunt, aut, lintri-
bus inventīs, sibi salūtem peperērunt.   In hīs fuit Ariovistus,
quī, nāviculam dēligātam ad rīpam nactus, eā prōfūgit; reliquōs
omnēs cōnsecūtī equitēs nostrī interfēcērunt.   Duae fuērunt
15 Ariovistī uxōrēs, ūna, Suēba nātiōne, quam domō sēcum dūxerat, altera Nōrica, rēgis Vocciōnis soror, quam in Galliā dūxerat
ā frātre missam: utraque in eā fugā periit; duae fīliae: hārum
altera occīsa, altera capta est.

C. Valerius Procillus, cum ā custōdibus in fugā trīnīs catēnīs
20 vīnctus traherētur, in ipsum Caesarem hostēs equitātū inse-
quentem incidit.   Quae quidem rēs Caesarī nōn minōrem quam
ipsa victōria voluptātem attulit, quod hominem honestissimum
prōvinciae Galliae, suum familiārem et hospitem, ēreptum ex
manibus hostium sibi restitūtum vidēbat, neque eius calamitāte
25 dē tantā voluptāte et grātulātiōne quicquam fortūna dēminue-
rat.   Is sē praesente dē sē ter sortibus cōnsultum dīcēbat, utrum
ignī statim necārētur, an in aliud tempus reservārētur; sortium
beneficiō sē esse incolumem.   Item M. Maecius repertus et ad
eum reductus est.

30   Hōc proeliō trāns Rhēnum nūntiātō, Suēbī quī ad rīpās Rhēnī
vēnerant domum revertī coepērunt.   Quōs ubi quī proximī
Rhēnum incolunt perterritōs sēnsērunt, īnsecūtī magnum ex
hīs numerum occīdērunt.   Caesar, ūnā aestāte duōbus maximīs
bellīs cōnfectīs, mātūrius paulō quam tempus annī postulābat
35 in hīberna in Sēquanōs exercitum dēdūxit.   Hībernīs Labiēnum
praeposuit; ipse in citeriōrem Galliam ad conventūs agendōs
profectus est.

IV. PHAEDRUS

60. The Wolf and the Lamb

Ad rīvum eundem lupus et agnus vēnerant,
sitī compulsī; superior stābat lupus
longēque īnferior agnus. Tunc fauce improbā
latrō incitātus iūrgiī causam intulit.
"Cūr," inquit, "turbulentam fēcistī mihi   5
aquam bibentī?" Lāniger contrā timēns:
"Quī possum, quaesō, facere quod quereris, lupe?
Ā tē dēcurrit ad meōs haustūs liquor."
Repulsus ille vēritātis vīribus,
"Ante hōs sex mēnsēs male," ait, "dīxistī mihi."   10
Respondit agnus, "Equidem nātus nōn eram."
"Pater hercle tuus ibi," inquit, "male dīxit mihi."
Atque ita correptum lacerat iniūstā nece.
Haec propter illōs scrīpta est hominēs fābula
quī fictīs causīs innocentēs opprimunt.   15

61. King Log and King Serpent

Athēnae cum flōrērent aequīs lēgibus,
procāx lībertās cīvitātem miscuit,
frēnumque solvit prīstinum licentia.
Arcem tyrannus occupat Pīsistratus.
Cum trīstem servitūtem flērent Atticī   20
(nōn quia crūdēlis ille, sed quoniam grave
omne īnsuētīs onus), et coepissent querī,
Aesōpus tālem tum fābellam rettulit.
Rānae vagantēs līberīs palūdibus
clāmōre magnō rēgem petiēre ā Iove   25
quī dissolūtōs mōrēs vī compescseret.

Pater deōrum rīsit, atque illīs dedit
parvum tigillum, missum quod subitō vadī
mōtū sonōque terruit pavidum genus.
Hoc mersum limō cum iacēret diūtius,
5 forte ūna tacitē prōfert ē stagnō caput,
et, explōrātō rēge, cūnctās ēvocat.
Illae, timōre positō, certātim adnatant,
lignumque suprā turba petulāns īnsilit.
Quod cum inquināssent omnī contumēliā,
10 alium rogantēs rēgem mīsēre ad Iovem,
inūtilis quōniam esset quī fuerat datus.
Tum mīsit illīs hydrum, quī dentē asperō
corripere coepit singulās. Frūstrā necem
fugitant inertēs; vōcem praeclūdit metus.
15 Fūrtim igitur dant Mercuriō mandāta ad Iovem,
adflīctīs ut succurrat. Tunc contrā deus:
"Quia nōluistis vestrum ferre," inquit, "bonum,
malum perferte."—"Vōs quoque, ō cīvēs," ait,
"hoc sustinēte, maius nē veniat malum."

62. The Jackdaw and the Peacock

20 Nē glōriārī libeat aliēnīs bonīs
Aesōpus nōbīs hoc exemplum prōdidit.
Tumēns inānī grāculus superbiā
pennās, pāvōnī quae dēciderant, sustulit,
sēque exōrnāvit. Deinde contemnēns suōs
25 sē immiscuit pāvōnum fōrmōsō gregī.
Illī impudentī pennās ēripiunt avī,
fugantque rōstrīs. Male mulcātus grāculus
redīre maerēns coepit ad proprium genus;
ā quō repulsus trīstem sustinuit notam.
30 Tum quīdam ex illīs, quōs prius dēspexerat,
"Contentus nostrīs sī fuissēs sēdibus,
et quod nātūra dederat voluissēs patī,
nec illam expertus essēs contumēliam,
nec hanc repulsam tua sentīret calamitās."

63. The Dog and His Reflection

Amittit meritō proprium, quī aliēnum appetit.
Canis per flūmen carnem cum ferret natāns
lymphārum in speculō vīdit simulācrum suum,
aliamque praedam ab alterō ferrī putāns
ēripere voluit; vērum dēcepta avididās   5
et quem tenēbat ōre dīmīsit cibum,
nec quem petēbat potuit adeō attingere.

64. The Lion's Share

Numquam est fidēlis cum potente societās:
testātur haec fābella prōpositum meum.
Vacca et capella et patiēns ovis iniūriae   10
sociī fuēre cum leōne in saltibus.
Hī cum cēpissent cervum vāstī corporis,
sīc est locūtus, partibus factīs, leō:
"Ego prīmam tollō, nōminor quoniam leō;
secundam, quia sum cōnsors, tribuētis mihi;   15
tum, quia plūs valeō, mē sequētur tertia;
malō afficiētur, sī quis quārtam tetigerit!"
Sīc tōtam praedam sōla improbitās abstulit.

65. The Frogs and the Sun

Vīcīnī fūris celebrēs vīdit nūptiās
Aesōpus, et continuō nārrāre incipit: 20
Uxōrem quondam Sōl cum vellet dūcere,
clāmōrem rānae sustulēre ad sīdera.
Convīciō permōtus, quaerit Iuppiter
causam querēlae. Quaedam tum stagnī incola,
"Nunc," inquit, "omnēs ūnus exūrit lacūs,   25
cōgitque miserās āridā sēde ēmorī.
Quidnam futūrum est, sī creārit līberōs?"

66. The Fox and the Tragic Mask

Persōnam tragicam forte vulpēs vīderat.
"Ō quanta speciēs," inquit, "cerebrum nōn habet!"
Hoc illīs dictum est, quibus honōrem et glōriam
fortūna tribuit, sēnsum commūnem abstulit.

67. The Wolf and the Crane

5 Quī pretium meritī ab improbīs dēsīderat,
bis peccat: prīmum, quoniam indignōs adiuvat;
impūne abīre deinde quia iam nōn potest.
Os dēvorātum fauce cum haerēret lupī,
magnō dolōre victus coepit singulōs
10 inlicere pretiō, ut illud extraherent malum.
Tandem persuāsa est iūreiūrandō gruis,
gulaeque crēdēns collī longitūdinem
perīculōsam fēcit medicīnam lupō.
Ā quō cum pactum flāgitāret praemium,
15 "Ingrāta es," inquit, "ōre quae ē nostrō caput
incolume abstulerīs, et mercēdem postulēs."

68. The Sparrow and the Hare

Sibi nōn cavēre et aliīs cōnsilium dare
stultum esse, paucīs ostendāmus versibus.
 Oppressum ab aquilā et flētūs ēdentem gravēs
20 leporem obiūrgābat passer: "Ubi pernicitās
nōta," inquit, "illa est? Quid ita cessārunt pedēs?"
Dum loquitur, ipsum accipiter necopīnum rapit,
questūque vānō clāmitantem interficit.
Lepus sēmanimus: "Mortis ēn sōlācium!
25 quī modo sēcūrus nostra inrīdēbās mala,
similī querēlā fāta dēplōrās tua."

69. The Wolf, the Fox, and the Ape

Quīcumque turpī fraude semel innōtuit,
etiam sī vērum dīcit, amittit fidem.
Hoc attestātur brevis Aesōpī fābula.
Lupus arguēbat vulpem fūrtī crīmine;
negābat illa sē esse culpae proximam.   5
Tunc iūdex inter illōs sēdit sīmius.
Uterque causam cum perōrāsset suam,
dīxisse fertur sīmius sententiam:
"Tū nōn vidēris perdidisse quod petis;
tē crēdō surripuisse quod pulchrē negās."   10

70. The Donkey and the Lion

Virtūtis expers verbīs iactāns glōriam
ignōtōs fallit, nōtīs est derīsuī.
Vēnārī asellō comite cum vellet leō,
contexit illum fruticē, et admonuit simul
ut īnsuetā vōce terrēret ferās,   15
fugientēs ipse exciperet. Hīc aurītulus
clāmōrem subitō tōtīs follit vīribus,
novōque turbat bēstiās mīrāculō,
Quae, dum paventēs exitūs nōtōs petunt,
leōnis adflīguntur horrendō impetū.   20
Quī, postquam caede fessus est, asinum ēvocat,
iubetque vōcem premere. Tunc ille īnsolēns:
"Quālis vidētur opera tibi vōcis meae?"
"Īnsignis," inquit, "sīc ut, nisi nōssem tuum
animum genusque, similī fūgissem metū."   25

71. The Stag at the Fountain

Laudātīs ūtiliōra quae contempserīs
saepe invenīrī, haec adserit nārrātiō.
Ad fontem cervus, cum bibisset, restitit,
et in liquōre vīdit effigiem suam.

Ibi, dum rāmōsa mīrāns laudat cornua
crūrumque nimiam tenuitātem vituperat,
vēnantum subitō vōcibus conterritus
per campum fugere coepit, et cursū levī
5 canēs ēlūsit. Silva tum excēpit ferum,
in quā, retentīs impedītus cornibus,
lacerārī coepit morsibus saevīs canum.
Tunc moriēns vōcem hanc ēdidisse dīcitur:
"Ō mē īnfēlīcem! Quī nunc dēmum intellegō
10 ūtilia mihi quam fuerint quae dēspexeram,
et quae laudāram quantum lūctūs habuerint."

72. The Fox and the Crow

Quī sē laudārī gaudet verbīs subdolīs
sērā dat poenās turpēs paenitentiā.
Cum dē fenestrā corvus raptum cāseum
15 comēsse vellet, celsā residēns arbore,
vulpēs hunc vīdit, deinde sīc coepit loquī:
"Ō quī tuārum, corve, pennārum est nitor!
Quantum decōris corpore et vultū geris!
Sī vōcem habērēs, nūlla prior āles foret."
20 At ille stultus, dum vult vōcem ostendere,
ēmīsit ōre cāseum; quem celeriter
dolōsa vulpēs avidīs rapuit dentibus.
Tum dēmum ingemuit corvī dēceptus stupor.

73. The Donkey and His Master

In prīncipātū commūtandō saepius
25 nīl praeter dominī nōmen mūtant pauperēs.
Id esse vērum parva haec fābella indicat.
Asellum in prātō timidus pāscēbat senex.
Is, hostium clāmōre subitō territus,
suādēbat asinō fugere, nē possent capī.
30 At ille lentus: "Quaesō, num bīnās mihi
clītellās impositūrum victōrem putās?"

Senex negāvit. "Ergō quid rēfert meā
cui serviam, clītellās dum portem meās?"

74. The Sheep, the Stag, and the Wolf

Fraudātor, hominēs cum advocat spōnsum improbōs,
nōn rem expedīre, sed malum augēre expetit.
Ovem rogābat cervus modium trīticī,   5
lupō spōnsōre. At illa, praemetuēns dolum:
"Rapere atque abīre semper adsuēvit lupus,
tū dē cōnspectū fugere vēlōcī impetū;
ubi vōs requīram, cum diēs advēnerit?"

75. The Aged Lion and the Donkey

Quīcumque amīsit dignitātem prīstinam   10
ignāvīs etiam iocus est in cāsū gravī.
Dēfectus annīs et dēsertus vīribus
leo cum iacēret, spīritum extrēmum trahēns,
aper fulmineīs ad eum vēnit dentibus,
et vindicāvit ictū veterem iniūriam.   15
Infestīs taurus mox cōnfōdit cornibus
hostīle corpus. Asinus, ut vīdit ferum
impūne laedī, calcibus frontem extudit.
At ille exspīrāns: "Fortēs indigne tulī
mihi īnsultāre; tē, nātūrae dēdecus,   20
quod ferre cōgor, certē bis videor morī.'

76. The Weasel and the Man

Mustēla ab homine prēnsa, cum īnstantem necem
effugere vellet, "Quaesō, parce," inquit, "mihi,
quae tibi molestīs mūribus pūrgō domum."
Respondit ille: "Facerēs sī causā meā,   25
grātum esset, et dedissem veniam supplicī.
Nunc, quia labōrās ut fruāris reliquiīs
quās sunt rōsūrī, simul et ipsōs dēvorēs,

nōlī imputāre vānum benificium mihi."
Atque ita locūtus improbam lētō dedit.
Hoc in sē dictum dēbent illī agnōscere
quōrum prīvāta servit ūtilitās sibi,
5 et meritum ināne iactant imprūdentius.

77. The Frog and the Ox

Inops, potentem dum vult imitārī, perit.
In prātō quondam rāna cōnspexit bovem,
et, tācta invidiā tantae magnitūdinis,
rūgōsam īnflāvit pellem; tum nātōs suōs
10 interrogāvit an bove esset lātior.
Illī negārunt. Rūrsus intendit cutem
maiōre nīsū, et similī quaesīvit modō
quis maior esset. Illī dīxērunt bovem.
Novissimē, indignāta dum vult validius
15 īnflāre sēsē, ruptō iacuit corpore.

78. The Dog and the Crocodile

Cōnsilia quī dant prāva cautīs hominibus
et perdunt operam, et dērīdentur turpiter.
Canēs currentēs bibere in Nīlō flūmine
ā corcodīlīs nē rapiantur trāditum est.
20 Igitur, cum currēns bibere coepisset canis,
sīc corcodīlus: "Quamlibet lambe ōtiō;
nōlī verērī!" At ille: "Facerem meherculēs,
nisi esse scīrem carnis tē cupidum meae."

79. The Frog and the Bulls

Humilēs labōrant, ubi potentēs dissident.
25 Rāna in palūde pugnam taurōrum intuēns,
"Heu quanta nōbīs īnstat perniciēs!" ait.
Interrogāta ab aliā cūr hoc dīceret,
dē prīncipātū cum illī certārent gregis,

longēque ab ipsīs dēgerent vītam bovēs:
"Est statiō sēparāta, ac dīversum genus;
sed pulsus regnō nemoris quī prōfūgerit
palūdis in sēcrēta veniet latibula,
et prōculcātās obteret dūrō pede.   5
Ita caput ad nostrum furor illōrum pertinet."

80. The Kite and the Doves

Quī sē committit hominī tūtandum improbō,
auxilia dum requīrit, exitium invenit.
Columbae saepe cum fūgissent mīluum,
et celeritāte pennae vītāssent necem,   10
cōnsilium raptor vertit ad fallāciam,
et genus inerme tālī dēcēpit dolō:
"Quārē sollicitum potius aevum dūcitis,
quam rēgem mē creātis, ictō foedere,
quī vōs ab omnī tūtās praestem iniūriā?"   15
Illae crēdentēs trādunt sēsē mīluō;
quī, rēgnum adeptus, coepit vēscī singulās,
et exercēre imperium saevīs unguibus.
Tunc dē reliquīs ūna: "Meritō plectimur."

81. The Eagle, the Cat, and the Sow

Aquila in sublīmī quercū nīdum fēcerat;   20
fēlēs, cavernam nancta, in mediā pepererat;
sūs, nemoris cultrīx, fētum ad īmam posuerat.
Tum fortuītum fēlēs contubernium
fraude et scelestā sīc ēvertit malitiā.
Ad nīdum scandit volucris; "Perniciēs," ait,   25
"tibī parātur, forsan et miserae mihi;
nam fodere terram quod vidēs cotīdiē
aprum īnsidiōsum, quercum vult ēvertere,
ut nostram in plānō facile prōgeniem opprimat."
Terrōre offūsō et perturbātīs sēnsibus,   30
dērēpit ad cubīle saetosae suis;

"Magnō," inquit, "in perīclō sunt nātī tuī;
nam simul exieris pāstum cum tenerō grege,
aquila est parāta rapere porcellōs tibi."
Hunc quoque timōre postquam complēvit locum,
5   dolōsa tūtō condidit sēsē cavō.
Inde ēvagāta noctū, suspēnsō pede,
ubi ēscā sē replēvit et prōlem suam,
pavōrem simulāns prōspicit tōtō diē.
Ruīnam metuēns, aquila rāmīs dēsidet;
10   aper, rapīnam vītāns, nōn prōdit forās.
Quid multa? Inediā sunt cōnsūmptī cum suīs,
fēlisque catulīs largam praebuērunt dapem.
    Quantum homo bilinguis saepe concinnet malī
documentum habēre stulta crēdulitās potest.

82. The Two Mules and the Robbers

15   Mūlī gravātī sarcinīs ībant duo:
ūnus ferēbat fiscōs cum pecūniā,
alter tumentēs multō saccōs hordeō.
Ille, onere dīves, celsā cervīce ēminet,
clārumque collō iactat tintinnābulum;
20   comes quiētō sequitur et placidō gradū.
Subitō latrōnēs ex īnsidiīs advolant,
interque caedem ferrō mūlum sauciant,
dīripiunt nummōs, neglegunt vīle hordeum.
Spoliātus igitur cāsūs cum flēret suōs,
25   "Equidem," inquit alter, "mē contemptum gaudeō;
nam nīl āmīsī, nec sum laesus vulnere."
    Hōc argūmentō tūta est hominum tenuitās;
magnae perīclō sunt opēs obnoxiae.

83. The Stag and the Oxen

Cervus, nemorōsīs excitātus latibulīs,
30   ut vēnātōrum fugeret īnstantem necem
caecō timōre proximam vīllam petit,

et opportūnō sē bovīlī condidit.
Hīc bōs latentī: "Quidnam voluistī tibi,
īnfēlīx, ultrō quī ad necem cucurrerīs,
hominumque tēctō spīritum commīserīs?"
At ille supplex, "Vōs modo," inquit, "parcite;   5
occāsiōne rūrsus ērumpam datā."
Spatium diēī noctis excipiunt vicēs.
Frondem bubulcus adfert, nīl ideō videt.
Eunt subinde et redeunt omnēs rūsticī:
nēmō animadvertit; trānsit etiam vīlicus,   10
nec ille quicquam sentit.   Tum gaudēns ferus
būbus quiētīs agere coepit grātiās,
hospitium adversō quod praestiterint tempore.
Respondit ūnus: "Salvum tē cupimus quidem;
sed ille, qui oculōs centum habet, sī vēnerit,   15
magnō in perīclō vīta vertētur tua."
Haec inter, ipse dominus ā cēnā redit,
et, quia corruptōs vīderat nūper bovēs,
accēdit ad praesaepe: "Cūr frondis parum est,
strāmenta dēsunt?   Tollere haec arānea   20
quantum est labōris?"   Dum scrūtātur singula,
cervī quoque alta cōnspicātur cornua;
quem convocātā iubet occīdī familiā
praedamque tollit.   Haec significat fābula
dominum vidēre plūrimum in rēbus suīs.   25

84. The Wolf and the Dog

Quam dulcis sit lībertās, breviter prōloquar.
Canī perpāstō maciē cōnfectus lupus
forte occucurrit.   Dein salūtātum invicem
ut restitērunt: "Unde sīc, quaesō, nitēs?
Aut quō cibō fēcistī tantum corporis?   30
Ego, quī sum longē fortior, pereō famē."
Canis simpliciter: "Eadem est condiciō tibi,
praestāre dominō sī pār officium potes."
"Quod?" inquit ille.   "Custōs ut sīs līminis,

ā fūribus tueāris et noctū domum."
"Ego vērō sum parātus: nunc patior nivēs
imbrēsque in silvīs asperam vītam trahēns.
Quantō est facilius mihi sub tēctō vīvere,
5 et ōtiōsum largō satiārī cibō!"
"Venī ergō mēcum." Dum prōcēdunt, aspicit
lupus ā catēnā collum dētrītum canī.
"Unde hoc, amīce?" "Nihil est." "Dīc, quaesō, tamen."
"Quia videor ācer, alligant mē interdiū,
10 lūce ut quiēscam, et vigilem nox cum vēnerit;
crepusculō solūtus quā vīsum est vagor.
Adfertur ultrō pānis; dē mēnsā suā
dat ossa dominus; frūsta iactant familia,
et quod fastīdit quisque, pulmentārium.
15 Sīc sine labōre venter implētur meus."
"Age, abīre sī quō est animus, est licentia?"
"Nōn plānē est," inquit. "Fruere quae laudās, canis!
Regnāre nōlō, līber ut nōn sim mihi."

85. Sister and Brother

Praeceptō monitus, saepe tē cōnsīderā.
20 Habēbat quidam fīliam turpissimam,
īdemque īnsignem pulchrā faciē fīlium.
Hī speculum, in cathedrā mātris ut positum fuit,
puerīliter lūdentēs forte īnspexerunt.
Hic sē fōrmōsum iactat; illa īrāscitur,
25 nec glōriantis sustinet frātris iocōs,
accipiēns quippe cūncta in contumēliam.
Ergō ad patrem dēcurrit laesūra invicem,
magnāque invidiā crīminātur fīlium,
vir nātus quod rem feminārum tetigerit.
30 Amplexus ille utrumque, et carpēns ōscula,
dulcemque in ambōs cāritātem partiēns,
"Cotīdiē," inquit, "speculō vōs ūtī volō:
tū, fōrmam nē corrumpās nēquitiae malīs;
tū, faciem ut istam mōribus vincās bonīs."

86. The Fox and the Grapes

Famē coācta vulpes altā in vīneā
ūvam appetēbat, summīs saliēns vīribus.
Quam tangere ut nōn potuit, discēdēns ait,
"Nōndum mātūra est; nōlō acerbam sūmere."
Quī, facere quae nōn possunt, verbīs ēlevant,   5
adscrībere hoc dēbēbunt exemplum sibi.

87. The Horse and the Boar

Equus sēdāre solitus quō fuerat sitim,
dum sēsē aper volūtat, turbāvit vadum.
Hinc orta līs est. Sonipēs, īrātus ferō,
auxilium petiit hominis, quem dorsō levāns   10
redīt ad hostem. Iactīs hunc tēlīs eques
postquam interfēcit, sīc locūtus trāditur:
"Laetor tulisse auxilium mē precibus tuīs;
nam praedam cēpī, et didicī quam sīs ūtilis."
Atque ita coēgit frēnōs invītum patī.   15
Tum maestus ille: "Parvae vindictam reī
dum quaerō dēmēns, servitūtem repperī."
    Haec īrācundōs admonēbit fābula
impūne potius laedī quam dēdī alterī.

88. The Fox and the Goat

Homō in perīclum simul ac vēnit callidus,   20
reperīre effugium quaerit alterius malō.
    Cum dēcidisset vulpēs in puteum īnscia,
et altiōre clauderētur margine,
dēvēnit hircus sitiēns in eundem locum.
Simul rogāvit esset an dulcis liquor   25
et cōpiōsus. Illa fraudem mōliēns:
"Dēscende, amīce! Tanta bonitās est aquae,
voluptās ut satiārī nōn possit mea."

Immīsit sē barbātus.   Tum vulpēcula
ēvāsit puteō, nīxa celsīs cornibus,
hircumque clausō līquit haerentem vadō.

89.   The Two Pouches

Pērās imposuit Iuppiter nōbīs duās:
proprīīs replētam vitiīs post tergum dedit,
aliēnīs ante pectus suspendit gravem.

Hāc rē vidēre nostra mala nōn possumus;
aliī simul dēlinquunt, cēnsōrēs sumus.

NOTES

For ease of reference, each note is numbered separately. Numbers in boldface type (e.g. **13**) refer to pages, numbers in lightface type (e.g. 13) refer to lines. Where there are two or more notes to a single line, they are distinguished by small letters in italics. The following abbreviations are used:

abl.: ablative
acc.: accusative
act.: active
adj.: adjective
adv.: adverb
c. (*circā*): about (*with approximate dates*)
cp.: compare
dat.: dative
e.g. (*exemplī grātiā*): for example
G.: Grammatical Outline (pp. 161-183). Reference is to sections.

gen.: genitive
i.e. (*id est*): that is
ind.: indicative
N., NN.: note, notes. N. **13** 5 = note on p. 13, line 5.
nom.: nominative
p., pp.: page, pages
pers.: person
plur.: plural
ı res.: present
sc. (*scīlicet*): understand, supply
sing.: singular

I. Aulus Gellius

(See pp. 1-3.)

Notes to Selection 1

13 1a **ā Samnītibus**: this phrase modifies *vēnērunt*, not *lēgātī*. Prepositional phrases in Latin are much more frequently adverbial than adjectival (cp. G. 4).

13 1b **Samnītibus**: the Samnites were a warlike race dwelling in a hilly region southeast of Rome. The Romans first came into armed conflict with them in the latter part of the fourth century B. C., but it was not until c. 275 B.C. that they were finally subdued.

13 1c **C. Fabricium Luscīnum**: for an explanation of the Roman name, see **8** 18 - **9** 29. The use of C. as the abbreviation of the *praenōmen* Gaius (and Cn. for Gnaeus) is a relic of the older form of the Latin alphabet, in which C represented the sound of G.

When Latin is read aloud, the *praenōmen* should be read as if printed in full, in the proper case (here *Gaium*). In oral English translation, the full name should be used in the nominative case (e.g. Gaius Fabricius Luscinus); it is customary in English contexts to use the English method of

79

pronouncing Latin names (contrast our customary pronunciation of the names Caesar and Cicero with the same names sounded as Latin words). To aid the student, the English pronunciation of all Latin and Greek names is indicated in the Vocabulary.

C. Fabricius Luscinus was consul in 282 B.C. and again in 278. The consuls, the chief magistrates of the Roman Republic, were two in number, and served for one year. Both consuls were vested with the full power of the office, and each acted as a check upon the other. Besides being the chief civil magistrates, the consuls acted as commanders-in-chief of the Roman army (see N. 21 14a, ¶2).

Fabricius was one of the most popular heroes in Roman history. His military exploits fall within the period (c. 285 - c. 265 B.C.) in which Rome was completing the extension of her power over the Italian peninsula. In later years Fabricius was revered as an example of the good old Roman virtues, and numerous anecdotes, semi-historical, semi-legendary, grew up about his name. The present story is one of these. Whatever truth this narrative may contain, it is a historic fact that Fabricius played a prominent part in the subjugation of the Samnites, and in his second consulship (278 B.C.) celebrated a triumph over them and their allies.

13 3 post redditam pācem: 'after the restoration of peace'; literally, 'after peace restored'. The English idiom here uses two nouns: one, 'restoration', an abstract noun of verbal origin; the other, 'peace', a noun in a prepositional phrase introduced by 'of'. For the same thought, Latin uses only one noun, pācem, and expresses the idea of the English abstract verbal noun 'restoration' by the use of the Perfect Passive Participle redditam. This is a characteristic Latin usage: e.g. ab urbe conditā, 'from the foundation of the city'; ante cīvitātem datam, 'before the bestowal of citizenship'. Where the English idiom differs from the Latin, it will generally be found that the English prefers the noun, the Latin the verb, the English the abstract expression, the Latin the concrete.

13 4a dōnō: 'as a gift'; Dative of Purpose. Cp. 'He gave it to me for a present'. So, Locum castrīs capit, 'He selects a place for a camp'. Cp. G. 14.

13 4b ut acciperet: 'to accept (it)'; a clause of Indirect Command or Request. Such a clause depends on a verb meaning to command, request, decree, or the like, and represents the substance of that which is commanded, requested, or decreed (here the direct request was accipe, 'accept'). The verb of the clause is in the subjunctive mood; affirmative clauses either have no introductory conjunction or are introduced by ut; negative clauses are introduced by nē or ut . . . nē: e.g. huic imperat adeat cīvitātēs, 'he orders him to visit the states' (direct, adī, 'visit'); suīs imperat, nē . . . tēlum reicerent, 'he ordered his men not to throw back a weapon' (direct, nōlīte reicere, 'don't throw back'). The Indirect Command is really a variety of the Subjunctive Substantive Clause (see G. 45, especially G. 45A); here the clause is used as the object of rogāvērunt.

13 5a Quae: 'these things', 'this'; to refer to something mentioned in a preceding sentence or clause, Latin often, as here, uses a relative where the English usage demands a demonstrative.

13 5b inquiunt: the only forms of the irregular verb inquam in general

SELECTION 2 **NOTES, AULUS GELLIUS** 81

use are the first pers. sing. pres. ind. act. *inquam*, 'I say', the third pers. sing. *inquit*, 'he, she, *or* it says', and the third plur. *inquiunt*, 'they say'. This verb is used only to introduce a direct quotation, and follows one or more words of the quotation.

The tense of *inquiunt* is the Historical Present, that is, the present tense used to represent vividly a past action or state of being. The Historical Present is not infrequent in English, especially in excited or informal narrative. It is much more common in Latin (the verb *inquam* regularly occurs in this tense), and should usually be translated by a past tense.

13 10 quicquam: the indefinite pronoun *quisquam*, *quicquam*, 'anyone, anything', is regularly found only in contexts in which a negative is expressed (as here, *numquam*) or implied.

13 11a quā: *ūsus est*, 'there is need', is used with the ablative of the thing needed, the dative (cp. G. 9) of the person who feels the need. So, *Mihi aquā ūsus est*, 'I need water'. A similar construction is found with *opus est*, 'there is need'.

13 11b nihil: 'not at all' (stronger than *nōn*). The accusative of a few nouns and pronominal adjectives may be used adverbially, as here (Adverbial Accusative): e.g. *magnam partem ex iambīs nostra cōnstat ōrātiō*, 'our speech consists mostly of iambi'.

13 11c ūsui: 'of use'; Dative of Purpose (see N. 13 4a). The combination of a Dative of Purpose with a Dative of Advantage or Disadvantage (see G. 8; here *quibus*) is so common that the construction is known as the "Double Dative": e.g. *Mihi auxiliō mittitur*, 'He is sent to help me' (literally, 'for assistance to me').

Notes to Selection 2

13 13 Hannibalem: Hannibal (247-182 B.C.) was the general of the Carthaginians in the Second Punic War (218-201 B.C.; for the name 'Punic', see N. 13 22). In this mighty struggle, waged between Rome and the north African city of Carthage for the mastery of the western Mediterranean region, Hannibal displayed the most brilliant generalship of ancient times. In fifteen years of campaigning on Italian soil, Hannibal was never defeated; but an attack upon Carthage itself by the almost equally brilliant Roman general Scipio (see N. 17 24c) necessitated Hannibal's return to Africa, where he finally met defeat at the battle of Zama (202 B.C.). Although Hannibal remained at Carthage for some time after the conclusion of the Second Punic War, he was finally forced to flee, and took refuge at the court of Antiochus (see next note). Here he continued to manifest his life-long hostility to the Romans. Relentlessly pursued by the Romans from refuge to refuge, Hannibal committed suicide in 182 B.C. The memory of Hannibal as the greatest single enemy of Rome was burned deeply into Roman consciousness, and it may perhaps be said that he occupies a greater place in Roman literature than any other non-Roman of historic times.

13 14 Antiochum: Antiochus III, surnamed 'the Great', was King of Syria from 223 to 187 B.C. His ambitious attempt to become master of the eastern Mediterranean region brought him into conflict with Rome. At the time at which the event here narrated is supposed to have taken place, Antiochus was preparing for war with Rome. This war, which actually broke out in 192 B.C., ended in 189 with the defeat of Antiochus by L. Scipio (see N. 18 12).

13 15 huiuscemodī: i.e. *huius-ce modī.* The emphatic demonstrative suffix *-ce,* 'here', regularly appears in the shortened form *-c* in fourteen of the thirty forms of *hic, haec, hoc.* The full suffix *-ce* is sometimes, as here, added to other forms of *hic.*

13 16 ingentīs: acc. plur. Note the quantity of the *-ī-* in the ending *-īs,* and contrast with the short *-is* of the gen. sing.

13 18 currūs cum falcibus: the Syrians and other inhabitants of Asia used war-chariots equipped with curved blades (here called *falcēs,* 'sickles', from their resemblance to the agricultural implement) projecting from the wheels and axles. These blades were intended to cut the enemy down as the charioteer drove at full speed through their ranks.

13 19a turribus: small turrets placed on the backs of the elephants. Each contained four soldiers, in addition to the mahout.

13 19b frēnīs, ephippiīs, monīlibus, phalerīs: the word *frēnum* signifies the combined bit and bridle. The former was sometimes made of silver or gold, the latter decorated with gems and metal ornaments. Among the Syrians and other Asiatics the use of such ornate equipment for both horse and rider was quite common. So the saddle (*ephippium*) is to be thought of as composed of, or covered with, brightly colored cloths; the horse as adorned with a necklet (*monīle*) of beads and shining metal disks; while both the harness of the steed and the armor of the warrior gleamed with highly-polished metal studs or bosses (*phalerae*).

13 20 aspicit: for the tense, see N. 13 5b, ¶2.

13 22 Poenus: this adjective, properly 'Phoenician', may be translated 'Carthaginian', since it was used by the Romans to refer to the inhabitants of Carthage, a people of Phoenician descent. A related word is the adjective *Poenicus* or *Pūnicus,* e.g. *bellum Pūnicum,* 'the Punic (i.e. Carthaginian) War'.

Notes to Selection 3

14 1a Milō was the most famous athlete of antiquity; the present anecdote is one of many told about his physical prowess. He was six times victor in the wrestling matches at the Olympic games (see N. 35 5), and was frequently victorious in other athletic contests.

14 1b Crotōniēnsis: note the use of an adjective where the English idiom employs a prepositional phrase, 'of Croton'; so *proelium Cannēnse* (28 28), 'the battle of Cannae'.

Croton (called Crotona by the Romans) was a Greek colony on the southeast coast of Italy. It was one of the leading cities of southern Italy, a region called *Magna Graecia,* 'Great Greece', because of its many flourishing Greek colonies.

14 2 nātū: the Ablative of Specification is used, as here, to limit the scope of a statement by denoting *that in respect to which* the statement is true. The statement *Grandis est,* 'He is great', would imply greatness in all respects; the addition of the Ablative of Specification *nātū*, 'in age', limits the scope of the statement to that one respect: *nātū grandis*, 'great in age', i.e. 'old'. So, *Frātrī celeritāte praestat*, 'He is superior to his brother in swiftness'.

14 3a dēsīsset: the contraction of *-ii-* to *-ī-* is not uncommon in the perfect infinitive and pluperfect subjunctive active.

14 3b forte (adv.): 'by chance'; from the noun *fors*, 'chance', not from the adj. *fortis, forte*.

14 4 proximē: though properly an adverb, *prope*, 'near' (with its comparative *propius* and its superlative *proximē*), is often used as a preposition governing the accusative case.

14 5a crēdō: a parenthetical remark of the narrator.

14 5b ūllae: *ūllus*, 'any', like *quisquam* (see N. 13 10), is generally found only in contexts in which a negative is expressed or (as here) implied.

14 7 dīdūcere et rescindere: Gellius is fond of using two or more virtually synonymous words to express one idea; cp. *dīscidit dīvellitque* (line 8); *retentīs inclūsīsque* (line 10). See 3 9-14.

14 9 laxāsset: in verbs with the Perfect Stem ending in *-v-*, forms based on this stem are often shortened by the omission of *-ve-* or *-vi-* before *-r-* and *-s-*; so *laxāsset* for *laxavisset*, *amārat* for *amaverat*.

Notes to Selection 4

14 12a Mōs: there is apparently no historical justification for ascribing this custom to the Romans of any period; it was probably invented in popular tradition for the purposes of this or similar stories.

14 12b cūriam: the Roman Senate-house was located in the Forum, the square or market-place which served as a civic and financial center for the Romans during the Republic.

14 12c praetextātīs: 'wearing the *toga praetexta*'. This was a toga with a purple border, worn by free-born boys until they became of age. At some time between the ages of 14 and 16 (the exact age in each case was fixed by the head of the family) the boy put aside the *toga praetexta*, and assumed the *toga virīlis*, which marked him as ready to undertake the responsibilities of Roman citizenship. The word *praetextātus* is therefore equivalent to 'minor', 'under the age of discretion'. The adjective *praetextus, -a, -um* is the perfect passive participle of *praetexō, praetexere, praetexuī, praetextus*, 'weave in front', 'weave at the edge', 'weave a border'.

14 13a Tum, cum: 'At a time when.'

14 13b maior: 'more important' than usual, 'rather important'; a common use of the comparative.

14 14a cōnsultāta . . . prōlāta est: the auxiliary often occurs only once in a sentence containing several participles, with all of which the auxiliary is to be taken.

14 14b cōnsultāta . . . est: for the mood, see G. 48, C 1.

14 14c ut eam rem nē quis ēnūntiāret: see N. 13 4b; the Indirect Command is here used as the subject of *placuit*, 'it was decreed' (direct *nē quis ēnūntiet*, 'let no one mention').

14 15a quis: the indefinite pronoun 'anyone, anything', is normally *aliquis, aliquid;* but after *sī, nisi, nē* (as here), and *num,* and in relative clauses, the pronoun *quis, quid* is used with the same meaning.

14 15b dēcrēta esset: the use of the subjunctive mood here is due to the fact that the author wishes us to take this verb, not as an addition of his own, but as representing part of the original decree [*priusquam dēcrēta erit,* 'before it is (literally 'shall have been') decided upon'; see N. **25** 13b].

When a verb, in a construction which normally requires the indicative, is subordinate to an Indirect Statement (G. 64), Indirect Question (G. 42), or Indirect Command (as here), it is placed in the subjunctive if the author wishes it to be taken as representing part of the original statement, question, or command; it remains in the indicative if the author wishes it to be taken as a remark of his own. Thus Cicero, discussing the decrees of the Senate at the time of the conspiracy of Catiline, says:

> . . . cēnsuērunt ut P. Lentulus, *cum sē praetūrā abdicāsset,* in custōdiam trāderetur; itemque utī C. Cethēgus, L. Statilius, P. Gabīnius, *qui omnēs praesentēs erant,* in custōdiam trāderentur,

'they decreed that Lentulus, *after resigning from the praetorship,* should be imprisoned, and also that Cethegus, Statilius, and Gabinius, *all of whom were present,* should be imprisoned'. Observe that Cicero wishes us to take the clause about the presence of the conspirators as a parenthetical remark of his own, but, by the use of the subjunctive *abdicāsset,* marks the clause about resignation from the praetorship as part of the original decree (*cum sē praetūrā abdicāverit,* 'when he has—literally, 'shall have'—resigned from the praetorship'; see G. 48B).

14 17 id dīcī nōn licēre: the Infinitive Clause *id dīcī* (see G. 63) is the subject of the infinitive *licēre.*

14 18 audiendī: 'of hearing'; the genitive of the gerund. The gerund is a verbal noun, with case-forms in the genitive, dative, accusative, and ablative. It may be formed by adding to the Present Stem the endings *-ndī* (gen.), *-ndō* (dat. and abl.), and *-ndum* (acc.); in the Fourth Conjugation, and in the Third Conjugation in *-iō,* the endings are *-endī, -endō,* etc. For example (First Conjugation, *portō, -āre, -āvī, -ātus*):

Gen.	*portandī,*	'of carrying'
Dat.	*portandō,*	'for carrying', 'carrying' (as object of certain verbs)
Acc.	*portandum,*	'carrying' (as object of prepositions)
Abl.	*portandō,*	'by carrying', 'carrying' (as object of prepositions).

So: II *movendī, -dō, -dum, -dō;* III *mittendī, -do, -dum, -dō;*
IV *audiendī, -dō, -dum, -dō;* IIIio *capiendī, -dō, -dum, -dō.*

The gerund has no nominative; the place of the nominative gerund is taken by the infinitive: e.g. 'Swimming is pleasant', *Natāre grātum est.* In the other cases, the gerund has the syntax of a noun; the accusative of the gerund is used only as the object of a preposition:

> *Homō bellandī cupidus est,* 'He is a man desirous of fighting';
> *Aqua ūtilis bibendō est,* 'Water is good for drinking';
> *Ōtium ad legendum nōn habēmus,* 'We have no leisure for reading';
> *Hominis mēns discendō alitur,* 'Man's mind is nourished by learning'.

The gerund must be carefully distinguished from the gerundive or future passive participle (e.g. *portandus, -a, -um;* see G. 69), which has several forms identical with those of the gerund. This distinction will not be difficult if it is kept in mind that the gerund is a *noun,* the gerundive or future passive participle an *adjective.*

14 21a Āctum (*esse*): the auxiliary *esse* is often omitted in the future active and perfect passive infinitive. The subject of the infinitive here is the clause *utrum vidērētur; agō* here has the meaning 'discuss'.

14 21b utrum: 'which of two (proposals)'; the alternative proposals (*ūnus . . . ut duās uxōres habēret,* and *ut ūna duōbus nūpta esset*) are introduced respectively by *-ne* and *an,* literally 'whether . . . or'; in translating, omit 'whether'.

14 22a ex . . . rē pūblicā: 'to the advantage of the state'.

14 22b ūnus . . . ut . . . habēret: the placing of one or more words of a clause before the conjunction which introduces the verb is quite common in Latin. For the mood of *habēret* (and *esset,* line 23), see G. 45, especially G. 45A.

14 23 esset: the copulative verb, not the auxiliary.

Notes to Selection 5

14 25 familiās: this old form of the genitive singular of *familia* is used in classical times only with the words *pater, māter, fīlius,* and *fīlia.*

14 28 quid sibi postulātiō istaec vellet: 'what their demand meant' (literally, 'what it wanted for itself'). This usage is derived from such expressions as *Quid tibi vīs?,* 'What do you want for yourself?', i.e. 'What is your purpose?', 'What do you mean?'

15 1a istaec: *istic, istaec, istuc* (like *iste, ista, istud*) properly means 'that . . . of yours'. Here *istaec* seems to echo the original question, as if addressed to one of the matrons by a Senator: "*Quid sibi postulātiō istaec vult?*", 'What does that demand of yours mean?' In the indirect form here, *istaec* is best translated 'that . . . of theirs'.

15 1b mediam cūriam: 'the middle of the Senate-chamber'; the adjective *medius, -a, -um,* 'middle', is often used partitively, as here. Other adjectives often so used are *summus,* 'highest'; *īmus,* 'lowest'; *prīmus,* 'first'; so *summus mōns,* 'the top of the mountain'.

15 2 quid . . . īnstitisset, quid . . . dīxisset, dēnārrat: in respect to the Sequence of Tenses (G. 58-G. 60) the Historical Present (N. 13 5b, ¶2) is frequently treated as a past tense.

15 4 utī: another form of the conjunction *ut.* Distinguish it carefully from *ūtī* (with long *u-*), the infinitive of *ūtor, ūtī, ūsus sum.*

15 6a honōris grātiā: *grātiā* and *causā,* both meaning 'for the sake of', govern the genitive case, and always follow the nouns which they govern. The common abbreviation 'e.g.' stands for *exemplī grātiā,* 'for the sake of example'.

15 6b datum (*est*): in the forms of the perfect indicative passive, the auxiliaries *est* and *sunt* are often omitted (cp. N. 14 21a).

15 7 praetextae (*togae*): see N. 14 12c.

Notes to Selection 6

15 8 P. Vergilius Marō, the greatest of Roman epic poets, was born in 70 B.C. near Mantua, north of the river Po.   His principal works were the Eclogues, a collection of pastoral poems; the Georgics, a poetical treatise on agriculture; and the Aeneid, a national epic in twelve books.   The last-named deals with the wanderings of the Trojan Aeneas, the reputed ancestor of Julius and Augustus Caesar, and of his adventures in Sicily, Africa, and Italy, as he sought the promised abodes for his fellow-wanderers; from Aeneas and his companions the Roman race was destined to be derived. Vergil died in 19 B.C., before he could put the finishing touches to the Aeneid.

15 9a ut . . . ēdit: *ut* with the indicative means 'as' (as here) or 'when' (see G. 38).

15 9b īnfōrmem: the notion that bear-cubs must be 'licked into shape' by the mother-bear is a bit of ancient folk-lore that has survived into modern times.

15 10 meī modifies *ingeniī.*

15 11 rudī . . . faciē et imperfectā: 'of rough and unfinished aspect'; the Ablative of Quality or Description is used to qualify a noun, either in the predicate, as here, or attributively, e.g. *vir magnā virtūte,* 'a man of great valor'.   In this construction, the noun in the ablative is always modified by an adjective.

15 12 iīs: another form of *eīs.*   In the plural of *is, ea, id* we find *iī* as well as *eī* for the nominative masculine, and *iīs* as well as *eīs* for the dative and ablative in all genders.

15 14a Aenēida: acc. sing., according to the Greek third declension.

15 14b ēlīmāvisset: the verb is derived from *līma, līmae,* f., 'a file', and means literally 'to file away (imperfections, rough spots, etc.)'.   Metaphors derived from the file are frequent in Roman literary criticism.   For the mood, see N. 14 15b, ¶2.

15 15 combūrerent: this request of Vergil's was of course never granted. Augustus commissioned Varius and Tucca, two authors who were Vergil's friends, to edit the poem, adding nothing, but excising anything which they deemed superfluous.   The poem as we have it contains a number of incomplete lines, and certain other minor imperfections which Vergil himself would probably have remedied.

Notes to Selection 7

15 16a Menander (c. 340-292 B.C.) is the chief representative of the playwrights of the Attic New Comedy, the 'Comedy of Manners', which supplanted the politico-satirical Old Comedy of Aristophanes.   Menander's portrayal of human character was so true that an ancient critic exclaimed, "Menander and Life!   Which of you has imitated the other?" **Philēmone:** Philemon (so in Greek; the Latin nominative is *Philēmō*), 361-262 B.C., was a rival of Menander in the field of the Attic New Comedy.

Though the comedies of Menander and Philemon survive only in fragments, we know that they served as models for the Roman playwrights

Plautus (see N. 34 14c) and Terence, whose plays, which have been preserved, exercised a powerful influence upon the great Molière.

15 16b in certāminibus comoediārum: Athenian dramas, both tragic and comic, were presented as part of religious festivals in honor of the god Dionysus. The presentations were in the form of a contest among the three playwrights whose plays had previously been adjudged the best among those presented for preliminary consideration. The plays of all three were presented to the entire Athenian populace on a single day, and the victor was chosen by a jury of citizens picked by lot.

15 19 bonā veniā: 'by your leave', 'begging your pardon'.

15 20 ērubēscis: the termination -scō of the first principal part of this verb shows that it belongs to a group of verbs known as 'inceptive' or 'inchoative': that is, verbs which denote *beginning* or *becoming*. Such verbs are always of the third conjugation; the -sc- appears only in the present system. So *dūrēscō, dūrēscere, dūruī*, 'become hard'; *advesperāscō, advesperāscere, advesperāvī*, 'grow toward evening', 'become dark.'

Notes to Selection 8

15 21 Sōcratis philosophī: Socrates, one of the founders of Greek philosophy, was born at Athens c. 470 B.C. A sculptor in his youth, he early abandoned this occupation to devote himself to the search for truth. This he sought, not in schools or in books, but in the market-place and streets of Athens, where he spent the day examining himself and others as to the fundamental concepts of human life and thought. The pursuit of dialectic, as he called his conversational method of investigation, fruitful as it was for the development of philosophy, naturally interfered seriously with his duties as provider for his wife and children; to this neglect is to be attributed the nagging of his wife Xanthippe, with whom, from the stand-point of every-day human affairs, we can surely sympathize.

15 23a Alcibiadēs (c. 450-404 B.C.) was a brilliant, but erratic and unscrupulous Athenian. Nephew and ward of the famous statesman Pericles (see N. 16 26c), Alcibiades also played an important role in the Athenian politics of his day. He was associated with Socrates to a considerable extent in his youth, but seems to have been little influenced by the latter's admirable ethical outlook.

15 23b Sōcratēn: acc. sing., according to the Greek first declension.

15 25 Quoniam . . . īnsuēscō et exerceor: see G. 37.

15 26 exerceor: 'I train myself'. This reflexive force seems to have been the original significance of the -r ending in primitive Latin. To this use of the verb the grammarians give the name 'Middle Voice'; thus: Active Voice (the subject performs the action) *Homo puerum exercet*, 'The man trains the boy'; Passive Voice (the subject is the recipient of the action) *Puer ab homine exercētur*, 'The boy is trained by the man'; Middle Voice (the subject acts upon himself), *Puer exercētur*, 'The boy trains himself', 'The boy exercises'. In classical Latin the primitive middle forms had already developed into the Passive Voice as we know it, while the true Middle survived only in a few usages (as here), and in the form of the so-called deponent verbs.

15 23-27 The impudent query of Alcibiades, and the calm but ironic reply of Socrates, with its veiled rebuke for Alcibiades' impudence, are thoroughly characteristic of the two men.

Notes to Selection 9

16 1 solitus (*esse*): see N. 14 21*a*. The verb *soleō* belongs to a group of verbs known as semi-deponents, that is, deponent only in the perfect system (perfect, pluperfect, and future perfect tenses). The group includes

audeō, audēre, ausus sum, 'dare';
fīdō, fīdere, fīsus sum, 'trust' (and the compounds of fīdō);
gaudeō, gaudēre, gāvīsus sum, 'rejoice'; and
soleō, solēre, solitus sum, 'be accustomed'.

16 2 ad . . . sōlem orientem: see the discussion in N. 13 3 of the Latin use of a participle where the English uses a noun of verbal origin.

16 3 īsdem: contracted from *iīsdem;* cp. N. 14 3*a*, and see N. 15 12.

16 4 tamquam . . . sēcessū . . . factō: cp. *quasi perfectō negōtiō*, 14 9.

Socrates' tremendous powers of concentration and detachment from his surroundings are well attested by his pupil Plato and by other contemporary writers. They are made the subject of unseemly jest by the comic playwright Aristophanes in his *Clouds.*

16 6 Temperantiā . . . tantā: see N. 15 11.

16 7 vīxerit: the perfect subjunctive is used in a Result Clause to emphasize the actual accomplishment of the result: e.g. *hostēs tam parātī ad dīmicandum fuērunt ut etiam ad galeās induendās tempus dēfuerit*, 'the enemy was so ready to fight that time was lacking even for putting on our helmets'.

16 8 pestilentiā: the famous plague of Athens, brought on by the crowding and the unsanitary conditions within the city during the early years of the Peloponnesian War. This war, which lasted from 431 to 404 B.C., was waged between Athens and Sparta; it takes its name from the Peloponnesus, the southern portion of Greece, in which Sparta was supreme. The war ended in the defeat of Athens and the loss of her maritime supremacy.

16 9 parcendī moderandīque: in accordance with the principle set forth in N. 13 3, ¶2, the student is advised to use English nouns in translating these verb-forms.

Notes to Selection 10

16 11*a* Alexandrī rēgis: Alexander the Great, son of King Philip of Macedon (see N. 38 12), was born in 356 B.C. In his youth he was the pupil of the great philosopher Aristotle (see N. 38 16). Upon the death of his father in 336, Alexander ascended the Macedonian throne. Quickly putting down uprisings in the Greek cities which his father had subdued, he proceeded upon a career of conquest which soon brought Eastern Europe, Asia Minor, and Egypt under his sway, with lasting results for the later history of these regions. His boundless ambition carried him even into India, where he waged the campaign mentioned in this story. He died in 323.

16 11b et capite et nōmine 'Būcephalās': for the ablatives, see N. 14 2. In Greek the name Bucephalas means 'ox-headed' (from *bous*, 'ox', and *kephalē*, 'head'); the horse was so called because of the extraordinary breadth of its head.

16 12a Ēmptum (*esse*): the omission of the subject accusative (*equum* or *eum*) is irregular (see G. 64).

16 12b Charēs of Mytilene (on the island of Lesbos) was an officer of Alexander's court, who wrote a series of anecdotes concerning his monarch's life and deeds.

16 12c talentīs: the talent was a Greek unit of weight; the Attic talent, here referred to, was equivalent to about 58 lbs. Here a talent of silver is meant. Though the evaluation of ancient monetary units in terms of modern money is generally inaccurate, and is especially so in these days of managed, devaluated, and constantly fluctuating currencies, it will be helpful to consider the Attic talent of silver as worth about $1200. The price of the horse would then be equivalent to $15,600.

16 13 sēstertia trecenta duodecim: a Roman unit of money was the sesterce (*sēstertius, sestertiī,* m.); we may consider it (with the same reservations as in the preceding note) as equivalent to $.05. For expressing fairly large sums of money the *neuter* plural *sēstertia* was used in the sense of 'thousands of sesterces', as here. We may therefore translate *sēstertia trecenta duodecim* 'three hundred and twelve thousand sesterces'. If we multiply 312,000 by $.05, we arrive at the same result as in the preceding note.

16 15 sēsē: another form of the reflexive personal pronoun *sē*, acc. The form *sēsē* is also used as equivalent to *sē* in the ablative.

16 16 bellō Indicō: Alexander's Indian campaign, which began in the summer of 327 B.C.

16 17 immīsit: used 'absolutely', i.e. without an object; this, if expressed, would be *equum*.

16 20 ē mediīs hostibus: see N. 15 1b.

16 22 dominī . . . sēcūrus: *sēcūrus, -a, -um,* 'free from care' (*sē-,* 'without', *cūra, cūrae,* f., 'care'), sometimes, as here, governs the genitive case; so, *poenae sēcūrus,* 'free from anxiety concerning punishment'.

16 23 animam exspīrāvit: according to more reliable sources, Bucephalas died of old age. It is characteristic of Gellius to prefer the more sensational account.

16 24 ob . . . honōrēs: 'for the glorification.'

16 25 Būcephalon: acc. sing., according to the Greek second declension.

Notes to Selection 11

16 26a Alcibiadēs: see NN. 15 23a and 15 23-27.

16 26b avunculum: *avunculus* is an uncle on one's mother's side, a mother's brother; an uncle on one's father's side is *patruus*.

16 26c Periclēn: for the form, see N. 15 23b. Pericles was a great Athenian statesman. Born c. 495 B.C., he rose to the highest position in the Athenian commonwealth. From 445 until his death in 429, with one brief interruption, he dominated the Athenian democracy. Under his leadership, Athens was beautified with such structures as the Odeum, the so-called

Theseum, and the magnificent Parthenon.   The period of his ascendancy was one of great brilliance in literature and the arts, and is justly called the Age of Pericles.

16 27 accessi . . . Antigenidam: Antigenidas of Thebes was a famous flute-player.   The statement that he was engaged to teach Alcibiades is of doubtful authenticity.
Unlike most verbs meaning *to command* (cp. N. 13 4*b*), *iubeō* takes as its object an infinitive substantive clause with subject accusative (G. 63).

17 1*a* tibiis: the tibiae were pipes, perforated at intervals to produce different notes, and fitted with a mouthpiece and vibrating reed, somewhat after the fashion of the modern clarinet.   They were always played in pairs (hence the plural), the two pipes being held together at the mouthpiece, and spreading out in the form of a V.   The translation 'flute' is, strictly speaking, inaccurate, since the modern flute lacks the vibrating reed; however, it is the customary rendition of *tibiae*, as is 'flute-player' of *tibicen.*

17 1*b* quod: a relative pronoun; the antecedent is *canere tibiis.*

16 26 - 17 4 Alcibiadēs . . . tibiās . . . abiēcit infregitque: the amplification of each part of the sentence by modifiers of various kinds, to include an entire and rather detailed narrative in a single sentence, is characteristic of Latin style.   The student, after grasping the thought as it is presented in the Latin, should translate into the relatively short sentences which are characteristic of English narrative.

Notes to Selection 12

17 6 Sibyllīnis: so called as originally owned by Sibylla, the *anus hospita* of line 7.   In the earlier writers, Sibylla is the proper name of a prophetess of Erythrae in Asia Minor, or of Cumae in Campania, near Naples; later writers use Sibylla as the title of any one of a number of prophetesses.   In English it is customary to speak of 'the Sibyl'.

17 7 Tarquinium Superbum: according to legend, Tarquin the Proud, of Etruscan descent, was the last king of Rome.   There seems to be no doubt that Rome was a monarchy early in its history, prior to the establishment of the Republic in the sixth century B.C., and that toward the end of the monarchical period Rome underwent an era of Etruscan domination; but present-day scholars regard as largely legendary the traditional account of the seven kings of Rome.

17 10 quasi . . . dēsiperet: the conjunctions *quasi, tamquam* or *tamquam si,* and *velutsi,* all meaning 'as if', and *quam si* 'than if', introducing imaginative comparisons, are followed by the subjunctive mood; the tense of the verb follows the rule of Sequence of Tenses (G. 58-G. 60), not, as one might expect, the tense-rule of the Condition Contrary to Fact (G. 51).

17 12 ecquid, the neuter of the interrogative pronoun *ecquis, ecquid,* '(is there) anyone (who)?', '(is there) anything (which)?', is here used in the Adverbial Accusative (N. 13 11*b*) as the equivalent of *num,* 'whether'.

17 13 sed enim: *enim,* which is usually explanatory, 'for', is used here in its rarer sense of 'indeed', strengthening and emphasizing the preceding word.   Note that *enim* is always postpositive, i.e. it never comes first in sentence or clause.

17 21a nusquam locī: 'nowhere in the world'; the Partitive Genitive (G. 5) is often used, as here, with adverbs of place. So, *ubinam gentium sumus?*, 'where in the world are we?' (literally, 'where of the nations').

17 21b sacrārium: the books were kept in an underground stone chest in the temple of Jupiter Capitolinus (see NN. 18 3a, 18 4b). In 83 B.C. they were destroyed by fire, and were replaced by a new collection from various sources. The books were later revised by order of Augustus, and transferred to his new temple of Apollo on the Palatine Hill (see N. 25 11b). They continued to be consulted occasionally until the beginning of the fifth century of our era, when they were burned by the Vandal Stilicho, commander of the armies of the Roman Empire.

17 22 quīndecimvirī: Roman governmental boards or commissions were regularly designated by the number of men which composed them. The scope of the commission's work was usually designated by a Dative of Purpose modified by a gerundive (future passive participle); the board here mentioned was known as *quīndecimvirī sacrīs faciundīs* (the form in *-undus* is equivalent to that in *-endus*), 'Commission of Fifteen for the Performance of the Sacred Rites'.

17 23 cum dī immortālēs . . . cōnsulendī sunt: on occasions of great emergency. The directions in the Sibylline books seem to have been of a ritualistic nature, and to have concerned themselves chiefly with methods of appeasing the gods.

Notes to Selection 13

17 24a M. Naevius: the fact that Naevius was tribune of the people in 184 B.C. sets the date for this story.

17 24b tribūnus plēbis: the office of tribune of the people was instituted in the fifth century B.C. as a protection for the common people against injustice at the hands of the nobility. The persons of the tribunes were sacrosanct (i.e. it was a dire offence against the Roman state religion to offer them violence); they could, by the use of their power of veto (*vetō*, 'I forbid'), restrain any magistrate from acting; they could also bring charges against an ex-magistrate before the assembly of the people, as is exemplified in this story.

17 24c Scīpiōnem Āfricānum: P. Cornelius Scipio, later surnamed Africanus (see 9 21-24). was born c. 235 B.C., a member of the *gēns Cornēlia*, one of the oldest patrician families in Rome. His early manhood was spent in the campaigns of the Second Punic War (see N. 13 13), in which he rose to the highest command; he served as consul (see N. 13 1c, ¶3) for the year 205. After his term of office, he succeeded, in spite of senatorial opposition, in carrying out his long-cherished plan of transferring the war to Africa. This move, as we have seen (N. 13 13), resulted in Hannibal's recall to Africa, and his ultimate defeat. Scipio now returned to Rome to celebrate a magnificent triumph; it was at this time that he was accorded the surname Africanus, 'Conqueror of Africa'. He was showered with every honor, and for nearly twenty years was considered the foremost citizen of the Republic. His last years, however, were darkened by such accusations as those mentioned in this Selection and the next; he died in retirement in the year 183 B.C.

17 25a ad populum: 'before an assembly of the people.'

17 25b Antiochō: see N. 13 14.

17 27 alia crimini daret: 'made other accusations'; literally, 'offered other things by way of accusation'. For the case of *crimini*, see 13 4a.

17 31 proeliō: the battle of Zama (see N. 13 13).

18 3a Iovī Optimō Maximō: *Iuppiter Optimus Maximus* was the cult-title of Jupiter worshipped in the temple on the Capitoline Hill (see N. 18 4b).

18 3b grātulātum: 'to give thanks'; the accusative supine of the verb *grātulor*, used to express purpose with the verb of motion *eāmus*.

The supine is a verbal noun, with case-forms in the accusative and ablative. The stem of the supine appears in the fourth principal part (third in the case of deponents), where it may be found by dropping the ending *-us* (or *-ūrus*); to the stem thus found, the endings *-um* (acc.) and *-ū* (abl.) are added. For example (First Conjugation, *portō, -āre, -āvī, -ātus*):

Acc. *portātum*, 'to carry' } see 'Uses of Supine', below.
Abl. *portātū*, 'to carry' }

So, II *vīsūm, vīsū*;   III   *dictum, dictū;*
IV *audītum, audītū;*   IIIio   *factum, factū.*

Uses of the Supine

1. The accusative supine is used to denote Purpose with verbs of motion (this construction is akin to the Accusative of End of Motion; see G. 13 and G. 14). The accusative supine may take an object in the proper case. So, *lēgātōs pācem petītum mittunt*, 'they send ambassadors to plead for peace'.

2. The ablative supine is used mainly as an Ablative of Specification (see N. 14 2): e.g. *Hoc est facile dictū, sed difficile factū*, 'This is easy to say, but hard to do'.

18 4a āvertit: this intransitive use of *āvertō* is unusual. *Sē āvertit* would be more regular.

18 4b Capitōlium: the Capitoline Hill, south-west of the Roman Forum (see N. 14 12b). On it was built the great temple of Jupiter which was the principal center of worship of the Roman state religion.

Notes to Selection 14

18 8 Petīliī quīdam: 'certain men named Petilius'.

18 9a M. . . . . Catōne: M. Porcius Cato, a genuine Roman of the old stamp, was born c. 234 B.C. in the town of Tusculum, in Latium. He distinguished himself in the Second Punic War; in 205 and 204 he served on the staff of Scipio Africanus in Sicily and in Africa. His life-long enmity toward the Scipios, exemplified by this story, may have been caused by his hatred of the Greek culture which they were instrumental in spreading at Rome. Cato became censor (see N. 29 15) in 184, and made violent attempts to stem the tide of luxury and refinement, an activity which won him the surname Censorius. He died in 149 B.C.

18 9b ut aiunt: the intrusion of these parenthetical words does not affect the construction. For *ut* meaning 'as', see N. 15 9a.

18 10 in eum: this use of *in* in the sense of 'against' is an outgrowth of its use with the Accusative of End of Motion (G. 13).

18 11 in eō bellō: see N. 13 14, ¶2.

18 12 L. Scīpiōnī Asiāticō: L. Cornelius Scipio, brother of Scipio Africanus, was consul in 190 B.C. He was sent to take charge of the war against Antiochus with the understanding that his brother would accompany him, as second-in-command (*lēgātus*, line 13). With the latter's advice and assistance, L. Scipio succeeded in defeating Antiochus in 189 at the battle of Magnesia, in Asia Minor. This victory earned him the surname of Asiagenus or Asiāticus, 'Conqueror of Asia'.

18 13 ē sinū togae: as the toga was thrown back over the shoulder, it formed a fold across the chest, which, in lieu of a pocket, was used for holding small articles.

18 15a inlātum: cp. N. 16 12a.

18 15b aerārium: the *aerārium populī Rōmānī*, or Roman state treasury, was located in the Temple of Saturn, in the Forum, at the foot of the Capitoline Hill. Here, in addition to currency and bullion, were kept official records, especially those which dealt with finance.

18 16 Sed enim: see N. 17 13; contrast with this the explanatory use of *enim* in line 12.

18 18a quod . . . poscerētur: *quod* in the sense 'the fact that' introduces a substantive clause; the verb of the clause is normally indicative: e.g. *Praetereō, quod ratiō poscitur*, 'I pass over the fact that an accounting is asked for'. Cp. G. 45, G. 63.

A verb in a construction which normally requires the indicative may be put in the subjunctive if the author wishes, without using formal Indirect Discourse, to indicate that the verb is to be taken as representing part of what someone else *says, thinks, knows, perceives,* or *commands*. So, *Paetus omnēs librōs, quōs pater suus relīquisset, mihi dōnāvit*, 'Paetus gave me all the books which (he said) his father had left' (*quos pater . . . relīquisset* instead of the formal *quōs patrem relīquisse dīxit*). This construction may be called Informal Indirect Discourse (cp. N. 14 15b, ¶2). In our present passage, we may translate 'the fact that, in his opinion, . . .'.

18 18b cui salūs imperiī āc reī pūblicae accepta referrī dēbēret: 'to whose account the salvation of the empire and commonwealth ought to be credited'; literally, 'to whom the salvation . . . , having been received (from him) ought to be credited'. In harmony with the occasion, Scipio is represented as thinking in terms of accounting. A banker, upon receiving funds for deposit, might acknowledge them with the formula *Tibi hanc pecūniam acceptam referō*, 'I credit to you this money, received (by me from you)', or *Tibi haec pecūnia accepta refertur*. It is the latter model which is followed here.

18 19 dēbēret: for the mood, see N. 18 18a, ¶2.

Notes to Selection 15

18 21 virtūtis dīvīnae: 'of god-like excellence'; the phrase conveys a connotation of supernatural gifts.

The words *virtūtis dīvīnae* are in the Genitive of Quality or Description.

A noun in this construction is always modified by an adjective. There is no difference in meaning between this construction and the Ablative of Quality or Description (N. 15 11), but the usage varies with different periods and authors: Cicero has *ācrī vir ingeniō*, Livy *vehementis vir ingeniī*, for 'a man of forceful nature'.

18 22 quod: relative pronoun.

18 24 ventitāre: 'to come frequently'; *ventītō* is the frequentative of *veniō*. Frequentative verbs denote repeated or intensive action; they are of the first conjugation, and are usually formed on the stem of the fourth principal part, occasionally on the present stem. Frequentatives end in *-tō, -tāre, -sō, -sāre*, or (as here) *-itō, -itāre*: e.g. *iactō, -āre*, 'toss about' (*iaciō*, 'throw'); *cursō, -āre*, 'keep running' (*currō*, 'run'); *dictitō, -āre*, 'keep saying' (*dīcō*, 'say').

18 27 id temporis: 'at that (point of) time'; *id* is Adverbial Accusative (see N. 13 11*b*) denoting time; *temporis* is Partitive Genitive.

18 28 lātrārent . . . incurrerent: see N. 18 18*a*, ¶2.

19 4 iūs . . . dīcēbat: the commander naturally had jurisdiction over all disputes arising among his soldiers.

19 5a ē mīlitibus . . . quispiam: with *quīdam, quispiam*, and other indefinites, as with certain numerals (cp. *ex quibus . . . ūnum*, **18 31;** *trīs . . . ex novem*, **17 12),** *ex* with the ablative is regularly used instead of the Partitive Genitive.

19 5b in iūre: 'on a legal matter,' 'in court'.

19 6a ex mōre: 'in accordance with the customary procedure'. When a law-suit could not be finished in one day, the defendant was forced either to submit to imprisonment, or to furnish the plaintiff security for his reappearance on the day and at the place (cp. *diem locumque*, line 6) set by the judge. The terms *vadimōnium prōmittere*, 'to furnish security (or bail)', and *vadārī*, 'to accept security (or bail)' were applied respectively to the defendant and the plaintiff.

There is a similar procedure in the civil law of the State of New York, but it is limited in its application to certain types of cases, such as personal injury, embezzlement, and the like, where there is a likelihood of the defendant's fleeing the jurisdiction.

19 6b in: here, and in line 10, *in* may be translated 'for'; the usage in these expressions is an extension of the Accusative of End of Motion; cp. *in diem posterum prōlāta est,* **14 14.**

19 7 vadimōnium prōmittī iubēret: see N. 16 27, ¶2.

19 9a sistant: apparently more than one defendant was involved.

19 9b tertiō: the Romans habitually counted both ends of a series; hence they called the day after the morrow 'the third day', where we should say 'two days later'. Cp. the French *huit jours* for 'a week', *quinze jours* for 'a fortnight' (= fourteen-nights).

19 10 vadārī: the unexpressed subject is *petītōrem*, 'the plaintiff'.

Notes to Selection 16

19 12a Chīlō was one of the ephors, or chief magistrates, of Sparta, c. 560 B.C. The ephors were five in number. They served to check the power of the Spartan kings in a manner somewhat analogous to that of the Roman tribunes of the people (see N. 17 24b); they also had extensive judicial and legislative functions.

19 12b ex illō inclutō numerō sapientium: Chilo was usually reckoned among the Seven Sages of Greece, to whom short and pithy maxims were attributed. To Chilo are sometimes ascribed the famous 'Know thyself' and 'Nothing to excess'. The other sages usually included in the list are Thales of Miletus, Solon of Athens, Bias of Priene, Pittacus of Mitylene, Cleobulus of Lindus, and Periander of Corinth.

19 13 in vītae . . . postrēmō: cp. *noctis extrēmō*, 18 24.

19 15 mihi aegritūdinī: see N. 13 11c.

19 16a profectō (adv.): 'indeed', 'certainly', 'assuredly'. This word, derived from *prō factō*, 'for a fact', is apt to cause the student trouble, since it is identical with certain participial forms of *prōficiō* and *proficīscor*.

19 16b capite: though the setting of this story is in Sparta, Gellius uses the terminology of the Roman courts. In its technical legal sense, *caput* means 'civil rights', 'citizenship'. The loss of civil rights was known as *capitis dēminūtiō*.

19 20 tolerātū: see N. 18 3b, under *Uses of the Supine*, ¶2.

19 24 quod . . . liquet: see N. 18 18a. The substantive clause here is in apposition with the noun *molestiam*.

Notes to Selection 17

19 26a Favōrīnus of Arelate (modern Arles, in southern France) was a sophist (see N. 28 2) and philosopher, an older contemporary of Gellius, who admired him greatly. Favorinus was an authority on both Greek and Roman antiquities, and wrote extensively in Greek.

19 26b veterum verbōrum cupidissimō: in the second century of our era the works of early Roman authors were much in vogue (see 2 20-25). The popularity of these early works resulted in the use of many archaic words by writers of the period, among them Gellius himself.

19 28 Curius . . . Fabricius . . . Coruncānius: M'. Curius Dentatus and Ti. Coruncanius were famous contemporaries of Fabricius (see N. 13 1c, ¶¶3, 4). Curius was consul in 290 B.C., and took an active part in the subjugation of the Samnites; Coruncanius, consul in 280, was renowned not only for his military successes against the Etruscans and King Pyrrhus (see N. 22 6a), but for his eminence as a jurist. The three worthies are often mentioned together as representatives of 'the good old days'. It should be kept in mind that they antedate the period of Favorinus by about four centuries; we may perhaps recapture the time-perspective in terms of our own day if we substitute Sir Walter Raleigh and Sir Francis Drake for Curius, Fabricius, and Coruncanius, King Alfred the Great for the Horatii, and the Britons for the Aurunci, Sicani, and Pelasgi.

19 29 Horātiī: the three brothers of the Horatian *gēns*, who, according to the legend, in the reign of Tullus Hostilius (traditionally placed in the middle of the seventh century B.C.; see N. 17 7), fought against the Curiatii, three brothers from Alba Longa, to determine whether Rome or

Alba was to be supreme.   The story furnished Corneille with the theme of his *Horace*.

19 30 Auruncōrum . . . Sicānōrum . . . Pelasgōrum: Genitive of Possession with *verbīs*, **20 1**.   The Aurunci were an ancient Italian tribe, the Sicani were early inhabitants of Sicily, and the Pelasgi in question were said to have been immigrants from Greece who had settled in Italy in remote antiquity.

20 2a Euandrī: Evander, according to the legend, established a Pelasgian colony on the site of Rome some years before the Trojan War (traditionally assigned to the twelfth century B.C.).

20 2b loquāre: the ending of the second person singular passive and deponent sometimes appears as *-re* instead of the more usual *-ris*.   For the mood and tense, see N. **17 10**.

20 2c abhinc multīs annīs: 'many years ago'; with *abhinc*, 'ago', and with other adverbs denoting prior or subsequent time (e.g. *ante* and *post* used adverbially), the Ablative of Degree of Difference (G. 26) is used.

20 4 Nōnne . . . tacēs: our idiom for this type of ironic rhetorical question would be 'Why don't you keep quiet?'

20 7 C. Caesare: see **4 11 – 7 17**.

20 8 Dē Analogiā: a non-extant treatise on grammar, written by Julius Caesar in the course of a journey from northern Italy to his army in Gaul. It was written from the standpoint of the Analogists, who believed that language is based on logical principles, and that word-forms should be strictly consistent throughout a language (e.g. either *ox, oxen, fox, foxen*, etc., or *fox, foxes, ox, oxes*, etc.).

20 10 scopulum: the comparison is drawn from navigation.

Notes to Selection 18

20 12a T. Mānlius Imperiosus Torquatus was consul in 347, in 344, and in 340 B.C.   He was regarded by the Romans as a model of military discipline.

20 12b locō: the noun *locus*, and others of kindred meaning (e.g. *pars, regiō, spatium, vestīgium*), and *liber* and *numerus*, are found in the construction of Place Where either with or without the preposition *in* (cp. G. 23).

20 14a torquem: a necklet of twisted metal (cp. *torqueō, torquēre, torsī, tortus,* 'twist'), often, as here, of gold, was a regular part of the accoutrement of a Gallic warrior.

20 14b quam . . . dētractam induit: when two actions are performed upon or by the same person or thing, the Latin idiom often uses a perfect passive participle to denote the first of these actions, a finite verb to denote the second, rather than two coordinate finite verbs.   So, *Librum ēmptum lēgī,* 'I bought the book and read it'; *Homō captus necātur,* 'The man is captured and killed'.

20 15a Q. Claudiī: Q. Claudius Quadrigarius was a historian of the first century B.C., who was noted for the simplicity and directness of his style. He wrote a history in the form of Annals, from the first book of which the excerpt here presented is taken.   This is an instance of how Gellius has preserved for us fragments of works which are otherwise lost.

20 15b **pugna illa**: the combat took place at the time of a Gallic invasion of Italy, c. 360 B.C. The two armies were drawn up on opposite sides of the river Anio, a tributary of the Tiber. The river was here crossed by a bridge (cp. *in ipsō ponte*, line 29). The story of the combat is probably historical, although some details (cp. N. 20 27b) have been added by later writers.

20 18 **cēterīs praestābat**: verbs compounded with *ad, ante, circum, com-* (the combining form of *cum*), *in, inter, ob, post, prae, prō, sub*, and *super* often govern an indirect object in the dative case. The instances of this construction fall under two heads:

A. Verbs which in their uncompounded form govern a direct object (e.g. *pōnō*, 'place', 'set'), when compounded govern two objects, one direct (acc.), the other indirect (dat.): *Honōrem salūtī antepōnit*, 'He places honor before safety'. Note that, though actually both *honōrem* and *salūtī* are objects of the compound verb *antepōnit*, in thought the acc. *honōrem* is governed by the simple verb, the dat. *salūtī* by the preposition.

B. Verbs which in their uncompounded form do not govern an object (e.g. *stō*, 'stand') when compounded govern only an indirect object in the dative: *Cēterīs praestat*, 'He excels (stands before) the others'.

20 19 **maximē proeliō commōtō**: 'when the battle had reached its highest pitch'.

20 20 **quiēscerent**: see N. 13 4b.

20 21 **conclāmat . . . vellet . . . prōdīret**: see N. 15 2.

20 24 **Doluit . . . flāgitium accidere**: verbs of emotion which involve perception often govern an Indirect Statement: e.g. *Haec perfecta esse gaudeō*, 'I rejoice that these things have been completed'.

20 27a **Scūtō pedestrī**: the *scūtum pedestre*, 'infantryman's shield', was a large rectangular shield, protecting almost the whole body. It was made of wood and leather.

20 27b **gladiō Hispānicō**: the Spanish sword was rather short, with double edge and sharpened point. Its mention here is an anachronism, since the Romans did not commence to use this weapon until the time of the Second Punic War (218-201 B.C.).

Notes to Selection 19

20 30 **suā disciplīnā**: 'in accordance with his training'; the Ablative of Accordance, without a preposition, is used to denote *that in accordance with which* something exists or is done: e.g. *cōnsuētūdine suā pauca respondit:* 'according to his custom, he made a brief reply'.

21 1a **cūnctābundus**: 'on the defensive'; literally, 'delaying', 'waiting (for the other to commence fighting)'.

21 1b **animō . . . cōnfīsus**: 'relying on his courage'; the verb *cōnfīdō* in the sense 'rely' is often used, as here, with the Ablative of Cause (G. 21): e.g. *nātūrā locī cōnfīdunt*, 'they rely on the nature of the place'. The use of a deponent perfect participle (see N. 16 1), where the English idiom requires the present, is quite common: e.g. *īsdem ducibus ūsus Numidās mittit*, 'employing the same men as guides, he dispatches the Numidians'.

21 3 **Dum . . . studet**: *dum* in the sense 'while' introduces the indica-

tive; the present tense is regularly used to express past time: e.g. *Alexander, dum pugnat, sagittā ictus est,* 'While Alexander was fighting, he was struck by an arrow'.

21 5a eī . . . successit: see N. 20 18, especially ¶B.

21 5b Gallicum gladium: the Gallic sword was a very long weapon, with sharp edges but a blunt point.

21 11 Ab: 'from' or 'after', not 'by'.

21 13 cum esset cōnsul: his third consulship in 340 B.C.

21 14a secūrī: the ablative singular in -ī is found in a few masculine and feminine nouns of the third declension. Among the most important of these, in addition to *secūris*, are *ignis, ignis,* m., 'fire,' *sitis, sitis,* f., 'thirst', and *turris, turris,* f., 'tower'.

When the consul was in the field, his attendants, called lictors (*līctōrēs*), carried an executioner's axe, *secūris*, in a bundle of rods, *fascēs*, with the axe-head protruding. The *fascēs* indicated the consul's power to have the soldiers beaten; the *secūris*, to have them beheaded. When the consul was in Rome, where he did not have the power of life and death, the *secūris* was not carried by his lictors. The present-day Italian *Fascisti* derive their name from the *fascēs* as a symbol of Roman governmental authority.

21 14b secūrī percussit: when applied to a consul, the expression *secūrī percutiō* means 'have a man beheaded'; the actual execution was of course performed by a lictor.

21 14c speculātum: see N. 18 3b, under *Uses of the Supine,* ¶1.

21 14d pugnā interdictā: the war between Rome and the Latins, her neighbors and for many years her allies, was so nearly a civil war that the consuls deemed it necessary to enforce the strictest discipline; among other measures, they forbade unauthorized combats.

21 11-15 Among Romans of a later date, a belief was current that T. Manlius owed his surname Imperiosus to this episode. However, we know from other sources that he inherited that name from his father, L. Manlius Imperiosus. It must be noted that the entire story of the punishment meted out by T. Manlius to his son rests on a much less secure historical basis than the story of his combat with the Gaul.

Notes to Selection 20

21 16a agrum Pomptīnum: a tract of land south of Rome, between the Alban hills and the sea.

21 16b insēderant: during a Gallic invasion of 349 B.C. (see N. 22 1b).

21 18 satis agentibus: 'who were greatly troubled'; *satis agō* in the sense 'be troubled', 'have one's hands full', is rather colloquial.

21 20 per . . . contemptum: the use of a prepositional phrase introduced by *per* in place of an adverb is not uncommon.

21 21 venīre et congredi: the subject of these infinitives (see N. 16 27, ¶2) is implied in the clause *sī — audēret.*

21 22 Valerius: M. Valerius Corvinus, consul in 348 B.C., held that magistracy at least five times more between that date and 299; he was dictator (see N. 35 30b, ¶2) in 342 and 301.

21 23 tribūnus mīlitāris: the 'military tribune', more commonly called *tribūnus mīlitum*, was one of the chief officers of the Roman legion; this office must not be confused with that of the *tribūnus plēbis* (N. **17** 24*b*).

21 27 vīs . . . dīvīna: 'a divine manifestation', 'a miracle'. The adjective *quaedam* is used, as often, to apologize for a rather bold expression: cp. *quōdam sēcessū mentis*, **16** 4.

21 28 imprōvīsus: in place of an adverb, Latin often employs an adjective in agreement with the subject: *laetus pergit*, 'he proceeds joyfully'.

22 1*a* Corvīnum: the surname is also found in the simple form Corvus. It is quite possible that the present story was invented to account for the name.

22 1*b* annīs quadringentīs quīnque post Rōmam conditam: for *post Rōmam conditam*, see N. **13** 3. The traditional date for the founding of Rome is 753 B.C.; in calculating from this date, it must be kept in mind that the Romans counted both ends of a series (cp. N. **19** 9*b*); 753 − 404 = 349 B.C.

22 3*a* statuam . . . statuendam cūrāvit: 'had a statue erected'; *rem faciendam cūrō* is the regular Latin idiom for 'have a thing done'. Note that *statuam* here is the direct object of *cūrāvit*, while *statuendam* is a gerundive (future passive participle) in agreement with *statuam*. So, *pontēs faciendōs cūrat*, 'he has bridges built'.

22 3*b* dīvus Augustus: Julius Caesar, Augustus, and most of their successors among Roman rulers were officially enrolled after death among the gods of the Roman state religion; they were thenceforth referred to as *dīvī*, i.e. 'deified' or 'divine'.

22 3*c* in forō suō: the *Forum Augustum*, 'Forum of Augustus'. In the closing years of the Republic, the old Forum (see N. **14** 12*b*) had become very crowded. During his dictatorship (see **6** 8-10) Julius Caesar added a new forum, called after him the *Forum Iūlium*. Augustus followed his example by constructing his own forum, which was dedicated in the year 2 B.C. In addition to a great temple of Mars the Avenger, the Forum of Augustus contained a series of statues of Roman heroes; that of Corvinus was one of these.

Notes to Selection 21

22 6*a* Pyrrhus rēx: Pyrrhus (319-272 B.C.), King of Epirus in northwestern Greece, was a military tactician of great skill, whose courage, however, was more than matched by his recklessness and instability. He seems to have been fired by an ambition to duplicate in the West the successes of his kinsman Alexander in the East (see N. **16** 11*a*). In 280 B.C. he came to Italy at the request of the inhabitants of Tarentum, the chief city of Magna Graecia (see N. **14** 1*b*, ¶2), to aid them in a war against the Romans. Though for a time the Romans were hard put to it, they succeeded in driving Pyrrhus out of Italy in 275 B.C.

22 6*b* ūnam atque alteram pugnās prōsperē pugnāsset: the battles of Heraclea, 280 B.C., and Asculum, 279, are meant; at both of these, the Romans were defeated with heavy losses. The word *prōsperē*, however, is scarcely appropriate: Pyrrhus himself lost so many men that he is said to have remarked, "If we defeat the Romans in one more battle, we shall be utterly ruined." The proverbial expression 'a Pyrrhic victory' is derived from this circumstance.

22 7 satis . . . agerent: see N. 21 18.

22 8a Ïtalia: Rome's Italian allies are meant. Rome was at this time the head of a military federation extending from the river Po southward to Magna Graecia. The eventual defeat of Pyrrhus and the Tarentines not only strengthened Rome's previous alliances, but brought the cities of Magna Graecia under her control.

22 8b Ambraciēnsis: Ambracia was a town in Epirus.

22 9a Tīmocharēs: nothing further is known of him, or of Nicias, mentioned in line 18.

22 9b C. Fabricium cōnsulem: his second consulship is evidently referred to here; see N. 13 1c, ¶3.

22 12 quoniam . . . ministrāret: for the normal mood with *quoniam*, see G. 37.

22 16 Valeriī Antiātis: Valerius Antias ('of Antium', a town of Latium, south of Rome) was a historian of the first century B.C.

22 17 Quadrīgārius: see N. 20 15a.

22 20 laudēs atque grātiās: i.e. a letter of praise and thanks. Like most soldiers of fortune, Pyrrhus manifested a generous, if somewhat erratic, spirit of chivalry. His magnanimity caused the Romans to regard him with much the same admiration which the Crusaders felt for their noble antagonist Saladin; the Romans never felt toward Pyrrhus the bitterness with which they regarded Hannibal.

Notes to Selection 22

22 22a circō maximō: the Circus Maximus was a huge, U-shaped, unroofed structure, with tier upon tier of seats, occupying the low ground between the Palatine and the Aventine Hills. It was about 650 yards long, and about 160 yards wide; estimates of its seating capacity under the later Emperors vary from 150,000 to 350,000. It was used principally for chariot-races.

22 22b vēnātiō, properly 'hunt', was the name applied to a cruel spectacle, not unlike the modern Spanish bull-fight, which was much enjoyed by the Romans. It consisted in a death-struggle between men and wild beasts; lions, tigers, bears, elephants, and even hippopotami and crocodiles were employed. *Vēnātiōnēs* were of two kinds; in one, the 'hunters' were trained animal-fighters, properly armed, who had a chance of leaving the arena alive; in the other, exemplified in this story, the human participants were condemned criminals, who were led into the arena unarmed, and whose death was a foregone conclusion. After its opening in 80 A.D., the great Flavian Amphitheatre, the so-called Colosseum, was the favorite setting for these spectacles; before that date they were presented either in the Circus Maximus or in the Forum, which was barred off for the purpose.

22 22c populō dabātur: under the Republic, victorious generals and other prominent citizens, under the Empire the Emperors, curried favor with the populace by the frequent presentation of such spectacles; they formed an important part of the *pānem et Circēnsēs*, the 'bread and Circuses', which the satirist Juvenal names as the sole desires of the Roman mob of his time (c. 100 A.D.).   Augustus, in a monument set up to commemorate his exploits, states that he displayed twenty-six *vēnātiōnēs*, in which 3500 wild beasts were killed; these numbers fade into insignificance before the prodigality of later Emperors.

22 26a cōnsulāris: a man who had once been consul was thenceforth called *cōnsulāris*, 'of consular rank'.

22 26b Androclus: in a later Greek version of this story, the name is given as Androcles, the form in which it most frequently appears in English; see George Bernard Shaw's witty play, *Androcles and the Lion*.

23 4 vidērēs: 'you might have seen'.   This potential use of the imperfect subjunctive to express *what might have happened* is regularly confined to the indefinite second person ('you' in the sense of 'one'), and to a few verbs, such as *crederēs, scīrēs, dīcerēs*, and, as here, *vidērēs*.

Notes to Selection 23

23 6 ā Caesare: 'by the Emperor'.   This story is supposed to have taken place in the time of Tiberius (14-37 A.D.), Caligula (37-41 A.D.), or Claudius (41-54 A.D.).   These three rulers, their predecessor Augustus (27 B.C.–14 A.D.), and their successor Nero (55-68 A.D.), bore the name Caesar as being related, in one way or another, to the great Julius; with the death of Nero, the Julio-Claudian line, as it is called, came to an end, but the name Caesar continued to be used as an Imperial title.   It survived in the modern titles of Kaiser and Czar.

23 8 prōvinciam . . . Āfricam: the Romans gave this name to the Carthaginian territory which they acquired as the result of the Third Punic War (149-146 B.C.); to this, subsequent acquisitions in the vicinity were added.

23 9 prōcōnsulāri imperiō: the province of Africa was governed at this time by a proconsul (i.e. *prō cōnsule*, 'in place of a consul') chosen by the Senate from among the ex-consuls.   The governor ruled the province by virtue of the proconsular authority *(prōcōnsulāre imperium)* conferred on him by the Senate.

23 12 dēfuisset: see N. 18 18a, ¶2.   Although the thought which Androclus refers to is his own, it belongs to a situation in the past; it is therefore treated as if it were the thought of someone else.

23 15 multō post: see N. 20 2c.

23 20 mītis et mānsuētus: see N. 21 28.

23 23 vulnere intimō: the Ablative of Separation, denoting *that from which something is removed or set free*, is used either with or without a preposition (*ab, dē,* or *ex*).   In general, the preposition is employed when the separation is physical (e.g. *sēcerne tē ā bonīs*, 'separate yourself from good men'), omitted when it is not (e.g. *līberā nōs metū*, 'free us from fear'); but there is no hard and fast rule, as may be seen from the present instance. [The Ablative of Place From Which with verbs of motion (G. 24, G. 32B) is a special category of the Ablative of Separation.]

Notes to Selection 24

23 29 mě vītae . . . **pertaesum est:** 'I became disgusted with the life'; the impersonal verb *pertaedet* (like the simple verb *taedet*), 'it disgusts', 'it wearies', governs the accusative of the person affected, the genitive of *that which causes the emotion*. *Taedet* and *pertaedet* are used as deponents in the perfect (cp. N. 16 1).

24 1 ad dominum . . . **Rōmam:** when two or more nouns denote End of Motion with one verb of motion, all are in the accusative: e.g. *litterae ad Caesarem in castra Alesiam dēferuntur*, 'the letter is brought to Caesar in camp at Alesia'.

24 2a mě . . . **damnandum cūrāvit:** see N. 22 3a.

24 2b reī capitālis damnandum: the genitive is used to denote the charge with verbs of *accusing, condemning*, and *acquitting:* e.g. *prōditiōnis damnātus est*, 'he was convicted of treason'.

Rēs capitālis denotes a crime which involves the loss of civil rights (*caput*, N. 19 16b), or of life; here the latter is meant, since a slave had no civil rights.

24 7 poenā: see N. 23 23.

24 7-9 leō . . . **eī dōnātus** (*est*), . . . **dōnātur aere:** these two expressions illustrate in passive form the two usages of *dōnō*, which do not differ in meaning: *hominī praemium dōnō* (G. 7A, G. 12), or *hominem praemiō dōnō* (G. 12, G. 18), 'I present a reward to the man', or 'I present the man with a reward', exactly as in English.

24 9 urbě tōtā: nouns modified by *tōtus* (and adjectives of kindred meaning, e.g. *omnis* and *ūniversus*, also *medius*) are found in the construction of Place Where either with or without the preposition *in*. Cp. N. 20 12b.

Notes to Selection 25

24 14 Polum: Polus of Sunium in Attica flourished in the fourth century B.C. He and Aristodemus (see N. 25 7b) are often coupled as the two most eminent tragic actors of their day.

24 16 Ēlectram Sophoclis āctūrus: i.e. the part of Electra in Sophocles' play of that name. On the Greek and Roman stage, as in Shakespeare's time, female parts were played by male actors.

The story on which Sophocles' Electra is based may be summarized as follows: Agamemnon, King of Mycenae, had sacrificed his daughter Iphigenia in order to secure a safe passage for the Greek army bound for Troy. Agamemnon's queen, Clytemnestra, embittered by the killing of Iphigenia, took Aegisthus to be her paramour in her husband's absence. On the latter's return, he was slaughtered by his wife, with the assistance of her lover. At the time of his death, Agamemnon had four children living, among them a daughter Electra, and a young son Orestes. Electra sent Orestes away for safe-keeping, in the hope that he would grow up to avenge their father's murder. As the play opens, Orestes, now a grown youth, sends a messenger to the palace at Mycenae with the report that he has been slain, and that two envoys are coming with an urn containing his ashes. Presently the two envoys, in reality Orestes and his friend Pylades, enter bearing an

urn, which they deliver to Electra. Believing it to contain her brother's
ashes, she bursts forth into a passionate lament, in the course of which the
brother and sister recognize each other. They now plot the murder of
Clytemnestra and Aegisthus; the play ends with the accomplishment of
their designs.

24 16-17 **Sophoclis . . . Oresti**: in Latin, the genitive singular ending
of Greek names in -*ēs* sometimes appears as -*is*, sometimes as -*ī*.
Sophocles (495-406 B.C.) was one of the three great playwrights of
Greek tragedy; the others were Aeschylus (525-456 B.C.) and Euripides
(480-406 B.C.). Of the three, Sophocles was the most beloved by the
Athenians. He won first place in the tragic contests (see N. 15 16b) more
than twenty times, and was never placed lower than second. He wrote
about 130 plays, of which seven and part of an eighth have come down to
us.

24 20 **Oresti**: Genitive of Possession, depending on *ossa* unexpressed.

24 21 **opplēvit omnia**: we should say 'filled the air'.

Notes to Selection 26

24 24 **Mīlētō**: Miletus was an important Greek city of Asia Minor,
which frequently, in its long history, had close relations with Athens.
However, the story of a Milesian embassy to Athens to ask for aid at a time
when Demosthenes was active in the Athenian Assembly has no historical
foundation; it was undoubtedly invented to provide a setting for this
anecdote. The anecdote itself is likewise pure invention: the same story is
told by Plutarch, but this time in connection with a bribe which Demosthenes was supposed to have received from Harpalus, the absconding treas-
urer of Alexander. Clever bits of repartee have a way of becoming attached to famous names, often with elaborate pseudo-historical settings.

24 25 **quī prō sēsē verba facerent**: '(men) to speak in their behalf'; a
Relative Clause of Purpose. Such a clause, introduced by a relative pronoun or relative adverb (e.g. *ubi, unde*), has its verb in the subjunctive
mood (cp. G. 36, G. 40). The antecedent is usually expressed in the main
clause: e.g. *puerum mīsī quī pānem emeret*, 'I sent a boy to buy bread'.
Sometimes, as here, the antecedent is not expressed (if expressed, the antecedent of *quī* would be the direct object of *advocāvērunt*).

24 26a **ad populum**: see N. 17 25a.

24 26b **Dēmosthenēs**: the great Athenian orator (381-322 B.C.). During his long career as a statesman, his talents were almost entirely devoted
to combatting the rising influence of Macedon under Philip (see N. 38 12);
his opposition to the latter found its most forceful expression in his famous
Philippics. Demosthenes' efforts were doomed to failure, as first Philip
and then Alexander rose to supremacy in the Greek world; but the orator
maintained the unequal struggle until his death. He made many bitter
enemies, and was accused by them of various misdeeds; the present tale is
an echo of these accusations.

24 28 **ex rē pūblicā**: see N. 14 22a.

24 30 **magnō . . . opere**: usually written as one word, *magnopere*.

25 1a **agī . . . coepta esset**: *coepī* is used in the active with active in-

finitives, in the passive with passive infinitives: e.g. *nāvem vidēre coepērunt,* 'they began to see the ship'; *nāvis vidērī coepta est,* 'the ship began to be seen'.

25 1b collum circumvolūtus: 'his neck wrapped'; literally, 'having wrapped his own neck'. The participle *circumvolūtus,* normally passive, 'having been wrapped', is here used with middle force (see N. 15 26), representing the subject as acting upon himself, or part of himself; it therefore takes a direct object, *collum;* the participle itself of course agrees with *Dēmosthenēs.* The construction here is probably an imitation of Greek usage rather than a survival of the primitive Latin Middle Voice.

25 2 synanchēn: accusative singular; so *argyranchēn,* line 4; cp. N. 15 23b.

25 3 eō: Ablative of Cause, neuter, referring to the preceding statement.

25 4 nōn synanchēn . . . sed argyranchēn: 'not a swollen throat, but a swollen purse'. In Greek, *synanche* means 'an inflammation of the throat' (from *syn-,* 'together', and the root of *ancho,* 'squeeze'. 'choke'); *argyranche* is a sarcastic coinage, with *argyr-,* from *argyros,* 'silver', substituted for *syn-:* 'a silver-strangling'. The witticism is also quoted as the invention of Demades, a rival of Demosthenes in Athenian politics.

25 7a glōriae: Dative of Purpose.

25 7b Aristodēmum: Aristodemus of Metapontum in Magna Graecia, later granted Athenian citizenship, was a celebrated tragic actor. In 346 B.C. he was associated with Demosthenes on a diplomatic mission. The story related in lines 7-10, if it has any basis in truth, may have arisen from a literal interpretation of a jesting remark of Demosthenes. In another passage, Gellius tells us that the same story was told of the orator Demades (see N. 25 4).

25 9 Talentum: see N. 16 12c.

Notes to Selection 27

25 11a Cicerō: M. Tullius Cicero, the famous Roman orator, statesman, and author, was born in 106 B.C. At the height of his career he was considered the ablest lawyer in Rome; in public life he rose through the various public offices to the consulship, which he held in 63 B.C. In that year he put down the conspiracy of Catiline, who had plotted to overthrow the government. This achievement, while winning him great acclaim, made him many enemies; these succeeded in having him banished for a time (58-57 B.C.). Cicero deplored, though he could not prevent, the ascendancy of Julius Caesar; he rejoiced at the latter's assassination (see 6 11-15), though he did not participate in it. He actively opposed Caesar's immediate successor Mark Antony, and was put to death by the latter's soldiers in 43 B.C.

A great number of Cicero's masterly speeches, both as statesman and as lawyer, have been preserved, as well as a large collection of letters. In the intervals of a busy life he wrote several able works on rhetoric and law, some charming essays, and a series of treatises in which he summarized for Roman readers the various schools of Greek philosophic thought. He is considered the greatest master of Latin prose style.

25 11b Palātiō: the Palatine Hill adjoined the Forum on the south. During the Republic, it was the most exclusive residential section of the city; during the Empire, the homes of the Emperors were located there. From the use of the word *Palātium* to denote the Imperial residence our word 'palace' is derived.

25 11c in praesēns: 'for the present'; though Cicero's income was large, he spent money freely, and was under frequent necessity of borrowing.

25 12a P. Sullā: P. Cornelius Sulla, a relative of the Dictator (see N. **26 8a**). He had been elected to the consulship for 65 B.C., but was convicted of corrupt election practices, and was expelled from that office and from the Senate.

25 12b quī tum reus erat: at this time (62 B.C.) Sulla was under accusation of having participated in the great Catilinarian conspiracy of 63 B.C. Though he had certainly taken part in an earlier plot (66-65 B.C.), he does not seem to have been guilty of active complicity in this one. He was defended both by Cicero and the latter's rival at the Bar, Hortensius; these eminent lawyers succeeded in winning him an acquittal.

25 12c mūtua . . . tacita: 'as a secret loan'; these adjectives modify *centēna mīlia*, 'hundred thousands', unexpressed; see the next note.

25 13a sēstertium vīciēns: *sēstertium* is an old form of the genitive plural of *sēstertius* (see N. **16 13**). The genitive depends on *centēna mīlia*, 'hundred thousands', understood; the omission of *centēna mīlia* was possible because it was only with units of 100,000 that a numeral adverb in *-iēns* (e.g. *vīciēns*, 'twenty times') was employed in monetary computations. The full expression would be *vīciēns centēna mīlia sēstertium*, 'twenty hundred thousands of sesterces', i.e. 2,000,000 sesterces, or (see N. **16 13**) approximately $100,000. That this was only part of the price, we learn from a letter of Cicero's, in which he states that the house cost 3,500,000 sesterces ($175,000).

25 13b priusquam: the temporal conjunctions *antequam* and *priusquam*, 'before', and *dum* and *dōnec*, 'until', may introduce a verb in the indicative mood if the action of the verb is regarded as a fact, either accomplished or certain of accomplishment: e.g. *sex annīs antequam ego nātus sum*, 'six years before I was born'; *mihi ūsque cūrae erit, dum, quid ēgeris, scierō:* 'I shall always be anxious until I know what you have done'.

When, however, an idea of anticipation, prevention, or purpose is involved, the verb introduced by *antequam*, *priusquam*, *dum*, or *dōnec* is in the subjunctive mood (Subjunctive of Anticipation): e.g. *mīlites, priusquam portae clauderentur, inrūpērunt*, 'the soldiers rushed in before the gates could be closed' (anticipation and prevention); *paucōs diēs morātus est, dum sē cōpiae adsequerentur*, 'he waited a few days, until the troops could catch up with him' (anticipation and purpose). In the present instance, the publicity given to Cicero's plan served to delay, if not to prevent, his purchase: *priusquam emeret*, 'before he had a chance to buy'.

25 14 quod . . . accēpisset: cp. N. **18 18a**.

25 15 pecūniam . . . ā reō accēpisset: lawyers were forbidden by Roman law to charge a fee. In actual practice, the law was constantly circumvented by the device of the *honōrārium*, a 'gift' by which the client showed his appreciation of successful legal services in his behalf. The stigma in this case seems to arise from the fact that, under the cloak of a loan, Cicero received a fee in advance, while his client was still under accusation (*reus*).

25 17 Adeō . . . vērum sit . . . sī . . . emerō: 'I am willing that it be considered the truth, if I actually buy'; literally, 'so let it be the truth, if I shall have bought'.

25 20 ἀκοινονόητοι (akoinonóĕtoi): 'lacking common sense'; an adjective, nom. plur. masculine. The use of Greek words in Latin is comparable to the use of French expressions in English, as we might say 'lacking in *savoir-faire*'.

25 21 prūdentis et cautī patris familiās esse . . . negāre: 'that it is (the characteristic) of a prudent and careful master of the household to deny'. The word *patris* is in the Predicate Genitive of Possession, which is frequently used to denote the person whose *characteristic*, or *duty*, or *natural function* something is: e.g. *mīlitis est pugnāre:* 'it is a soldier's business to fight'. Cp. 'Theirs not to reason why'.

25 22 familiās: see N. 14 25.

Notes to Selection 28

25 24a Antōnius Iuliānus, who had come to Rome from the province of Spain, was a teacher and friend of Gellius.

25 24b rhētor: the study of rhetoric, of which Julianus was a professor, dealt with the principles of eloquence, and included some instruction in language and literature. As a practical preparation for public life, rhetoric was the subject most highly esteemed in Rome; it was the first in which a state-supported professorship was established. This professorship, endowed by the Emperor Vespasian (69-79 A.D.), was first filled by the great educator Quintilian.

25 26a montem Cispium: the Cispian Hill was the northern spur of the Esquiline, north-east of the Forum. At this time it was thickly covered with cheap tenement-houses.

25 26b īnsulam: 'tenement-house'; originally the term *īnsula* denoted any dwelling *isolated* from others by a surrounding alley-way; in later usage it is applied to a tenement housing several families, as distinguished from a *domus*, or home of a single well-to-do family.

25 27 4. multīs arduīsque tabulātīs ēditam: because of high land-values, the *īnsulae* were built to a considerable height, and were veritable fire-traps. Augustus found it necessary to limit the height of such buildings to 68 feet, which, with Roman methods of construction, would allow for six or seven stories. The poet Martial (40-104 A.D.) complains of having to live up three steep flights.

26 2 ut nē: the use of *ut nē* instead of the simple *nē*, which we have already met in Indirect Command (cp. N. 14 14c), is also fairly common in negative Clauses of Purpose when, as here, it is desired to attach the negative to a word or words other than the verb (here *tam adsiduē*).

26 3a vēnum: this use of the Accusative of Purpose (Figurative End of

Motion, G. 14) without a preposition is a survival of a very ancient usage; cp. the use of the accusative supine (N. **18** 3*b*), and the construction of End of Motion with names of cities, etc. (G. 32A). From *vēnum dō*, 'offer for sale', 'sell', the verb *vēndō* is derived.

26 3*b* **hercle:** 'indeed', 'surely'; originally a vocative ('O Hercules!'), this word degenerated through constant use into an interjection or adverb with intensive force.

26 5 **Q. Claudiī:** see N. **20** 15*a*.

26 6 **Archelāus,** a Greek by birth, commanded the armies of King Mithridates (see N. **27** 19*a*) in the First Mithridatic War (88-84 B.C.).

26 7 **quō remediō . . . dēfenderēs:** 'by what remedy you might ward off'. This Indirect Question represents an original Deliberative Subjunctive, *Quō remediō defendam?*, 'By what remedy shall I ward off?'.

The Deliberative Subjunctive is used in questions which ask for instructions, or which involve perplexity, surprise, or indignation. So, *quid faciam?*, 'what shall I do?'; *huius condiciōnēs audiāmus?*, 'shall we listen to his terms?'.

26 8*a* **L. Sulla:** L. Cornelius Sulla, who later assumed the surname Felix, 'the Lucky', was born in 138 B.C., of an aristocratic but impoverished family. In 107 he saw service in Africa under C. Marius (see N. **57** 7), later to be his bitter enemy. In 88 he held the consulship, and was given charge of the war against Mithridates, an assignment which Marius violently but unsuccessfully opposed. Upon Sulla's departure for the East, Marius took control at Rome, and slaughtered Sulla's supporters. Marius remained supreme at Rome while Sulla conducted his eastern campaign, including the siege of Piraeus mentioned here.

By 84 B.C. Mithridates was willing to listen to terms; Sulla returned to Italy in 83, and avenged the death of his followers by slaying the adherents of Marius, who had since died. In 82 Sulla was made dictator; in defiance of precedent (see N. **35** 30*b*, ¶2), he was given an unlimited term. He devoted nearly three years to re-fashioning the government along aristocratic lines; when his task was completed, he abdicated in 79 B.C. He died in the following year; his reactionary legislation did not long survive him.

26 8*b* **Piraeum:** Piraeus was a peninsula on which the harbors of Athens were located (see N. **39** 3); in the First Mithridatic War, the Athenians sided with Mithr dates.

26 9 **turrim:** the accusative singular in -*im* is found in a few masculine and feminine nouns of the third declension. Cp. N. **21** 14*a*.

26 11*a* **alūmine:** the ancient *alūmen* was not identical with, but was very closely related to, the substance which we commonly call 'alum'. Concerning the latter, more fully called 'potash alum' (potassium-aluminum sulphate), Smith's Inorganic Chemistry (Revised by James Kendall; New York, The Century Co., 1926), 883, says, "An aqueous solution of this salt . . . is used for fire-proofing draperies, because the crystals deposited in the fabric melt easily, and the fused material protects the fibers from access of oxygen."

26 11*b* **oblita esset:** *oblitus*, from *oblino*, is not to be confused with *oblitus*, from *oblīvīscor*.

Notes to Selection 29

26 12a **Arïŏn**: Herodotus (fifth century B.C.), the 'Father of History', from whom Gellius copied this tale, states that Arion was the foremost lute-player of his time, the late seventh century B.C. To him are attributed certain innovations in the musico-poetical form known as the dithyramb, the forerunner of Greek tragedy. It is, however, a matter of doubt whether Arion is a historical personage.

26 12b **fidicen**: 'lute-player' (compare *tibïcen*, 17 1); the Romans used the word *fidēs, fidium,* f. plur., to denote a stringed instrument, a 'lute', 'cithern', 'lyre', or 'harp'. The *fidicen* chanted to the accompaniment of his instrument.

26 12c **locŏ . . . Mēthymnaeus, terrã . . . Lesbius**: for the ablatives, see N. 14 2. We would say 'a native of the town of Methymna on the island of Lesbos'. Methymna was a town in the northern part of the island of Lesbos, off the coast of Asia Minor; the island is famous as the birthplace of the poets Sappho and Alcaeus.

26 14a **Corinthï**: the city of Corinth, on the isthmus of that name, was one of the richest and most cultured in Greece. The crossing of the isthmus afforded the shortest route between the Adriatic and the Aegean; Corinth owed her wealth to her favorable location on this trade route.

26 14b **Periander** was 'tyrant' of Corinth from c. 625 to 585 B.C. In early Greek history, the term 'tyrant' does not carry with it any connotation of cruelty or despotism; it merely means a usurper, a ruler who has acquired power unconstitutionally, usually by wresting it from the hereditary king. The term is also applied to the immediate descendants of such a ruler. The first tyrant of Corinth was Periander's father Cypselus, who seized the kingship about 655 B.C. Periander himself raised Corinth to a point of great magnificence and power; he was numbered among the Seven Sages of Greece (see N. 19 12b), and, like most 'tyrants', was a patron of literature and the arts.

26 28 **vestïmenta**: the ceremonial costume of the lute-player was rich and ornate.

26 30 **cïnctus, amïctus, ŏrnãtus**: the first of these participles refers to an ornamental belt or girdle, the second to a mantle or cloak, the third to a wreath and other embellishments.

26 31a **summã puppï**: see N. 15 1b.

26 31b **carmen . . . 'orthium'**: the Greeks gave the name of *nomos orthios*, 'high song', to a high, clear melody; in this case probably a hymn to Apollo, the patron god of the lute-player. Apollo is often represented with a lute.

Notes to Selection 30

27 3a **pium**: 'kindly'; our word 'pious' is by no means an exact translation of the Latin *pius*. The Latin word conveys the idea of dutifulness, first toward the gods, then toward the state, one's parents and grandparents, one's family, and, in general, one's fellow-men; derived from this is the meaning here exemplified of kindliness and solicitude for the welfare of others.

27 3b Delphinus: it was an ancient belief that the dolphin was kindly disposed toward humans, and that it was very fond of music. The dolphin was also connected with the worship of Apollo (cp. N.26 31b); under the name of Apollo Delphinius, the god was regarded as a protector of sea-farers.

27 5 Taenarum in terram Lacōnicam: see N. 24 1. Taenarum was the name of a promontory and a town in the extreme southern part of Laconia, the land of which Sparta was the capital. The town was famous for its temple of Poseidon, god of the sea.

27 7 tālem . . . quālis: correlatives, 'such as', 'in the same guise as'.

27 9a istaec: cp. N. 15 1a.

27 9b quasi: 'on the ground that'; literally, 'as if'; cp. N. 17 10.

27 10 nautās inquisītos . . . interrogāvit: see N. 20 14b.

27 15 ire infitiās: this seems to be another example of figurative End of Motion, in the primitive construction without a preposition (cp. N. 26 3a); cp. our 'take refuge in denial'.

27 17 simulācra duo: actually one statue in two parts. In reality, the statue was probably a thank-offering dedicated by a rescued sea-farer, and was meant to represent a sea-divinity astride a dolphin (perhaps Apollo Delphinius: see N. 27 3b). Later, when the true significance of the statue was forgotten, the story of Arion and the Dolphin would be the natural outcome of an attempt to explain the work of art.

Notes to Selection 31

27 19a Mithridātēs VI Eupator, born c. 132 B.C., was King of Pontus, a small Graeco-Oriental kingdom of Asia Minor. In his attempts to enlarge his sphere of sovereignty by the addition of other territories in and near Asia Minor, he was repeatedly checked by the Romans, who looked unfavorably upon the growth of any strong power in the East. Matters came to open warfare in 89-88 B.C.; as we have seen (N. 26 8a, ¶2), Sulla met with some success in this First Mithridatic War. Mithridates was by no means crushed, however, and after some inconclusive clashes war began again in 74 B.C. After several Roman generals had fought with varying success, Pompey the Great brought the war to a victorious conclusion in 65 B.C. The death of Mithridates, mentioned in this story, occurred in 63 B.C.

27 19b ille: here used in the sense of 'the famous', as often; when so used it usually follows the noun it modifies.

27 23 ultima rēgnī: Mithridates died at Panticapaeum, located on what are now called the Straits of Kerch, between the Black Sea and the Sea of Azov.

27 24 suō sē ipse gladiō trānsēgit: according to more trustworthy tradition, Mithridates was unable to inflict the death-stroke himself, and was killed at his own request by one of his men.

27 26 Q. Ennius, 239-169 B.C., the 'Father of Latin Poetry', was born at Rudiae in Calabria, in southern Italy, a town of predominantly Greek culture. Ennius spent most of his life at Rome, where he lived in modest circumstances, but on friendly terms with such outstanding men as Cato and Scipio; he made the latter the subject of an epic poem. His works,

which have come down to us only in fragments, included over twenty
tragedies and two comedies on Greek models, several books of Saturae (see
N. 32 3), and, most important of all, eighteen books of *Annals*, an epic on
the rise of Rome, in which Ennius was in many ways the fore-runner of
Vergil.

27 27 Oscē: Oscan was an ancient Italic language, related to Latin, and
was spoken by the Samnite tribes dwelling in central and southern Italy.

27 30 quemque: from *quisque*.

27 31 quam sī . . . esset: see N. 17 10.

Notes to Selection 32

28 1 causārum: here, and in lines 6 and 7, *causa* is used in the sense of
'case', 'law-suit'.

28 2 Prōtagorae: Protagoras (c. 485 - c. 410 B.C.) of Abdera in Thrace
was the first and among the most eminent of the Sophists. These were
professional teachers of practical knowledge, who emphasized the arts of
public speaking and argumentation. Protagoras paid great attention to
correctness of speech. In the field of ethics, he is famous for his dictum
that man is the measure of all things, that is, that there is no absolute standard of right or wrong. In religion, Protagoras was an agnostic, holding
man incapable of knowledge concerning the divine.

28 3 grandem pecūniam: Protagoras' fee for a course was said to be 100
minae. Since the *mina* was one-sixtieth of a talent (N. 16 12c), 100 minae
may be considered the equivalent of $2000.

28 5a priusquam disceret: see N. 25 13b; here the idea of purpose is
involved.

28 5b pepigit . . . ut . . . daret: see G. 45, especially G. 45A.

28 6 quō prīmō diē: by a common Latin idiom, the 'antecedent' of the
relative pronoun is incorporated in the relative clause.

28 13a utrōque modō: 'in either event'; see N. 20 30.

28 13b fore utī reddās: *fore* is an indeclinable form of the future infinitive of *sum*. The clause *utī reddās* is a substantive clause (G. 45B) used
as the subject of *fore* in Indirect Statement. Thus *Disce . . . fore utī
reddās* is equivalent to *Disce tē redditūrum esse*. The use of *fore ut* with the
subjunctive of a verb in place of the future infinitive of that verb is rather
common, especially in the passive (to avoid the infinitive in *-um īrī*). The
use of this circumlocution is necessary in the case of verbs which lack the
fourth principal part (e.g. *sciō fore ut discās*, 'I know that you will learn').

28 16 secundum tē: *secundum* is here used as a preposition governing
the accusative case, with the meaning 'in favor of'; it usually means 'according to'.

28 25 diem longissimam: *diēs* is normally masculine; when it denotes a
set date, as here, it is generally feminine.

Notes to Selection 33

28 28 proelium Cannēnse: see N. 14 1b. In 216 B.C., Cannae, a town
in Apulia, was the scene of Rome's most disastrous defeat in the Second
Punic War (see N. 13 13). The Romans lost about 40,000 men.

28 29 mandāvitque eīs pactusque est: 'he instructed them and agreed': i.e. he instructed them to lay the terms before the Romans, and he agreed to abide by them if they were accepted.

28 30 vidērētur: *vidētur* is often used impersonally in the sense, 'it seems advisable', 'it seems good'.

28 31a alterī: 'the one side or the other', as it might turn out when the exchange was accomplished.

28 31b plūrēs (modifies *quōs*): 'in excess' of the number which they returned. The exchange was to be made man for man, as far as possible; then the side which had no more captives was to ransom its remaining men at the rate specified.

28 32a pondō lībram et sēlībram: 'a pound and a half by weight'. *Pondō* is ablative, from an old word related to *pondus, ponderis,* n. From *pondō* as here used comes our word 'pound'.

The Roman *lībra,* 'pound' (cp. our abbreviation 'lb.'), weighed 327.4 grams, not quite three-quarters of our pound avoirdupois (453.6 grams).

28 32b Hoc . . . iūsiūrandum eōs adēgit: 'he compelled them (to take) the following oath'; in the idiom exemplified here, *adigō* governs two accusatives: (1) the accusative of *iūsiūrandum,* (2) the accusative of the person forced to take the oath.

29 5 postlīminiō: when a Roman was captured by an enemy, he became his captor's slave, and thereby suffered complete loss of his Roman civil rights (*maxima capitis dēminūtiō;* see N. 19 16b). If, however, he returned to Rome, he was entitled to resume his civil status. This right was known as *postlīminium;* the derivation of the word is uncertain. It is best left untranslated, and used as a technical legal term in its Latin form: 'the right of *postlīminium'.*

29 7 nē . . . redīre vellent reproduces rather faithfully the direct *nōlīte redīre.*

29 11 religiōne: 'religious scruple'; this is a common meaning of *religiō,* which usually refers to a tenet or article of religion rather than to a whole body of religious beliefs.

29 15 cēnsōrēs: two censors were elected every five years from among the ex-consuls. They held office for eighteen months. Their primary duty, from which their name is derived, was to take the census; in addition to this they supervised the letting of public contracts. They also prepared the official list of the Senate, excluding therefrom any whom they deemed unworthy. Closely connected with the last-named prerogative was their supervision of the public morals; for conduct unbecoming a Roman citizen they could degrade a man from his rank, and brand his name on their rolls with the censorial stigma, the *nota cēnsōria.* A man so treated was said to suffer *ignōminia,* 'public disgrace'.

29 18 Cornēlius . . . Nepōs: see 3 23 - 4 10. The work which is here referred to, the *Exempla,* seems to have been a series of moral anecdotes; it survives only in a few quotations and references.

29 21 vidērētur: see N. 28 30.

Notes to Selection 34

29 25 Sertōrius: Q. Sertorius was a revolutionary general of the early first century B.C.; had he lived in less disturbed times, he would probably have been one of Rome's great heroes. Though a member of Marius' party (see N. 26 8a), he distrusted the old general in political matters, and strove constantly to mitigate the violence of those turbulent years. At the end of 83 B.C. he was sent to Nearer Spain as Governor by the Marian extremists, who were glad to be rid of him. In Spain he fought with varying fortunes against Sulla's appointees; for a time he withdrew to Africa, but returned to head a revolt of the natives. Though claiming to rule as a Roman Governor, he set up what was practically an independent Romano-Iberian government, and defied all attempts to dislodge him. Finally the Senate sent Pompey the Great against him; Sertorius countered by making an alliance with Mithridates (see N. 27 19a). It was not until 74 B.C., when Pompey received reinforcements from Rome, that the tide turned; Sertorius was moving toward inevitable defeat when he was murdered by a treacherous subordinate in 72 B.C.

29 28 religiōnēs: see N. 29 11.

29 29a quid: 'at all'; literally 'any'; see NN. 14 15a and 13 11b.

29 29b istae: *iste*, properly 'that . . . of yours' (see N. 15 1a) is often used, as here, with a connotation of contempt or dislike.

29 31 ā Lusitānō . . . quōdam: the Lusitanians inhabited the southwestern part of Spain. They were devoted adherents of Sertorius.

29 32a Hanc . . . conloquī . . . persuāsit: in the sense 'convince', *persuādeō* governs the Indirect Statement; as always, the personal object of *persuādeō* is in the dative (here *omnibus*).

29 32b Diānae: deer were sacred to Diana, the goddess of the chase; she is often represented as attended by one of the creatures. It must also be noted that Diana was the sister of Apollo, god of prophecy.

30 1 cum dīxerat: see G. 48, C2.

Notes to Selection 35

30 6 multīs diēbus post: see N. 20 2c.

30 10 in quiēte: 'in a dream'; *quiēs* is frequently used in the sense of 'sleep'.

30 11a consuērat: see N. 14 9.

30 11b quod opus esset factō: 'what had to be done'. With *opus est*, 'there is need', the ablative (see N. 13 11a) neuter of the perfect passive participle is used impersonally as a substantive: e.g. *cōnsultō opus est*, 'there is need of deliberation' (from *cōnsulō, cōnsulere, cōnsuluī, cōnsultus*, 'deliberate').

30 12 praedīcere: distinguish between *praedīcō, praedīcere*, 'foretell' and *praedīcō, praedīcāre*, 'state'; note the quantity of the *-i-* in each case.

30 6-14 Sertorius staged this deception on the eve of the battle of the river Sucro in south-east Spain, in 75 B.C.; it had the effect of greatly strengthening the morale of his native troops.

30 17 cum Sertōriō faciēbant: 'sided with Sertorius'.

30 18 quamquam . . . esset: *quamquam*, 'although', may introduce a Concessive Clause (cp. G. 47); the verb is normally indicative: e.g. *illōs, quamquam sunt hostēs, tamen monēre volō*, 'although they are enemies, I wish to warn them'. For the subjunctive here, see N. 14 15b, ¶2.

Notes to Selection 36

30 20a Aesōpus: Aesop, generally assigned to the sixth century B.C., is reputed to have been a native of Phrygia, in Asia Minor. He is said to have been a slave of a Greek master, but later to have been freed. The fables in the collection which bears his name spring from various sources: it was the custom to ascribe to Aesop any fable of unknown authorship. Many of the tales were handed down in Greek folk-lore from remote antiquity; others were borrowed from the East.

30 20b sapiēns existimātus est: Pliny (first century A.D.) calls him *fābellārum philosophus* (*fābella* is a diminutive of *fābula*).

30 26 quis: see N. 14 15a.

30 27 sēmet: the suffix *-met* is added to the personal pronouns for emphasis; cp. *nōsmet*, 31 29.

30 28 id . . . temporis, ut: 'at such a time, that' (cp. N. 18 27). In the sense of 'such', *is, ea, id* is often defined, as here, by a Result Clause.

30 29 appetat messis: 'the harvest approaches'.

30 30 tempestīviōrēs: see N. 14 13b.

31 2 Dum . . . iret: see N. 25 13b, ¶2. In this clause the idea of purpose is so strong that one may translate, 'In order that she might go meanwhile'.

Notes to Selection 37

31 7a fac . . . eās et rogēs: an urgent command may be expressed by the present subjunctive (G. 39) preceded by the imperative *fac*. Cp. our 'Do come!'.

31 7b amīcōs: the object of *rogēs*, or rather of *eās-et-rogēs* regarded as a single verb; cp. our colloquial 'go ask'. Cp. also *īmus et cognātōs . . . ōrāmus*, lines 18-19.

31 10 pullī . . . circumstrepere ōrāreque: in vivid narrative the infinitive may be used in place of a past tense of the indicative. This usage is known as the Historical (or Descriptive) Infinitive. The subject of the Historical Infinitive is in the nominative case (cp. G. 16): e.g. *Nihil Sēquanī respondēre, sed in eādem trīstitiā tacitī pormanēro*, 'the Sequani made no reply, but remained plunged in the same gloom, without a word', 53 8.

31 12 qui . . . roget: see N. 24 25.

31 18 Quin . . . īmus: in the sense 'why not', *quīn* introduces the indicative (as here) or the imperative.

Notes to Selection 38

31 27 Valeant: 'May they fare well!'; i.e. 'Farewell to them!'

32 1 In ipsō . . . vertitur: 'It hinges (i.e. 'depends'; literally 'turns', 'revolves') upon the man himself'.

32 3 Q. Ennius in Satiris: for Ennius, see N. 27 26; his *Satirae* (or *Saturae*) were four or more books of miscellaneous verse in different metres. In Ennius' day the term *satira* (or *satura*) had not yet acquired the connotation of biting criticism; it simply meant 'miscellany'.

32 4 versibus quadrātis: the so-called *versus quadrātus*, 'squared verse', was the Trochaic Tetrameter, composed of four double trochees ($\stackrel{\angle}{\smile} - \smile$ the single trochee is $\stackrel{\angle}{\smile}$). The trochee is sometimes replaced by a spondee ($- -$) or a tribrach ($\smile\smile\smile$). The last half of the last double trochee is composed of a single syllable.

The two verses quoted in lines 7-8 may be scanned as follows (see pp. 150-151):

$$\stackrel{\angle}{\smile}|-\smile| \quad \stackrel{\angle}{} -| \ -\ - \ \mathbf{|} \ \stackrel{\angle}{} \ \smile\ |- \ - \ \mathbf{|}\stackrel{\angle}{\smile}|\smile$$

Hoc e|rit ti|b(i) argu|mentum **|** semper | in promp|tu si|tum

$$\stackrel{\angle}{} \ \smile\ | - \ - |\stackrel{\angle}{\smile}| \ - \ \mathbf{|} \ \stackrel{\angle}{} \ -| \ \smile\smile\smile\mathbf{|} \stackrel{\angle}{\smile}|-$$

ne quid | exspec|tes a|micos **|** quod tu|t(e) agere **|** possi|es.

The stress-accent of the metre is like that of Longfellow's 'Tell' me not in | mourn'ful numbers | life' is but an | emp'ty dream'; but the Latin verses depend for their effect on quantity (i.e. length and shortness of syllables) rather than on stress.

32 5 operae·pretium: 'worth while'.

32 8a quid exspectēs amicōs: the double accusative with *exspectō* is unusual; the normal construction is *aliquid ab aliquō exspectō*.

32 8b tūte: a strengthened form of *tū*, nominative.

32 8c possiēs: an old form equivalent to *possīs*.

Notes to Selection 39

32 9 Metelli Numidicī: Q. Caecilius Metellus was consul in 109 B.C. He received his surname of Numidicus as a result of victories over Jugurtha, King of Numidia in Africa. Metellus served as censor (see N. 29 15) in 102 B.C.

32 15 vīvī possit: 'it is possible to live'; literally, 'it can be lived'. The passive of intransitive verbs is often used impersonally: so *vīvitur*, 'people live', 'life goes on' (literally, 'it is lived'); *pugnātur*, 'there is a battle'. This impersonal usage is common with the gerundive (future passive participle): *vīvendum est*, 'one must live' (literally, 'it is to be lived'); *pugnandum est*, 'one must fight'.

32 17a Q. Metellum . . . nōn oportuisse . . . cōnfitērī: the impersonal verb *oportet*, 'it is necessary', 'it is fitting', often has as its subject an Infinitive Clause (G. 63): *eum īre oportet*, 'it is necessary that he go', 'he must go'. So also *decet*, 'it is fitting'; see lines 23-25, *Metellum . . . decuit . . . dīcere*.

32 17b cui cōnsilium esset: 'since it was his intention'. A relative clause with its verb in the subjunctive may express Cause (cp. G. 36, G. 46): *dērīsus est ā cēterīs, quī illa vitia nōn agnōscerent*: 'he was ridiculed by the others, since they did not acknowledge those faults'. Cp. N. 24 25.

32 17c ad uxōrēs dūcendās: the regular Latin expression for 'marry' is *in mātrimōnium dūcō*, 'lead into matrimony', when used of a man; *nūbō*, 'assume the bridal veil', when used of a woman.

32 19a rei uxōriae: 'marriage'.   The use of a circumlocution composed of *rēs* and the appropriate adjective instead of a simple noun is quite common: so *rēs rūstica*, 'agriculture'; *rēs dīvīna*, 'worship'.

32 19b T. . . . Castricius: a teacher of rhetoric.   He flourished at the time of the Emperor Hadrian (117-138 A.D.), who regarded him with great esteem.

32 22a dum modo . . . sint: 'provided that they be'.   Clauses of Proviso are introduced by *dum*, by *modo*, or (as here) by *dum modo*, all meaning 'provided that'; the verb is in the subjunctive mood: e.g. *dum rēs maneant, verba fingant arbitrātū suō,* 'provided that the things remain the same, let them fashion the words as they please'.

32 22b vēri similēs: *similis* governs either the genitive (as here) or the dative.   Usage varies among the different authors: either the genitive or the dative is used with nouns denoting things, while the genitive is more common with nouns denoting persons.

32 23 Metellum . . . decuit . . . dīcere: see N. 32 17a.

32 27 quae . . . comprehenderētur: see N. 18 18a, ¶2: this clause is to be taken as representing a thought present in Metellus' mind.   We may bring out the force of the subjunctive by adding the words 'as well he knew'.

32 29a facile: adverb.

32 29b quod fuit . . . vērissimum: this relative clause describes—and anticipates—the Indirect Statement *cīvitātem salvam esse . . . nōn posse* (see N. 29 32a).

Notes to Selection 40

33 1a Pȳthagorae: Pythagoras of Samos (sixth century B.C.) founded at Croton (see N. 14 1b, ¶2) a school of philosophy and an ideal community.   Pythagoras taught not only a philosophical system but also a complete way of life, which reminds us somewhat of monasticism, if tradition has represented it correctly (see N. 33 24).   The philosophy of Pythagoras rested on the theory that number is the basic principle of the universe.   Prominent among his doctrines was that of metempsychosis, or transmigration of souls.   Pythagoras was regarded by his followers with religious veneration; 'the master has said it' (Greek *autos ephā*, Latin *ipse dīxit*) silenced any dispute on matters of doctrine.

33 1b recipiendī instituendīque discipulōs: the construction of gerund governing the accusative, here used, is much less common than that of the gerundive (future passive participle) modifying a noun (e.g. *causārum ōrandārum*, 28 1).

33 2 adulēscentēs: accusative, object of ἐφυσιογνωμόνει (see the next note).

33 3 ἐφυσιογνωμόνει (ephysiognōmónei:) 'he physiognomized': the imperfect ind. act. third pers. sing. of φυσιογνωμονέω (*physiognōmonéo*), 'physiognomize', 'judge a man's character by his features'.   Gellius himself defines the word in the next sentence.

33 6 recipī . . . tacēre: the subject of these infinitives is the unexpressed antecedent of *quī*.

33 13 ἀκουστικοί (akoustikoí): 'hearers'; the word is derived from ἀκούω (akoúo), 'hear'; cp. our word 'acoustic'.

33 17 μαθηματικοί (mathēmatikoí): 'mathematicians'; the rest of the sentence gives the derivation of the word.

33 18a geōmetriam: Pythagoras made notable contributions to geometry, whether or not he invented the proposition which bears his name. The subject was highly regarded by the Greeks: Plato is said to have inscribed on his door, 'Let no one ignorant of geometry enter here!'.

33 18b gnōmonicam: the insertion of *gnōmonica*, 'the art of the sundial', in this list of studies is apparently due to a misunderstanding on Gellius' part of a technical term in the source which he follows. The main subjects of the Pythagorean curriculum, in addition to geometry and music, were arithmetic and astronomy.

33 19a mūsicam: Pythagoras was the first to study the mathematical basis of harmony. It was from this standpoint that music formed a part of the Pythagorean curriculum.

33 19b μαθήματα (mathḗmata): the acc. plur. of μάθημα, μαθήματος (*máthēma, mathḗmatos*), n., 'a subject of study', from μανθάνω (*mantháno*), 'learn'.

33 21 mundī: the Greek word *cosmos* originally meant 'order', 'orderly arrangement'; Pythagoras, impressed by the ordered, mathematical interrelation of the heavenly bodies, is said to have been the first to use the word in the sense of 'universe'. Now *cosmos* also meant 'adornment' (originally 'neat arrangement', hence 'embellishment'; cp. our word 'cosmetic'); the Romans therefore translated *cosmos* in the sense 'universe' by their own word for 'adornment', namely *mundus;* this identification was doubtless fostered by the existence of a (perhaps related) adjective *mundus, -a, -um,* 'neat', 'orderly'.

33 22 φυσικοί (physikoí): 'physicists', 'students of nature', from φύσις (*phýsis*), 'nature'.

33 24 in medium: 'into a common treasury'. This account of the existence of a community of property among the followers of Pythagoras rests on a somewhat untrustworthy tradition.

Notes to Selection 41

33 27 P. Crassus Mūciānus: P. Licinius Crassus Dives Mucianus (born Q. Mucius Scaevola, adopted by P. Licinius Crassus Dives; see 9 25-29), was consul in 131 B.C.; at the same time he held the office of *pontifex maximus,* or chief priest of the Roman state religion. In 133 B.C., Attalus III, King of Pergamum, a kingdom in Asia Minor, had died, bequeathing his kingdom to the Roman people. While the Romans were preparing to organize this legacy into the province of Asia, they were temporarily checked by a pretender named Aristonicus, who attempted to make himself king of Pergamum. The consul Crassus was sent against him; the Roman suffered defeat at Leucae, mentioned in line 28, and was captured and killed in 130 B.C. by some Thracian troops of Aristonicus. The latter, however, was finally defeated by the Romans, and the province was organized according to plan.

33 28 Leucās: Leucae was a city on the coast of Pergamum.

34 1 arietem: the battering-ram commonly used by the Romans consisted of a huge beam, the striking end of which was heavily sheathed with metal, often fashioned to represent a ram's head.

34 2a architectona: for the form, cp. N. 15 14a. Many Greek cities employed a public architect, who served as consultant to the various administrative boards of the city.

34 2b Mylasēnsium: Mylasa was a city of Caria in Asia Minor, south of Pergamum.

34 3 mālis: from *mālus, mālī*, m., 'mast'. Note the quantity of the *-ā-; mălus, -a, -um,* 'bad', has a short *-a-*.

34 10a dictitābat: see N. 18 24.

34 10b virgīs . . . cecīdit: cp. N. 21 14b; *virgīs caedō* is the regular expression for 'have a man beaten'.

This act of Roman severity so impressed itself upon the people of Asia Minor that for generations they called anyone who administered harsh chastisement a 'Licinius'.

Notes to Selection 42

34 14a epigrammata: 'epitaphs'; the word *epigramma*, borrowed from the Greek, signifies etymologically 'a writing upon', 'an inscription'. The modern meaning of the word 'epigram' arose from the fact that the short verse-form suitable for inscriptions lent itself readily to the brief expression of a witty and ingenious turn of thought.

34 14b Cn. Naevii: Cn. Naevius, the most original of the Roman playwrights, was born in Campania (see line 18) in the early part of the third century B.C. His literary activity began with the presentation of a drama in 235. He wrote tragedies, chronicle plays based on Roman history, and comedies, including both imitations of Greek models and original plays on Roman themes. His outspoken criticism of the Roman aristocracy resulted in his imprisonment; released, he retired from Rome. In his old age, he composed the *Bellum Pūnicum*, an epic based on the First Punic War (264-241 B.C.), in which he himself had served. His influence on later Latin literature was considerable, but of his works only fragments have survived.

34 14c Plauti: T. Maccius Plautus, the greatest Roman comic playwright, was born at Sarsina in Umbria c. 250 B.C. Like Shakespeare, he gained his knowledge of the stage from practical experience. His dramatic activity extended from 204 to his death in 184. He devoted himself entirely to the writing of comedies, basing them on the works of Menander, Philemon, and other playwrights of the Attic New Comedy (see N. 15 16a). His plays therefore have a Greek setting, but with a liberal admixture of Roman color, and with a rather coarse vigor that was Plautus' own. Twenty comedies, which have come down to us, and a twenty-first, which has survived in part, probably comprise the group of twenty-one recognized as genuine by the Roman critic Varro (see N. 34 25). The influence of Plautus upon modern comedy has been very great.

34 15a M. Pācuvii: M. Pacuvius is the least important of the three poets here mentioned. **Nephew and pupil of the poet Ennius** (see N. 27 26), he was born at Brundisium in south-eastern Italy in the year 220 B.C. At Rome he devoted his time to writing and painting. His works included at least twelve tragedies, one chronicle play, and *Saturae* (see N. 32 3); none of them has come down to us save in inconsiderable fragments.

34 15b ipsī fēcērunt: the authenticity of all three epitaphs, particularly the first, is open to question.

34 16 nōbilitātis . . . grātiā et venustātis: Gellius sometimes uses *grātiā*, properly 'for the sake of', in a meaning approaching 'on account of', 'because of'; cp. *artis grātiā*, 26 14.

34 17 dūxī: 'I have judged', 'I have considered'; a not infrequent meaning of *dūcō* is 'consider', 'reckon'.

34 18 superbiae Campānae: the Campanians were noted for their arrogance.

34 20-23 The epitaph is in the old Saturnian metre, a native Italian measure based largely on stress-accent, while the later Latin metres, borrowed from the Greek, depend on quantity (cp. N. 32 4). The details of the Saturnian metre are too little known to permit of marking the points of stress with any certainty.

34 20 foret: the forms *forem, forēs*, etc., are sometimes used instead of *essem, essēs*, etc.; cp. *fore*, N. 28 13b.

34 21 Camēnae: these were native Italian goddesses of springs and wells, whom the Romans identified with the Greek Muses, goddesses of poetry.

34 22 Orchi . . . thēsaurō: 'to the store-house of Orcus'. Orcus is a name, possibly of Greek origin, used to designate the god who ruled over the underworld. This god was also called *Dīs pater;* see N. 47 32.

34 23 loquier: an old form of the infinitive *loquī.*

34 25 M. Varrōne: M. Terentius Varro, author and antiquarian, was born in 116 B.C. at Reate, in the Sabine country. In the course of his long life (he died in 27 B.C.) he wrote an incredible number of volumes. Among these were several books of *Saturae*, a collection of historico-philosophical essays, a book of Portraits of seven hundred famous men, each picture accompanied by a eulogy in verse and an account in prose (the epitaph of Naevius is traced by some to this source), a series of treatises on literature (one of these was the *De Poetis*, mentioned here), a great work on Antiquities, Human and Divine, an Encyclopedia of Liberal Arts, a commentary on the Civil Law, a Geography, a work on the Latin Language, a treatise on Agriculture, and Epistles on various subjects. Of all these, only the treatise on Agriculture and part of that on the Latin Language have come down to us.

34 26-28 These verses are in the Dactylic Hexameter; each verse comprises six feet; the foot is either a dactyl ($\stackrel{\smile}{-}\smile\smile$) or a spondee($\stackrel{\smile}{-}-$); the last foot of the verse always has two syllables, the first long, the second long or short (cp. p. 151, ¶C). The verses may be scanned as follows (the caesura, or verse-pause, is marked by ||):

‿ – | ‿   – | ‿   – | ‿ || – | ‿ ∪∪ ‿∪
Postquam (e)st | mort(em) ap|tus Plau|tus, || Co|moedia | luget,

‿ – | ‿ – | ‿ || – | ‿ – | ‿∪ ∪| ‿ ∪
scaena (e)st | deser|ta, || dein | Risus, | Ludus, Io|cusque

‿ ∪∪| ‿ ∪ ∪| ‿ || ∪ ∪ | ‿ – | ‿ ∪ ∪| ‿ –
et Nume|r(i) innume|ri || simul | omnes | conlacri | marunt.

The word *dēsertā* in the second verse, though nominative, ends in long -*a*
by poetic license (the nominative -*a* was originally long).
34 26 est . . . aptus: from *apiscor*.
34 28 Numerī innumerī: 'Numbers (i.e. 'rhythms', 'measures') innumerable'; the reference is to the great multitude and metrical variety of
Plautus' verses. For 'numbers' in this sense cp. 'Tell me not in mournful
numbers . . .'.
35 1–4 These verses are in the Iambic Senarius (see p. 151, ¶2):

∪ ∪‿| –   ‿ |– ∪∪| – || ‿ | – ‿| ∪∪
Adules|cens t(am) et|si prope|ras || hoc | te sa|xulum

∪∪‿ | – ∪∪|– || ‿| ∪   ‿ | –   ‿ |∪‿
rogat ut | s(e) aspici|as, || dein|de quod | scriptum (e)st | legas:

– ‿ | ∪‿| – || ∪∪‿| – ∪| ∪∪
hic sunt | poe|tae || Pa|cuvi | Marci | sita

–   ‿ | ∪‿| – || ‿|∪‿| – ‿ | ∪‿
oss(a) hoc | vole| bam || nes|cius|n(e) esses. | Vale.

35 1a Adulēscēns: addressed to the passer-by. Ancient epitaphs betray a pathetic eagerness to attract the attention of the passer-by (the
graves were frequently by the side of a road), and, if possible, to induce him
to read aloud the name of the deceased.
35 1b tam etsī (usually written in one word, *tametsī*): 'although'.
35 4 hoc . . . nescius nē essēs: the accusative *hoc* (referring to the
preceding statement) is the object of *nescius essēs*, which in meaning is
equivalent to a transitive verb (e.g. *ignōrārēs, nescīrēs*). For the mood of
essēs, see G. 45A.

Notes to Selection 43

35 5 Diagorās of Rhodes won the boxing contest at the Olympic games
in 464 B.C. A statue of Diagoras was set up at Olympia (the inscribed
base still exists), and the great Pindar wrote his Seventh Olympian Ode in
his honor.
The Olympic Games were the greatest of the Pan-Hellenic contests.
They were held every fourth summer, at Olympia in Elis, in honor of Zeus.
Only Greeks might compete, and they flocked to the games from all over
the Greek world. The prize for winning a contest was only a simple wreath
(see line 7), but such a victory was considered the most glorious of all
honors. The importance of the Olympic games to the Greeks may be
judged from the fact that they reckoned time by Olympiads (four-year
periods), beginning with the first recorded victory in 776 B.C.
35 6 pancratiastēn: for the form, see N. 15 23b. The *pancration*

(Greek *pan-* 'all', 'every', *kratos*, 'strength') was a contest which combined boxing and wrestling, with no holds barred.

35 12a nostrīs: i.e. Roman.
35 12b quō tempore: see N. 28 6.
35 13 apud Cannās: see N. 28 28.

Notes to Selection 44

35 19a Fabricius Luscīnus: see N. 13 1c, ¶¶3, 4.
35 19b rēbus gestīs: 'exploits'; cp. N. 32 19a. *Rem gerō* means 'manage affairs' in any field of endeavor, but particularly in the military and governmental sphere. The account of his exploits which Augustus set up in various parts of the Roman Empire was called *Rēs Gestae Dīvī Augustī* (see N. 22 3b). In a general sense *rēs gestae* means 'history'.
35 20 P. Cornēlius Rūfīnus: consul in 290 and in 277 B.C. The first part of this story apparently has to do with his second consulship, when Rome was engaged in her struggle with Pyrrhus (see N. 22 6a).
35 23 neque amīcō ūtēbātur: 'nor was he on friendly terms with him'; *amīcō* is in agreement with the unexpressed complement of *ūtēbātur*, which, if expressed, would be *eō*.
Ūtor is frequently used in such a way that the leading idea is expressed by a predicate noun or adjective in agreement with the complement of *ūtor:* e.g. *eōrum operā fortī fidēlīque ūsus sum*, 'their assistance, which I employed, was steadfast and loyal'.
35 29 vēndat: i.e. into slavery.
35 30a cōnsulātū et dictātūrā functum: *fungor* means 'discharge (an obligation)', 'serve (a term as an official)'; for the use of the ablative, see G. 28.
35 30b dictātūrā: the exact date of Rufinus' dictatorship is not known; it probably followed soon after his first consulship (290 B.C.).
In the early Republic, the dictatorship was an extraordinary magistracy, filled only in times of great emergency. The dictator served for a specific purpose, and his term was limited to six months. He was superior to all other magistrates, and had the power of life and death over the citizens even within the city walls (his lictors everywhere carried the *secūris* in the *fascēs:* cp. N. 21 14a, ¶2).
36 1a cēnsor: Fabricius was censor (see N. 29 15) in 275 B.C.
36 1b senātū: see N. 23 23.
36 1c decem pondō lībrās: see N. 28 32a.
36 2 argentī factī: 'wrought silver'; that is, silver tableware. Such luxury was just coming in through the close contact between Rome and the cities of Magna Graecia during the Pyrrhic War; to an old-fashioned Roman like Fabricius it seemed scandalous. The history of Rome is full of unsuccessful attempts to regulate luxury by legislative and censorial action.

Notes to Selection 45

36 3a C. Caesar cōnsul: Caesar's first consulship, in 59 B.C. (see 4 17 - 5 5). As this narrative shows, he was already displaying dictatorial ten-

dencies; but the republican feeling in the Senate was still too strong to admit of tame submission.

36 3b M. Catōnem: M. Porcius Cato, statesman of the first century B.C. To distinguish him from his ancestor Cato 'the Censor' (see N. 18 9a), later generations called him *Uticēnsis*, 'of Utica', from the place of his death. Born in 95 B.C., he entered public life at the age of thirty; from then on he was a staunch upholder of republican institutions, and a bitter opponent of monarchical tendencies wherever they manifested themselves. In 63, with Stoic severity, he argued for the death penalty for the Catilinarian conspirators, and carried his point against the arguments of Caesar. As this account shows, he opposed the power of the First Triumvirate (see 4 24-30). When Caesar left Rome to conquer Gaul, he did not wish to have Cato in the city; he accordingly contrived to have him sent on a governmental mission to Cyprus during 58-56 B.C. In 54 Cato became praetor; in the Senate he criticized Caesar's harsh treatment of the Gauls, and even proposed that he be delivered into their hands for punishment. When the Civil War between Caesar and Pompey broke out, Cato naturally sided with the latter, and was high in the councils of the Republican army. After Pompey's defeat, Cato commanded part of the Republican forces in Africa (47-46 B.C.). When it became apparent that Caesar was victorious, Cato, who had been entrusted with the defense of the city of Utica, there took his own life.

36 3c Catōnem sententiam rogāvit: *rogō*, like other verbs meaning 'ask', and also those meaning 'teach' and 'conceal', governs two accusatives, one of the person, the other of the thing: e.g. *tē mūsicam doceō*, 'I teach you music'; *amīcum pecūniam cēlō*, 'I hide the money from my friend'.

Senātōrem sententiam rogō is the technical term for asking for a senator's vote in the course of polling the Senate on a motion. In the passive, *senātor sententiam rogātur*, the accusative of the thing is kept as a Retained Object.

36 7 quicquid dē aliā rē vellet et quoad vellet: this privilege was frequently made use of. In 43 B.C., at a meeting of the Senate, some minor motions concerning the Appian Road, the Mint, and the Festival of the Lupercalia were before the house. Cicero rose, made a brief reference to the business at hand, and then launched into a political speech against Antony (the 'Seventh Philippic'; see N. 25 11a). Of the whole speech, which covers nine pages in a modern edition, only the first twenty-seven words and the last seven are concerned with the motions before the Senate.

The verb *vellet* (in both its occurrences) is in the subjunctive mood because the clauses *quicquid . . . vellet* and *quoad vellet* are integral, inseparable parts of the subjunctive substantive clause *ut . . . dīceret* (see G. 45A): without the words *quicquid dē aliā rē vellet* and *quoad vellet*, the substantive clause *ut . . . dīceret* would be meaningless. The verb *vellet* is therefore felt as part of the substantive clause, and is put in the subjunctive. This construction, known as Subjunctive of Integral Part (less accurately Subjunctive by Attraction), is comparatively rare; students should *never* account for a subjunctive by reference to it until they have exhausted the possibility of other explanations.

36 8 viātōrem: 'bailiff'; the *viātor* was a minor attendant of a magistrate, who at his direction escorted recalcitrant persons into his presence (hence the name; cp. *via*), and executed arrests and seizures. During sessions of the Senate, the presiding magistrate's *viātor* took the place of the modern sergeant-at-arms.

36 9a **prēndī loquentem et in carcerem dūcī**: this is the only recorded instance of such tactics on the part of a consul.

36 9b **carcerem**: the Prison was a small, very ancient structure about fifty yards away from the Curia, where the Senate sat. Considerable portions of it are still preserved.

36 11 **mittī**: 'released', 'dismissed'.

Notes to Selection 46

36 12 **Prōtagoram**: see N. 28 2.

36 13 **librō**: the *Protagoras* of Plato portrays the famous sophist at the height of his career. The dialogue is concerned with the question of whether virtue can be taught.

36 15 **Abdēra**: neuter plural; see N. 24 1.

36 16 **Dēmocritus** of Abdera, called the 'Laughing Philosopher', was born c. 460 B.C. He was a pupil of Leucippus, who was the first to formulate the atomic theory, the doctrine that all matter is composed of minute, indivisible particles. In his prolific writings, Democritus developed and spread the atomic theory.

The fact that Democritus was at least ten, and probably twenty or twenty-five years younger than Protagoras seriously diminishes the credibility of this story. The ancients were very fond of inventing anecdotes which brought together famous men of the same city or period. The story, drawn from Greek sources, is significant, however, as illustrating the Greeks' admiration for geometry (see N. 33 18a).

36 17 **virtūtis et philosophiae grātiā**: see N. 34 16.

36 22 **quasi orbem**: 'circle, so to speak'; *quasi* (like *quīdam*, N. 21 27), is used to apologize for an unusual expression: cp. *ratiōne quasi geōmetricā*, lines 23-24.

36 26 **in modum eundem**: 'in the same manner'. With *modus*, 'manner', and similar words, the accusative with *ad* or *in* is used where we say 'in this manner', etc.

Notes to Selection 47

37 3a **Croesī**: Croesus was King of Lydia, in Asia Minor, from c. 560 to 547 B.C. His kingdom was a very wealthy one, and his name became proverbial for riches. He carried on an extensive campaign of conquest in Asia Minor, but proved to be an enlightened ruler. He was very friendly to the Greeks, and lived on peaceful terms with his neighbors, the Medes. When, however, the Persian Cyrus conquered the Medic kingdom, Croesus felt himself threatened by the might of Persia. Partly for this reason, partly to avenge the downfall of the Medic king, partly in the hope of conquering additional territory, Croesus declared war on Cyrus. The former was defeated at Sardis (the city mentioned in line 6). According to

Herodotus, from whom this story is taken, Croesus was spared by Cyrus, who kept him at his court.

37 3*b* cum iam fārī per aetātem posset: 'when he had arrived at the age of speech'; literally, 'when he could already have spoken as far as his age was concerned'. For this use of *per*, cp. *id tibi per mē facere licet*, 'you may do it as far as I am concerned'.

37 5 habitus est: 'was considered'.

Notes to Selection 48

37 12*a* Taurus: L. Calvisius Taurus, a famous Platonist, was born in Beirut in Syria. His period of greatest activity falls in the middle of the second century of our era. He was the director of the Platonic Academy at Athens, and taught both Gellius and the famed sophist Herodes Atticus. Among his works were commentaries on several Platonic dialogues, and a treatise which compared the doctrines of Plato and Aristotle. Affable and kindly, if a bit pedantic, in manner, he had a strong and noble character, and was far superior to most of his contemporaries, the '*philosophi*' mentioned in line 28.

37 12*b* cum . . . tum: 'not only, but also'. This is one of the most troublesome uses of *cum*. The verb introduced by *cum* in this construction is regularly in the indicative mood.

37 15 Euclīdem: Euclides of Megara (c. 450-380 B.C.) was the founder of the Megarian school of philosophy. This group blended the doctrines of Socrates with those of the Eleatic school, which taught the essential unity of all existence. Euclides of Megara is not to be confused with Euclides (Euclid) the mathematician, who lived in the late fourth and early third century B.C.

37 16-19 Megara (the form is neuter plural) was the capital of a little state which lay between Attica and Corinth. Since it was on the Isthmus, it had ports on both the Corinthian and the Saronic Gulfs, leading respectively to the Adriatic and the Aegean. In 432 B.C., using a manufactured grievance as a pretext, Athens passed the decree mentioned here, shutting the ports and markets of her Empire to the Megarians. The decree was intended to force the Megarians by economic pressure to return to the Athenian Empire, which they had left in 446. This and similar measures were among the chief causes of the Peloponnesian War (see N. 16 8).

37 16-17 ut . . . ut: after the intervention of two clauses, *quī . . . esset* and *sī . . . inventus esset*, the conjunction *ut* is repeated for the sake of clarity.

37 20 et esse Athēnīs et audīre Sōcratēn: Socrates could rarely be induced to leave his beloved Athens.

37 22 sub noctem: in expressions of time, *sub* means 'toward', 'just before'.

37 23 caput . . . vēlātus: see N. 25 1*b*.

37 24 domō suā Megarīs: cp. N. 24 1.

37 26 mīlia passuum paulō amplius vīgintī: 'a little more than twenty miles'. *Mille passūs*, literally 'a thousand paces' (plural *mīlia passuum*, 'thousands of paces') is the regular Latin expression for 'a mile'.

By a peculiar idiom, *amplius* and *plūs*, 'more', are introduced paren-
thetically into numerical expressions in the sense of 'more than' without
affecting at all the construction into which they are introduced: e.g. *librōs
plūs ducentōs scrīpsit*, 'he wrote more than two hundred books'. Note
that *amplius* and *plūs*, however, may themselves be modified by an Ablative of Degree of Difference (here *paulō*).
37 30 dōnec . . . ēdormiant: see N. 25 13*b*.

Notes to Selection 49

38 2 Pīsistratus became 'tyrant' (see N. 26 14*b*) of Athens in 560 B.C.
He reigned as a benevolent despot; during his rule (560-527) and that of
his sons and successors (527-510), Athens experienced a great advance in
the arts.
38 4*a* Xerxēs, King of Persia (486-465 B.C.). His father Darius had
directed and led a Persian invasion into Greece (492-490), but had suffered
defeat at Marathon (490), and had died (486) while preparing for another
expedition. Xerxes took up his father's plan, and in 480 led his army
across the Hellespont. After Xerxes forced the pass at Thermopylae, the
Athenians temporarily abandoned their city, which the Persian occupied
and burned. Xerxes was defeated by the Greeks at the battle of Salamis
(480 B.C.), and his forces were driven out of Greece by the Greek victories
at Plataea and Mycale (479 B.C.).
38 4*b* Athēnārum potītus: *potior* governs either the ablative (G. 28) or
the genitive, as here.
38 5 in Persās: 'to Persia'; literally, 'to the Persians'. Latin often
uses the name of the inhabitants where we prefer to use the name of the
country.
38 6 Seleucus had been an officer in the army of Alexander the Great.
In the struggles for mastery which followed the conqueror's death, Seleucus
emerged in 312 B.C. as king of a realm which later came to include Syria,
Mesopotamia, Iran, and the greater part of Asia Minor. He died in 281
B.C.; his descendants, the Seleucid dynasty, ruled in the East until the
middle of the first century B.C. Antiochus III (see N. 13 14) was one of
these.
38 7 Nīcānōr: the surname is also given as Nicator. In either case, it
means 'the Conqueror'.
38 8*a* in Aegyptō: at Alexandria, which was founded by Alexander in
332 B.C.
38 8*b* Ptolemaeīs rēgibus: Ptolemy was a Macedonian, a general of
Alexander the Great, whom the latter sent to Egypt as Governor in 323
B.C. After Alexander's death Ptolemy continued to rule Egypt, and set
himself up as king in 306 or 305. He thus founded the dynasty of the
Ptolemies, who ruled Egypt until the death of Cleopatra, the last of the
line, in 30 B.C.
The Library at Alexandria, the greatest in the ancient world, was established either by the founder of the dynasty, Ptolemy I Soter, or by his suc-
cessor, Ptolemy II (283-247 B.C.). The Library formed part of the great
Museum, or University, of Alexandria.

38 10 bellō Alexandrīnō: this name is given to the campaign which Caesar waged in Egypt (see **6** 2-4) in the years 48-47 B.C. Some scholars believe that it was not the great Library that was burned, but a large store of books which were awaiting export, and that this fact gave rise to the story of the burning of the Library. The matter is complicated by the fact that there was a smaller library at Alexandria, and it is impossible to determine which one is meant by later references to 'the Library'.

Notes to Selection 50

38 12 Philippus: Philip was born in 383 B.C., son of Amyntas, King of Macedon. At the age of fifteen he was sent to Thebes (cp. N. 41 20*a*) as a hostage; he remained there for three years, and was strongly influenced by the culture of the Greek city. In 359 he became ruler of Macedon. Soon after he came to power, he seized the gold-mines of Mt. Pangaeus, in Thrace. With the revenue derived from these, he built up a strong army, and embarked upon a program of bribery which bought him friends in every important city of Greece. It is the best proof of Demosthenes' integrity of character that he constantly opposed Philip's campaign of aggrandizement (see N. **24** 26*b*). In a series of wars and diplomatic manoeuvers, between 359 and 338 Philip made himself master of Greece, and imposed upon the Greek cities the federal union which they had been unable to develop for themselves. He was planning to invade Persia at the head of an army of Macedonians and Greeks when he was assassinated in 336, leaving his plan of conquest for his son to execute.

38 14 Feruntur: 'are circulated', 'are in circulation'.

38 16 Aristotelī: Aristotle was born at Stagira, a Greek colony of Chalcidice, in 384 B.C. In 365 he became the pupil of Plato, with whom he remained until the latter's death in 347. Five years later, Philip entrusted to Aristotle the education of Alexander, as he announces his intention of doing in the letter which Gellius here translates. Aristotle remained in Macedon until 335, when Alexander set forth on his career of conquest. The young king sent his teacher many rare specimens of animal life which he encountered on his expeditions, as well as large sums of money for purposes of research. In 335 Aristotle returned to Athens and opened his school, the 'Lyceum'. Here he lectured on rhetoric and philosophy. After the death of Alexander in 323, Aristotle was forced to leave Athens because of the violent anti-Macedonian reaction; he died in the following year.

Aristotle is numbered with Socrates and Plato as one of the founders of Greek philosophy in the form in which it influenced future ages. He differs from his illustrious predecessors in his emphasis upon the facts of the physical world; he turned his searching intellect upon almost every department of human knowledge, collecting, systematizing, codifying. In the domain of logic, in which he did his most original work, he invented the syllogism, the basic instrument of deductive reasoning. Among his extant works are treatises on logic, literature, ethics, government, and natural science.

38 17 Alexandrum: see N. **16** 11*a*.

38 19*a* Expōnenda est: *expōnō* here means 'translate'.

38 19b ad hanc ferme sententiam: 'in about the following vein'; cp. N. 36 26.

38 20 Philippus Aristoteli Salūtem Dīcit: the stock Latin formula for beginning a letter; it takes the place both of our salutation and of our complimentary close and signature. The last two words are often abbreviated *S.D.;* sometimes we find *S.P.D.*, *salūtem plūrimam dīcit.*

38 21 scītō: 'you shall know', 'I wish you to know'; *scītō* is the future imperative second pers. sing. act. The future imperative is rarely used save in laws, official declarations, and formal announcements.

38 22 proinde . . . quam: 'so much . . . as'.

38 23 quod . . . contigit: see N. 18 18a, ¶1. The clause is in apposition with *eō*, which is neuter.

38 24 fore ut . . . exsistat: see N. 28 13b.

II. Cornelius Nepos

(See pp. 3-4.)

Notes to Selection 51

39 1a bellō Persicō: the second Persian invasian, under Xerxes, is meant (see N. 38 4a).

39 1b Themistoclēs, the great Athenian statesman, was born c. 524 B.C. He began public life by serving as archon (a high Athenian magistracy) in 493-492. At that time he began the development and fortification of the harbors at Piraeus as part of his program to make Athens a strong sea power. This work was interrupted by the first Persian invasion, in which Themistocles fought at the battle of Marathon (490); it was later resumed. In 482 Themistocles sponsored a decree whereby the proceeds of the state silver mines were used to increase the Athenian fleet. In 480 he was elected *stratēgus,* or general, of the Athenian forces. The Greeks' crushing victory at Salamis was due to his plan of abandoning Athens, taking to the ships, and forcing the Persians to give battle in the narrow straits. Had the Greeks heeded his bold advice to follow up their victory, the war might have been over that year. For his services Themistocles was honored at Sparta; but his own Athenians, with characteristic ingratitude, did not re-elect him as *stratēgus* for the next year. His influence was still strong at Athens, however, and he continued the development of the Piraeic harbors. There followed the incident here narrated, in which Themistocles used— and lost—his popularity with the Spartans for the benefit of his native state. In spite of all he had done, his very successes, and a certain arrogance of manner, earned him the jealousy and ill-will of his fellow-citizens; in 471 he was ostracized (see N. 40 28); in his absence charges of treason were brought against him, and he was condemned to death; he fled to Persia, where he was hospitably received by the King; there he died c. 459 B.C.

39 2 Phalēricō portū neque magnō neque bonō Athēniēnsēs ūterentur: see N. 35 23. Athens is an inland city: before the construction of the Piraeic harbors, the Athenians used the open road-stead of Phalerum, east of the peninsula of Piraeus. This 'Phaleric Harbor', as Themistocles saw, could never have served as the main port of a great maritime power.

39 3 **triplex Piraei portus:** the peninsula of Piraeus, about four and one-half miles south-west of Athens, contains three harbors, anciently called Cantharus, Zea, and Munichia; the first was the main port, and is often called *the* harbor of Piraeus.

39 4 **iis . . . ut:** see N. 30 28.

39 5 **ūtilitāte superāret:** Themistocles seriously proposed abandoning the inland city and making Piraeus the capital. Sentiment prevented the adoption of this eminently practical plan; the two cities were later made virtually one by the connecting fortifications of the Long Walls.

39 6a **restituit:** after their destruction by the Persians.

39 6b **causam . . . quā negārent:** 'a pretext, on the basis of which to state (that) . . . not'. For the mood of *negārent*, see N. 24 25.

39 9 **quae . . . possīderent:** see N. 24 25.

39 10 **longē aliō spectābat:** 'had a far different purpose'; more literally, 'looked in a far different direction'.

39 11 **atque:** 'than'; with *alius* and other words denoting difference, *atque* is to be translated 'than'; with *īdem* and other words denoting sameness, *atque* is to be translated 'as'.

39 19 **reliquī lēgātī ut tum exīrent:** see N. 14 22b.

39 23 **Quō factum est:** 'Thus it came about'; literally, 'By this it was brought about'. See G. 45B.

39 25 **magistrātūs:** the ephors (see N. 19 12a).

39 26 **dedit operam:** 'made it his business'.

40 1 **superesse:** 'remained (to be completed)'.

40 4 **aeqᵘᵘm esse:** 'it was proper'; the subject of *esse* is the infinitive clause *illōs . . . mittere*. In that clause, *illōs* is the subject, *virōs* the object, of *mittere*.

40 5 **Gestus est eī mōs:** 'they complied with his request'; *alicui mōrem gerō* is a Latin idiom for 'humor someone', 'be obliging to someone'.

40 6 **functī summīs honōribus:** see N. 35 30a; *honor* is often used, as here, in the sense of 'public office'.

40 7 **praedīxit:** 'he instructed'.

40 8 **prius . . . quam:** more often found written together, as one word, *priusquam*.

40 11 **quod . . . possent:** cp. N. 32 29b; here the relative clause describes the action of *deōs . . . saepsisse*.

40 12 **deōs pūblicōs . . . (deōs) patriōs . . . penātēs:** the *dī pūblicī* are the gods of the whole Greek people, the *dī patriī* the gods of Athens in particular, the *penātēs* the household gods of each Athenian family. (For the use of the Roman religious term *penātēs* in a Greek context, cp. N. 43. 15).

40 13 **quō facilius . . . possent:** 'in order that they might more easily be able'; a Purpose Clause containing a comparative (here *facilius*) is regularly introduced by *quō*, 'in order that'. In this construction, *quō* is really an Ablative of Degree of Difference, 'by which'. So, *medicō pecūniam dat, quō sit studiōsior*, 'he gives the doctor money, in order that he may be more attentive'.

40 14 in eō: 'in (doing) this', i.e. in fortifying Athens.

40 15a prōpugnāculum oppositum . . . barbarīs: 'a bulwark opposed to the barbarians'; *esse* is used as a copulative verb, not as an auxiliary with *oppositum*.

40 15b apud quam . . . cōpiās . . . fēcisse: when the relative, as here, introduces a coordinate clause (cp. N. 13 5a) in an Indirect Statement, the verb is put in the infinitive with subject accusative. Here *apud quam* is equivalent to *et apud eam*.

40 16 bis: see 39 11-12.

40 17 qui . . . intuerentur: see N. 32 17b.

Notes to Selection 52

40 22a Aristīdēs was born at Athens about the middle of the sixth century B.C. In the battle of Marathon he served as a commander. He held the position of chief archon (see N. 39 1b) in 489 B.C. In politics, he was a conservative, and favored the development of the army rather than the navy; in both respects he was an opponent of Themistocles. He was highly esteemed for his integrity, and in 477 was entrusted with the task of apportioning the sums to be contributed by the member-states of the newly-formed Delian League.

40 22b aequālis ferē . . . Themistoclī: 'of about the same age as Themistocles.' The form *Themistoclī* may be taken either as genitive (see N. 24 16-17), or as dative according to the Latin third declension. The adjective *aequālis*, 'of the same age', governs either of these cases.

40 24 In hīs: 'In the case of these men'.

40 26 post hominum memoriam: 'within the memory of mankind'.

40 28 testulā illā: 'by the well-known *ostracon*'; i.e. by the institution of ostracism. This mild form of banishment was introduced into Athenian law by Clisthenes in 507 B.C., to enable him to rid the city of those who sympathized with the deposed 'tyrants'. As the institution developed, it was used to remove temporarily those who had incurred the suspicion of their fellow-citizens as being too powerful or too ambitious for the good of the democracy. It was used not to punish treasonable acts, but to forestall them.

The mechanism of this "energetic precaution of political hygiene", as it has been called, was as follows: once each year the Assembly of the People was asked whether it wished to employ the device of ostracism. No discussions were held, no names were mentioned; the vote was by show of hands. If the vote was in the affirmative, a separate meeting was held, at which, again without discussion, each citizen could deposit a ballot with the name of the man whom he wished sent away. The ballot used was an *ostracon* (hence 'ostracism'), 'fragment of earthenware pottery', 'potsherd', on which the name was scratched. If a man's name appeared on the majority of the ballots cast, provided the majority totalled at least 6000 votes, he was forced to leave Athens within ten days. The term of ostracism was normally ten years (the *decem annōrum lēgitima poena* of 41 1), but the sentence might be retracted before the full term had run. In any event, ostracism was not considered a disgrace; the exile's wealth was not confiscated, and when he returned (having learned his lesson, it was hoped) he was eligible to all the offices in the state.

The ostracism of Aristides took place in 482, at the time when Themistocles was pushing his naval program (see N. 39 1*b*) with all his energy. *Ostraca* bearing the names of Aristides and of Themistocles have been discovered in the excavations at Athens.

40 28 - 41 1 According to another form of the story, the conversation took place when the voter, unable to write, and not knowing Aristides, asked him to write 'Aristides' on the *ostracon*.

40 32 cūr: 'because of which'; relative, not interrogative.

41 2 populī scītō: in reference to a decree of the Roman people, the expression regularly used is *plēbis scītum*, whence our 'plebiscite'.

41 3 restitūtus est: under pressure of the impending Persian invasion, the Athenians passed, late in 481, a decree permitting all those who had been ostracized to return.

Notes to Selection 53

41 4 Lȳsander was the admiral of the Spartan fleet in 406 B.C., toward the end of the Peloponnesian War. In this year, he inflicted a crushing defeat upon the Athenians at Notium; in 405, with the power of admiral but without the title, he defeated them again at Aegospotami, thus practically winning the war for the Spartans. The end of the war came in 404, leaving Lysander in virtual control of Greece.

It was Lysander's ambition to make Sparta the mistress of the Greek world, and himself the master of Sparta. He set about insuring Spartan supremacy by establishing an oligarchy of ten nobles, backed by a Spartan garrison, in every important city of Greece. His methods were cruel, grasping, and unscrupulous; his motto was "Cheat children with dice, and men with oaths".

In 403, when his brother nominally, and he really, commanded the Spartan fleet, he went so far as to ravage cities in the district subject to Pharnabazus, the satrap, or royal governor, of the Persian territory about the Hellespont. Persia was at this time allied with Sparta, and Pharnabazus complained to the ephors. Feeling against Lysander's excesses had been growing at Sparta, and he was summoned home.

41 6 esse perlātum: 'that news had been brought'; the infinitive lacks a subject accusative because it is impersonal (see N. 32 15).

41 12 dum signātur: the report was in the form of a scroll, tied with thread; the knot was sealed with wax, which was imprinted with the satrap's seal. The ceremonies attending the sealing must have afforded opportunity for the substitution mentioned in lines 12-13.

41 15 maximum magistrātum: *magistrātus* is here used collectively, 'a board of magistrates'; the ephors are meant.

41 16 testimōniī locō: 'to serve as evidence'.

41 14-19 Disgraced by this disclosure, Lysander voluntarily left Sparta for Africa. He returned in 399; in 395 he was killed in a battle between the Spartans and the Thebans.

Notes to Selection 54

41 20a Epaminōndam: Epaminondas was born c. 420 B.C. at Thebes in Boeotia, a region of Greece which adjoined Attica on the north-west. It was largely due to his efforts that Thebes enjoyed a brief period of supremacy in Greek affairs. This began with the victory won by his brilliantly original military tactics at Leuctra (371 B.C.; see N. 42 23), and ended with his death at Mantinea (362 B.C.).

41 20b fuisse . . . ferentem: 'was disposed to endure'; the use of the present participle with *sum* is rare, except for those participles which have virtually become adjectives (e.g. *patiēns, excellēns*). That *ferentem* is felt as a true participle is shown by the fact that it governs an object, *iniūriās*. When such a participle is used with *sum*, it regularly denotes, as here, a permanent characteristic, not a mere momentary action or state.

41 22-29 Cum—incolumem: these events took place in 368 B.C.; it must be noted that they are later than those narrated below, 41 30 - 42 33. In 368 the Thebans sent a force to rescue Pelopidas (see N. 42 1), who had been treacherously imprisoned by Alexander, 'tyrant' of Pherae in Thessaly. As this narrative shows, the attempt was unsuccessful, but in the following year Epaminondas returned as official commander of a new contingent, which forced Alexander to release Pelopidas.

41 23 praeficere exercituī nōluissent: after Epaminondas' second Peloponnesian campaign (summer, 369), he failed of re-election to the board of 'Boeotarchs', as the seven generals in command of the military forces of the Boeotian league were called.

41 24 eō: 'to such a point'.

41 27 prīvātus, numerō mīlitis: 'without command, with the rank of a common soldier'. Cp. our term 'private' as a military title. For *numerō*, see N. 20 12b.

41 30 cum . . . dūxisset: in 370, the Arcadians asked the help of the Thebans in a dispute which they were having with Sparta. Epaminondas, seeing a good opportunity to enhance the prestige of Thebes and lower that of Sparta, persuaded the Thebans to send him south with an army. He accomplished his mission in Arcadia, but pressed on into Laconia with 50,000 men; he besieged Sparta, pillaged Laconia, and won freedom for the Messenians (see N. 42 29b).

42 1 Pelopidās was one of the seven heroes who, in 379, had rid Thebes of its pro-Spartan magistrates and the Spartan garrison (see N. 41 4, ¶2). He was associated with Epaminondas in most of the latter's projects and campaigns.

42 2-13 Hī—imperium: this part of Nepos' narrative is apparently based on misinformation: see N. 42 14c.

42 3a ob eamque rem: when *-que* is used with a group of words beginning with a monosyllabic preposition, the conjunction is often attached to the word following the preposition.

42 3b iīs: Dative of (Advantage or) Disadvantage; we should say either 'the command was withdrawn from them' or 'their command was cancelled'. With verbs signifying removal, the Dative of Advantage or Disadvantage naturally denotes in most instances the person *from* whom something is removed; hence this construction is often called 'Dative of Separation' (cp. N. 23 23): e.g. *hunc mihi timōrem ēripe*, 'snatch away this fear from me' (i.e. 'for my advantage', *mihi*). This construction applies only to persons, since a thing can scarcely be thought of as deriving advantage or suffering disadvantage.

42 4 praetōrēs: here used in its military sense, 'generals'; the Boeotarchs are meant (see N. 41 23).

42 14a reditum est: see N. 32 15.

42 14b collēgae eius . . . accūsābantur: Pelopidas was brought up first; presumably the other colleague (see line 1) next; Epaminondas would have been tried next in any event.

42 14c hōc crīmine: the tradition which Nepos here follows seems to be incorrect; the charge on which the Boeotarchs were brought up was apparently that of exceeding the limit of their instructions, not that of their term of office. As we have seen (N. 41 30), Epaminondas went much further than the mere accomplishment of his mission.

42 15 accūsābantur: presumably before the federal court of the Boeotian League.

42 16 factum (*esse*): cp. N. 39 23.

42 18 quid dīceret: 'anything to say'; literally, 'what he might say': see N. 26 7.

42 21 quōminus . . . subīret: 'to undergo'. A verb of *preventing* or *refusing* may govern a subordinate clause with its verb in the subjunctive mood introduced by *quōminus* (i.e. *quō minus*, 'by which the less') or *quīn* (i.e. *quī ne*, 'by which not'; *quī* here is an old form of the abl.). The English idiom requires a gerund or infinitive: *nihil obstat quōminus eat*, 'nothing hinders his going'; *nōn recūsant quīn servī fiant*, 'they do not refuse to become slaves'.

42 23 Leuctra: in 371 Sparta invaded Boeotia with 10,000 men for the purpose of destroying the Boeotian League, which had been re-established in 375-374 after having been in abeyance for eleven years. The Boeotians, led by Epaminondas, numbered only 7,000, but the military genius of the commander effected the defeat, at Leuctra, a little Boeotian town, of the hitherto invincible Spartans.

42 24a ante sē imperātōrem: 'before his generalship', 'before he became general'. Note how this expression illustrates the Latin preference for the concrete; cp. N. 13 3.

42 24b sē: by a natural oversight, Nepos uses the reflexive, which is inappropriate in the supposed epitaph, though it would be in place in the report of Epaminondas' speech (cp. *suō*, line 22).

42 24c quōs . . . nemō . . . ausus sit: 'although no one dared'; a relative clause with its verb in the subjunctive may express Concession (cp. G. 36, G. 47): *C. Fabriciī memoriam coluit, quem numquam vīdisset*, 'he cherished the memory of C. Fabricius, although he had never seen him'. Cp. NN. 24 25, 32 17b.

42 29a prius . . . quam: see N. 40 8.

42 29b Messēnē restitūtā: *Messēnē* is ablative. It is not quite correct to speak of the 'restoration' of Messene; it was a new city, built on and around the ruins of the Messenians' ancient stronghold, Ithome. The

Messenians, inhabiting the south-western portion of the Peloponnese, had for centuries been dominated by the Spartans, who kept them in virtual serfdom.   Epaminondas liberated them, and built Messene for them as a strongly fortified capital; thenceforth they were formidable rivals of Sparta in Peloponnesian affairs.

42 30 eōrum: i.e. the Spartans'.

Notes to Selection 55

42 34a Hannibal: see N. 13 13.

42 34b paternum: cp. N. 14 1b.

43 1 opum indigēret: *egeō* and *indigeō*, 'need', 'be in want', govern either the ablative (see N. 23 23) or, as here, the genitive.

43 2 ut omittam: 'to say nothing of', 'not to mention'.

43 3 Philippum: Philip V of Macedon (221-179 B.C.); in 215 his envoys signed a treaty of alliance with Hannibal at the latter's camp in Italy (hence *absēns*, 'in his absence'); Philip thus entered the Second Punic War on the Carthaginian side.   He made a separate peace with Rome in 205 B.C.

43 4 Antiochus: see N. 13 14.

43 5 rubrō marī: by *rubrum mare* Nepos means not what we call the Red Sea (the narrow strip of water separating Egypt from Arabia), but what is now known as the Arabian Sea.   For the rhetorical effect Nepos mentions the extreme eastern portion of Antiochus' empire; his capital was Antioch on the Orontes, twenty miles distant from the Mediterranean.

43 8 rēgī: 'in the eyes of the king'; a usage akin to the Dative of Advantage or Disadvantage.

43 9a tamquam: cp. N. 27 9b.

43 9b alia . . . sentīret: 'he held different views', 'his sentiments were different' (cp. N. 13 3, ¶2).

43 9c atque: see N. 39 11.

43 13 Hamilcar was the leader of the Carthaginians in the First Punic War.   After the Roman victory in 241 B.C., he devoted himself to building up the Carthaginian power in Spain.   He died in 229 B.C.

43 14a nōn amplius novem: see N. 37 26, ¶2.

43 14b novem annōs nātō: 'nine years old'; age is usually expressed in Latin by the Accusative of Extent (G. 15) with the participle *nātus*, 'having been born'.

43 15 Iovī Optimō Maximō: Baal, the supreme deity of the Phoenicians and their descendants, is meant.   It is the custom of Roman authors to use the names of analogous Roman divinities (see N. 18 3a) when referring to foreign gods.

43 16 dum cōnficiēbātur: the use of the imperfect is exceptional; see N. 21 3.

43 18 dubitāret dūcere: when *dubitō* governs the infinitive, it means 'hesitate'; see G. 62.

43 21 tenentem: agrees with *mē*, to be supplied from line 20 as the subject of *iūrāre*.

43 25 mē cēlāris: see N. 36 3c.   Here the accusative of the thing is implied in *sī quid . . . cōgitābis*.

Notes to Selection 56

43 28 Antiochō fugātō: at the battle of Magnesia (see N. 18 12). By the terms of the treaty of peace, Hannibal was to be surrendered to the Romans, but Antiochus allowed him to escape.

43 29a Crētam: with Greek geographical names, the Accusative of End of Motion is sometimes found without a preposition, even when the names do not fall within the categories of G. 32 (Crete is a *large* island).

43 29b Gortȳniōs: see N. 38 5. Gortyna was a city on the southern coast of central Crete.

43 30 quō sē cōnferret: see N. 26 7.

43 34 summās (*amphorās*): see N. 15 1b.

44 3 statuās aēneās . . . complet: ancient bronze statues were usually cast hollow.

44 3-7 Hannibal's ruse seems to have succeeded.

Notes to Selection 57

44 8a Prusiae: Prusias was King of Bithynia, in Asia Minor; it was to his court that Hannibal came after his experience with the Cretans. In 186 Prusias, with Hannibal's aid, attacked Eumenes of Pergamum, a Roman ally. Roman intervention caused Prusias to make peace. The exact circumstances under which Prusias sent the embassy here mentioned to Rome are not known, but it is probable that the events here narrated took place in 182 B.C.

44 8b Flāmininum: T. Quinctius (or Quintius) Flamininus was consul in 198 B.C. He distinguished himself in Rome's second war against Philip V of Macedon (200–197 B.C.; cp. N. 43 3).

44 14a suum . . . sibi: these two reflexives refer to the subject of *peterent*, the verb which governs the clause in which they appear, while the reflexive *sē* (in *sēcum*) refers to the subject of *habēret*.

44 14b sibi . . . dederet: the joining of this affirmative clause to the negative *nē . . . habēret* by the use of *-que*, without an intervening *ut*, is very awkward.

44 15 illud recūsāvit, nē . . . postulārent: 'he objected to their demanding'; *nē . . . postulārent* is a substantive clause of Indirect Command in apposition with *illud*.

44 18 locō: see N. 20 12b.

44 20 ūsū venīret: the origin of the idiom *ūsū venit*, 'it happens', is uncertain.

44 22 puer: 'a slave'.

III. Julius Caesar

(See pp. 4-7.)

Notes to Selection 58

45 1 ad hunc locum: 'to this point' (in the narrative).

45 2 Galliae Germaniaeque: by *Gallia*, Caesar means the region bounded on the West and North by the Bay of Biscay and the English

Channel, on the North and East by the Rhine and the Alps, and on the South by the Mediterranean and the Pyrenees, comprising modern France and Belgium, with parts of Holland, Germany, and Switzerland. The term *Germania* he applies to an undefined region north and east of the Rhine, and north of the Alps.

45 5 sunt principēs quī: not 'there are leaders who' but 'those men are leaders who'.

45 6 eōrum iūdiciō: 'in their judgment' (see N. 20 30); *eōrum* refers to the Gauls in each particular group.

45 7 quōrum ad arbitrium . . . summa . . . redeat: 'so that to their decision . . . the supreme control . . . is referred'. A relative clause with its verb in the subjunctive mood may, as here, express Result (cp. G. 36, G. 41): *neque is sum quī perīculō terrear*, 'I am not such a man that I am frightened (or 'as to be frightened') by danger'. Cp. NN. 24 25, 32 17b, 42 24c. The antecedent of *quōrum* is the same as that of *quī*, line 6.

45 9 auxiliī: see N. 43 1.

45 12 summā: 'entirety'.

45 14 numerō: 'rank', 'repute', 'account'.

45 15a plēbēs: the more usual form of the nominative singular is *plēbs*.

45 15b habētur: see N. 37 5.

45 16 nūllō adhibētur cōnsiliō, 'is not made party to any deliberation'.

45 17 aere aliēnō: *aes aliēnum*, literally 'another man's money', is the regular Latin expression for 'debt'.

45 18 sēsē . . . dicant: 'they surrender themselves'; *dīcant* is a form of *dīcō*, *dīcāre*, not of *dīcō*, *dīcere;* note the quantity of the -*i*-, and cp. N. 30 12.

45 19a in: 'over'; cp. N. 18 10.

45 19b Sed: 'To resume' (after the interruption of *Nam . . . servōs*, lines 15-19).

45 20 druidum: Caesar's discussion of the Druids which is included in this Selection is our most important source of knowledge concerning that ancient Gallic priesthood. Caesar's informant was probably Diviciacus, a Gallic nobleman who Cicero tells us was himself a Druid.

45 22 religiōnēs: 'matters of religion', 'religious questions'; see N. 29 11.

45 23 hī . . . eōs: the Druids and the Gauls, respectively.

45 25 sī quod . . . facinus: after *sī*, *nisi*, *nē*, and *num*, and in relative clauses (cp. N. 14 15a), the indefinite adjective *quī*, *quae* (or *qua*), *quod*, 'some', 'any', is regularly used instead of the indefinite adjective *aliquis*, *aliqua*, *aliquod*, 'some', 'any'.

45 27a praemia: 'awards' to be paid the aggrieved parties.

45 27b Sī quī . . . prīvātus . . . (*sī quī*) populus: see N. 45 25.

45 28a dēcrētō nōn stetit: with *stō* meaning 'abide (by)' the ablative is used without a preposition; the classification of the ablative is uncertain. Compare the cardinal principle of the Common Law, *stāre dēcīsīs*, 'to abide by the decisions (of previous judges)'.

45 28b stetit . . . interdīcunt: the perfect is used in the first verb to show that the failure to abide by the decree precedes the excommunication (see G. 49): the English idiom requires the present tense in both verbs.

45 29 Quibus est ita interdictum: 'those upon whom such a sentence of excommunication has been passed'; *interdīcō* governs the dative of the person, the ablative (of Separation) of the thing forbidden.

46 1a numerō . . . habentur: cp. *habētur locō*, **45** 15, and see N. **20** 12b.

46 1b hīs . . . dēcēdunt (*dē viā*): 'get out of their way'; for *hīs* cp. N. **42** 3b.

46 6–7 aut . . . aut: literally 'either . . . or'; in this context, the English idiom requires the omission of 'either'.

46 6 quī: this is an unusual form of the indefinite pronoun (see N. **14** 15a) instead of the more usual *quis*.

46 7 plūrēs: 'several'.

46 9 quae regiō: the vicinity of the modern Chartres.

46 14 illō (adverb): 'there', 'thither'.

46 21a Graecīs . . . litterīs: in very early times the Greeks had established the colony of Massilia (Marseilles) in southern Gaul.

46 21b Id: the custom of not committing their tenets to writing.

46 23 velint: the subjunctive is due to the fact that the clause *quod . . . velint* is subordinate to the quasi-Indirect Statement *īnstituisse* (*videntur*); cp. N. **14** 15b, ¶2. The indicative mood of *discunt* is due to the fact that the clause *eōs quī discunt* is merely the equivalent of a noun, e.g. *discipulōs*.

46 24 quod: 'a thing which'; relative, referring to the thought of *litterīs cōnfīsōs, minus memoriae studēre;* the relative is then further explained by the substantive clause *ut . . . remittant.*

46 26a remittant: 'relax'.

46 26b In prīmīs: 'especially'.

46 28 excitārī: 'men are aroused'; impersonal passive (see N. **32** 15).

46 33a incidit: perfect indicative (G. 48A); the English idiom here requires the present.

46 33b quod: cp. N. **46** 24.

46 33c Caesaris: in the Commentaries, Caesar always refers to himself, in his capacity of governor and general, in the third person. This device does much to lend an air of impartiality to the account.

46 33d quotannīs: 'every year'; literally, 'in as many years as there are': *quot annīs.*

46 35 ut . . . amplissimus, ita plūrimōs: we would say, 'the more distinguished . . . , the more numerous'.

46 36 ambactōs clientēsque: 'servitors and dependents'. There is some uncertainty as to the exact meaning of *ambactus*, a Gallic word.

47 1 Hanc ūnam: emphatic: 'This is the only . . . which'.

47 3 religiōnibus: 'religious observances'; cp. NN. **29** 11, **45** 22.

47 17 Mercurium: see N. **43** 15, second sentence. The same remark applies to the other names of divinities occurring in this passage.

47 18 ferunt: 'they proclaim'.

47 25 cēperint: see N. **18** 18a, ¶2.

47 32 Dīte patre: *Dīs pater*, 'Father Dis', god of the underworld, corresponded to the Greek Pluto.

47 34 noctium: the English 'fortnight' (i.e. 'fourteen nights') is a relic of this custom.

47 35 mēnsum: this form of the genitive plural of *mēnsis* is found in Caesar, his predecessors, and his contemporaries; later writers use *mēnsium*.

48 4 dōtis nōmine: 'in the nature of dowry', 'as dowry'.

48 11 uxōribus: the plural is used to correspond with *virī*, line 8; the Gauls were monogamous.

48 12 in servīlem modum: see N. 36 26.   At Rome, slaves were always examined under torture; it is to this practice that Caesar refers.

48 15 vīvīs cordī: 'dear to their hearts when they were alive'.   In the idiom *hoc mihi cordī est,* 'this is dear to my heart', the case and syntax of *cordī* are uncertain; many scholars take *cordī* as dative (see N. 13 11c), others as ablative (Place Where).

48 16 suprā hanc memoriam: 'before the present generation'; cp. N. 40 26.

48 17a cōnstābat: 'it was generally believed'.

48 17b iūstīs fūnebribus: 'the regular funeral rites'.

48 25 quae vīsa sunt occultant: i.e. *quae eīs occultanda vīsa sunt, occultant.*

48 29 student: this verb connotes enthusiastic devotion; to say that the Germans were not enthusiastically devoted to sacrifices does not of course imply that they did not practice them at all.   The same remark holds for *Agrī cultūrae nōn student,* line 35.

48 30 eōs sōlōs . . . Sōlem et Vulcānum et Lūnam: a hundred and fifty years later, Tacitus reports that the Germans worship, among others, divinities whom he equates with Mercury, Hercules, Mars, and Isis. Since Tacitus made a much more thorough study of the Germans than Caesar did, either Caesar was misinformed, or the Germans had changed their basic religion in the interval.

48 37 in annōs singulōs: 'for each year'.   See N. 13 1a.

49 1 quīque ūnā coiērunt: 'and (to those) who have banded together'; the principle on which these last-named groups were formed is unknown, but they were presumably composed of those who did not belong to, or for some reason would not work with, a clan (*gēns*) or group of kinsmen (*cognātiō*).

49 2a vīsum est: see NN. 28 30, 48 25.

49 2b agrī: Partitive Genitive with *quantum.*

49 4 studium . . . cultūrā commūtent: with *mūtō* and *commūtō,* 'change', 'exchange', we find an Accusative of the Direct Object and an Ablative of Means; either (as here) the former denotes the thing given in exchange, the latter the thing received, or *vice versa.*   Thus 'I exchanged my sword for a ploughshare' is either *gladium arātrō mūtāvī* or *gladiō arā-trum mūtāvī.*

49 12a Hoc: refers to *solitūdinēs habēre,* and is further explained by the appositives *fīnitimōs cēdere, neque quemquam . . . audēre.*   Cp. N. 46 24.

49 12b proprium: 'a characteristic'.

49 23 profiteantur: for the mood, see N. 13 4b.

49 27 hīs: see N. 42 3b.

49 31 Suēbōrum: the *Suēbī* here mentioned by Caesar dwelt on the river Main.   The name *Suēbī* is a Roman adaptation of a primitive Germanic word; its root is related to that of the Latin *suus.*   The name apparently meant 'their own men', either in the sense of 'men under *their own* rule', i.e. 'independent', or 'men belonging to *their own* race', i.e. not oreigners or slaves.   It has survived in the name of the modern Swabia.

49 33 singula mīlia: 'a thousand each', 'a thousand apiece'.

49 36 ratiō atque ūsus: 'theory and practice'.

49 37 maximam partem: see N. 13 11b.

50 3 ā puerīs: 'from boyhood'; cp. N. 42 24a.

50 5 eam . . . ut: see N. 30 28.

50 6–8 neque . . . et: correlatives (cp. *et . . . et, neque . . . neque*), but we can scarcely say 'neither . . . and'. One way to handle the difficulty is to translate *neque* by a simple negative, 'not', and to bring out the correlative force by strengthening the translation of *et* to 'and moreover'.

50 6 vestītūs: Partitive Genitive with *quicquam*.

50 8 laventur: see N. 15 26.

50 9a eō: 'on this account', explained by the clause *ut . . . habeant*.

50 9b quae bellō cēperint: the antecedent of *quae* would, if expressed, be the object of *vēndant*. For the mood of *cēperint*, cp. *ea quae bellō cēperint . . . dēvovent*, 47 25, and see N. 18 18a, ¶2.

50 9c quibus vēndant: '(men) to whom to sell' (see N. 24 25); the antecedent of *quibus* would, if expressed, be the object of *habeant*.

50 10 quō . . . dēsiderent: *quō* here means 'because'. When a possible reason is introduced, as here, merely to deny its validity, the verb is in the subjunctive: *pugilēs ingemīscunt, nōn quod doleant, sed quia prōfundendā vōce corpus intenditur*, 'boxers groan, not because they are in pain, but because in giving vent to the voice the body is made taut'.

50 11 iūmentīs . . . importātīs . . . ūtuntur: see N. 35 23, ¶2. The word *iūmentīs* here refers only to horses, although *iūmentum* is usually used to mean any draught-animal.

50 14 summī . . . labōris: literally, 'of the utmost laboriousness' (see N. 18 21, ¶2); i.e. 'capable of the utmost exertion'.

50 15 pedibus: 'on foot'; this idiom arose out of usages in which the Ablative of Means is appropriate, e.g. *pedibus eō*, 'go on foot', literally 'go by means of one's feet'; the use of the expression was then extended to contexts in which, as here, the feet are not the means of the action.

50 16 eōdem . . . vestīgiō: see N. 20 12b.

50 17 mōribus: see N. 20 30.

50 19 quemvīs numerum: 'any number whatsoever'; *quemvīs* is from *quīvīs*, i.e. *quī vīs*, literally 'which (ever) you wish'. The adverb *quamvīs*, 'however', is similarly formed from the adverb *quam*.

50 26 Hercyniam silvam: the Hercynian forest was a vast wooded area extending from the sources of the Danube to the Carpathian mountains.

50 27a Eratosthenī (dative): Eratosthenes of Cyrene (third century B.C.), a geographer, astronomer, and mathematician at Alexandria.

50 27b quibusdam Graecīs: we would say 'certain *other* Greeks'.

50 28 Volcae Tectosagēs: the *Volcae* were a Celtic race of which the *Tectosagēs* formed a subdivision (our words Wales and Welsh are related to the word *Volcae*). In translating, use both names, employing the English method of pronunciation (see Vocabulary).

50 31 quā ante: 'as before'; literally 'in which (they were) before'.

50 33 prōvinciārum: the Roman provinces are meant.

50 35a adsuēfactī: in agreement with *Gallī*, the unexpressed subject of *comparant*.

50 35b nē . . . quidem: 'not even'.
50 36 illīs: the Germans.

Notes to Selection 59

51 1a Bellō Helvetiōrum cōnfectō: these words sum up the narrative of Book 1, Chapters 1-29, which immediately precede the present passage. Caesar spent the spring of 58 B.C., the first year of his provincial governorship (see 4 31 - 5 14) in preventing the Helvetians, a Gallic tribe, from carrying out a mass migration in search of new homes, a movement which he held was inimical to the interests of Rome and her Gallic allies. Defeating the Helvetians in a series of battles, he forced them to relinquish their plan and return to their homes in what is now Switzerland. The events narrated in this Selection, which comprises the rest of Book 1, took place during the summer of the same year.

51 1b tōtīus ferē Galliae: here Caesar uses *Gallia* in the narrower sense of Celtic or Central Gaul, by far the largest of the three parts into which Gaul as a whole was divided. Caesar's authority as Roman Governor did not extend beyond the boundaries of the Roman Province of Transalpine Gaul, which lay immediately to the south of Celtic Gaul. The states or tribes (*cīvitātēs*) of Celtic Gaul were independent at this time, but some were bound to Rome by treaties of alliance.

51 2 intellegere sēsē (*dīxērunt*): Caesar often omits a verb of saying governing an Indirect Statement.

51 3a tametsī . . . repetīsset: *tametsī*, 'although', normally introduces the Indicative Mood; cp. N. 30 18, and see N. 14 15b, ¶2.

51 3b prō veteribus Helvetiōrum iniūriīs populī Rōmānī: 'for the ancient wrongs which the Helvetians had inflicted on the Roman people'; the two genitives *Helvetiōrum* and *populī Rōmānī* are connected with the noun *iniūriīs* (see G. 4), the former in a subjective, the latter in an objective relation. In 107 B.C., the Helvetians had killed a Roman consul and humiliated his army.

51 5 ex ūsū: 'to the advantage'; cp. N. 14 22a.

51 6 eō cōnsiliō: explained by the clauses which follow.

51 8 ex magnā cōpiā: sc. *locōrum*.

51 10 stīpendiāriās: predicative, 'as tributaries'.

51 10-12 Petīvērunt—licēret: the fact that the Gallic leaders considered it politic to ask Caesar's permission to call a council shows how commanding a position over the nominally independent Gallic states Caesar's Helvetian victories had gained him. It must be understood that Caesar was not to be present at the first meeting of the council.

51 11 in diem certam: see N. 28 25.

51 14 nē quis ēnūntiāret: that which they were not to divulge was not the plan of holding a meeting, but rather the proceedings of the meeting itself.

51 15 nisi (*eī*) quibus . . . mandātum esset: 'except those to whom it should be entrusted'.

51 17 Eō conciliō dīmissō: we are not given an account of the meeting, but what must have happened there may easily be deduced from what follows.

51 18 sēcrētō refers to the manner of holding the meeting, in occultō to the place where it was to be held.

51 19 agere: 'deal', 'hold a conference'.

51 20 Caesarī: the Dative of Advantage or Disadvantage is occasionally used where the English idiom would lead us to expect a genitive, especially in connection with words denoting parts of the body.

51 21 id: direct object of *contendimus*, 'we strive for'; *id* is explained by the substantive Purpose Clause *nē . . . ēnūntientur*, which is in apposition with it.

51 23 ēnūntiātum erit: impersonal (N. 32 15): 'a report is divulged'.

51 25 Dīviciācus: see N. 45 20.

51 26 factiōnēs . . . duae: cp. 45 3-5.

51 27a Aeduī . . . Arvernī: the Aedui, allies of Rome, were a powerful people dwelling between the upper reaches of the Saône and the Loire; their rivals, the Arverni, were their neighbors to the southwest.

51 27b cum . . . multōs annōs contenderent: 'when they had been fighting for many years'.

51 28a factum est: see N. 39 23.

51 28b Sēquanīs: the Sequani dwelt on the opposite (eastern) side of the Saône from the Aedui. Bitter enmity between the two peoples had arisen from constant disputes over the rights to collect tolls on that river; the Sequani therefore naturally allied themselves with the Arverni.

51 30 XV: *quīndecim*.

51 32 ad centum et vīgintī mīlium numerum: 'about 120,000'; literally, 'to the number of 120,000'.

52 4 frāctī: sc. *Aeduī*.

52 5a hospitiō et amīcitiā: 'cordial relationship and friendship'. *Hospitium* between states bound them to extend hospitality to each other's envoys; cp. N. 62 1.

52 5b plūrimum . . . potuerant: 'had been most powerful'.

52 6 obsidēs: 'as hostages'.

52 9 quōminus . . . essent: see N. 42 21.

52 12 vēnī: in 61 B.C. The Senate, in spite of its professed friendship with the Aedui, did not desire to embroil itself with Ariovistus, and went no further than to pass a rather perfunctory decree, the terms of which are given below (54 28-31).

52 17 tertiam partem: the rich lands of modern Alsace.

52 18 dē alterā parte tertiā: 'from a second third'.

52 19 paucīs mēnsibus ante: see N. 20 2c.

52 20a Harūdum: the Harudes were a German tribe dwelling near the river Elbe.

52 20b XXIIII: *vīgintī quattuor*.

52 20c quibus . . . parārentur: see N. 24 25.

52 22 neque . . . cōnferendus est Gallicus (*ager*) cum Germānōrum agrō: we say "B is not to be compared with A" when we mean that A is immeasurably superior to B; here the idea is expressed in the reverse order.

52 25 ut semel . . . vīcit . . . imperat: 'ever since he conquered, he has been ruling'.

52 26 Magetobrigam: a Gallic town of unknown location.

52 27 nōbilissimī cuiusque (*Gallī*): 'of all the noblest (Gauls)'; literally, 'of each noblest (Gaul)'. *Quisque* is often so used with the superlative.

52 28a exempla: 'punishments'; literally 'examples' to deter others.

52 28b ad: 'according to', 'in response to'.

52 31 quid . . . auxiliī: cp. N. 49 2b.

53 2 Rhēnum trāducātur: some verbs compounded with *circum* and *trāns* may govern two accusatives, one depending on the verb proper, the other on the prefix. The active form would have been *nē Ariovistus maiōrem multitūdinem Rhēnum trādūcat;* in the passive, *multitūdō* is the subject, and *Rhēnum* a Retained Object (cp. N. 36 3c).

53 9 respondēre: see N. 31 10.

53 11 Hōc: 'to this degree' (G. 26); explained by the following *quod*-clause.

53 13 nē . . . quidem: 'not even'.

53 14 velut sī . . . adsit: see N. 17 10.

53 15 tamen: 'at any rate'.

53 16 recēperint . . . sint: for the mood, see N. 32 17b.

53 20 sibi . . . cūrae: see N. 13 11c.

53 21 beneficiō suō: during Caesar's consulship (59 B.C.), Ariovistus was recognized as a king by the Roman Senate; Caesar claims a large share of the credit for obtaining this recognition for him.

53 24a secundum: 'in addition to'.

53 24b multae rēs eum hortābantur quārē . . . putāret: 'many considerations inclined him to think'; literally, 'many considerations urged him, as a result of which fact he thought'; for the mood of *putaret*, see N. 45 7.

53 24-54 1 multae rēs—putābat: this passage is typical of the reasoning whereby Caesar sought to justify his intervention in Gallic affairs (cp. 6 27-32).

53 25 in prīmīs: 'in the first place'.

53 29a quod: 'a thing which'.

53 29b in: 'in view of'.

53 31 Germānōs cōnsuēscere . . . perīculōsum (*esse*) **vidēbat:** 'he perceived that it was dangerous for the Germans to become accustomed'; *Germānōs cōnsuēscere* is an Infinitive Clause (G. 63) used as the subject of *esse*, unexpressed.

53 33 neque sibi hominēs . . . temperātūrōs exīstimābat: 'and he did not think that men would refrain'. The dative of the reflexive is used with *temperō* in the sense 'refrain', followed by *quīn* or *quōminus* (cp. N. 42 21).

53 35a Cimbrī Teutonīque: Germanic tribes which overran Gaul and penetrated into Northern Italy in the closing years of the second century B.C.; see N. 57 7.

53 35b prōvinciam: the Roman Province of Transalpine Gaul (see 5 4-10).

53 37 Rhodanus: the Rhône, which could be forded, did not interpose any real barrier.

54 1a mātūrrimē: a short form of the superlative. The superlative of *mātūrus* is regularly *mātūrissimus*.

54 1b (*sibi*) **occurrendum** (*esse*) **putābat:** 'he believed that it was necessary for him to attend'; for the impersonal use of the gerundive, cp. N. 32 15.

54 5 medium utrĭusque: 'midway between them both'.

54 6 rē pūblicā: 'official business'.

54 7 Sī quid mihi . . . opus esset: 'If I needed anything'; *quid* is the subject of *esset*, while *opus* is in the predicate; the construction is therefore different from that explained in N. 13 11*a*.

54 8 quid . . . mē: both accusative, objects of *vult*. *Volō* may govern two objects, one of the person, the other of the thing, where we say 'want something *from* someone', or . . . *of* someone'.

54 12 mīrum: 'a cause for wonder'.

54 16-18 tantō—appellātus esset: see N. 53 21.

54 19 ut . . . gravārētur neque . . . putāret: this clause explains *hanc grātiam*, 'such gratitude'; cp. N. 30 28.

54 20 dīcendum sibi . . . putāret: cp. N. 54 1*b*.

54 21 quam multitūdinem . . . amplius: 'any number in addition' (to those already brought over).

54 24 illī . . . illīs: the Sequani and the Aedui respectively. The former had exacted hostages from the latter (see 52 6-7), and now, though willing to return them, were prevented from doing so by their nominal ally and real master, Ariovistus.

54 27 sī nōn impetrāret: sc. *Caesar*.

54 28-31 quoniam—dēfenderet: see N. 52 12.

54 28 M. Messālā M. Pīsōne cōnsulibus: 'in the consulship of Messala and Piso': 61 B.C. The Romans regularly dated the year by the names of the consuls in the Ablative Absolute with *cōnsulibus*.

54 29 quod commodō reī pūblicae facere posset: 'in so far as he could do so consistently with the welfare of the (Roman) republic'. For the case of *commodō*, see N. 20 30.

54 31 sē: repeated (cp. *sēsē*, line 28) after the intervening clause *quoniam—dēfenderet* for the sake of clearness.

54 35 ad: see N. 52 28*b*.

55 1 quemadmodum . . . ūtātur: 'how to use'; cp. N. 26 7.

55 7*a* iniūriā: 'unjustly'; see N. 20 30.

55 7*b* eō . . . quod convēnit: 'that which was agreed upon'.

55 9*a* frāternum nōmen: cp. 53 26-27.

55 9*b* Quod: 'In regard to the fact that'.

55 12 quid . . . Germānī . . . virtūte possint: 'of what deeds of valor the Germans are capable'; literally, 'what they can (do) by means of their valor'.

55 13 XIIII: *quattuordecim*.

55 14 et: correlative with *eōdem tempore*, with which it may be joined in translation: 'at the same time as'.

55 15 Trēverīs: the Treveri were a Gallic tribe dwelling in northeastern Gaul; their territories bordered upon the Rhine.

55 17*a* nē obsidibus quidem datīs: 'not even by giving hostages' (G. 30).

55 17*b* pācem Ariovistī: 'peace with Ariovistus' (G. 4).

55 18 pāgōs centum Suēbōrum: cp. 49 32, and N. 49 31.

55 23*a* resistī: see N. 32 15.

55 23*b* rē frūmentāriā: 'grain supply'; cp. N. 32 19*a*.

55 23*c* quam celerrimē potuit: the addition of a form of *possum* to the superlative with *quam* heightens the emphasis: *quam celerrimē*, 'as swiftly as possible'; *quam celerrimē potuit*, 'as swiftly as he possibly could'.

55 24 **magnīs itineribus**: 'by means of forced marches'.

55 27 **quod**: the relative pronoun sometimes, as here, agrees in number and gender with a predicate noun in its own clause (here *oppidum*) rather than with its antecedent (here *Vesontiōnem*).

55 32 **dūcendum**: *dūcō* here means 'prolong'.

55 33 **ut circinō circumductum**: 'as if drawn by a pair of compasses'.

55 35*a* **quod est nōn amplius pedum sēscentōrum**: 'which extends no more than six hundred feet'; literally, 'which is of six hundred feet, not more'; cp. N. 37 26, ¶2.

55 35*b* **quā**: 'where'. The mountain completes the circle almost formed by the loop in the river.

56 1 **ex utrāque parte**: 'on either side'.

56 10 **aciem**: 'keenness', 'sharpness'.

56 13*a* **tribūnīs mīlitum**: see N. 21 23.

56 13*b* **praefectīs**: 'officers' (of the auxiliary corps).

56 14 **Caesarem secūtī**: those mentioned here were young men of noble families, most of them without previous military training, who had joined Caesar's staff for the experience and prestige to be gained there.

56 15*a* **ūsum**: 'experience'.

56 15*b* **Quōrum alius aliā causā inlātā**: 'each one of these alleging a different pretext'. This idiom, in which *alius* is used in two different cases in the same sentence, is quite common: *alius aliud vult*, 'one man wants one thing, another another thing', 'each man wants a different thing'.

56 16 **quam sibi ad proficīscendum necessāriam esse dīceret**: 'so that he might claim it necessitated his departure' (N. 24 25); literally, 'which he might say was necessary to him for departing'.

56 24*a* **centuriōnēs**: the centurions, usually hard-bitten soldiers who had risen from the ranks, formed the backbone of the Roman army. Each commanded a company (*centuria* or *ōrdō*) which in Caesar's army normally numbered about sixty men. There were sixty such companies in a legion.

56 24*b* **quī . . . equitātuī praeerant**: 'the cavalry officers'.

56 25 **Quī . . . ex hīs**: 'those of them who'.

56 28 **rem frūmentāriam ut . . . supportārī posset**: i.e. *ut rēs frūmentāria supportārī posset*. The preceding accusatives *angustiās* and *magnitūdinem* led Caesar to place *rem frūmentāriam* in the accusative also, thus bringing it outside the clause of which it is logically the subject.

56 30*a* **signa ferrī**: 'the march to begin'; literally, 'the standards to be carried', the military technical term for the order to proceed.

56 30*b* **iussisset**: see N. 14 15*b*; the direct form would be *iusseris*.

56 30*c* **dictō audientēs**: 'obedient to his command'; when *audiō* means 'obey', it may govern the dative like other verbs of similar meaning. For *fore . . . audientēs*, cp. N. 41 20*b*.

56 32 **omnium . . . ōrdinum . . . centuriōnibus**: 'the centurions of all the companies' (see N. 56 24*a*). Ordinarily only the six highest-ranking centurions of each legion participated in councils of war, but in this instance Caesar was desirous of reaching all his men through their immediate superiors.

56 34a **quod** . . . **putārent:** 'because, as he said, they believed' (N. 18 18a, ¶2).

56 34b **quam in partem** . . . **quō cōnsiliō dūcerentur:** Indirect Questions depending on *quaerendum aut cōgitandum.*

56 36 **mē cōnsule:** 59 B.C. (cp. N. 54 28); see N. 53 21.

56 37 **cur** . . . **quisquam** . . . **iūdicet?:** 'why should anyone believe?'; see N. 26 7, ¶2.

57 1 **Mihi** . . . **persuādētur:** 'I am convinced'; a verb which, like *persuādeō*, regularly governs the dative case, cannot have a personal subject in the passive; the impersonal third person singular is therefore used, literally 'persuasion is brought to bear upon (*to*) me'.

57 3 **Quod sī:** 'But if'.

57 6 **periculum:** 'trial', 'test'.

57 7 **Cimbris et Teutonīs ā C. Mariō pulsīs:** C. Marius was born c. 156 B.C. near Arpinum in Central Italy, of sturdy farmer folk. As a young man he served in the Roman army in Spain. After a period of political activity at Rome, he won military renown in Africa, where he served against Jugurtha of Numidia, first under the consul Metellus (109-108 B.C.), then as consul himself (107). In 106 he brought the Jugurthine War to a successful conclusion, thus gaining recognition as Rome's most competent general. When the Germanic hordes of the Cimbri and the Teutoni, which had overrun Gaul with irresistible force, destroyed two Roman armies which had been sent against them (105), Marius was elected consul for 104 to meet the emergency, though precedent forbade re-election after so short an interval. He reorgani: ed the army, trained it thoroughly, and finally succeeded in defeating the Teutoni in 102 B.C., the Cimbri in the following year. To make it possible for him to accomplish this, he was re-elected consul, in even greater defiance of precedent, for the years 103, 102, and 101 B.C. See also N. 26 8a.

57 8 **meritus** (*esse*) **vidēbātur:** 'plainly deserved'; literally, 'was seen to have deserved'; *meritus esse* is deponent.

57 9a **servīlī tumultū:** see G. 25. A great uprising of slaves, under the gladiator Spartacus, had occurred in 73-71 B.C. Many of these were of Germanic origin, and had received training as gladiators (*ūsus ac disciplīna quam ā nōbīs accēperant,* line 10), which should have rendered them more formidable.

57 9b **quōs:** i.e. the slaves; the antecedent is implied in the word *servīlī.*

57 10 **tamen aliquid** . . . **sublevābant:** 'helped somewhat, at any rate'; *aliquid* is Adverbial Accusative (N. 13 11b).

57 11 **bonī:** Partitive Genitive with *quantum.*

57 12 **inermēs:** even at the beginning of the uprisings, when the slaves were as yet unarmed, they caused great consternation.

57 13a **timuistis,** . . . **superāvistis:** the members of the council are addressed as representing the Roman people in general.

57 13b **victōrēs:** the slaves met with a great measure of success before they were finally crushed.

57 16 **qui tamen:** 'and yet they', i.e. the Helvetians. The argument is *ā fortiōrī:* we have defeated the Helvetians, the Helvetians have often (*plērumque*) defeated the Germans, therefore we can defeat the Germans.

57 17 adversum proelium: at Magetobriga (cp. 52 25-26).
57 19 castrīs sē . . . **tenuisset:** 'had hidden himself in (literally 'by means of') camp'.
57 20a suī potestātem fēcisset: 'given them an opportunity to fight with him'.
57 20b (Gallōs) dēspērantēs iam dē pugnā: 'the Gauls, who were at last giving up hope of battle'.
57 22 Cui ratiōnī . . . **locus fuit:** 'a plan for which there was an opening'. For the 'incorporation of the antecedent' cp. N. 28 6. *Ratiōne* is of course to be supplied with *hāc,* line 23.
57 24 capī: 'deceived'.
57 25 Quī suum timōrem in simulātiōnem . . . **cōnferunt:** 'Those who attribute their fear to a pretended concern'.
57 28 Leucī Lingonēs: two Gallic tribes who were neighbors of the Sequani on the north and west.
57 31 Quod: 'as to the fact that'.
57 32 quibuscumque . . . **dictō audiēns nōn fuerit:** see N. 56 30c, here the entire expression *dictō audiēns sum* is regarded as a verb of obeying, and governs the dative *quibuscumque.* The clause *quibuscumque* . . . *fuerit* is to be regarded as a substantive in the dative case, serving as the object of *defuisse,* and as Dative of Disadvantage with *avaritiam esse convictam:* 'I know that whoever has had an army mutiny against him has either managed badly (N. 35 19b) and been lacking in good fortune, or, through the discovery of some crime (which he committed) has had his rapacity proved (to the army)'. Caesar means that mutiny can arise only out of one of two circumstances: a commander's persistent lack of good fortune (the Romans were very superstitious about *fēlīcitās,* 'good luck'), or his criminal rapacity.
57 37 dē quārtā vigiliā: 'during the fourth watch'. The Romans divided the hours between sunset and sunrise into four equal *vigiliae,* 'watches', which naturally varied in duration with the seasons.
58 4 praetōria cohors: the Praetorian Cohort formed the general's private bodyguard, and occupied a position of great honor in the army.
58 6 mīrum in modum: 'in a remarkable way'; see N. 36 26.
58 8 princeps: 'first of all'.
58 11a cum tribūnīs . . . **et** . . . **centuriōnibus ēgērunt:** 'took the matter up with their tribunes and centurions'.
58 11b prīmōrum ōrdinum centuriōnibus: 'the centurions of the highest ranking companies'. The legion was divided into ten cohorts, each of which contained six companies (*centuriae, ōrdinēs*). The six companies of the highest ranking cohort were called *prīmī ōrdinēs,* and their centurions were the six who regularly attended the councils of war (see N. 56 32).
58 12 satis facerent: 'make amends'.
58 13 suum iūdicium . . . **esse:** 'that the discretion was theirs'.
58 15 exquīsītō: 'ascertained'.
58 16 mīlium (passuum) amplius quinquāginta circuitū: 'by a circuitous route of over fifty miles'; cp. N. 37 26. Caesar was evidently trying to avoid places which would have given Ariovistus an opportunity for ambuscade (cp. *locīs apertīs,* line 17).

58 19 certior factus est: 'he was informed': a favorite idiom of Caesar's; the active is *aliquem certiōrem faciō*, 'I inform someone'.

58 20 mīlia passuum quattuor et vīgintī: see G. 15.

58 23 id per sē fierī licēre: 'he had no objection to its being done'; see N. 37 3*b*.

58 24 accessisset: sc. *Caesar*.

58 25 exīstimāret: sc. *Ariovistus*.

58 26 petentī: sc. *Caesarī*.

58 28 cognitis suīs postulātīs: 'once his demands were understood'.

58 29 fore utī . . . dēsisteret: see N. 28 13*b*.

58 31 ultrō citrōque: 'back and forth'; in Latin the adverbs are in the reverse order.

58 34 aliā ratiōne: 'otherwise'; literally, 'according to (any) other plan'.

58 35 tollī: 'to be cancelled' (by Ariovistus). ·

58 36 Gallōrum equitātuī: in the Gallic campaigns Caesar had no Roman cavalry.

58 37 Gallīs equitibus: 'from the Gallic cavalry'; see N. 42 3*b*.

59 1 eō mīlitēs . . . impōnere: 'to mount the soldiers upon them'; literally, '. . . thereupon'.

59 3*a* sī quid opus factō esset: see N. 30 11*b*.

59 3*b* nōn inrīdiculē: 'not without wit'.

59 5 in cohortis praetōriae locō: see 58 2-4, and N. 58 4.

59 6 ad equum rescrībere: 'was (actually) enrolling them among the *equitēs*'.   The point of the jest lies in the fact that the term *equitēs Rōmānī*, which originally denoted the Roman cavalry, had come to be used as the title of the lesser nobility, the 'Roman knights'.   The old term for 'enrolling in the cavalry', *ad equum rescrībere*, had therefore assumed the sense of 'raising to knighthood'.

59 7*a* Plānitiēs . . . magna: the plain of Alsace.   It was in this region that all the subsequent events narrated in this Selection took place.

59 7*b* satis: 'rather', 'fairly'.

59 9 erat dictum: 'had been agreed'.

59 10 passibus ducentīs ab eō tumulō: 'two hundred paces away from that mound'; to denote the distance which separates two points, Caesar uses either the Ablative of Degree of Difference, as here, or the Accusative of Extent, as in *aequum spatium*, line 8.

59 12 ex equīs: we would say 'on horseback'.

59 15 quod . . . appellātus esset: cp. N. 18 18*a*.

59 16 mūnera: it was the custom of the Roman Senate to send gifts to those whose kingly title it recognized.

59 18*a* tribuī depends on *cōnsuēsse*.

59 18*b* aditum: 'means of approach' (to the Senate).

59 21 quam veterēs . . . causae: 'how ancient (were the) causes (which)'.

59 22 ipsīs (= *Rōmānīs*) cum Aeduīs intercēderent: 'existed between the Romans and the Aeduans'.

59 23 ut: 'how'.

59 26 suī: genitive singular neuter of the possessive adjective, used substantively: 'of their own'.

59 27 grātiā: 'influence'.

59 28 quod . . . ad amīcitiam populī Rōmānī attulissent: 'what they had brought to the Roman alliance'; i.e. what they already had when they became Roman allies, namely their independence and the leadership of Gaul.

59 29 quis . . . posset?: 'who could?' The Deliberative Subjunctive of the Direct Discourse (*quis possit*) is retained, with the necessary change of tense (G. 60), in the indirect. Cp. N. 26 7.

59 32 at: 'at any rate'.

60 4 ūnō . . . proeliō: cp. 52 26.

60 9 per populum Rōmānum: 'through (the interference of) the Romans'.

60 10 remittētur: 'is remitted', 'is cancelled'; i.e. if the Gauls are freed by the Romans from their obligations to Ariovistus.

60 14 nisi rogātus: 'without being asked'.

60 16-17 Galliam . . . Galliae: Ariovistus means the part of Gaul north of the Roman province.

60 18 cūr . . . vēnerīs: 'that you have come'; cp. NN. 40 32, 45 7.

60 19a haec . . . Gallia: 'this (part of) Gaul'; see N. 60 16-17.

60 19b illa: the Roman Province of Transalpine Gaul.

60 19c Ut: 'just as'.

60 19d mihi concēdī nōn oportēret: 'it would not be right to yield to me'. The impersonal passive infinitive¦ (N. 32 15) is the subject of *oportēret*.

60 24 bellō Allobrogum proximō: the Allobroges, a Gallic tribe inhabiting the most northern part of the Roman Province, had revolted and been subdued three years before.

60 25a ipsōs: sc. *Aeduōs*.

60 25b contentiōnibus: cp. 51 27-52 10.

60 27 quem exercitum . . . habēs: see N. 28 6.

60 31 multīs nōbilibus prīncipibusque: Caesar had many bitter enemies among the Roman aristocracy; cp. NN. 36 3a, 36 3b, and the whole of Selection 45.

60 32 id . . . compertum habeō: 'I have learned this'; literally, 'I possess this having been learned'. This is an interesting forerunner of the use of the derivatives of *habeō* as auxiliary verbs in the Romance languages.

61 1 in eam sententiam . . . quārē . . . nōn posset: 'to explain why he could not'; literally, 'toward this idea, why . . . '. Cp. N. 38 19b.

61 5a Rutēnī: a Gallic tribe dwelling between the territory of the Arverni and the Roman Province.

61 5b Q. Fabiō Maximō: consul in 121 B.C., in which year he and Cn. Domitius Ahenobarbus administered a severe defeat to several Gallic tribes.

61 6 neque in prōvinciam (eōs) redēgit: 'and did not include them in the Province'; i.e. left them independent.

61 7 antīquissimum quodque tempus: 'the records of antiquity'; literally, 'each most ancient period'; cp. N. 52 27.

61 10a suīs lēgibus ūtī: 'to be independent'; literally, 'to use its own laws'.

61 10*b* **voluit: sc.** *senātus.*

61 17 **committendum** (*esse*) **nōn putābat ut . . . dīcī posset:** 'he did not think that the matter should be so conducted that it might be said'.

61 18 **per fidem:** 'through their trust (in his integrity)'.

61 19*a* **elātum est:** 'was reported', 'became known'; cp. N. **41** 6.

61 19*b* **quā adrogantiā . . . ūsus:** 'with (literally 'using') what arrogance'.

61 20 **Galliā Rōmānīs interdīxisset:** 'had ordered the Romans out of Gaul'; see N. **45** 29.

61 22 **ut:** 'how'.

61 26 **sī . . . minus** is often used in the sense of *sī . . . nōn.*

61 28*a* **causa** (*esse*) **vīsa nōn est:** 'there did not seem to be (sufficient) reason'.

61 28*b* **eō magis:** 'all the more'; for the case of *eō*, see G. 26; it is explained by the following *quod*-clause.

61 30 **sēsē magnō cum perīculō . . . missūrum:** 'that it would be very dangerous to send'; literally, 'that he would send (if he should do so) with great danger'.

61 31 **obiectūrum:** 'place at the mercy of'.

61 32 **C. Valerium Procillum:** a Romanized Gaul, a member of the tribe of the Helvii, who dwelt within the Province.

61 34*a* **C. Valeriō Flaccō:** Governor of the Roman Province of Transalpine Gaul in 83 B.C. Note that the Gaul Caburus, in receiving Roman citizenship (*cīvitās*) from C. Valerius Flaccus, adopted the latter's *praenōmen* and *nōmen*, and kept his Gallic name as a *cognōmen* (see **8** 18 - **9** 12).

61 34*b* **et propter fidem . . . et propter . . . scientiam . . . et quod . . . esset:** reasons for Procillus' suitability as an envoy.

61 35 **quā multā . . . Ariovistus . . . ūtēbātur:** 'which Ariovistus spoke fluently'.

61 36 **in eō:** 'in his case'.

61 37 **peccandī . . . causa:** 'reason for acting unjustly': Caesar thought that, as a Gaul, Procillus would avoid the almost certain doom that a Roman would have met at Ariovistus' hands.

62 1 **hospitiō Ariovistī ūtēbātur:** 'was on terms of mutual hospitality with Ariovistus'. Among the Romans *hospitium*, 'guest-friendship', was a solemn relationship between two men of different cities which bound each to offer the hospitality and protection of his home to the other and his kin.

62 4 **An**, 'or', is regularly used to introduce the second part of a disjunctive question; sometimes, as here, the first part (e.g. 'Was it for some honest purpose?') is omitted, and the use of *an* with the second alternative serves to indicate remonstrance, surprise, reproof, or irony. In such cases, it is better not to translate *an*.

62 6 **castra prōmōvit:** *castra prōmoveō* is the technical term for moving one's camp to a location nearer the enemy. Ariovistus was north of Caesar, and therefore moved south to meet him.

62 7 **cōnsēdit:** still to the north of Caesar's position.

62 8 **ultrā:** having passed Caesar's camp (*praeter castra*, line 7), Ariovistus was now 'beyond' him to the south-east. He was thus in a position to cut Caesar off (*interclūderet*, line 10) from supplies coming from the

South, until, as we shall see, Caesar established a small camp still further south.

62 12 ut . . . nōn deesset: the use of *ut* . . *nōn* in a Purpose Clause is most exceptional. It is probably to be explained on the ground that *nōn deesset* is thought of as equivalent to *adesset*, 'might be at hand'.

62 14 castrīs continuit: cp. N. 57 19.

62 18a ex omnī cōpiā: 'from the entire army'.

62 18b singulī (*equitēs*) **singulōs** (*peditēs*): 'each cavalryman (choosing) a single infantryman'. These infantrymen (denoted by *hīs, hōs, hī,* and *hōrum* below) served as assistants to the cavalrymen.

62 19 sē . . . recipiēbant: 'would return' (if they had occasion to ride away from them).

62 20a dūrius: 'unusually hazardous'.

62 20b concurrēbant: 'would run up to assist them'.

62 20c sī quī: see N. 46 6.

62 21 quō: 'in any direction'.

62 23 iubīs sublevātī: 'hanging on to (literally, 'supported by') the horses' manes'.

62 32a numerō: this apparently superfluous Ablative of Specification is often used by Caesar.

62 32b expedīta: 'light-armed'; the adjective agrees with *mīlia*, instead of with *hominum*, as we might expect.

62 34 Nihilō sētius: 'none the less'. Cp. N. 61 28b.

62 36 auxiliōrum: 'auxiliary troops'.

63 1 īnstitūtō suō: 'in accordance with his established practice'.

63 7 pugnātum est: see N. 32 15.

63 10 proeliō . . . dēcertāret: i.e. in a decisive battle with all his forces, instead of in the skirmishes which had occurred thus far.

63 13 utrum . . . necne: 'whether or not'.

63 14 fās: 'fated'.

63 16a praesidiō . . . utrīsque castrīs: 'to protect each camp'; see N. 13 11c.

63 16b quod satis esse vīsum est: i.e. a sufficient number of soldiers.

63 17 alāriōs: 'auxiliary troops', made up of non-Romans.

63 18 minus . . . valēbat: 'was weaker'.

63 19a prō: 'in comparison with'.

63 19b ad speciem: i.e. to deceive Ariovistus into thinking that they, too, were legionaries.

63 25 circumdedērunt: not, of course, in a complete circle, but in a great semicircle covering the wings and rear.

63 26 Eō . . . imposuērunt: cp. N. 59 1.

63 27a proficīscentēs 'the men as they went forth'.

63 27b passīs manibus: 'with hands outstretched' (in an attitude of supplication). *Passīs* is from *pandō*.

63 29 singulīs legiōnibus singulōs lēgātōs et quaestōrem: i.e. one high-ranking officer in charge of each legion. Caesar had six legions; one of these he placed in charge of a Quartermaster-General (*quaestor*), the other five each under a Lieutenant-General (*lēgātus*).

63 30a testēs suae . . . virtūtis: the men naturally fought more valiantly when they felt that their bravery would be noted and rewarded.

63 **30***b* **ab dextrŏ cornū:** 'on the right wing'.

63 **31** **eam partem:** i.e. the corresponding (left) wing of the enemy.

63 **32** **commīsit:** 'commenced'.

63 **35** **Relictīs:** 'cast aside'.

63 **36** **phalange:** 'phalanx', a dense formation of soldiers with shields interlocked.

64 **2** **ā sinistrŏ cornū . . . ā dextrŏ cornū:** i.e. on the enemy's left and right, corresponding to Caesar's right and left.

64 **4** **P. Crassus:** son of Caesar's associate in the First Triumvirate (see **4** 24-30).

64 **5** **expedītior:** 'less encumbered', 'able to move more easily'.

64 **6***a* **tertiam aciem:** this had been kept in reserve.

64 **6***b* **labōrantibus nostrīs subsidiō:** 'to aid our men who were hard-pressed'; see N. **13** 11*c*.

64 **9** **fugere:** in spite of the semicircle of wagons which was supposed to prevent flight (cp. **63** 25-26).

64 **11** **vīribus cōnfīsī:** see N. **21** 1*b*.

64 **12** **Ariovistus . . . prŏfūgit:** we know nothing further of his career, save that he died within five years of this battle.

64 **14** **Duae . . . uxōrēs:** among the Germans polygamy seems to have been practiced only by the chiefs, probably for reasons of state, as in this instance (cp. *rēgis Vocciōnis soror*, line 16).

64 **16***a* **Nŏrica:** the Norici dwelt in the region between the Danube and the Alps.

64 **16***b* (*in matrimōnium*) **dūxerat:** see N. **32** 17*c*; *duxerat* in the preceding line has of course the ordinary meaning 'had brought'.

64 **19***a* **C. Valerius Procillus:** see **61** 32-37.

64 **19***b* **trīnīs catēnīs vīnctus:** 'bound by three chains'; the distributive numeral *trīnī, -ae, -a*, 'three at a time', 'three by three', is employed because *catēnae* is regularly used in the plural to refer to a single chain (cp. *litterae*, 'an epistle', and our word 'scissors').

64 **20** **equitātū:** in military expressions the Ablative of Accompaniment occurs without *cum* (cp. G. 19). This usage probably developed from the attitude of officers who regarded soldiers as the means by which, rather than as persons in whose company, military objectives are attained.

64 **23** **hospitem:** 'guest-friend'; cp. N. **62** 1.

64 **26** **cōnsultum** (*esse*): see N. **32** 15.

64 **28** **M. Maecius:** see **62** 1.

64 **31***a* **qui . . . incolunt:** 'those who dwell'.

64 **31***b* **proximī Rhēnum:** 'nearest the Rhine'; cp. N. **14** 4.

64 **33** **duŏbus . . . bellīs:** the campaign against the Helvetians (see N. **51** 1*a*) and that against Ariovistus.

64 **34** **tempus annī:** it was now the latter part of September.

64 **35***a* **in hiberna in Sēquānōs:** 'to winter-quarters in the territory of the Sequani'. See N. **24** 1. The fact that Caesar quartered his troops among the Sequani instead of withdrawing them to the Province shows that he was definitely committed to a policy of conquest.

64 **35***b* **Labiēnum:** T. Labienus, a Lieutenant-General (*lēgātus*), was Caesar's right-hand man throughout the Gallic Wars.

64 **36***a* **citeriōrem Galliam:** the Province of Cisalpine Gaul (i.e. Gaul on this side—the Roman side—of the Alps). This comprised the northern part of the Italian peninsula, from the River Rubicon to the Alps. It was called 'Gaul' because it was largely inhabited by Gallic tribes which had crossed the Alps in the fifth and fourth centuries B.C.

64   36b ad conventūs agendōs: 'to hold court'. As provincial governor, Caesar had judicial as well as military duties. In addition, he preferred to winter in Northern Italy so as to keep in closer touch with the political situation in Rome.

IV. PHAEDRUS

(See pp. 7-8)

The Metre of the Fables

1. The following is a brief statement of some important principles of Latin verse.

A. **Quantity.** A syllable is long if it contains (1) a long vowel, (2) a diphthong, or (3) a vowel, even if short, immediately followed by two consonants. In the last-named instance, the two consonants need not be in the same word. Thus in the verse

fugitant inertēs; vōcem praeclūdit metus, **66 14,**

the syllables *-tēs, vō-,* and *-clū-* are long because each contains a long vowel; the syllable *prae-* is long because it contains a diphthong; the syllables *-tant, -ner-, -cem,* and *-dit* are long because each contains a vowel immediately followed by two consonants (in the last two examples the second consonant belongs to the next word). A syllable which belongs to none of these groups is short: so *fu-, -gi-, i-, me-,* and *-tus.*

Note: In determining quantity, *h* does not count as a consonant, *qu* regularly counts as a single consonant, while *x* and *z* each count as two consonants. A syllable containing a short vowel followed by a mute (*b, p, ph, d, t, th, g, c, qu, ch*) and a liquid (*l, m, n, r*) may for the purposes of verse be either long or short.

B. **Elision.** A vowel at the end of a word is elided if the next word in the verse begins with a vowel or *h-:*

Ant(e) hōs sex mēnsēs mal(e), ait, dīxistī mihi, **65 10.**

Elision also takes place if a word ends in a vowel followed by *-m,* and the next word in the verse begins with a vowel or *h-:*

Tum quid(am) ex illīs, quos prius dēspexerat, **66 30.**

Tunc moriēns vōc(em) hanc ēdidisse dīcitur, **70 8.**

Inverse elision occurs when a word ending in a vowel or *-m* is followed by the word *est:*

Haec propter illōs scrīpta (e)st hominēs fābula, **65 14.**

Hoc illīs dictum (e)st, quibus honōrem et glōriam, **68 3.**

The present practice in reading is to omit the elided letters entirely; in the classical period they may have been sounded lightly, or blended with the following (or, in the case of inverse elision, with the preceding) syllable.

C. Syllaba Anceps. In all Latin verse, the last syllable of the line may be either long or short, regardless of the normal structure of the metre in which the syllable appears. It is therefore called *syllaba anceps*, 'the doubtful syllable'.

2. The metre of the Fables is the Iambic Senarius, a verse consisting of six (*sēnī*) Iambi: $\overset{1}{\smile}\perp \mid \overset{2}{\smile}\perp \mid \overset{3}{\smile}\perp \mid \overset{4}{\smile}\perp \mid \overset{5}{\smile}\perp \mid \overset{6}{\smile}\perp$

Any of the first five Iambi may be replaced by one of the following feet, with the limitations noted:

Spondee	$- \perp$
Dactyl	$- \smile \smile$
Tribrach	$\smile \smile \smile$
Anapaest	$\smile \smile \perp$
Proceleusmatic	$\smile \smile \smile \smile$

The accents noted above apply only when these feet are substituted for Iambi. The Anapaest is usually restricted to the first and fifth feet; the Proceleusmatic appears only in the first foot.

The sixth foot, because it contains the Syllaba Anceps (see 1C above), may appear either as an Iambus ($\smile \perp$) or as a Pyrrhic ($\smile \smile$).

A caesura, or break in the verse (*caesūra*, 'cutting'), will usually be found just before the stressed syllable of the third foot, less often just before the stressed syllable of the fourth foot; it is marked by the symbol $\|$.

The following verses exemplify the points noted above:

$- \perp \mid\quad \smile \perp \mid - \quad\| \smile \smile \mid \smile \perp \mid - \perp \mid \smile \smile \perp$
Ad ri|v(um) eun|dem $\|$ lupus | et ag|nus ve|nerant, 65 1.

$\smile \perp \mid - \quad \perp \quad \mid - \perp \mid - \quad\| \perp \mid - \perp \mid \smile \smile$
Athe|nae cum | flore|rent $\|$ ae|quis le|gibus, 65 16.

$- \perp \mid - \quad \perp \quad \mid - \|\smile \smile \smile \quad \perp \mid \quad \smile \smile \perp \mid \smile \smile$
Qui pos|sum, quae|so, $\|$ face|re quod | quereris, | lupe, 65 7.

$- \perp \mid \smile \perp \mid \smile \quad\| \smile \smile \mid - \perp \mid - \perp \mid \smile \smile$
Respon|dit ag|nus: $\|$ "Equi|dem na|tus non | eram, 65 11.

$\smile \smile \perp \mid \smile \perp \mid - \perp \mid - \quad\| \perp \mid - \quad\smile \smile$
alium | rogan|tes re|gem $\|$ mi|ser(e) ad | Iovem, 66 10.

$\smile \smile \smile \smile \mid - \quad \perp \mid - \quad\| \smile \smile \mid - \perp \mid - \quad\perp \mid \smile \smile$
Ita caput | ad nos|trum $\|$ furor | illo|rum per|tinet, 73 6.

Notes to Selection 60

(Cp. LA FONTAINE, FABLES 1.10, LE LOUP ET L'AGNEAU)

65 2*a* **sitī**: see N. 21 14*a*.
65 2*b* **superior**: 'upstream'; literally, 'higher'.
65 3 **fauce**: 'hunger'; literally, 'throat'.
65 4 **latrō**: i.e. the Wolf.
65 6 **contrā**: '(said) in reply'.
65 7 **Quī**: 'how'; an old ablative form of *quī, quae, quod*.
65 8 **ad meōs haustūs**: 'to where I am drinking'; literally, 'to my draughts'.

65 10a Ante hōs sex mēnsēs: 'six months ago'.
65 10b male . . . dīxistī mihi: 'you slandered me'.
65 13 (agnum) correptum lacerat: see N. 20 14b.

Notes to Selection 61

(Cp. LaFontaine, Fables 3.4, Les Grenouilles qui demandent un Roi)

65 17 miscuit: 'threw into confusion'.
65 18 frēnum: 'restraint', 'sobriety'; literally, 'bridle'. The figure is taken from horsemanship; cp. our word 'unbridled'.
65 19 Arcem tyrannus occupat Pīsistratus: see N. 38 2. The seizure of the citadel of course betokened the coup d'état by which Pisistratus became 'tyrant'.
65 22 īnsuētīs: 'to those who are not accustomed (to it)'.
65 23 Aesōpus: see N. 30 20a.
65 24 līberīs palūdibus: 'in the freedom of their marshes'; literally, 'in their free marshes'. Latin poets frequently omit the preposition in the construction of Ablative of Place Where; cp. G. 23.
65 25 petiēre: in the third person plural perfect indicative active, the ending -ēre is sometimes found instead of -ērunt.
66 2a subitō modifies missum.
66 2b vadī is to be taken with mōtū sonōque in the next verse.
66 4 diūtius: 'for a rather long time'; cp. N. 14 13b.
66 5 ūna: sc. rāna.
66 7 positō: i.e. dēpositō, 'discarded', 'dismissed'.
66 8 lignum . . . suprā: the poets often reverse the order of preposition and noun.
66 9 Quod: i.e. the Log.
66 10 alium rogantēs rēgem: '(messengers) requesting another king'.
66 14a inertēs: 'unskillfully'.
66 14b vōcem praeclūdit metus: i.e. they were speechless with terror.
66 16 contrā: see N. 65 6.
66 18 ait: sc. Aesōpus.

Notes to Selection 62

(Cp. LaFontaine, Fables 4.9, Le Geai paré des plumes du Paon)

66 20 Nē glōriārī (nōbīs) libeat aliēnis bonīs: 'so that we may not be disposed to glorify ourselves with possessions belonging to another'. Glōriārī is the subject of the impersonal verb libeat.
66 23 pāvōnī: see N. 42 3b.
66 29 trīstem sustinuit notam: 'suffered severe chastisement'.
66 34 tua . . . calamitās: 'you, in your wretchedness'; literally, 'your wretchedness'. Phaedrus is peculiarly fond of using an abstract noun to denote a person or persons possessing the quality which the noun signifies.

Notes to Selection 63

(Cp. LaFontaine, Fables 6.17, Le Chien qui lâche sa proie pour l'ombre)

67 1 meritō: adverb.
67 5a vērum: adverb, 'but'.
67 5b dēcepta aviditās: 'he, in his misguided greed'; cp. N. 66 34.
67 6 et . . . nec: cp. N. 50 6-8.
67 7 nec . . . potuit adeō: 'still less was he able'.

Notes to Selection 64

(Cp. LaFontaine, Fables 1.6, La Génisse, la Chèvre, et la Brebis en société avec le Lion)

67 8 fidēlis: 'trustworthy', 'safe'.
67 10 patiēns . . . iniūriae: 'tolerant of mistreatment'.
67 13 partibus factīs: i.e. when the prey had been divided into four parts.
67 14 prīmam and the other ordinal numerals which follow all modify *partem* or *pars* unexpressed.
67 16 plūs valeō: 'I am stronger'.
67 17 malō adficiētur: 'he will be severely punished'.
67 18 improbitās: we may translate 'His Royal Wickedness' on the model of 'His Royal Highness'. Cp. N. 66 34.

Notes to Selection 65

(Cp. LaFontaine, Fables 6.12, Le Soleil et les Grenouilles)

67 19 celebrēs: 'crowded'.
67 20 continuō: 'straightway'.
67 21 Uxōrem . . . dūcere: see N. 32 17c.
67 26a miserās: sc. *nōs.*
67 26b āridā sēde: see N. 65 24.
67 27 creārit: shortened form of *creāverit;* see N. 14 9.

Notes to Selection 66

(Cp. LaFontaine, Fables 4.14, Le Renard et le Buste)

68 1 Persōnam tragicam: the Greek tragic actor wore a mask which covered not only the face, but the greater part of the head.
68 3 illis: 'in the interest of those' (G. 8).

Notes to Selection 67

(Cp. LaFontaine, Fables 3.9, Le Loup et la Cicogne)

68 5 pretium meritī: 'a recompense for services'.
68 6 bis peccat: 'commits two errors'. The first is an error from the ethical, the second from the practical standpoint.

68 7a **deinde:** 'secondly'.
68 7b **iam:** 'then', i.e. after he has served them.
68 8 **fauce:** see N. **65** 24.
68 9 **singulōs:** '(the other creatures) one by one'.
68 11 **persuāsa est gruis:** this use of *persuadeō* in the passive with a personal subject is most irregular; the normal construction would be *gruī persuāsum est;* cp. N. **57** 1.
68 12 **crēdēns:** 'entrusting'.
68 13 **perīculōsam:** i.e. to herself.
68 15a **ōre** . . . **ē nostrō:** see N. **66** 8.
68 15b **quae** . . . **abstulerīs et** . . . **postulēs:** see N. **32** 17b.

Notes to Selection 68

(CP. LAFONTAINE, FABLES 5.17, LE LIÈVRE ET LA PERDRIX)

68 21 **Quid:** 'Why'; see N. **13** 11b.
68 24a **sēmanimus:** shortened form of *sēmianimus,* used for metrical reasons.
68 24b **Mortis** . . . **sōlācium:** 'consolation for my death'.
68 25 **modo:** 'just now'.
68 26 **similī:** 'like (my own)'; cp. line 19, *flētūs ēdentem gravēs.*

Notes to Selection 69

(CP. LAFONTAINE, FABLES 2.3, LE LOUP PLAIDANT CONTRE LE RENARD PAR-DEVANT LE SINGE)

69 1 **turpī fraude:** 'for (literally 'by means of') base fraudulence'.
69 4 **arguēbat** . . . **fūrtī crīmine:** 'accused of theft'; literally, 'accused by a charge of theft'. The word *crīmine* is really superfluous.
69 5 **culpae proximam:** 'guilty'; literally, 'next to the guilt', i.e. connected with it.
69 9 **Tu—petis:** addressed to the Wolf.
69 10 **tē—negās:** addressed to the Fox.

Notes to Selection 70

(CP. LAFONTAINE, FABLES 2.19, LE LION ET L'ANE CHASSANT)

69 11 **Virtūtis expers verbīs iactāns glōriam:** 'One who lacks valor, but exalts his own glory with words'.
69 12a **ignōtōs:** here has an active meaning, 'those who do not know (him)'.
69 12b **nōtīs est dērīsuī:** 'is an object of ridicule to those who know him' (see N. **13** 11c.).
69 13 **asellō comite:** G. 30.
69 15 **insuētā:** 'unfamiliar' to the wild beasts.
69 16a **fugientēs ipse exciperet:** '(saying) that he himself would intercept them as they fled'. Under the influence of *terrēret,* the subjunctive is used here irregularly instead of the Infinitive with Subject-Accusative: *sē exceptūrum esse.*

uy 100 hic: adverb.
69 22 premere: 'restrain'.
69 24 nōssem: shorter form of nōvissem (see N. 14 9), from nōscō.

Notes to Selection 71

(Cp. LaFontaine, Fables 6.9, Le Cerf se voyant dans l'eau)

69 26 Laudātīs (esse) ūtiliōra (ea) quae contempserīs saepe invenīrī: 'that the things which you have despised are often found to be more useful than the things which you have praised'. Laudātīs is the ablative plural neuter of the perfect passive participle of laudō, used as a substantive in the Ablative of Comparison, 'than the praised things'.
70 3 vēnantum: 'of the huntsmen'; in the present participle, the genitive plural in -um instead of -ium is occasionally found in verse.
70 5 Silva . . . excēpit ferum: 'the Stag took refuge in the woods'; literally, 'the woods received the wild animal'.
70 6 retentīs: by the branches of the trees.
70 7 lacerārī coepit: the regular construction would be lacerārī coeptus est: see N. 25 1a.
70 9 mē īnfēlīcem: Accusative of Exclamation; cp. our 'Poor me!'.
70 10 quam: 'how'.

Notes to Selection 72

(Cp. LaFontaine, Fables 1.2, Le Corbeau et le Renard)

70 13 sērā dat poenās turpēs paenitentiā: 'suffers a disgraceful penalty, and repents too late'. Poenam dō is the regular idiom for 'suffer a punishment'; sērā paenitentiā is Ablative Absolute; literally, 'repentance being late'.
70 17 qui . . . est nitor!: 'how remarkable is the sheen'; literally, 'what a sheen there is'.
70 19 prior: 'superior'.
70 21 ōre: 'from his beak'; the Ablative of Place From Which is often found in verse without a preposition; cp. G. 24, and N. 65 24.
70 23 corvī dēceptus stupor: cp. dēcepta aviditās, 67 5, and NN. 67 5b, 66 34.

Notes to Selection 73

(Cp. LaFontaine, Fables 6.8, Le Vieillard et l'Ane)

70 24a In principātū commutandō: 'In a change of government'; cp. N. 13 3.
70 24b saepius: 'too often'; literally, 'more often (than is right)'.
70 29 fugere: poetical construction, instead of the regular ut fugeret.
70 30 bīnās . . . clītellās: 'two saddles'; for the use of the distributive adjective, see N. 64 19b; the plural clītellae is used of a single saddle.
71 1 quid rēfert meā: 'what concern is it of mine'. The impersonal verb rēfert, 'it concerns', 'it is of interest' (to be distinguished carefully from rēferō, 'carry back'), is used with the genitive of nouns (e.g. rēgis rēfert, it

concerns the king'); but instead of the genitive of a personal pronoun, the ablative singular feminine of the corresponding possessive adjective is used: *tuā refert,* 'it concerns you'.

71 2a clītellās . . . meās: '(only) my own saddle'; i.e. no additional burden.

71 2b dum portem: N. 32 22a.

Notes to Selection 74

71 3 spōnsum: 'to serve as sureties', 'to guarantee his credit'; supine (N. 18 3b). The verb *advocat* implies motion.

71 5 Ovem rogābat . . . modium: N. 36 3c. *Rogō* here means 'request as a loan'.

71 6 lupō spōnsōre: 'offering the Wolf as guarantor'.

71 9 diēs: the day for the repayment of the loan.

Notes to Selection 75

(CP. LaFontaine, Fables 3.14, Le Lion devenu vieux)

71 12 Dēfectus: 'overcome'.

71 19a Fortēs . . . mihi īnsultāre: 'that brave creatures behaved insolently toward me'; Infinitive Clause, object of *tulī*.

71 19b indignē: 'with indignation'.

Notes to Selection 76

71 25 causā meā: 'for my sake'; instead of the genitive singular of the pronoun, the ablative singular feminine of the corresponding possessive adjective is used; cp. N. 15 6a, and N. 71 1.

71 26 supplicī (*tibi*): 'to your prayers'; literally, 'to (you,) a suppliant'.

71 28a sunt: the subject is *mūrēs;* the mice are again referred to by the word *ipsōs.*

71 28b et joins *dēvorēs* with *fruāris.*

72 1a imputāre . . . mihi: 'charge to my account', i.e. try to make it seem that I am indebted to you.

72 1b benficium: shortened form of *beneficium,* used for metrical reasons.

72 3 Hoc in sē dictum (*esse*): 'that this is directed against themselves'.

72 5a et: 'while'.

72 5b imprūdentius: 'unwisely'; the force of the comparative (cp. N. 70 24b) is better left untranslated.

Notes to Selection 77

(CP. LaFontaine, Fables 1.3, La Grenouille qui veut se faire aussi grosse que le Bœuf)

72 6 dum vult: 'in wishing', 'in his desire'.

72 14a Novissimē: 'finally'.

72 14b indignāta: 'indignant'; cp. N. 21 1b, end.

Notes to Selection 78

72 18 Canēs currentēs bibere: the same strange account is given by Pliny the Elder (Natural History 8.148) and by Macrobius (Satires 2.2.7).

72 19 corcodīlis: this form is used instead of *crŏcodīlĭs* for metrical reasons.

72 21 Quamlibet . . . ōtiŏ: 'as unhurriedly as you wish'; the omission of *cum* with an abstract noun in the Ablative of Manner is irregular when, as here, the noun is not modified by an adjective (cp. G. 20). Perhaps, however, *quamlibet* is thought of as supplying the place of an adjective.

Notes to Selection 79

(CP. LAFONTAINE, FABLES 2.4, LES DEUX TAUREAUX ET LA GRENOUILLE)

72 24 labōrant: 'suffer'; cp. N. 64 6*b*.

72 28 gregis: to be taken with *prīncipātū*.

73 2-6 "Est stātiŏ—pertinet": the reply of the first Frog.

73 3 quī prŏfūgerit: 'whichever (of the two bulls) flees'.

73 5 prŏculcātās (*nōs*) obteret: see N. 20 14*b*.

73 6 caput ad nostrum: 'to our welfare'; for the order, cp. *ōre . . . ē nostrō*, 68 15.

Notes to Selection 80

73 13 potius . . . quam: 'rather . . . than'.

73 14 ictŏ foedere: 'under the terms of a formal treaty'; literally, 'a treaty having been struck' (Ablative Absolu, e). The Romans spoke of *striking* a treaty because, as part of the ceremony, a sacrificial animal was killed by the blow of an axe.

73 15 quī . . . praestem: N. 24 25.

73 17 singulās: in early Latin, which Phaedrus here imitates, *vēscor* is found with an object in the accusative (cp. G. 28).

73 19*a* dē reliquīs ūna: cp. N. 19 5*a*.

73 19*b* meritō: adverb.

Notes to Selection 81

(CP. LAFONTAINE, FABLES 3.6, L'AIGLE, LA LAIE, ET LA CHATTE)

73 20 in sublīmī quercū: 'high in an oak'; cp. N. 15 1*b;* cp. also *in mediā (quercū)* and *ad īmam (quercum)* below.

73 21 pepererat: i.e. had given birth to a litter of kittens, and had made a home for them there.

73 26 et: 'also'.

73 27 fodere . . . quod vidēs . . . aprum, . . . quercum vult evertere: literally, 'as to the fact that you see the Sow dig, she wishes to overthrow the oak'; we may perhaps translate 'If you see the Sow digging, it is because she wishes . . .'.

73 29 in plānō: 'on level ground'.

73 31 suīs: genitive of *sūs*.

74 2a simul: 'as soon as'; *simul atque* is regularly used to mean 'as soon as' in prose.

74 2b pāstum: 'to feed' (N. 18 3b).

74 6 suspēnsō pede: 'on tiptoe'; a vivid expression.

74 9 Ruīnam: 'the collapse (of the oak)'.

74 10 forās: 'out of doors'; an old Accusative of End of Motion, which has become an adverb.

74 11a Quid multa?: 'To make a long story short'; literally 'Why (should I relate) many things?'.

74 11b (*aquila et aper*) **sunt cōnsūmptī:** see G. 71; the gender of *aper* is masculine, even when, as here, it denotes a female.

74 11c cum suīs: 'with their offspring'; contrast *suīs* (from *suus, -a, -um*) with *suīs*, 73 31.

74 13a bilinguis: we should say 'two-faced'.

74 13b malī: to be taken with *quantum*.

Notes to Selection 82

(Cp. LaFontaine, Fables 1.4, Les deux Mulets)

74 16 fiscōs: 'baskets' used to hold and transport money. From this usage is derived our word 'fiscal', i.e. 'monetary'.

74 18 onere dīves: 'with his precious burden'; literally, 'wealthy in respect to his burden' (N. 14 2).

74 22 mūlum: i.e. the Mule who carried the money.

74 24 (*mūlus*) **Spoliātus:** 'the Mule who had been robbed'.

74 27a Hōc argūmentō: N. 20 30.

74 27b hominum tenuitās: 'poor men'; cp. N. 66 34.

74 28 perīclō: this short form of the word *perīculum* is used for metrical reasons.

Notes to Selection 83

(Cp. LaFontaine, Fables 4.21, L'œil du Maître)

74 29 latibulis: see N. 70 21.

74 30 vēnātōrum: 'at the hands of the huntsmen'.

74 31 vīllam: 'farmhouse'.

75 2a Hīc: adverb.

75 2b latentī (*cervō*): Indirect Object of *inquit* unexpressed.

75 2c Quidnam voluistī tibi: see N. 14 28.

75 3 qui . . . cucurrerīs: 'that you have run'; N. 45 7.

75 4 spīritum: 'your life'.

75 5 modo: 'only'.

75 6 occāsiōne . . . datā: 'when opportunity offers'.

75 7 Spatium diēī noctis excipiunt vicēs: 'The change of night succeeds the period of day'; a highly 'poetical' statement of the simple fact of nightfall.

75 8a Frondem: 'fodder'.

75 8b ideō: 'even so', 'in spite of this'.

75 12 būbus: dative plural of *bos*.

73 13 Ille. I.e. *dominus;* see line 17.
75 16 vertētur: 'will be involved'.
75 17 Haec inter: 'Meanwhile'.
75 18 corruptōs: 'mistreated', 'showing evidences of neglect'.
75 20 Tollere: i.e. sweep away.
75 23 convocātā . . . familiā: the word *familia* is here used collectively to mean 'the slaves of the household'. This is a regular meaning of *familia;* the idea of our word 'family' is usually conveyed in Latin by the word *domus.*
75 24 praedam: 'as booty'; in apposition with *quem.*

Notes to Selection 84

(Cp. LaFontaine, Fables 1.5, Le Loup et le Chien)

75 28a salūtātum . . . restitērunt: by a slight extension of its regular usage, the Accusative Supine is here used with a verb denoting cessation of motion (*resistō* in the sense 'halt'); cp. N. **18** 3b, cp. also our expression 'come to a stop'.
75 28b invicem: 'each other'; literally, 'in turn'.
75 29-31 "Unde—famē": the Wolf is the first speaker.
75 32a simpliciter: 'frankly'.
75 32b Eadem est condiciō tibi: 'the same terms (of employment) are open to you'.
75 33 pār officium: 'the same service (as I do)'.
75 34 ut sīs: Substantive Clause explaining *officium.*
76 1 et: joins *tueāris* with *sīs* (**75** 34).
76 4a Quantō: 'How much' (G. 26).
76 4b est: we would say 'would be'.
76 5 ōtiōsum: agrees with *mē,* the unexpressed subject of *satiārī.*
76 7a ā catēnā: an unusual construction; we should expect the Ablative of Means. The preposition, however, expresses the idea of 'from' rather than that of 'by': 'from wearing a chain'.
76 7b canī: see N. 51 20.
76 11 quā vīsum est: 'where I please'; cp. N. **28** 30.
76 11-14 crepusculō—pulmentārium: the Dog hastens to speak of additional advantages, to cover up the vital drawback of his situation.
76 13 iactant familia: see N. **75** 23. The number of *iactant* corresponds to the meaning, not to the grammatical number, of the subject.
76 14 pulmentārium (*est mihi*): 'is my relish'.
76 16a Age: 'come now!', 'see here!'. This imperative form is regularly used to attract attention to an important utterance.
76 16b abīre . . . quō: 'to go away somewhere'.
76 16c est (*tibi*) **animus:** 'you have the desire'.
76 17 Fruere: present imperative, second person singular.
76 18 Rēgnāre nōlō, līber ut nōn sim mihi: 'I do not wish (even) to be king at the cost of my freedom'; literally, '. . . with the result that I be not free'. For the case of *mihi,* see G. 8.

Notes to Selection 85

76 19 monitus . . . consīdērā: 'be warned and examine'; see N. 20 14b.
76 20 turpissimam: 'very ugly'.
76 21 pulchrā: 'handsome'.
76 22 speculum . . . inspexerunt: *inspiciō* may govern a direct object, as here.
76 24 sē: subject of *esse* unexpressed.
76 25 nec . . . sustinet: 'and could not bear'.
76 26a accipiēns . . . in contumēliam: 'taking as an insult'.
76 26b cūncta: 'everything (that he said)'.
76 27 laesūra: 'determined to inflict injury'.
76 29 vir nātus: '(though) of male sex'; literally, 'born a male'.
76 31 in ambōs: 'between them both'.
76 33 fōrmam: 'handsome appearance'.
76 34 vincās: 'overcome', i.e. cause people to forget it.

Notes to Selection 86

(Cp. LaFontaine, Fables 3.11, Le Renard et les Raisins)

77 5a facere quae nōn possunt: i.e. *ea quae facere nōn possunt*.
77 5b ēlevant: 'belittle'.

Notes to Selection 87

(Cp. LaFontaine, Fables 4.13, Le Cheval s'étant voulu venger du Cerf)

77 7-8 Equus—vadum: i.c. *aper, dum sēsē volūtat, vadum, quō equus sitim sēdāre solitus fuerat, turbāvit.*
77 9 irātus ferō: 'angry at the beast' (G. 11).
77 11a redīt: contracted from *rediit*. Cp. N. 14 3a.
77 11b hunc: i.e. the Boar.
77 15 invītum: sc. *equum*.
77 19 impūne: 'without seeking revenge'. The experience of the Sequani with Ariovistus (51 28 - 52 21) affords an excellent illustration of this Fable.

Notes to Selection 88

(Cp. LaFontaine, Fables 3.5, Le Renard et le Bouc)

77 23 altiōre: 'too high' (for her to climb).
78 2 nīxa . . . cornibus: 'climbing up his horns'. For the tense of *nīxa*, see N. 21 1b, end; for the case of *cornibus*, see G. 18.

Notes to Selection 89

(Cp. LaFontaine, Fables 1.7, La Besace)

78 4 Pērās . . . duās: 'two pouches' forming a *mantica*, or double wallet. This article of luggage, much used in ancient times, was slung over the shoulder, so that one pouch hung down in front, the other behind.
78 5a replētam: sc. *pēram*.
78 5b dedit: 'has placed'.
78 6 aliēnis (*vitiīs*) **gravem**: cp. *propriīs replētam vitiīs*, line 5.
78 8 simul: cp. N. 74 2a.

GRAMMATICAL OUTLINE

This outline comprises the main points of grammar which are essential both for an understanding of the text and as a basis for later studies.   In the sections numbered G. 1 - G. 74 are set forth the constructions which the student is supposed to have learned previously.   The examples in these sections are either taken from or based upon the text; the complete context is therefore available in every instance.   Students are advised to read sections G. 1 - G. 74 as soon as possible, and to give special study to any points which have not previously been learned.

New constructions are listed in this outline by title only, with reference in each case to the note in which the construction is explained (for the notes, see pp. 79-160).   As the work progresses, the student should make this outline the basis of frequent grammatical review; whether a given point has been covered as yet may easily be ascertained by comparing the number of the note cited with the page and line numbers of the current assignment.

The topics are taken up in the following order:

Uses of the Cases: G. 1-G. 33
    Nominative: G. 1-G. 2
    Genitive: G. 3-G. 6
    Dative: G. 7-G. 11
    Accusative: G. 12-G. 17
    Ablative: G. 18-G. 31
    Accusative, Ablative, and Locative (Special Expression of Place Relations): G. 32
    Vocative: G. 33

Substantive Use of Adjectives: G. 34

Uses of the Moods: G. 35-G. 65
    Indicative: G. 35-G. 38
    Subjunctive: G. 39-G. 45
    Indicative and Subjunctive: G. 46-G. 60

Cum-Clauses: G. 46-G. 48

Conditional Sentences: G. 49-G. 51

Tenses of Indicative and Subjunctive: G. 52-G. 60

Infinitive: G. 61-G. 64

Imperative: G. 65

Verbal Nouns with Case-forms

Participles: G. 66-G. 69

Agreement: G. 70-G. 74

Minor grammatical points, with references to the notes in which they are explained, are listed in an Index, pp. 185-186. For the abbreviations used, see p. 79.

Uses of the Cases

NOMINATIVE

G. 1   Nominative as Subject of Finite Verb.   The subject of a finite verb is in the nominative case.   (The term 'finite' is used to distinguish the forms of the indicative, subjunctive, and imperative moods from those of the infinitive mood.)

Lēgātī . . . vēnērunt, 'Ambassadors came', **13 1.**

G. 2   Predicate Nominative.   A noun or pronoun in the predicate referring to the subject of a finite verb (see G. 1) is in the nominative case.

iūdex . . . fuī, 'I was a judge', **19 16.**

Nominative Subject of Historical Infinitive: N. 31 10.

GENITIVE

G. 3   Genitive of Possession.   Possession may be expressed by the genitive case.

Māter *Papīrī*, 'Papirius' mother', **14 15.**

G. 4   Genitive of Connection.   Connection between one noun and another may be expressed by the genitive case; the noun in the genitive is in an adjectival relation to the other.

splendōrem *domūs*, 'the splendor of your home', **13 6.**

mendāciī cōnsilium, 'the idea of a lie', **14 21.**

G. 5 Partitive Genitive (Genitive of the Whole). The whole of which a part is mentioned may be expressed by the genitive case.

> reliquum *mercēdis*, 'the remainder of the fee', 28 9.

G. 6 Genitive with Adjectives. A noun in the genitive case may be used to complete the meaning of certain adjectives denoting *desire, knowledge, memory, fulness, power, sharing,* and *guilt,* and their opposites.

> Corinthiī . . . *praedae* . . . cupidī, 'Corinthians desirous of plunder', **26** 20.

Genitive with *Causā* and *Grātiā:* N. 15 6a.
of Quality or Description: N. 18 21.
of the Charge: N. 24 2b.

Predicate Genitive of Possession: N. 25 21.

DATIVE

G. 7 Dative of the Indirect Object. The dative case denotes the indirect object of

> A. Transitive verbs of *giving, telling, owing, showing,* or of kindred meaning.
>> reddō *iīs* . . . līneāmenta, 'I give them features', **15** 12.
> B. Certain intransitive verbs, e.g. *imperō, placeō, persuādeō.* For these verbs, the Vocabulary, where they are marked 'w. dat.', will be the student's best guide.
>> *hīs . . . membrīs* . . . imperare possum, 'I can command these parts of my body', **13** 9.

G. 8 Dative of Advantage or Disadvantage (Dative of Reference, Dative of Interest). The person to whose advantage or disadvantage something is done or exists may be denoted by the dative case.

> victōriam *vōbīs* peperī, 'I gained a victory for you', **18** 1.

G. 9 Dative of Possession. When the fact of possession is the main thought of a sentence or clause, the dative case denoting the possessor may be used with the verb *sum.*

> *eī servō* Androclus nōmen fuit, 'that slave had the name
> of Androclus', 22 26.

G. 10   Dative of the Person Obligated (Dative of Agent).
When obligation or necessity is denoted by a combination of the
gerundive (future passive participle) and the verb *sum*, the
person obligated may be denoted by the dative case.

> *amīcō* . . . caput perdendum fuit, 'my friend had to
> lose his civil status', 19 18.

G. 11   Dative with Adjectives.   A noun in the dative case
may be used to complete the meaning of certain adjectives denoting *nearness, friendliness, likeness, fitness,* and their opposites.

> nautās, ut . . . amīciōres . . . *sibi,* Corinthiōs dēlēgit,
> 'he chose Corinthian sailors, as being more friendly
> to him, 26 18.

Dative of Purpose: N. 13 4*a.*
"Double Dative": N. 13 11*c.*
Dative of Indirect Object with Compound Verbs: N. 20 18.
"Dative of Separation": N. 42 3*b.*

ACCUSATIVE

G. 12   Accusative of Direct Object.   The direct object of a
transitive verb is in the accusative case.

> obtulērunt . . . *pecūniam,* 'they offered money', 13 4.

G. 13   Accusative of End of Motion (Place to Which).   The
place to or toward which motion is directed may be denoted by
the accusative case with the preposition *ad,* 'to', 'toward', *in,*
'into', 'to', or *sub,* '(to a place) under' (but see G. 32A).

> Venit ad *senātum* . . . matrum . . . caterva, 'a band
> of matrons comes to the senate', 14 25.
> immissīs in *cavernās* arboris digitīs, 'his fingers thrust
> into the hollows of the tree', 14 6.
> sub *Gallicum gladium* successit, 'he got up close under
> the Gallic sword', 21 5.

G. 14   Accusative of Purpose (Figurative End of Motion).
When purpose is expressed by a noun, the noun may be in the
accusative case with the preposition *ad,* less frequently *in.*

ōrnātus erat . . . ad *proelium,* 'it had been equipped for battle', 16 14.

multa ad *splendōrem* . . . dēfierī, 'many things are lacking (that make) for splendor', 13 5.

leōne in *vēnātum* profectō, 'when the lion had gone off to hunt' (here the literal and the figurative End of Motion are blended), 23 30.

G. 15 Accusative of Extent. The extent of time or space may be expressed by the accusative case without a preposition.

triennium tōtum . . . in eōdem specū . . . vīximus, 'for three whole years we lived in the same cave', 23 26.

mīlia passuum . . . vīgintī . . . redībat, 'he would return (a distance of) twenty miles', 37 20.

G. 16 Accusative as Subject of Infinitive. The subject of an infinitive is in the accusative case.[1]

cum . . . arcessī . . . *tībīcinem* iussisset, 'when he had ordered that a flute-player be summoned', 16 26.

G. 17 Accusative with Prepositions. Certain prepositions govern the accusative case, e.g. *ante, apud, contrā, inter, ob, per, post, propter, trāns.* The Vocabulary, where these are marked 'w. acc.', will be the student's best guide.

apud *rēgem*, 'at the court of the king', 13 14.

Adverbial Accusative: N. 13 11*b*.

Two Accusatives with Verbs of Asking, Teaching, and Concealing: N. 36 3*c*.

ABLATIVE

G. 18 Ablative of Means. The means or instrument by which an action is accomplished may be denoted by the ablative case without a preposition.

librum . . . *manibus* . . . dīscidit, 'he tore the book to pieces with his hands', 18 17.

exercitum *īnsignibus* . . . micantem, 'an army gleaming with ornaments', 13 17.

G. 19 Ablative of Accompaniment. The person or thing by

---

[1] See N. 31 10.

which another person or thing is accompanied may be denoted
by the ablative case with the preposition *cum*, 'with'.

  cum . . . *fīliīs* introīre, 'to enter with their sons', 14 12.
  elephantōs cum *turribus*, 'elephants with turrets', 13 18.

G. 20 Ablative of Manner. The manner in which an act is
performed may be denoted by the ablative case with the preposition *cum*, 'with'. If the noun in the ablative is modified by
an adjective, *cum* is sometimes omitted.

  cōntiō . . . Scīpiōnem . . . cum *laetitiā* . . . prōsecuta
      est, 'the assemblage escorted Scipio with joy', 18 7.
  utrīsque *summō studiō* pugnantibus, 'while each side
      fought with utmost energy', 20 19.

G. 21 Ablative of Cause. Cause may be expressed by a
noun in the ablative case without a preposition.

  quasi anus *aetāte* dēsiperet, 'as if the old woman were
      weak-minded with age', 17 9.

G. 22 Ablative of Personal Agent. With verbs in the passive voice, the person by whom the action is performed is regularly denoted by the ablative case with the preposition *ab*.

  Menander ā *Phīlemone* . . . vincēbātur, 'Menander
      used to be defeated by Philemon', 15 16.

G. 23 Ablative of Place Where. The place where a thing
is or an action occurs may be denoted by the ablative case with
the preposition *in*, 'in' or 'on', or *sub*, 'under' (but see G. 32C²).

  In *librīs* . . . scrīptum est, 'It has been set forth in
      books', 13 13.
  īnsidēns in *eō*, 'sitting on it', 16 16.
  sub *tēctō* vīvere, 'to live under a roof', 76 4.

G. 24 Ablative of Place from Which. The place from which
motion starts may be denoted by the ablative case with the
preposition *ab*, '(away) from', *dē* '(down) from', or *ex*, 'from',
'out of'. But see G. 32B.

  Fabricius manūs ab *auribus* ad oculōs . . . dēdūxit,
      'Fabricius moved his hands from his ears to his
      eyes', 13 7.

---

² See also NN. 20 12*b*, 24 9.

dē *locō* hominem . . . dēiēcit, 'he hurled the man down from his position', 21 4.

ē *mediīs hostibus* rēgem . . . rettulit, 'he carried the king back from the midst of the enemy', 16 20.

G. 25 Ablative of Time at or within Which. The time at or within which something exists or is done may be denoted by the ablative case; usually without a preposition, but sometimes with *in*, 'in', 'on'.

(dies) *quō* Hannibalem . . . vīcī, '(a day) on which I defeated Hannibal', 17 30.

(pestilentia) quae *in* bellī . . . *principiīs* . . . cīvitātem dēpopulāta est, '(a plague) which ravaged the state in the early days of the war', 16 8.

G. 26 Ablative of Degree of Difference. The amount by which one term of a comparison differs from another may be denoted by the ablative case without a preposition.

Tarquinius id *multō* rīsit magis, 'Tarquin laughed at this much more heartily (than he had done before)', 17 13.

G. 27 Ablative of Comparison. When the first term of a comparison is a noun in the nominative or the accusative case, the second term may be denoted by the ablative case without a preposition; *quam* is not used in this construction.

hīs antīquiōrcs Horātiī, 'thc brothcro Horatiuo, morc ancient than these', 19 29.

G. 28 Ablative with Certain Verbs. The verbs *ūtor*, 'use', *fruor*, 'enjoy', *fungor*, 'discharge', *potior*, 'gain possession of', and *vēscor*, 'eat', and their compounds, may govern a noun or pronoun in the ablative case.

aetātis suae *verbīs* ūsī sunt, 'they used words belonging to their own generation', 20 1.

G. 29 Ablative with Adjectives. A noun in the ablative case may be used to complete the meaning of the adjectives *dignus* and *indignus*.

alia . . . indigna *tālī virō*, 'other things unworthy of such a man', 17 27.

G. 30 Ablative Absolute. A noun or pronoun in the ablative case, together with a participle, adjective, or noun, also in the ablative case, may be used in an absolute (i.e. separated, independent) construction. The two parts of this construction have a relation to each other similar to that of the subject of a sentence to its predicate. The entire Ablative Absolute is loosely connected with the rest of the sentence. There is no explicit indication of how the facts stated in the Ablative Absolute are related to those stated in the rest of the sentence: this must be inferred from the context. The Ablative Absolute usually takes the place of a clause of Time, Cause, Circumstance, Concession, or Condition. Examples of the first four are given in order below.

> Lēgātī . . . *memorātīs multīs rēbus* . . . obtulērunt . . . pecūniam, 'The ambassadors, when they had mentioned many services, offered money', or '. . . having mentioned many services . . .' (literally, 'many things having been mentioned'), 13 1.
>
> puer *mātre urgente* . . . consilium capit, 'since his mother insisted, the boy adopted a plan' (literally, 'his mother insisting'), 14 20.
>
> *metū magnō* ea congressiō . . . facta est, 'amidst great anxiety, that combat took place' (literally, 'the anxiety being great'), 20 29.
>
> *pugnā interdictā*, hostem . . . occīderat, 'though combat had been forbidden, he had killed an enemy' (literally, 'combat having been forbidden'), 21 14.

G. 31 Ablative with Prepositions. Certain prepositions govern the ablative case: e.g. *prō, sine.* The Vocabulary, where these are marked 'w. abl.', will be the student's best guide.

> (pretium) quod erat petītum prō *omnibus*, '(a price) which had been asked for them all', 17 19.

Ablative with *Ūsus Est* and *Opus Est*: N. 13 11a.
  of Specification: N. 14 2.
  of Quality or Description: N. 15 11.
  of Accordance: N. 20 30.
  of Separation: N. 23 23.

ACCUSATIVE, ABLATIVE, AND LOCATIVE

G. 32 Special Expression of Place Relations. Names of towns, cities, and small islands, and a few other nouns (e.g.

domus, 'home', *rūs,* 'country')[3] are not used in expressions of place relations in the same way as the vast majority of nouns (see G. 13, G. 23, and G. 24).

A. **End of Motion (Place to Which):** accusative case without a preposition.

> *Rōmam* dēductus (sum), 'I was brought to Rome', **24 1.**

B. **Place from Which:** ablative case without a preposition.

> *domō* . . . ēgreditur, 'she went forth from home', **14 24.**

C. **Place Where:** locative case without a preposition.

> *Athēnīs* Ēlectram . . . actūrus, 'about to act the part of Electra at Athens', **24 16.**

VOCATIVE

G. 33 Direct Address. The vocative is the case of direct address.

> Quaesō, . . . *Philēmō,* . . . dīc mihi, 'Pray, Philemon, tell me', **15 18.**

SUBSTANTIVE USE OF ADJECTIVES

G. 34 Certain adjectives may be used substantively (i.e. as nouns), especially in the plural. When so used, they are masculine if they refer to persons, neuter if they refer to things.

> *cēterōrum* . . . petulantiam, 'the insolence of other persons', **15 26.**
> sunt *maiōra,* 'there are greater things', **36 30.**

Uses of the Moods
INDICATIVE

G. 35 Indicative in Direct Statement, Question, or Exclamation. The indicative mood is used in a simple sentence, or in the main clause of a complex sentence, to declare something to be a fact, or to inquire or exclaim about a fact.

---

[3] See N. 43 29*a.*

Lēgātī . . . *vēnērunt*, 'The ambassadors came', 13 1.
*Putās*ne . . . satis esse haec, 'Do you think these are enough?', 13 21.

G. 36 Indicative in Relative Clause. The verb of a simple relative clause is in the indicative mood.

memorātīs . . . rēbus, quās . . . *fēcerat*, 'having mentioned the things which he had done', 13 2.

G. 37 Indicative in Causal Clause. *Quod, quia,* or *quoniam,* 'because', may introduce a causal clause; the verb is in the indicative mood.

sermōne . . . dēsitō ūteris, *quod* . . . intellegere nēminem *vīs*, 'you use obsolete language, because you want no one to understand', 20 2.

G. 38 Indicative in Temporal Clause with *Ubi, Ut, Postquam*. *Ubi* or *ut*, 'when', or *postquam*, 'after', may introduce a temporal clause; the verb is regularly in the perfect indicative.

Hoc illa *ubi audīvit*, . . . egreditur, 'When she heard this, she went forth', 14 24.

Indicative in Temporal Clause with *Antequam*, etc.: N. 25 13*b*.
Indicative with *Dum*, 'While': N. 21 3.
Indicative in Substantive Clause with *Quod*, 'the fact that': N. 18 18*a*.
Indicative in Concessive Clause with *Quamquam*: N. 30 18.

SUBJUNCTIVE

G. 39 Independent Subjunctive. The subjunctive mood may be used in a simple sentence, or in the main clause of a complex sentence, to express the ideas listed below. No introductory particle is ordinarily used for the affirmative; the negative introductory particle is regularly *nē*.

A. Suggestion or Exhortation (Hortatory Subjunctive) addressed to a group of which the speaker is a member.

eāmus, 'let us go', 18 2.
Nē . . . *sīmus* . . . ingrātī, 'Let us not be ungrateful', 18 1.

B. **Command (Jussive Subjunctive)**

sēsē *sistant* illō in locō, 'let them present themselves in that place', 19 9.

C. **Wish (Optative Subjunctive)**

Cīvis . . . mē *compīlet*, 'May a citizen rob me!', 35 29.

G. 40 **Subjunctive of Purpose.** The purpose of an act or state of being may be expressed by the subjunctive mood introduced by *ut* affirmative, *nē* or *ut nē* negative.[4]

exerceor, *ut* . . . petulantiam . . . *feram*, 'I train myself in order to endure insolence', 15 26.

cum . . . facere id vidērētur, *nē* reliquum . . . *daret*, 'since it seemed that he was doing this in order not to give the remainder', 28 7.

G. 41 **Subjunctive of Result.** The result of an act or state of being may be expressed by the subjunctive mood introduced by *ut* affirmative, *ut* . . . *nōn* negative. The main clause usually contains a word of incomplete significance (e.g. *tam, ita*, 'so', *tantus*, 'so large') which the result clause completes.

Temperantiā . . . fuisse eum *tantā* . . . ut . . . valetūdine integrā *vīxerit*, '. . . he was a man of such moderation, that he lived in perfect health', 16 6.

precum . . . miseritī sunt *hāctenus, ut* eī necem . . . *nōn adferrent*, 'they took pity on his prayers to this extent, that they did not kill him', 26 23.

G. 42 **Subjunctive of Indirect Question.** An Indirect Question is a subordinate clause introduced by an interrogative pronoun (e.g. *quis*, 'who'), an interrogative adjective (e.g. *quantus*, 'how large'), an interrogative adverb (e.g. *ubi*, 'where'), or an interrogative particle (e.g. *num, -ne, an*, 'whether'); the verb is in the subjunctive mood.

experīrī . . . volēns, *an* ūllae . . . reliquae vīrēs *adessent*, 'wishing to discover, whether any strength was left', 14 5.

percontāta est . . . *quidnam* . . . patrēs *ēgissent*, 'she

---

[4] See N. 40 13.

asked what in the world the senators had done', 14 16.

G. 43 Subjunctive in Fear-Clause. A clause dependent on a verb denoting *fear* is introduced by *nē* when the clause is affirmative, *ut* (or *nē nōn*) when the clause is negative; the verb so introduced is in the subjunctive mood.

> verēns, *nē dederētur*, 'fearing that he would be surrendered', 43 28.

G. 44 Subjunctive with Negative Expression of Doubt. With negative expressions of doubt, a clause introduced by *quīn*, 'that', is used; the verb is in the subjunctive mood.

> haudquāquam dubitantēs, *quīn perīsset*, 'not doubting at all, that he had perished', 27 1.

G. 45 Subjunctive in Substantive Clauses. A clause with its verb in the subjunctive mood may be used with the syntax of a noun in the nominative or accusative case: i.e. as the subject or object of a verb, in the predicate with a copulative verb, or in apposition with a noun or pronoun. Such clauses, for the most part, fall into two main classes:

A. **Subjunctive Substantive Clauses introduced by *Ut*[5] Affirmative, *Nē* or *Ut Nē* Negative**: used with verbs, nouns, and adjectives denoting *desire, intention, agreement, permission, endeavor, utility, necessity, custom*, or the like.

> pactus . . . est *ut* . . . permūtātiō *fieret*, 'he agreed that an exchange should be made', 28 30.
> volēbam nescius *nē essēs*, 'I desired that you be not unaware', 35 4.
> erat . . . iūs senātōrī, *ut* . . . *dīceret*, 'a senator had the right to speak', 36 6.

Clauses of this type, although they resemble Purpose Clauses (G. 40), were probably developed from the Subjunctive of Wish (G. 39)

---

[5] Clauses of this type sometimes appear in the affirmative without any introductory conjunction.

B. Subjunctive Substantive Clauses introduced by *Ut* Affirmative, *Ut* . . . *Nōn* Negative: used with verbs of *causing* or *happening*.

Accidit . . . *ut* . . . *cēnārent*, 'It happened that they were dining', **44** 8.

factum . . . *ut* . . . *nōn oboedīrent*, '. . . it came about that they did not obey', **42** 16.

Clauses of this type resemble Result Clauses (G. 41).

Subjunctive of Indirect Command or Request: N. 13 4*b*.
of Subordinate Verb in Indirect Discourse: N. 14 15*b*.
with *Quasi, Tamquam*, etc.: N. 17 10.
of Informal Indirect Discourse: N. 18 18*a*, ¶2.
of Anticipation: N. 25 13*b*, ¶2.
in Clause of Proviso: N. 32 22*a*.
of Integral Part: N. 36 7, ¶2.
with *Quīn* and *Quōminus:* N. 42 21.

Subjunctive Relative Clauses:
of Purpose: N. 24 25.
of Cause: N. 32 17*b*.
of Concession: N. 42 24*c*.
of Result: N. 45 7.

INDICATIVE AND SUBJUNCTIVE

Cum Clauses

G. 46 Subjunctive in *Cum* Causal Clause. A clause denoting cause may be introduced by *cum*, 'since'; the verb is in the subjunctive mood.

nihil decuit aliud dīcere, . . . praesertim *cum* dē eā rē *dīceret*, etc., 'it was not fitting for him to say anything else, especially since he was discussing a matter, etc.', **32** 25.

G. 47 Subjunctive in *Cum* Concessive Clause. A concessive clause (i.e. a clause denoting a state of affairs in spite of which something exists or is done) may be introduced by *cum*, 'although'; the verb is in the subjunctive mood.

cum . . . *superātus esset*, nēminem . . . *dēscīvisse*, 'although he had been defeated, . . . no one deserted', **30** 17.

G. 48 Indicative or Subjunctive in *Cum* Temporal Clauses.
Clauses denoting time may be introduced by *cum*, 'when'; the
mood of the verb varies with the tense, and with the nature of
the clause.

A. **Present:** when the clause introduced by *cum*,
'when', refers to the present, concerning either a general
truth or a particular state of facts, the indicative is
used: present for incomplete action, perfect for complete
(G. 58).

> *cum* mē *vincis*, nōnne ērubēscis?, 'when you defeat
> me, do you not blush?', **15** 19.

> *cum superāvērunt*, animālia ... immolant, 'when
> they are victorious, they sacrifice animals',
> **47** 26.

B. **Future:** when the clause introduced by *cum*,
'when', refers to the future, concerning either a general
truth or a particular state of facts, the indicative is used:
future for incomplete action, future perfect for completed
action (see G. 58).

> *cum* ... bellum *parābis*, tē ipsum frūstrāberis,
> 'when you make ready for war, you will be
> deceiving yourself', **43** 26.
> id mihi, *cum redierō*, nūntiāte, 'report it to me
> when I return', cp. **31** 4.

C. **Past:** here a further subdivision is necessary:

1. When a clause introduced by *cum*, 'when', is
used with *tum*, 'then', *eō tempore*, 'at that time', or
the like, or when the author wishes to emphasize the
time-element to the exclusion of other concepts, the
indicative mood is used, in any appropriate tense of
the past.

> *Tum, cum* ... rēs ... quaepiam *cōnsul-*
> *tāta* ... *est*, 'At a time when a certain
> matter had been discussed', **14** 13.

2. When a clause introduced by *cum*, 'when',
'whenever', refers to a general truth or practice in

the past, the indicative is used, in any appropriate tense of the past.

> Id *cum dīxerat,* ūniversī . . . pārēbant, 'Whenever he said this, they all obeyed', **30** 1.

3. (*"Cum* Circumstantial") When a clause introduced by *cum*, 'when', refers to the past, with such exceptions as are noted in subdivisions 1 and 2 just above, the verb is in the imperfect or pluperfect subjunctive (see G. 58, G. 60).

> *Cum* . . . artem āthlēticam *dēsīsset,* iterque *faceret* . . . , quercum vīdit, 'When he had given up athletics, and was making a journey, he saw an oak-tree', **14** 2.

Conditional Sentences

A conditional sentence normally contains two parts: a condition (usually introduced in Latin by *sī*, 'if', *nisi*, 'if not', 'unless', or *sīn*, 'but if'), and a conclusion; in the conditional sentence *sī quī excellit, succēdit,* 'if anyone is preeminent, he succeeds to the office', the condition is *sī quī excellit,* the conclusion is *succēdit.* A conditional sentence may usually be assigned to one of three types (G. 49, G. 50, and G. 51).

G. 49 Conditions of Fact (Simple Conditions). These deal with the present, past, or future, with reference either to a particular state of facts or to a general truth; there is no implication as to the reality of the supposition. The mood is indicative; any tense may be used. In the condition-clause, the tense regularly denotes the completeness or non-completeness of the verb in that clause with reference to the verb in the conclusion (see G. 58): the present, imperfect, and future for incomplete action, the perfect, pluperfect and future perfect for completed action.

> *sī* quī . . . *excellit* . . . , *succēdit,* 'if anyone is preeminent, he succeeds to the office', **46** 6.
> *sī* quod *est* facinus *admissum,* . . . dēcernunt, 'if any crime is committed, they render the decision', **45** 25.

mentiēbātur . . . , *sī* mendācium *prōderat*, 'he would lie, if a lie was to his advantage', 29 26.

sī quid *dicētur, advertētis*, 'if anything is said, you will pay attention', cp. 31 24.

sī contrā tē līs *data erit*, mercēs mihi . . . *dēbēbitur*, 'if the case is decided against you, a fee will be due me', 28 15

NOTE: the so-called Future More Probable (More Vivid, Shall-Will) Condition is merely a Condition of Fact referring entirely to the future; see the last two examples cited just above.

G. 50 Future Less Probable Conditions (Less Vivid, Should-Would, Ideal). These deal with the future, and imply that the supposition is rather unlikely to be realized. The mood is subjunctive, in either the present or the perfect tense.

neque, aliter *sī faciat*, ūllam . . . *habeat* auctōritātem, 'if he were to do otherwise, he would have no authority', 45 11.

G. 51 Conditions Contrary to Fact. These deal with the present and the past; they imply that the supposition is false. The mood is subjunctive; the imperfect is used to refer to present time, the pluperfect to refer to past time.

Sī sine uxōre vīvere *possēmus*, . . . omnī eā molestiā *carērēmus*, 'If we were able to live without a wife, we should be free from all that unpleasantness', 32 12.

Sī annālem . . . ūndēvīcēnsimum . . . *lēgissēs, docuisset* tē . . . Archelāus, 'If you had read the nineteenth Annal, Archelaus would have instructed you', 26 4.

Tenses of Indicative and Subjunctive
INDICATIVE

G. 52 The **Present Indicative** represents an act or state of being as *in progress*, or as *generally true at the time of speaking.*

"Quae *facimus*," inquiunt, ' "We are doing this," they say', 13 5.

illa bestia . . . fētum *ēdit* īnfōrmem, 'that animal gives birth to offspring that are shapeless', 15 9.

G. 53 The **Imperfect Indicative** represents an act or state of being as *in progress at a past time*, or as *habitual* or *repeated at a past time*.

> *Ostendēbat* eī Antiochus . . . cōpiās, 'Antiochus was showing troops to him', 13 15.
>
> *Dicēbat* P. Vergilius, 'Vergil used to say', 15 8.

G. 54 The **Future Indicative** represents an act or state of being as *occurring at a future time*, or as *in progress at a future time*.

> frūmentum . . . *metēmus*, 'we shall reap the grain', 31 29.
>
> mercēs . . . *dēbēbitur*, 'a fee will be owing', 28 16.

G. 55 The **Perfect Indicative** represents an act or state of being as *completed at the time of speaking*, or as *having occurred at a past time*.

> dominus . . . *mīsit*, quī amīcōs roget, 'the master has sent a man to ask his friends', 31 11.
>
> Lēgātī . . . *vēnērunt*, 'Ambassadors came', 13 1.

G. 56 The **Pluperfect Indicative** represents an act or state of being as *already completed at a past time stated or implied*.

> memorātīs . . . rēbus, quās . . . *fēcerat*, obtulērunt . . . pecūniam, 'having mentioned things which he had done, they offered money', 13 2.

G. 57 The **Future Perfect Indicative** represents an act or state of being as *already completed at a future time stated or implied*.

> sī iūdicēs prō causā meā *sēnserint*, nihil tibi . . . dēbēbitur, 'if the judges decide (literally, 'will have decided') in my favor, nothing will be owing to you', 28 20.

Historical Present: N. 13 5b, ¶2.

SUBJUNCTIVE

In general, each tense of the subjunctive mood (Present, Imperfect, Perfect, Pluperfect) has the force of the indicative

tense of the same name (see G. 52, G. 53, G. 55, G. 56); in addition, each may have a future force. Since, however, subjunctive verbs are, for the most part, subordinate (but see G. 39, G.
50, and G. 51), and so generally represent relative rather than
absolute time, it is convenient to treat the tenses of the subjunctive by reference to the rule of Sequence of Tenses. It must be
noted that, corresponding to the diversity of human expression,
a great variety of combinations of tenses is possible; the following rules, however, will be found to apply to the tenses of
subordinate subjunctive verbs in the majority of instances.

G. 58 **Relative Completeness.** A subordinate verb is said
to denote *completed action* if, at the time of the leading verb, the
action of the subordinate verb is no longer in progress, but is
quite finished, i.e. if the action of the subordinate verb entirely
precedes that of the leading verb. A subordinate verb is said
to denote *incomplete action* if, at the time of the leading verb, the
action of the subordinate verb is either still in progress or has
not yet begun, i.e. if the action of the subordinate verb is *contemporary with* or *subsequent to* the action of the leading verb
('state of being' may be substituted for 'action' throughout).

G. 59 **Tense-Sequence with Present and Future Verbs
(Primary Sequence).** With a leading verb denoting present or
future time, the subordinate verb is in the *present* subjunctive if
its action is *incomplete*, in the *perfect* subjunctive if its action is
completed (see G. 58).

> *exerceor*, ut . . . *feram*, 'I train myself, that I may
> endure', **15 26.**
> rēctēne . . . *fēcerim* nōndum mihi . . . *liquet*, 'it is not
> yet clear to me whether I acted rightly', **19 24.**

G. 60 **Tense-Sequence after Past Verbs (Secondary Sequence).** After a leading verb denoting past time, the subordinate verb is in the *imperfect* subjunctive if its action is
incomplete, in the *pluperfect* subjunctive if its action is *completed*
(see G. 58).

> Cum . . . artem āthlēticam *dēsīsset*, iterque *faceret*
> . . . quercum *vīdit*, 'When he had given up ath-
> letics, and was making a journey, he saw an oak-
> tree', **14 2.**

Special Sequence in Result Clause: N. 16 7.

INFINITIVE

G. 61 Infinitive, without Subject, as Noun. A verb in the
infinitive mood, without a subject, may be used as a noun in the
relation of subject or object of a verb, or in the predicate with a
copulative verb, or in apposition with a noun or pronoun.

> *nāscī* contigit, 'his birth (literally, 'to be born') oc-
> curred', **38 23.**
> *īre* . . . coepit, 'he began to go'[6], **18 4.**
> Mōs fuit . . . *introīre*, 'It was the custom to enter', **14
> 12.**
> rēs didicerant . . . difficillimās, *tacēre audīreque*, 'they
> had learned two very difficult things, to keep silent
> and to listen', **33 13.**

G. 62 Complementary Infinitive. A verb which cannot
govern an object, but which looks toward an action or state of
being which can be performed only by or predicated only of its
own subject (e.g. *possum*, 'be able', *soleō*, 'be accustomed') requires an infinitive to *complete* its meaning.

> *imperāre* possum, 'I am able to command', **13 9.**
> Solitus est . . . *ventitāre*, 'he was accustomed to come
> repeatedly', **18 23.**

NOTE: the term Complementary Infinitive is often applied to
any infinitive depending on another verb, if the subject of the
infinitive and the subject of the other verb are the same. See
the second example under G. 61.

G. 63 Infinitive in Substantive Clause. A clause composed
of an infinitive with subject accusative may be used with the
syntax of a noun in the nominative or accusative case: i.e. as
the subject or object of a verb, in the predicate with a copulative
verb, or in apposition with a noun or pronoun.

> *id dīcī* nōn licet, 'that the matter be mentioned is not
> permitted', cp. **14 17.**
> cum . . . *arcessī* . . . *tībīcinem* iussisset, 'when he had
> ordered a flute-player to be summoned', **16 26.**
> *Immortālēs* . . . sī fās foret *flēre*, 'If it were permissible
> for immortals to mourn', **34 20.**

---

[6] See G. 62, *Note.*

Hoc proprium virtūtis exīstimant, . . . *fīnitimōs cēdere*, 'They consider this a characteristic of valor, namely, for one's neighbors to depart', **49 12**.

G. 64   Indirect Statement. An Indirect Statement is a subordinate clause which depends on a verb of *telling, knowing, thinking, perceiving*, or the like;[7] the clause reports the substance of what is *told, known, thought*, or *perceived*. In Indirect Statement, the main verb of the original direct statement is represented by a verb in the infinitive mood, with subject accusative. The subject accusative is regularly expressed unlike the subject of a finite verb (see G. 1), which is so often indicated by a personal ending.

The tense of the infinitive reproduces as closely as possible the tense of the verb in the original direct statement: if the original statement was in the present, the present infinitive is used; if the original statement was in any of the past tenses, the perfect infinitive is used; if the original statement was in the future, the future infinitive is used.

> Dīcēbat P. Vergilius *parere sē* versūs, 'Vergil used to say that he produced verses' (direct: "*Versūs pariō*", 'I produce verses'), **15 8**.
>
> Cum M. Naevius . . . dīceret *accēpisse eum* . . . pecūniam, 'When Naevius said that he (Scipio) had received money' (direct: "*Pecūniam accēpit*", 'He received money'), **17 24**.
>
> animadvertēbat . . . *xercitum* . . . *peritūrum* (*esse*), 'he perceived that the army would perish' (direct, "*Exercitus perībit*", 'The army will perish'), **42 6**.

NOTE: when a copulative verb is in the infinitive in Indirect Statement, a noun or adjective in the predicate of course agrees in case with the subject accusative of the infinitive.

> quōs esse dīcēbat . . . *ōrācula*, 'which she said were oracles', **17 8**.

Historical Infinitive: N. 31 10.

---

[7] See N. 20 24.

IMPERATIVE

G. 65 The imperative mood may be used to express a *command*, *entreaty*, or *admonition*.

> *Disce,* . . . adulēscēns, 'learn, youth', 28 13.
>
> Quaesō, . . . *dīc* mihi, 'Pray, tell me,' 15 18.
>
> *Vīve* . . . mōribus praeteritīs, 'live according to ancient customs', 20 6.

Verbal Nouns With Case-Forms

Gerund: N. 14 18.

Supine: N. 18 3b.

Participles

The participle is a verbal adjective. As an adjective, it agrees in number, gender, and case with the noun or pronoun it modifies; as a verb, it may govern cases, and has voice and tense. The tense expressed by a participle is regularly relative to that of the main verb of the sentence or clause in which the participle appears. The Latin verb has four participles: Present Active, Perfect Passive, Future Active, and Future Passive (Gerundive).

G. 66 The **Present Active Participle** represents an act or state of being as *going on at the time of the main verb*.

> convertēbat . . . exercitum īnsignibus . . . *micantem,* 'he was manœuvring an army gleaming with ornaments', 13 17.

G. 67 The **Perfect Passive Participle** represents an act as *already completed at the time of the main verb*.

> quercus . . . *dīducta* . . . rediit, 'the oak, having been rent asunder, sprang back', 14 8.
>
> ut . . . praedae . . . in eō bellō *captae* ratiōnem redderet, 'that he render an account of the booty captured in that war', 18 10.

G. 68 The **Future Active Participle** represents an act or state of being as *destined or intended to take place at a time subsequent to that of the main verb.*

> cōpiās . . . quās bellum . . . *factūrus* comparāverat, 'troops which he, being about to make war, had mustered', 13 16.

G. 69 The **Future Passive Participle** or **Gerundive** is always passive in relation to the noun or pronoun which it modifies, but its force is rarely as purely temporal as is the case with the other participles; sometimes it is virtually timeless. In conjunction with the verb *sum* (see G. 10), and occasionally elsewhere, this participle expresses necessity, obligation, or propriety.

> *dīlacerandum* hominem ferīs praebuit, 'it gave the man to the wild beasts to be torn to pieces', 14 10.
>
> exitum . . . *miserandum* et *mīrandum*, 'a departure worthy of pity and wonder' (literally, 'to be pitied and wondered at'), 14 1.
>
> cōntiō, quae ad sententiam . . . *ferendam* convēnerat, 'the assemblage, which had convened to pass judgment' (literally, 'for judgment to be passed'; see G. 14), 18 4.
>
> ēloquentiae *discendae* . . . cupidus fuit, 'he was desirous of learning the art of public speaking' (literally, 'desirous of the art . . . to be learned'), 28 1.
>
> ōrātiō . . . quam . . . dīxit . . . dē *dūcendīs* uxōribus, 'the speech which he delivered concerning the taking of wives' (literally, 'concerning wives to be taken'), 32 9.
>
> dī . . . *cōnsulendī* sunt, 'the gods are to be consulted' (i.e. 'ought to be' or 'must be consulted'), 17 23.

Agreement

G. 70 Agreement of Verb with Subject. A verb agrees with its subject in person and number; when a participle forms part of a finite verb, it agrees with the subject in number, gender, and case. When one verb has two or more subjects, it either agrees with the nearest subject or is plural.

rēs . . . *cōnsultāta est*, 'a matter was discussed', **14** 13.

pauca . . . quae *dignitās* . . . atque *glōria postulābat*, 'a few words, which dignity and glory demanded', **17** 28.

ego et *lcō* . . . *vīximus*, 'the lion and I lived', **23** 26.

G. 71 Agreement of Adjective with Noun. An adjective agrees with the noun it modifies in number, gender, and case. When an adjective belongs to more than one noun of the same gender, it may either agree with the nearest, or be plural in that gender; if there is a difference of gender among the nouns, the adjective may either agree with the nearest, or be masculine plural if any of the nouns denotes a man, feminine plural if none denotes a man, but at least one a woman, neuter plural if all denote things.

Ostendēbat . . . *cōpiās ingentīs*, 'He was displaying huge forces', **13** 15.

Navem . . . et *nautās* . . . *Corinthiōs* dēlēgit, 'He chose a Corinthian ship and sailors', **26** 18.

G. 72 Predicate Adjective. An adjective in the predicate with a copulative verb agrees in number, gender, and case with the subject of the verb.

perīcula sunt . . . *maxima*, 'the risks are very great', **26** 1.

G. 73 Agreement of Appositive. A noun or pronoun in apposition with another agrees with it in case.

ad *C. Fabricium* . . . , *imperātōrem* . . . vēnērunt, 'they came to C. Fabricius, a commander', **13** 1.

G. 74 Agreement of Relative Pronoun. A relative pronoun agrees with its antecedent in number and gender; its case is determined by its use in the clause which it introduces.

rēbus, quās . . . fēcerat, 'deeds which he had done', **13** 3.

INDEX TO NOTES ON MINOR
POINTS OF GRAMMAR

This index contains references to points not listed in the Grammatical Outline. Reference is to notes; '13 3' means 'note to page 13, line 3'.

INDEX TO PROPER NAMES IN TEXT

All proper names occurring in the text are listed; only the first occurrence in each Selection is noted. Numbers in parentheses refer to passages in the Introduction and Notes in which these names or related topics are discussed. In the alphabetical order, the abbreviations of *praenōmina* (see pp. 8-9) are disregarded: e.g. M. Tullius Cicero is listed as if Tullius Cicero.

SUPPLEMENTARY INDEX TO IMPORTANT NOTES

This index lists references to important notes which are not covered either by the Grammatical Outline (pp. 161 to 183), the Index to Notes on Minor Points of Grammar (pp. 185 to 186), or the Index to Proper Names in Text (pp. 187 to 190).

TABLE OF CORRESPONDENCES BETWEEN THE SELECTIONS AND THE COMPLETE WORKS OF THE AUTHORS

I. Aulus Gellius, *Noctēs Atticae*

Sel.	Gellius	Sel.	Gellius	Sel.	Gellius
1.	1.14	18.	9.13	35.	15.22
2.	5.5	19.	9.13	36.	2.29
3.	15.16	20.	9.11	37.	2.29
4.	1.23	21.	3.8	38.	2.29
5.	1.23	22.	5.14	39.	1.6
6.	17.10	23.	5.14	40.	1.9
7.	17.4	24.	5.14	41.	1.13
8.	1.17	25.	6.5	42.	1.24
9.	2.1	26.	11.9	43.	3.15
10.	5.2	27.	12.12	44.	4.8
11.	15.17	28.	15.1	45.	4.10
12.	1.19	29.	16.19	46.	5.3
13.	4.18	30.	16.19	47.	5.9
14.	4.18	31.	17.16,17	48.	7.10
15.	6.1	32.	5.10	49.	7.17
16.	1.3	33.	6.18	50.	9.3
17.	1.10	34.	15.22		

II. Cornelius Nepos, *Vītae*

Sel.	Nepos	Sel.	Nepos	Sel.	Nepos
51.	2.6-7	54.	15.7-8	56.	23.9
52.	3.1	55.	23.1.3; 23.2	57.	23.12
53.	6.4				

III. C. Iulius Caesar, *Dē Bellō Gallicō*

Sel. 58: 6.11; 6.13-20; 6.21.1-3; 6.22-23; 4.1.3-6, 8-9; 4.2; 6.24.
Sel. 59: 1.30-54.[8]

---

[8] The following passages have been converted from Indirect Discourse to Direct Discourse: 1.31.2-16, 32.4-5, 34.2-4, 36, 40.2-15, 44, 45, 47.6.

IV. Phaedrus, *Fābulae Aesōpiae*

Sel.	Phaedrus	Sel.	Phaedrus	Sel.	Phaedrus
60.	1.1	70.	1.11	80.	1.31
61.	1.2	71.	1.12	81.	2.4
62.	1.3	72.	1.13	82.	2.7
63.	1.4	73.	1.15	83.	2.8
64.	1.5	74.	1.16	84.	3.7
65.	1.6	75.	1.21	85.	3.8
66.	1.7	76.	1.22	86.	4.3
67.	1.8	77.	1.24	87.	4.4
68.	1.9	78.	1.25	88.	4.9
69.	1.10	79.	1.30	89.	4.10

VOCABULARY

An asterisk marks the form before which it appears as not found in actual use.

The material in square brackets relates to etymology. Only those derivations are given which are deemed instructive or interesting. It is not intended to imply that the word in question is in every case directly and solely derived from the forms given in brackets; occasionally intermediate forms are omitted for the sake of brevity. Within the square brackets, the colon is used as a sign of derivation, with the earlier forms following.

Proper names are given here only to indicate their form and the pronunciation to be used when they occur in English contexts (see N. 13 1c, ¶2). Since all significant proper names are treated in the Notes (see Index to Proper Names, pp. 187-190), only the briefest possible identification is given below. In the alphabetical order, the abbreviations of *praenomina* (see pp. 8 and 9) are disregarded in listing full Roman names: e.g. M. Tullius Cicero is listed as if Tullius Cicero. A Key to the symbols used to indicate the English pronunciation of proper names will be found below after the List of Abbreviations.

LIST OF ABBREVIATIONS

abl.: ablative	*impers.:* impersonal
acc.: accusative	*indecl.:* indeclinable
adj.: adjective	*indef.:* indefinite
adv.: adverb	*infin.:* infinitive
comp.: comparative	*intrans.:* intransitive
cp.: compare	*interj.:* interjection
conj.: conjunction	*interrog.:* interrogative
dat.: dative	*m.:* masculine
defect.: defective	*n.:* neuter
demonstr.: demonstrative	*nom.:* nominative
distr.: distributive	*num.:* numerical
f.: feminine	*part.:* participle
fut.: future	*pass.:* passive
gen.: genitive	*perf.:* perfect
imperf.: imperfect	*pers.:* personal

pl.: plural
poss.: possessive
p.p.p.: perfect passive participle
prep.: preposition
pron.: pronoun
reflex.: reflexive
rel.: relative

s.: singular
sc.: supply, understand
subjv.: subjunctive
subst.: substantive
superl.: superlative
trans.: transitive
w.: with

KEY TO PRONUNCIATION OF ANGLICIZED PROPER NAMES

ā as in fāte
â as in senâte
ă as in făt
ä as in ärm
ą as in ąll
à as in sofà
ą as in whąt
ē as in mēte
ê as in êvent
ĕ as in mĕt
ē as in hēr
ī as in īce
ĭ as in ĭt
ō as in ōld
ô as in ôbey
ŏ as in nŏt
ô as in côrk

ū as in ūse
û as in ûnite
ŭ as in ŭp
û as in fûr
ų as in rųle
ų as in pųll
ȳ as in bȳ
ў as in babў
c as in call
g as in go
ġ as in caġe
n as in ink
qu as in quit
s as in sit
ş as in hiş
z as in zebra
ʒ as in azure

Vocabulary

ā, ab, abs, *prep. w. abl.:* away from, from; against; *to denote a side or direction,* at, on; *with pass.,* by

Abdēra, Abdērōrum, *n. pl.:* a city in Thrace (ăbdē'ra)

ab-dō, -dere, -didī, -ditus [ab, dō]: put away; conceal, hide

ab-dūcō, -dūcere, -dūxī, -ductus [ab, dūcō]: lead away

ab-eō, -īre, -iī, -itūrus [ab, 2.eō]: go away; get away, get off

abhinc, *adv.* [ab, *cp.* hinc]: ago, since

ab-iciō, -icere, -iēcī, -iectus [ab, iaciō]: throw away, cast down

ablēgō, -āre, -āvī, -ātus [ab, lēgō (*delegate*)]: send away

abrogō, -āre, -āvī, -ātus [ab, rogō]: repeal, annul

abs: *see* **ā**

absēns, *gen.* **absentis,** *adj.* [absum]: absent

ab-solvō, -solvere, -solvī, -solūtus [ab, solvō]: set free, discharge, absolve

abstinentia, -ae, *f.* [abs, teneō]: abstinence, self-restraint, integrity

abstulī: *see* **auferō**

absum, abesse, āfuī, āfutūrus [ab, sum]: be away, be absent

abundē, *adv.* [abundō (*overflow*): ab, undō (*flow*): unda]: abundantly, fully

ac: *see* **atque**

ac-cēdō, -cēdere, -cessī, -cessūrus [ad, cēdō]: go to, approach

ac-cidō, -cidere, -cidī [ad, cadō]: happen

ac-cipiō, -cipere, -cēpī, -ceptus [ad, capiō]: receive, accept; take on board

accipiter, accipitris, *m.:* hawk

accūrātus, -a, -um, *adj.* [accūrō (*take care*): ad, cūrō]: careful, exact

accūsātor, accūsātōris, *m.* [accūsō]: accuser

accūsō, -āre, -āvī, -ātus [ad, *cp.* causa]: accuse

ācer, ācris, ācre, *adj.:* sharp; violent; keen, brave, fierce

acerbus, -a, -um, *adj.* [*cp.* ācer]: bitter

acervus, -ī, *m.:* pile, heap

aciēs, aciēī, *f.* [*cp.* ācer]: sharp edge; keenness, sharpness; army (*in order of battle*), line of battle

āctor, āctōris, *m.* [agō]: actor

ad, *prep. w. acc.:* to, towards; to the number of; at, by, near; for

adaequō, -āre, -āvī, -ātus [ad, aequō]: make equal; equal, keep up with

adamō, -āre, -āvī, -ātus [ad, amō]: fall in love with, become fond of

ad-dō, -dere, -didī, -ditus [ad, dō]: put to, place upon; add

ad-dūcō, -dūcere, -dūxī, -ductus [ad, dūcō]: lead to; induce; bring, bring to

1. adeō, *adv.* [ad, 1.eō]: to such a degree, so very; indeed, truly; *with a negative,* still less

2. ad-eō, -īre, -iī, -itūrus [ad, 2.eō]: go to, approach

adequitō, -āre, -āvī, -ātus [ad, equitō (*ride*): eques]: ride to

adessent: *see* **adsum**

adferō, adferre, attulī, allātus [ad, ferō]: carry to, bring to; adduce, allege, assign; *w. reflex. pron.,* betake oneself; employ

197

ad-ficiō, -ficere, -fēcī, -fectus [ad, faciō]: do to, treat, affect; afflict, overcome; brand

adfīnis, -e, adj. [ad, fīnis]: neighboring, adjoining; subst. m., relation by marriage

ad-flīgō, -flīgere, -flīxī, -flictus [ad, flīgō (strike)]: overwhelm with blows, overcome, beat

ad-hibeō, -hibēre, -hibuī, -hibitus [ad, habeō]: bring to; apply to, bring to bear, employ; summon

ad-igō, -igere, -ēgī, -āctus [ad, agō]: drive to; urge, force; cause to take an oath

adipīscor, adipīscī, adeptus sum [ad, apīscor]: obtain, get, attain

aditus, -ūs, m. [2.adeō]: approach, means of approach

ad-iungō, -iungere, -iūnxī, -iūnctus [ad, iungō]: join to, fasten on, draw near; add

ad-iuvō, -iuvāre, -iūvī, -iūtus [ad, iuvō]: help

administer, administrī, m. [administrō]: helper; minister

administrō, -āre, -āvī, -ātus [ad, ministrō]: manage, control

admīrātiō, -iōnis, f. [admīror]: wonder, astonishment, admiration

admīror, -ārī, -ātus sum [ad, mīror]: wonder at, admire

ad-mittō, -mittere, -mīsī, -missus [ad, mittō]: send to, let go; admit; allow

admodum, adv. [ad, modus]: to full measure; very, extremely

ad-moneō, -monēre, -monuī, -monitus [ad, moneō]: warn, admonish

adnatō, -āre [ad, natō]: swim to

ad-nītor, -nītī, -nīxus (or -nīsus) sum [ad, nītor]: strive

adnō, -āre, -āvī [ad, nō (swim)]: swim to

ad-olēscō, -olēscere, -olēvī, -ultus [ad, *alēscō (grow): alō]: grow up; ripen

ad-orior, -orīrī, -ortus sum [ad, orior]: rise against; attack

ad-quiēscō, -quiēscere, -quiēvī [ad, quiēscō]: become quiet, rest

adrogāns, gen. adrogantis, adj. [adrogō (claim): ad, rogō]: arrogant, haughty

adrogantia, -ae, f. [adrogāns]: arrogance, haughtiness

ad-scrībō, -scrībere, -scrīpsī, -scrīptus [ad, scrībō]: assign, ascribe; add in writing, add

ad-serō, -serere, -seruī, -sertus [ad, serō (bind)]: claim, assert

ad-sideō, -sidēre, -sēdī [ad, sedeō]: sit by; lay siege to

adsiduus, -a, -um, adj. [ad, sedeō]: persistent, diligent, constant

adsignō, -āre, -āvī, -ātus [ad, signō]: mark out, assign; ascribe

ad-sistō, -sistere, -stitī [ad, sistō]: stand by; attend

adsuē-faciō, -facere, -fēcī, -factus [adsuēscō, faciō]: accustom, train

ad-suēscō, -suēscere, -suēvī, -suētus. [ad, suēscō (become accustomed)]: become accustomed; p.p. p. adsuētus, -a, -um: accustomed

ad-sum, -esse, -fuī, -futūrus [ad, sum]: be present, be at hand

adulēscēns, gen. adulēscentis, adj. [adolēscō]: young, youthful; subst. m., youth, young man

adulēscentia, -ae, f. [adulēscēns]: youth

adūlor, -ārī, -ātus sum: fawn, flatter

ad-veniō, -venīre, -vēnī, -ventūrus [ad, veniō]: come to, approach

adventō, -āre [adveniō]: advance, approach

adventus, -ūs, m. [adveniō]: approach, arrival

adversārius, -a, -um, adj. [adversus]: hostile; subst. m.: enemy, opponent

adversum or adversus, adv. and prep. w. acc. [advertō]: in opposition; against, toward

adversus, -a, -um, adj. [advertō]: turned toward, facing; opposed, contrary, unfavorable, unpropi-

tious (*see also preceding entry*)
ad-vertō, -vertere, -vertī, -versus
[ad, vertō]: turn to, direct; notice,
give heed
ad-vesperāscit, -vesperāscere, *impers.* [ad, vesperāscit (*becomes
evening*): vesper]: it approaches
evening, it is twilight
advocō, -āre, -āvī, -ātus [ad, vocō]:
summon; call to aid
advolō, -āre, -āvī, -ātūrus [ad, 2.
volō]: fly to, fly near; rush upon
aedēs, aedis, *f.*: temple, sanctuary;
pl. dwelling, house
aedificium, aedificiī, *n.* [aedēs, fa-
ciō]: building
aedificō, -āre, -āvī, -ātus [aedēs,
faciō]: build
aeditumus, -ī, *m.* [aedēs]: custodian
of a temple, sacristan
Aeduus, -a, -um, *adj.*: Aeduan, of
the Aedui, *a Gallic people; subst.
m. pl.*, the Aedui (ĕd′ûàn, ĕd′ûĭ)
aegrē, *adv.* [aeger (*ill*)]: with difficulty, hardly; aegrē patior: be
displeased
aegritūdō, aegritūdinis, *f.* [aeger
(*ill*)]: illness; uneasiness, grief
Aegyptus, -ī, *f.*: Egypt
Aenēis, Aenēidos, *f.*: the Aeneid, *a
poem of Vergil* (ĕnē′ĭd)
aēneus, -a, -um, *adj.* [aes]: of copper; of bronze, brazen
aequālis, -e, *adj.* [aequō]: of the
same age, equally old
aequiperō, -āre, -āvī, -ātus [aequus]:
equal, rival
aequitās, -ātis, *f.* [aequus]: fairness,
equity; evenness, calmness
aequō, -āre, -āvī, -ātus [aequus]:
make equal, equalize
aequus, -a, -um, *adj.*: even, level;
fair, reasonable; favorable, friendly
aerārium, aerāriī, *n.* [aerārius (*monetary*): aes]: treasury
aes, aeris, *n.*: copper, bronze;
money; aes aliēnum: debt

Aesōpus, -ī, *m.*: Aesop, *the Greek
fabulist* (ē′sŏp)
aestās, -ātis, *f.*: summer
aestimātiō, -iōnis, *f.* [aestimō]: valu-
ation, appraisal
aestimō, -āre, -āvī, -ātus: estimate,
appraise
aestus, -ūs, *m.*: heat; waves, sea,
tide
aetās, -ātis, *f.* [aevum]: age; generation, time
aevum, -ī, *n.*: time; age
Āfrica, -ae, *f.*: Africa
ager, agrī, *m.*: productive land,
field; farm; territory, district
agnōscō, agnōscere, agnōvī, agnitus
[ad, (g)nōscō]: recognize; acknowledge
agnus, -ī, *m.*: lamb
agō, agere, ēgī, āctus: lead; discuss,
confer; perform, do, transact;
enact, act
aiō, *defect.*: say
āla, -ae, *f.*: wing
alacritās, -ātis, *f.* [alacer (*lively*)]:
liveliness, eagerness, cheerfulness
ālārius, -a, -um, *adj.* [āla]: pertain-
ing to the wing (of an army);
subst. m. pl., auxiliary troops
albus, -a, -um, *adj.*: white
Alcibiadēs, Alcibiadis, *m.*: *an Athenian* (ălsĭbī′ădēs)
āles, *gen.* ālitis, *adj.* [āla]: winged;
subst. m. and f.: winged creature,
bird
Alexander, Alexandrī, *m.*: *a king of
Macedonia*
Alexandrīa, -ae, *f.*: *a city in Egypt*
Alexandrīnus, -a, -um, *adj.*: Alexan-
drian, of Alexandria
aliēnus, -a, -um [alius]: of another,
belonging to another; foreign,
strange; out of place, inappropriate
aliō, *adv.* [alius]: to another place,
elsewhere; in another direction,
toward a different purpose
aliquamdiū, *adv.* [aliquī, diū]: for
some time, for a while

aliquī, aliqua, aliquod, *indef. adj.:* some, any

aliquis, aliqua, aliquid, *indef. pron.:* someone, something; anyone, anything

aliter, *adv.* [alius]: in another way, otherwise; aliter . . . aliter: in one way . . . in another

alius, alia, aliud, *adj.:* another, other, different; *in distr. clauses,* alius . . . alius, aliī . . . aliī: one . . . another, some . . . others; *used twice in the same clause,* one . . . one . . . , another . . . another: *e.g.* alius aliā ex nāvī: one from one ship, another from another

allātus, -a, -um: *see* adferō

alligō, -āre, -āvī, -ātus [ad, ligō (*bind*)]: bind to, tie to; tie up

Allobrogēs, Allobrogum, *m. pl.:* a *Gallic people* (ălŏb'rŏgēş)

alō, alere, aluī, altus: feed, nourish

alter, altera, alterum: the other (of two); one (of two); alter . . . alter: the one . . . the other

altitūdō, altitūdinis, *f.* [altus]: height

altus, -a, -um, *adj.* [alō]: high, tall; deep

alūmen, alūminis, *n.:* alum

ambactus, -ī, *m.:* vassal, dependent

am-: *see* ambi-

ambi-, amb-, am-, an-, *prefix:* around, round about

ambiguus, -a, -um, *adj.* [ambigō (*drive about*): ambi-, agō]: doubtful, wavering

ambitus, -ūs, *m.* [ambiō (*go around*): ambi-, 2.eō]: corruption, bribery

ambō, ambae, ambō, *adj.* [*cp.* ambi-]: both

Ambraciēnsis, -e, *adj.:* Ambracian, of Ambracia *in Greece* (ămbrā'-shǐá)

āmentia, -ae, *f.* [āmēns (*mad*): ā, mēns]: madness, senselessness

amiciō, amicīre, ——, amictus [ambi-, iaciō]: wrap around, cloak

amīcitia, -ae, *f.* [amīcus]: friendship

amīcus, -a, -um, *adj.* [amō]: friendly; *subst. m.,* friend; *superl. as subst. m.,* very good friend

ā-mittō, -mittere, -mīsī, -missus [ā, mittō]: send away, dismiss; lose

amō, -āre, -āvī, -ātus: love

amphora, -ae, *f.:* two-handled vessel, jar

am-plector, -plectī, -plexus sum [am-, plectō (*weave*)]: embrace

amplius, *adv.* [amplus]: more, further

amplus, -a, -um, *adj.:* large, ample, abundant, extensive, generous

1. an, *conj.: in disjunctive questions,* or; *in simple indirect questions,* whether

2. an-: *see* ambi-

anceps, *gen.* ancipitis, *adj.* [2.an-, caput]: two-headed; double, twofold; doubtful, perilous

Androclus, -ī, *m.: a slave* (ăn'drŏclŭs)

angustiae, angustiārum, *f. pl.* [angustus (*narrow*)]: narrow pass, defile

anima, -ae, *f.:* soul, life

animad-vertō, -vertere, -vertī, -versus [animus, advertō]: give attention to, observe, notice, realize

animal, animālis, *n.* [anima]: animal

animus, -ī, *m.:* mind, spirit, heart

annālis, -e, *adj.* [annus]: of a year; *subst. m.* (*sc.* liber): chronicle, annals

annus, -ī, *m.:* year; *pl.* age

ante, *adv. and prep. w. acc.:* before

anteā, *adv.:* formerly

ante-stō, -stāre, -stetī [ante, stō]: excel, surpass, be superior

Antiās, *gen.* Antiātis, *adj.: see* Valerius

Antigenidās, Antigenidae, *m.: a Greek musician* (ăntĭgěn'ĭdăs)

Antiochīnus, -a, -um, *adj.:* of Antiochus

Antiochus, -ī, *m.: a king of Syria* (ăntĭ'ŏcŭs)

antīquitās, -ātis, *f.* [antīquus]: antiquity

antīquitus, *adv.* [antīquus]: in former times, of old

antīquus, -a, -um, *adj.* [ante]: ancient, of old time

Antōnius Iūliānus: *a professor of rhetoric* (ăntō'nĭŭs jūlĭā'nŭs)

anus, -ūs, *f.*: old woman

aper, aprī, *m.*: wild boar, wild sow

aperiō, aperīre, aperuī, apertus: uncover, open; *p.p.p.* apertus, -a, -um: uncovered, open; *adv.* apertē: openly

apertus: *sce* aperiō

apīscor, apīscī, aptus sum: attain, get, get possession of

Apollō, Apollinis, *m.*: *god of prophecy* (ápŏl'ō)

apologus, -ī, *m.*: fable

ap-pāreō, -pārēre, -pāruī, -pāritūrus [ad, pāreō]: appear

appellō, -āre, -āvī, -ātus: address, speak to; call, name

ap-petō, -petere, -petīvī (*or* -petiī), -petītus [ad, petō]: strive for, seek; approach, draw near

ap-pōnō, -pōnere, -posuī, -positus [ad, pōnō]: place at, place near

ap-prehendō, -prehendere, -prehendī, -prehēnsus [ad, prehendō]: seize

approbō, -āre, -āvī, -ātus [ad, probō]: approve, favor; prove

aptus, -a, -um, *adj.*: suited, apt (*also see* apīscor)

apud, *prep. w. acc.*: before, in the presence of; among, with, in, at; at the house of

aqua, -ae, *f.*: water

aquila, -ae, *f.*: eagle

āra, -ae, *f.*: altar

arāneum, -ī, *n.*: cobweb

arbitrium, arbitriī, *n.* [arbiter (*judge*)]: judgment, decision

arbitror, -ārī, -ātus sum [arbiter (*judge*)]: think, consider

arbor, arboris, *f.*: tree

arceō, arcēre, arcuī [*cp.* arx]: keep

away, hold off; hinder, prevent

arcessō, arcessere, arcessīvī, arcessītus: send for, summon

Archelāus, -ī, *m.*: *a Greek general* (ärkĕlā'ŭs)

architectōn, *acc.* architectona, *m.*: architect

ārdeō, ārdēre, ārsī, ārsūrus [*cp.* āridus]: be on fire, burn, blaze

arduus, -a, -um, *adj.*: lofty

argenteus, -a, -um, *adj.* [argentum]: of silver, made of silver

argentum, -ī, *n.*: silver

argūmentum, -ī, *n.* [arguō]: argument, proof, evidence; story, plot

arguō, arguere, arguī, argūtus: prove, declare; accuse, charge

argyranchē, argyranchēs, *f.*: *a word coined in jest,* 'silver-constriction'

āridus, -a, -um, *adj.* [*cp.* ārdeō]: dry, parched

ariēs, ariētis, *m.*: ram, battering-ram

Ariōn, Ariōnis, *m.*: *a Greek musician* (ărĭ'ŏn)

Ariovistus, -ī, *m.*: *a German king* (ărĭŏvĭs'tŭs)

Aristīdēs, Aristīdis, *m.*: *an Athenian statesman* (ărĭstī'dēş)

Aristodēmus, -ī, *m.*: *a Greek actor* (ărĭstŏdē'mŭs)

Aristotēlēs, Aristotēlis, *m.*: *Aristotle, a Greek philosopher* (ăr'ĭstŏt'l)

arma, armōrum, *n.pl.*: arms, weapons

armilla, -ae, *f.* [armus (*upper arm*)]: bracelet, armlet

armō, -āre, -āvī, -ātus [arma]: arm, equip

artificium, artificiī, *n.* [artĭfex (*artist*): ars, faciō]: craft, art, trade

ars, artis, *f.*: skill; art

Arvernī, Arvernōrum, *m. pl.*: *a Gallic people* (ärvēr'nī)

arx, arcis, *f.* [*cp.* arceō]: citadel, fortress

asellus, -ī, *m.* [asinus]: little donkey, donkey, ass

Asia, -ae, *f.*: Asia

asinus, -ī, *m.*: donkey, ass

asper, aspera, asperum, *adj.*: rough, harsh, violent; hard

aspiciō, aspicere, aspexī, aspectus [ad, speciō]: look at, behold

asportō, -āre, -āvī, -ātus [abs, portō]: carry away

astūtus, -a, -um, *adj.* [astus (*craftiness*)]: crafty, cunning; shrewd

at, *conj.*: but

Athēnae, Athēnārum, *f.pl.*: Athens (ăth'ĕng)

Athēniēnsis, -e, *adj.*: Athenian, of Athens (ăthē'nĭăn)

āthlēta, -ae, *m.*: athlete

āthlēticus, -a, -um, *adj.*: athletic

atque *or* ac, *conj.*: and moreover, and; *with words denoting sameness,* as; *with words denoting difference,* than

atrōx, *gen.* atrōcis, *adj.*: savage, fierce

attentus, -a, -um, *adj.* [attendō (*stretch toward*): ad, tendō (*stretch*)]: attentive, intent

attestor, -ārī, -ātus sum [ad, testor]: prove, confirm

Attica, -ae, *f.*: the region around Athens (ăt'ĭcă)

Atticus, -a, -um, *adj.*: Attic, Athenian (ăthē'nĭăn)

at-tingō, -tingere, -tigī, -tāctus [ad, tangō]: touch; reach, arrive at

at-tribuō, -tribuere, -tribuī, -tribūtus [ad, tribuō]: assign; ascribe

auctōritās, -ātis, *f.* [auctor (*producer*): augeō]: authority, prestige, influence

auctus, -a, -um: *see* augeō

audāx, *gen.* audācis, *adj.* [audeō]: daring, bold

audeō, audēre, ausus sum [avidus]: dare

audiō, audīre, audīvī, audītus: hear, listen to; *w. dat.,* obey

audītor, audītōris, *m.* [audiō]: hearer, pupil

auferō, auferre, abstulī, ablātus [ab, ferō]: carry away; receive

augeō, augēre, auxī, auctus: increase, enlarge, extend; *p.p.p.*

auctus, -a, -um: increased, enriched

Augustus, -ī, *m.*: *the founder of the Roman Empire* (ăgŭs'tŭs)

aureus, -a, -um, *adj.* [aurum]: golden

auris, auris, *f.*: ear

aurītulus, -ī, *m.* [aurītus (*long-eared*): auris]: little long-eared creature, donkey

aurum, -ī, *n.*: gold

Auruncī, Auruncōrum, *m. pl.*: *an Italic people* (ᾱrŭn'sī)

aut, *conj.*: or; aut . . . aut: either . . . or

autem, *conj.*: however, moreover; but, now

auxiliārius, -a, -um, *adj.* [auxilium]: auxiliary

auxilium, auxiliī, *n.* [*cp.* augeō]: help, aid

avāritia, -ae, *f.* [avārus]: greed, avarice

avārus, -a, -um, *adj.* [aveō (*desire*)]: greedy

ā-vertō, -vertere, -vertī, -versus [ā, vertō]: turn aside, turn away

aviditās, -ātis, *f.* [avidus]: eagerness, greed

avidus, -a, -um, *adj.* [aveō (*desire*)]: greedy, eager

avis, avis, *f.*: bird

avunculus, -ī, *m.* [avus (*grandfather*)]: maternal uncle, mother's brother

baiulus, -ī, *m.*: porter

barbarus, -a, -um, *adj.*: foreign: uncivilized, barbarous

barbātus, -a, -um, *adj.* [barba (*beard*)]: bearded; *subst. m.* bearded creature, goat

bellātor, bellātōris, *m.* [bellō]: warrior

bellicōsus, -a, -um, *adj.* [bellicus (*military*): bellum]: warlike

bellō, -āre, -āvī, -ātus [bellum]:
wage war, fight
bellum, -ī, n.: war
bene: see bonus
beneficium, beneficiī, n. [bene,
faciō]: bcncfit, service, kindness
benevolus, -a, -um, adj. [bene, 1.
volō]: well-wishing, kindly, kind,
generous
benficium = beneficium
bēstia, -ae, f.: beast, animal
bibō, bibere, bibī: drink
bīduum, -ī, n. [bi- (twice), diēs]:
period of two days, two days
biennium, bieniī, n. [bi- (twice),
annus]: period of two years, two
years
bilinguis, -e, adj. [bi- (twice),
lingua]: two-tongued, hypocritical
bīnī, -ae, -a, distr. num. adj. [bis]:
two by two, two at a time; two
bis, num. adv.: twice
Bīthȳnia, -ae, f.: a region of Asia
Minor (bĭthĭn'ĭà)
blandīmentum, -ī, n. [blandior (caress): blandus]: caress, fondling
blandus, -a, -um, adj.: caressing,
coaxing, charming
Boeōtī, Boeōtōrum, m. pl.: Boeotians, inhabitants of Boeotia in
Greece (bēō'shĭàn̄s, bēō'shĭà)
bonitās, -ātis, f. [bonus]: goodness
bonus, -a, -um, adj.: good, kind;
fine; comp. melior, melius: better;
superl. optimus, -a, -um: best,
very good; adv. bene: well
bōs, bovis, dat. and abl. pl. būbus, m.
and f.: ox, bull, cow
bovīle, bovīlis, n. [bōs]: ox-stall,
stall
brevī: see brevis
brevis, -e, adj.: short, brief, small;
adv. brevī: shortly, in a short
time
Britannia, -ae, f.: Britain
bubulcus, -ī, m. [bōs]: ox-driver,
herdsman
Būcephalās, Būcephalae, m.: Alexander's horse (bū̆sĕf'àlàs)

Būcephalos, acc. Būcephalon, f.:
Bucephalus, a town in India
(bū̆sĕf'àlŭs)
C.: Gaius (gā'yŭs)
cadō, cadere, cecidī, cāsūrus: fall
Q. Caecilius Metellus Numidicus:
a Roman consul (quĭn'tus sĕsĭl'ĭŭs
mĕtĕl'ŭs nŭmĭd'ĭcŭs)
caecus, -a, -um, adj.: blind
caedēs, caedis, f. [caedō]: slaughter,
killing
caedō, caedere, cecīdī, caesus: cut,
strike, kill
caelestis, -e, adj. [caelum]: of
heaven; subst. m. pl., heavenly
beings, gods
Caesar, Caesaris, m.: see Iūlius
calamitās, -ātis, f.: calamity, disaster
calliditās, -ātis, f. [callidus]: shrewd-
ness, cleverness
callidus, -a, -um, adj. [calleō (be
callous)]: practised, shrewd, clever
L. Calvisius Taurus: a philosopher
(lū'shĭŭs cälvĭsh'ĭŭs tạ'rŭs)
calx, calcis, f.: heel
Camēnae, Camēnārum, f. pl.: goddesses of springs and fountains;
Muses (càmē'nē)
Campānus, -a, -um, adj.: Campa-
nian, of Campania in Italy (càmpā'nĭàn, càmpā'nĭà)
campus, -ī, m.: plain, field
canis, canis, m. and f.: dog
Cannae, Cannārum, f. pl.: a city in
Italy (căn'ē)
Cannēnsis, -e, adj.: of Cannae
canō, canere, cecinī: sing, play
cantō, -āre, -āvī, -ātus [canō]: sing
cantor, cantōris, m. [canō]: singer,
poet
cantus, -ūs, m. [canō]: song
capella, -ae, f. [capra (she-goat)]:
little she-goat, she-goat
capessō, capessere, capessīvī, ca-
pessītus [capiō]: take hold of with
zeal, undertake
capiō, capere, cēpī, captus: take,

seize, capture; adopt, conceive; experience, suffer

capitālis, -e, *adj.* [caput]: involving life or civil rights, capital; punishable by death

Capitōlium, Capitōliī, *n.:* the Capitol, *temple of Jupiter at Rome*

captīvus, -a, -um, *adj.* [capiō]: taken prisoner, captive; *subst.* *m.,* captive, prisoner

captus, -ūs, *m.* [capiō]: capacity

caput, capitis, *n.:* head; civil rights

carcer, carceris, *m.:* prison, jail

careō, carēre, caruī, caritūrus: be without, be free from

cāritās, -ātis, *f.* [cārus]: affection

carmen, carminis, *n.* [canō]: song; poem

Carnūtēs, Carnūtum, *m. pl.: a Gallic people* (cärnū'tēg)

carō, carnis, *f.:* meat, flesh

carpō, carpere, carpsī, carptus: pluck, snatch

carrus, -ī, *m.:* cart, wagon

Carthāginiēnsis, -e, *adj.:* of Carthage, Carthaginian (cärthā́gǐn'-ĭán)

Carthāgō, Carthāginis, *f.:* Carthage, *a city of North Africa* (cär'thǎg)

caseus, -ī, *m.:* cheese

cassita, -ae, *f.* [cassis (*helmet*)]: crested lark, lark

castellum, -ī, *n.* [castrum]: fortress, stronghold

T. Castricius: *a teacher of rhetoric* (tī'tǔs cǎstrǐsh'ǐǔs)

castrum, -ī, *n.:* fortress; *usually pl.,* castra, castrōrum: camp

cāsus, -ūs, *m.* [cadō]: fall; accident, chance; calamity

catēna, -ae, *f.:* chain; *often pl. to denote a single chain*

caterva, -ae, *f.:* troop, band

cathedra, -ae, *f.:* arm-chair, chair

Catō, Catōnis, *m.: see* **Porcius**

catulus, -ī, *m.:* young animal; puppy; kitten

cauda, -ae, *f.:* tail

caudex, caudicis, *m.:* trunk of a tree, log

causa, -ae, *f.:* cause, reason; lawsuit, case; **causam ōrō:** plead a case; *abl. governing a preceding gen.,* **causā:** for the sake of

cautus, -a, -um, *adj.* [caveō]: careful, wary, cautious

caveō, cavēre, cāvī, cautus: be on one's guard, take care; provide

caverna, -ae, *f.* [cavus]: hollow, cavity

cavillātiō, -iōnis, *f.* [cavillor]: mockery, jest

cavillor, -ārī, -ātus sum [cavilla (*mockery*)]: jeer, mock, jest

cavus, -a, -um, *adj.:* hollow; *subst. n.,* opening, hole

cēdō, cēdere, cessī, cessūrus: go away, go; *w. dat.,* yield

celeber, celebris, celebre, *adj.:* frequented, much visited; honored, celebrated

celer, celeris, celere, *adj.:* swift, quick

celeritās, -ātis, *f.* [celer]: speed, swiftness

cella, -ae, *f.* [cp. cēlō]: store-room, sanctuary, shrine

cēlō, -āre, -āvī, -ātus: hide from, keep ignorant of; conceal

celsus, -a, -um, *adj.* [cellō (*tower*)]: lofty

cēna, -ae, *f.:* dinner

cēnō, -āre, -āvī, -ātus [cēna]: dine

cēnseō, cēnsēre, cēnsuī, cēnsus: estimate; propose, move; resolve, decree; think, believe

cēnsor, cēnsōris, *m.* [cēnseō]: censor, *a Roman magistrate*

cēnsūra, -ae, *f.* [cēnsor]: *the magistracy of the censor,* censorship

centum, indecl. num. adj.: a hundred

centuriō, -iōnis, *m.* [centuria (*company of one hundred men*): centum]: *commander of a company,* centurion

cerebrum, -ī, *n.:* brain

cernō, cernere, crēvī, crētus: see;

distinguish, discern; decide, decree

certāmen, certāminis, *n.* [certō]: decisive battle; contest

certātim, *adv.* [certō]: in rivalry, in competition

certō, -āre, -āvī, -ātus [certus]: vie with, compete, struggle, fight

certus, -a, -um, *adj.* [cernō]: determined, fixed, certain; certior fīō: be informed; *adv.* certō: certainly, surely

cerva, -ae, *f.* [cervus]: female deer, doe

cervīx, cervīcis, *f.*: nape of the neck; neck; shoulders

cervus, -ī, *m.*: male deer, stag

cessātor, cessātōris, *m.* [cessō]: loiterer, idler

cessō, -āre, -āvī, -ātus [cēdō]: loiter, linger; pause, cease

cēterī, -ae, -a, *adj.*: other, remaining

Charēs, Charētis, *m.*: a Greek historian (cā′rēs)

Chīlō, Chīlōnis, *m.*: a Spartan magistrate (kī′lō)

cibārius, -a, -um, *adj.* [cibus]: of food; rēs cibāria: food supply

cibus, -ī, *m.*: food

Cicerō, Cicerōnis, *m.*: *see* Tullius

Cimberius, Cimberiī, *m.*: a German leader (sĭmbē′rĭŭs)

Cimbrī, Cimbrōrum, *m. pl.*: a Germanic people (sĭm′brī)

cingō, cingere, cīnxī, cīnctus: surround, encompass, gird

circinus, -ī, *m.* [circus]: pair of compasses

circiter, *adv. and prep. w. acc.* [circus]: about, around

circuitus, -ūs, *m.* (*cp.* circumeō]: circuit, circuitous route

circum, *adv. and prep. w. acc.* [circus]: around, round about

circum-dō, -dare, -dedī, -datus [circum, dō]: place around; surround

circum-dūcō, -dūcere, -dūxī, -ductus [circum, dūcō]: lead around, draw around

circum-eō, -īre, -iī, -itūrus [circum, 2.eō]: go around

circum-ferō, -ferre, -tulī, -lātus [circum, ferō]: carry around, circulate

circum-fundō, -fundere, -fūdī, -fūsus [circum, fundō]: pour around; *pass. w. middle force* (Note 15 26): surround

circum-plector, -plectī, -plexus sum [circum, plectō (*weave*)]: embrace

circum-sistō, -sistere, -stetī [circum, sistō]: stand around

circum-spiciō, -spicere, -spexī, -spectus [circum, speciō]: look around at, look around

circum-stō, -stāre, -stetī [circum, stō]: stand around

circum-strepō, -strepere, -strepuī, -strepitus [circum, strepō (*make a noise*)]: make a noise around

circum-veniō, -venīre, -vēnī, -ventus [circum, veniō]: go around, surround; trick, abuse

circumvolō, -āre, -āvī, -ātūrus [circum, 2.volō]: fly around

circus, -ī, *m.*: circle; race-course, circus

Cispius, -a, -um, *adj.*: Cispian; mōns Cispius: the Cispian Hill, in Rome (sĭs′pĭăn)

citerior, citerius, *adj.* [cis (*on this side*)]: on this side, nearer, hither

citō, -āre, -āvī, -ātus [cieō (*stir*)]: put in quick motion, rouse; urge; summon

citrō, *adv.* [cis (*on this side*)]: to this side, hither; ultrō citrōque: back and forth, to and fro

cīvis, cīvis, *m.*: citizen, fellow-citizen

cīvitās, -ātis, *f.* [cīvis]: citizenship; state

clāmitō, -āre, -āvī, -ātus [clāmō]: shout

clāmō, -āre, -āvī, -ātus: call, shout

clāmor, clāmōris, *m.* [clāmō]: loud call, shout

clandestīnus, -a, -um, *adj.* [clam (*silently*): cēlō]: secret, hidden

clāritūdŏ, clāritūdinis, *f.* [clārus]:
brightness; clarity, clearness
clārus, -a, -um, *adj.*: clear, bright;
brilliant; famous
classis, classis, *f.*: fleet
Q. Claudius Quadrīgārius: *a Roman
historian* (quĭn'tŭs clạ'dĭŭs quạd-
rīgā'rĭŭs)
claudŏ, claudere, clausĭ, clausus
[*cp.* clāvis (*key*)]: close, shut; shut
in, hem in
clēmenter, *adv.* [clēmēns (*mild*)]:
mildly, leniently, with clemency
cliēns, clientis, *m.*: dependant, client; vassal
clītellae, clītellārum, *f. pl.*: pack-
saddle, saddle
Cn.: Gnaeus (nē'ŭs)
co-: *see* com-
coāctus: *see* cōgŏ
co-eŏ, -īre, -iī, -itūrus [co-, 2.eŏ]: go
together, come together, meet
coepī, coepisse, coeptus, *defect.*:
begin, commence
cōgitŏ, -āre, -āvī, -ātus [co-, agitŏ
(*set in motion*): agŏ]: consider,
ponder, think
cognātiŏ, -iōnis, *f.* [cognātus]:
blood-relationship; group of
blood-relations
cognātus, -a, -um, *adj.* [co-, (g)nās-
cor]: related by blood; *subst. m.*,
blood-relation, kinsman
cognōmen, cognōminis, *n.* [co-,
nōmen[1]]: surname
cognōminŏ, -āre, -āvī, -ātus [cognō-
men]: provide with a surname,
surname
cognōscŏ, cognōscere, cognōvī, cognitus [co-, (g)nōscō]: become ac-
quainted with, learn, examine; *in
perf. system,* know
cōgŏ, cōgere, coēgī, coāctus [co-,
agŏ]: drive together; compel
cohors, cohortis, *f.*: *the tenth part
of a legion,* division, cohort; body,
band, group

collēga, -ae, *m.* [con-, lēgŏ (*delegate*)]:
partner in office, colleague
collum, -ī, *n.*: neck
colŏ, colere, coluī, cultus: cultivate;
inhabit; worship; cherish
colōnia, -ae, *f.* [colōnus (*farmer*):
colŏ]: colony
columba, -ae, *f.*: dove, pigeon
com-, con-, co-, *prefix* [*cp.* cum]: together, with; *w. intensive force:*
thoroughly, completely
combūrŏ, combūrere, combussī,
combustus: burn up, burn
comedŏ, comēsse, comēdī, comēsus
[com-, 2.edŏ]: eat up, eat
comes, comitis, *m. and f.* [com-, *cp.*
2.eŏ]: companion, comrade
comitor, -ārī, -ātus sum [comes]:
accompany
commeātus, -ūs, *m.* [commeŏ]: pro-
visions, supplies
commemorŏ, -āre, -āvī, -ātus [com-,
memorŏ]: recall to memory, relate
commentārius, commentāriī, *m.*
[commentor]: note, memoran-
dum; *pl.* memoirs, commentaries
commentīcius, -a, -um, *adj.* [com-
mīnīscor]: fabricated, feigned,
false
commentor, -ārī, -ātus sum [com-
mīnīscor]: comment upon (*orally
or in writing*)
commeŏ, -āre, -āvī, -ātūrus [com-,
meo (*go*)]: go to and fro, frequent,
visit
commīnīscor, commīnīscī, commentus sum [com-, *cp.* mēns]:
devise, contrive
comminus, *adv.* [com-, manus]:
hand to hand, in close quarters
com-mittŏ, -mittere, -mīsī, -missus
[com-, mittŏ]: bring together; en-
gage in, begin; entrust, commit;
act, commit, do
commodus, -a, -um, *adj.* [com-,
modus]: suitable, convenient; ad-

---

[1] The *g* in *cognōmen* is due to a false analogy with *cognōscō*.

vantageous; *subst. n.*, convenience, advantage, interest
com-moneō, -monēre, -monuī, -monitus [com-, moneō]: remind, impress upon; admonish, instruct
com-moveō, -movēre, -mōvī, -mōtus [com-, moveō]: set in violent motion, move, disturb
commūnicō, -āre, -āvī, -ātus [*cp.* commūnis]: share, divide with; deposit in a joint fund; communicate, impart
commūnis, -e, *adj.*: common, general
commūtō, -āre, -āvī, -ātus [com-, mūtō]: change entirely, change
cōmoedia, -ae, *f.*: comedy
comparō, -āre, -āvī, -ātus [com-, parō]: prepare; procure, get, purchase; suborn, instigate
com-pellō, -pellere, -pulī, -pulsus [com-, pellō]: drive together, assemble; drive, force, compel
com-periō, -perīre, -perī, -pertus (*or* **com-perior, -perīrī, -pertus sum**) [com-, pariō]: find out, learn; *impers. pass.*, information is found, guilt is established
com-pescō, -pescere, -pescuī [com-, parcō]: repress, check
competītor, competītōris, *m.* [competō (*compete*): com-, petō]: rival, competitor
compīlō, -āre, -āvī, -ātus [com-, pīlō (*steal*)]: plunder, pillage, rob
com-pleō, -plēre, -plēvī, -plētus [com-, *pleō (fill)*]: fill up, fill
complōrō, -āre, -āvī, -ātus [com-, plōrō (*bewail*)]: bewail, lament
complūrēs, complūria, *adj.* [com-, plūs]: several, many
com-pōnō, -pōnere, -posuī, -positus [com-, pōnō]: put together, join; compose; contrive, feign
com-prehendō, -prehendere, -prehendī, -prehēnsus [com-, prehendō]: seize, grasp; perceive, comprehend; surround, include, embrace

con-: *see* com-
con-cēdō, -cēdere, -cessī, -cessus [con-, cēdō]: *intrans.*, go away; *w. dat.*, yield; *trans.*, grant, concede, allow
con-cidō, -cidere, -cidī [con-, cadō]: fall together, collapse
concilium, conciliī, *n.* [con-, calō (*summon*)]: meeting, council
concinnō, -āre, -āvī, -ātus: cause, produce
con-cipiō, -cipere, -cēpī, -ceptus [con-, capiō]: take, receive; imagine, think; adopt; compose
concitō, -āre, -āvī, -ātus [con-, citō]: set in motion, arouse, incite, agitate
conclāmō, -āre, -āvī, -ātus [con-, clāmō]: shout together, shout aloud
con-currō, -currere, -currī (*or* **-cucurrī**), **-cursūrus** [con-, currō]: run together, assemble
condemnō, -āre, -āvī, -ātus [con-, damnō]: condemn, find guilty
condiciō, -iōnis, *f.* [con-, *cp.* diciō]: agreement, contract, terms
con-dō, -dere, -didī, -ditus [con-, dō]: put together, build; establish, found; put away, store; conceal, hide
cōn-ferō, -ferre, -tulī, -lātus [con-, ferō]: bring together, bring; compare; bring to bear, employ; postpone; *w. reflex. pron.*, betake oneself, go
cōn-ficiō, -ficere, -fēcī, -fectus [con-, faciō]: collect; make ready; complete, finish; overcome, overwhelm
cōnfidentia, -ae, *f.* [cōnfīdō]: confidence, boldness
cōn-fīdō, -fīdere, -fīsus sum [con-, fīdō (*trust*)]: *w. dat.*, trust; *w. abl.*, rely on
cōn-firmō, -āre, -āvī, -ātus [con-, firmō]: strengthen, establish, corroborate; assert; assure, reassure
cōn-fiteor, -fitērī, -fessus sum

208

VOCABULARY

[con-, fateor (*acknowledge*)]: confess

cŏn-fodiŏ, -fodere, -fŏdī, -fossus [con-, fodiō]: dig up, dig

cŏnfŏrmŏ, -āre, -āvī, -ātus [con-, fōrmō (*shape*): fōrma]: shape, form, fashion

cŏnfūtŏ, -āre, -āvī, -ātus: defeat in argument, refute

con-gerŏ, -gerere, -gessī, -gestus [con-, gerō]: bring together, heap up; build

con-gredior, -gredī, -gressus sum [con-, gradior]: come together, meet; meet in strife, fight

congressiŏ, -iōnis, *f.* [congredior]: meeting; combat

con-iciŏ, -icere, -iēcī, -iectus [con-, iaciō]: throw together; throw, hurl

coniectūra, -ae, *f.* [coniciō]: conjecture, guess

coniūnctim, *adv.* [coniungō]: jointly

con-iungŏ, -iungere, -iūnxī, -iūnctus [con-, iungō]: fasten together, join; *p.p.p.* coniūnctus, -a, -um: joined, connected

con-labefīŏ, -labefierī, -labefactus sum [con-, labefīō (*be shaken*)]: be ruined, be overthrown

conlacrimŏ, -āre, -āvī, -ātus [con-, lacrimō]: weep together

conlaudŏ, -āre, -āvī, -ātus [con-, laudō]: praise highly, extol

conlocŏ, -āre, -āvī, -ātus [con-, locō (*place*): locus]: put together; station, place, erect

conloquium, conloquiī, *n.* [conloquor]: conference

con-loquor, -loquī, -locūtus sum [con-, loquor]: speak with, converse, confer

cŏnor, -ārī, -ātus sum: try, attempt

cŏnsanguineus, -a, -um, *adj.* [con-, sanguis (*blood*)]: related by blood, kindred; *subst. m. pl.*, kinsmen

cŏn-sciscŏ, -sciscere, -scīvī, -scītus [con-, sciscō (*decide*): sciō]: determine, decree; necem cŏnsciscŏ,

w. dat. of reflex. pron., commit suicide

cŏn-scrībŏ, -scrībere, -scrīpsī, -scrīptus [con-, scrībō]: write together; compose, write; enlist, enroll

cŏnsecrātus, -a, -um, *adj.* [cōnsecrō (*dedicate*): con-, sacrō (*dedicate*): sacer]: hallowed, holy, sacred

cŏnsēnsus, -ūs, *m.* [cōnsentiō (*agree*): con-, sentiō]: agreement, consent

cŏn-sequor, -sequī, -secūtus sum [con-, sequor]: follow up, follow; reach, arrive at; attain, acquire

cŏn-serŏ, -serere, -seruī, -sertus [con-, serō (*weave*)]: connect, join; manūs conseruntur (*literally*, hands are joined): they fight hand to hand

cŏnservŏ, -āre, -āvī, -ātus [con-, servō (*save*)]: keep safe, preserve, save

cŏnsīderŏ, -āre, -āvī, -ātus [con-, sīdus]: regard closely, examine; consider, reflect upon

cŏn-sīdŏ, -sīdere, -sēdī, -sessūrus [con-, *cp.* sedeō]: sit down; settle, encamp

cŏnsilium, cŏnsiliī, *n.* [cōnsulō]: council; deliberation; resolution, plan; judgment, wisdom

cŏn-sistŏ, -sistere, -stitī [con-, sistō]: stand, take a stand, halt; consist of, consist in

cŏnsors, cŏnsortis, *m. and f.* [con-, sors]: partner

cŏnspectus, -ūs, *m.* [cōnspiciō]: sight, view

cŏn-spiciŏ, -spicere, -spexī, -spectus [con-, speciō]: look at attentively, get sight of, observe

cŏnspicor, -ārī, -ātus sum [con-, *cp.* speciō]: get sight of, perceive, see

cŏnstantia, -ae, *f.* [cōnstāns (*steady*): cōnstō]: firmness, constancy, perseverance

cŏnsternŏ, -āre, -āvī, -ātus: terrify, alarm, dismay

cōn-stituō, -stituere, -stituī, -stitū-
tus [con-, statuō]: set, place, station; build, establish, constitute;
determine, resolve, decide

cōn-stō, -stāre, -stitī, -stātūrus
[con-, stō]: be firm, persevere;
impers., be certain, be known, be
agreed

cōn-suēscō, -suēscere, -suēvī, -suē-
tus [con-, suēscō (*become accustomed*)]: become accustomed; *in
perf. system*, be accustomed;
p.p.p., cōnsuētus, -a, -um: accustomed

cōnsuētūdō, cōnsuētūdinis, *f.* [cōn-
suēscō]: custom, habit

cōnsul, cōnsulis, *m.:* consul, *a
Roman magistrate*

cōnsulāris, -e, *adj.* [cōnsul]: of consular rank; *subst. m.*, ex-consul

cōnsulātus, -ūs, *m.* [cōnsul]: *the
magistracy of a consul*, consulship

cōnsulō, cōnsulere, cōnsuluī, cōnsultus: consult; *w. dat.*, have regard for, take care of; discuss,
consider

consultō, -āre, -āvī, -ātus [cōnsulō]:
reflect, deliberate; consider, discuss; consult

cōnsultum, -ī, *n.* [cōnsulō]: decree,
decision

cōn-sūmō, -sūmere, -sūmpsī,
-sūmptus [con-, sūmō]: devour,
consume; destroy

cōn-surgō, -surgere, -surrēxī, -sur-
rēctus [con-, surgō (*rise*)]: rise,
stand up

contāgiō, -iōnis, *f.* [con-, tangō]: in-
fection, contagion

con-tegō, -tegere, -tēxī, -tēctus
[con-, tegō (*cover*)]: cover, conceal

con-temnō, -temnere, -tempsī,
-temptus [con-, temnō (*despise*)]:
despise, disdain

contemptus, -ūs, *m.* [contemnō]:
contempt, scorn

con-tendō, -tendere, -tendī, -tentus
[con-, tendō (*stretch*)]: strain;

strive for; hasten; dispute, fight;
assert, maintain

contentiō, -iōnis, *f.* [contendō]: exertion; strife, contention, dispute

contentus, -a, -um, *adj.* [contineō]:
content, satisfied

con-terreō, -terrēre, -terruī, -terri-
tus [con-, terreō]: terrify

contestor, -ārī, -ātus sum [con-,
testor]: call to witness; **lītem contestor**: institute a law-suit

con-texō, -texere, -texuī, -textus
[con-, texō (*weave*)]: weave, construct

con-tineō, -tinēre, -tinuī, -tentus
[con-, teneō]: hold together,
bound, limit; restrain; include

con-tingō, -tingere, -tigī, -tāctus
[con-, tangō]: touch; reach, attain; happen

continuus, -a, -um, *adj.* [contineō]:
uninterrupted, continuous; *adv.*

continuō: without interruption,
immediately

cōntiō, -iōnis, *f.* [co-, veniō]: assembly, meeting; public address

contrā, *adv. and prep. w. acc.: adv.*,
opposite, on the other side, in opposition; in reply; on the contrary; *prep.*, against, facing

con-trahō, -trahere, -trāxī, -tractus
[con-, trahō]: draw together, collect, assemble

contrōversia, -ae, *f.* [contrō: contrā,
vertō]: controversy, dispute

contubernium, contuberniī, *n.* [con-,
taberna]: dwelling together, com-
panionship

con-tueor, -tuērī, -tuitus sum [con-,
tueor]: look at, gaze upon

contumēlla, -ae, *f.:* insult, abuse;
disgrace

conturbō, -āre, -āvī, -ātus [con-,
turbō]: disturb

con-vellō, -vellere, -vellī, -vulsus
[con-, vellō (*pull*)]: tear away,
tear to pieces, rend apart

con-veniō, -venīre, -vēnī, -ventūrus
[con-, veniō]: come together,

meet; come, present oneself; be agreed on, be settled; *impers.*, it is agreed, an agreement is reached

conventus, -ūs, *m.* [conveniō]: meeting, assembly; judicial session, court

con-vertō, -vertere, -vertī, -versus [con-, vertō]: turn around, turn; manoeuvre; attract; convert, change

convīcium, convīciī, *n.:* outcry, clamor

con-vincō, -vincere, -vīcī, -victus [con-, vincō]: overcome, convict; expose; prove incontestably

convīvium, convīviī, *n.* [con-, vīvō]: banquet

convocō, -āre, -āvī, -ātus [con-, vocō]: call together, summon

co-orior, -orīrī, -ortus sum [co-, orior]: arise, break forth

cōpia, -ae, *f.* [co-, *ops]: supply; abundance, plenty; opportunity; resources, wealth; *pl.*, forces, troops

cōpiōsus, -a, -um, *adj.* [cōpia]: furnished abundantly, well supplied; abundant, copious

cor, cordis, *n.:* heart; cordī: dear to one's heart

cōram, *adv. and prep. w. abl.: adv.*, in (his, their) presence, openly, face to face; *prep.*, in the presence of, before

corcodīlus = crocodīlus

Corinthius, -a, -um, *adj.:* Corinthian, of Corinth (cŏrĭn'thĭán)

Corinthus, -ī, *f.:* Corinth, *a city in Greece* (cŏr'ĭnth)

Cornēlius Nepōs: *a Roman biographer* (cŏrnē'lĭŭs nē'pŏs)

P. Cornēlius Rūfīnus: *a Roman consul* (pŭb'lĭŭs cŏrnē'lĭŭs rf̄ī'nŭs)

P. Cornēlius Scīpiō Āfricānus: *a Roman general* (pŭb'lĭŭs cŏrnē'lĭŭs sĭp'ĭō ăfrĭcā'nŭs)

L. Cornēlius Scīpiō Asiāticus: *a Roman general* (lū'shĭŭs cŏrnē'lĭŭs sĭp'ĭō ăzĭăt'ĭcŭs)

P. Cornēlius Sulla: *a Roman politician* (pŭb'lĭŭs cŏrnē'lĭŭs sŭl'á)

L. Cornēlius Sulla Fēlīx: *a Roman general and dictator* (lū'shĭŭs cŏrnē'lĭŭs sŭl'á fē'lĭx)

cornū, -ūs, *n.:* horn, antler; wing (*of an army*), flank

corōna, -ae, *f.:* crown, wreath

corōnō, -āre, -āvī, -ātus [corōna]: crown, wreathe

corpus, corporis, *n.:* body; flesh, corpulence

cor-rigō, -rigere, -rēxī, -rēctus [con-, regō]: correct

cor-ripiō, -ripere, -ripuī, -reptus [con-, rapiō]: seize, snatch

cor-rumpō, -rumpere, -rūpī, -ruptus [con-, rumpō]: destroy, ruin, waste; spoil, injure

Ti. Coruncānius: *a Roman hero* (tĭbē'rĭŭs cŏrŭncā'nĭŭs)

corvus, -ī, *m.:* crow, raven

cotīdiānus, -a, -um, *adj.* [cotīdiē]: daily

cotīdiē, *adv.* [quot, diēs]: every day, daily

crās, *adv.:* tomorrow

Crassus: *see* Licinius

crēdō, crēdere, crēdidī, crēditus, *w. dat.:* trust; believe

crēdulitās, -ātis, *f.* [crēdulus (*easy of belief*): crēdō]: ready belief, credulity

cremō, -āre, -āvī, -ātus: burn, cremate

creō, -āre, -āvī, -ātus: create, beget; make, elect

crepusculum, -ī, *n.* [creper (*gloomy*)]: twilight, dusk, early evening

Crēta, -ae, *f.:* Crete (crēt)

Crētēnsis, -e, *adj.:* Cretan; *subst. m. pl.*, the Cretans (crē'tán)

crīmen, crīminis, *n.* [*cp.* cernō]: charge, accusation; crime, fault; crīminī dō: offer by way of accusation, accuse of

crīminor, -ārī, -ātus sum [crīmen]: accuse, charge

crocodīlus, -ī, *m.:* crocodile

Croesus, -ī, *m.*: *a king of Lydia* (crē'sŭs)

Crotōniēnsis, -ē, *adj.*: of Croton *in Italy* (crō'tŭn)

cruciātus, -ūs, *m.* [cruciō (*torture*): crux (*gallows*, *cross*)]: torture, torment

crūdēlis, -e, *adj.* [crūdus (*bloody*): *cp.* cruor]: cruel, unmerciful

crūdēlitās, -ātis, *f.* [crūdēlis]: cruelty, harshness

cruentus, -a, -um, *adj.* [*cp.* cruor]: bloody, blood-stained; bloodthirsty, cruel

cruor, cruōris, *m.*: blood, gore

crūs, crūris, *n.*: leg

cubiculum, -ī, *n.* [cubō (*recline*)]: bedchamber

cubīle, cubīlis, *n.* [cubō (*recline*)]: nest, lair

culpa, -ae, *f.*: fault, error, guilt

cultrīx, cultrīcis, *f.* [colō]: (female) inhabitant

cultūra, -ae, *f.* [colō]: cultivation, culture; agrī cultūra: cultivation of the soil, agriculture

cultus, -ūs, *m.* [colō]: care, cultivation; culture, civilization

1. cum, *conj.*: when, whenever; since; although; cum . . . tum: not only . . . , but also

2. cum, *prep. w. abl.*: with, together with

cumulus, -ī, *m.*: heap, pile

cūnctābundus, -a, -um, *adj.* [cūnctor]: delaying, lingering; on the defensive

cūnctor, -ārī, -ātus sum: delay, hesitate

cūnctus, -a, -um, *adj.* [co , iungō]: all in a body, all together, whole, entire

cuneus, -ī, *m.*: wedge; wedge-shaped formation

cupiditās, -ātis, *f.* [cupidus]: desire, greed, covetousness

cupidus, -a, -um, *adj.* [cupiō]: desirous, eager, fond

cupiō, cupere, cupīvī, cupītus: desire, wish

cūr, *adv. and conj.*: why; for what reason; wherefore; that

cūra, -ae, *f.*: trouble, care; anxiety, concern

cūria, -ae, *f.*: senate-house

M'. Curius Dentātus: *a Roman hero* (mā'nĭŭs cū'rĭŭs děntā'tŭs)

cūrō, -āre, -āvī, -ātus [cūra]: care for, take care of, administer, supervise; rem faciendam cūrō: have a thing done

currō, currere, cucurrī, cursūrus: run

currus, -ūs, *m.* [currō]: chariot

cursus, -ūs, *m.* [currō]: running, course; speed

custōdiō, custōdīre, custōdīvī, custōdītus [custōs]: watch, guard; hold in custody

custōs, custōdis, *m. and f.*: guard, keeper, custodian

cutis, cutis, *f.*: skin

damnō, -āre, -āvī, -ātus [damnum (*penalty*)]: condemn, convict

*daps, dapis, *f.*: often *pl.*, feast, banquet

dē, *prep. w. abl.*: down from, from; out of, of; because of; concerning

dēbeō, dēbēre, dēbuī, dēbitus [dē, habeō]: owe; be under obligation; ought, must

dēbilis, -e, *adj.*: weak; lame, disabled

dē-cēdō, -cēdere, -cessī, -cessūrus [dē, cēdō]: go away, depart, withdraw; decease, die

decem, *indecl. num. adj.*: ten

dē-cernō, -cernere, -crēvī, -crētus [dē, cernō]: decide, decree

dēcertō, -āre, -āvī, -ātus [dē, certō]: fight a decisive battle, fight out; contend

decet, decēre, decuit, *impers.*: it is fitting, it is suitable, it is proper

1. dē-cidō, -cidere, -cidī [dē, cadō]: fall down, fall off

2. dē-cīdō, -cīdere, -cīdī, -cīsus

[dē, caedō]: cut off, cut away; decide, determine

decimus, -a, -um, adj. [decem]: tenth

dē-cipiō, -cipere, -cēpī, -ceptus [dē, capiō]: deceive, cheat

dēclāmō, -āre, -āvī, -ātus [dē, clāmō]: declaim, lecture

dēclārō, -āre, -āvī, -ātus [dē, clārō (make clear): clārus]: disclose, demonstrate, show; state, declare

decor, decŏris, m. [decet]: grace, beauty

decorō, -āre, -āvī, -ātus [decus]: adorn, embellish

dēcrētum, -ī, n. [dēcernō]: decree, resolution

dē-currō, -currere, -currī, -cursūrus [dē, currō]: run down, flow down

decus, decoris, n. [decet]: grace, dignity; adornment, honor

dēdecus, dēdecoris, n. [dē, decus]: disgrace, dishonor

dēditīcius, -a, -um, adj. [dēditus: dēdō]: surrendered; subst. m. pl., prisoners of war, captives

dē-dō, -dere, -didī, -ditus [dē, dō]: give up, surrender; devote; p.p.p. dēditus, -a, -um: surrendered; devoted, addicted

dē-dūcō, -dūcere, -dūxī, -ductus [dē, dūcō]: bring down; lead away, withdraw; draw out, unsheathe

deerit: see dēsum

dēfatigo, -āre, -āvī, -ātus [dē, fatīgō (tire)]: tire out, exhaust

dēfendō, dēfendere, dēfendī, dēfēnsus: ward off, repel, avert; defend, protect

dēfēnsiō, -iōnis, f. [dēfendō]: defense

dēfēnsor, dēfēnsōris, m. [dēfendō]: defender

dē-ferō, -ferre, -tulī, -lātus [dē, ferō]: carry off, remove; drive away; report; bring down, transmit; bestow, confer

dē-ficiō, -ficere, -fēcī, -fectus [dē,

faciō]: withdraw, desert; overcome; be lacking, be wanting; p.p.p. dēfectus, -a, -um: abandoned; overcome

dē-fīō, -fierī [dē, fīō]: be lacking, be wanting

dēfōrmis, -e, adj. [dē, fōrma]: misshapen, deformed

dēfōrmitās, -ātis, f. [dēfōrmis]: ugliness, deformity

dē-fugiō, -fugere, -fūgī, -fugitūrus [dē, fugiō]: run away, flee, escape

dēgō, dēgere, dēgī [dē, agō]: pass, spend, live

dē-iciō, -icere, -iēcī, -iectus [dē, iaciō]: hurl down, cast down

deinceps, adv. [dein (then, cp. deinde), capiō]: in succession, one after another; in regular order; then, thereafter

deinde, adv.: then, thereupon, next

dēlectō, -āre, -āvī, -ātus: delight, charm, please

dēlēctus, -ūs, m. [2.dēligō]: choice; conscription, draft of soldiers

1. dēligō, -āre, -āvī, -ātus [dē, ligō (bind)]: tie down, bind fast

2. dē-ligō, -ligere, -lēgī, -lēctus [dē, legō]: choose, pick out, select

dē-linquō, -linquere, -līquī, -lictus [dē, linquō]: fail, be wanting; commit a fault, do wrong

dēlīrō, -āre [dē, līra (furrow)]: be deranged, be crazy, rave

dē-litēscō, -litēscere, -lituī [dē, latēscō (be hidden): lateō]: hide, conceal oneself

delphīnus, -ī, m.: dolphin

dēmēns, gen. dēmentis, adj. [dē, mēns]: insane, raving

dē-metō, -metere, -messuī, -messus [dē, metō]: mow, reap

dē-minuō, -minuere, -minuī, -minūtus [dē, minuō]: lessen; take away

dēmiror, -ārī, -ātus sum [dē, mīror]: wonder at, wonder, be amazed

dē-mittō, -mittere, -mīsī, -missus [dē, mittō]: send down, let down, cast down; **caput dēmittō**: hang one's head

Dēmocritus, -ī, *m.: a Greek philosopher* (dĕmŏc'rĭtŭs)

dēmōnstrō, -āre, -āvī, -ātus [dē, mōnstrō (*show*)]: point out, show

Dēmosthenēs, Dēmosthenis, *m.: a Greek orator* (dĕmŏs'thĕnēş)

dēmoror, -ārī, -ātus sum [dē, moror]: delay; linger, tarry, stay

dē-mulceō, -mulcēre [dē, mulceō (*stroke*)]: stroke gently, caress

dēmum, *adv.* [*cp.* dē]: at last, at length

dēnārrō, -āre, -āvī, -ātus [dē, nārrō]: relate, narrate

dēnegō, -āre, -āvī, -ātus [dē, negō]: refuse, deny, say no

dēnī, -ae, -a, *distr. num. adj.* [decem]: ten by ten, ten each

dēnique, *adv.* [*cp.* dē]: at last, finally

dēns, dentis, *m.*: tooth

dēnūntiō, -āre, -āvī, -ātus [dē, nūntiō]: announce, declare

dēnuō, *adv.* [dē, novus]: anew, once more

dē-pellō, -pellere, -pulī, -pulsus [dē, pellō]: drive out, drive away, expel

dē-perdō, -perdere, -perdidī, -perditus [de, perdō]: ruin, destroy

dē-pingō, -pingere, -pīnxī, -pictus [dē, pingō (*paint*)]: depict, describe

dēplōrō, -āre, -āvī, -ātus [dē, plōrō (*lament*)]: bemoan, lament

dē-pōnō, -pōnere, -posuī, -positus [dē, pōnō]: put down, put away; lay up, deposit

dē-populor, -ārī, -ātus sum [dē, populor]: lay waste, ravage, plunder

dē-pugnō, -āre, -āvī, -ātus [dē, pugnō]: fight decisively, fight to a finish, fight out

dē-rēpō, -rēpere, -rēpsī [dē, rēpō (*creep*)]: creep down, crawl down

dē-rīdeō, -rīdēre, -rīsī, -rīsus [dē, rīdeō]: laugh at, scorn, deride

dērīsus, -ūs, *m.* [dērīdeō]: derision, scorn

dērogō, -āre, -āvī, -ātus [dē, rogō]: repeal, restrict; take away

dē-scendō, -scendere, -scendī, -scēnsūrus [dē, scandō]: climb down, come down, descend

dē-scīscō, -scīscere, -scīvī, -scītus [dē, scīscō (*decide*): sciō]: withdraw, desert, revolt

dē-scrībō, -scrībere, -scrīpsī, -scrīptus [dē, scrībō]: write down; describe, define

dē-serō, -serere, -seruī, -sertus [dē, serō (*bind*)]: leave, forsake, desert

dēsertor, dēsertōris, *m.* [dēserō]: deserter

dē-sideō, -sidēre, -sēdī [dē, sedeō]: sit idle

dēsīderō, -āre, -āvī, -atus [dē, sīdus]: desire, long for; ask, demand

dēsidia, -ae, *f.* [*cp.* dēsideō]: idleness, inactivity

dē-siliō, -silīre, -siluī, -sultūrus [dē, saliō]: leap down, jump down

dē-sinō, -sinere, -siī, -situs [dē, sinō (*leave*)]: leave off, give up, cease; *p.p.p.* **dēsitus, -a, -um:** abandoned, obsolete

de-sipiō, -sipere [dē, sapiō (*be wise*)]: be senseless, act foolishly

dē-sistō, -sistere, -stitī, -stitūrus [dē, sistō]: leave off, cease, desist from

dēspērō, -āre, -āvī, -ātus [dē, spērō]: be hopeless, despair

dē-spiciō, -spicere, -spexī, -spectus [dē, speciō]: look down upon; despise

dē-stituō, -stituere, -stituī, -stitūtus [dē, statuō]: leave, abandon

dē-sum, -esse, -fuī, -futūrus [dē, sum], *w. dat.*: be lacking, be wanting

dēsuper, *adv.* [dē, super]: from above

dē-tergeō, -tergēre, -tersī, -tersus

[dē, tergeō (*wipe*)]: wipe away,
cleanse

dēterior, dēterius, *adj.* [*cp.* dē]:
lower, worse, poorer

dē-terō, -terere, -trīvī, -trītus [dē,
terō (*rub*)]: rub away, wear away,
wear

dē-terreō, -terrēre, -terruī, -territus
[dē, terreō]: frighten off; deter,
prevent, hinder

dē-trahō, -trahere, -trāxī, -tractus
[dē, trahō]: draw off, take away,
remove

dētrīmentum, -ī, *n.* [dēterō]: loss,
damage, detriment

de-ūrō, -ūrere, -ussī, -ustus [dē,
ūrō]: burn away, burn up

deus, -ī, *nom. pl.* dī, diī, deī; *dat. and
abl. pl.* dīs, diīs, deīs, *m.*: god,
deity

dē-vehō, -vehere, -vexī, -vectus [dē,
vehō]: carry down, convey, transport

dē-veniō, -venīre, -vēnī, -ventūrus
[dē, veniō]: come, arrive, reach

dēvorō, -āre, -āvī, -ātus [dē, vorō
(*swallow*)]: gulp down, devour

dē-voveō, -vovēre, -vōvī, -vōtus
[dē, voveō]: vow, devote

dexter, dextera, dexterum (*or* dex-
tra, dextrum), *adj.*: right (*as opposed to left*)

dī: *see* deus

dī-: *see* dis-

Diagorās, Diagorae, *m.*: *a Greek athlete* (dĭăg'ōrăs)

Diāna, -ae, *f.*: *goddess of the chase*
(dĭăn'à)

diciō, -iōnis, *f.* [*cp.* 2.dīcō]: sovereignty, authority, jurisdiction

1. dicō, -āre, -āvī, -ātus [*cp.* 2.dīcō]:
dedicate, devote

2. dīcō, dīcere, dīxī, dictus: say,
tell; iūs dīcō: administer justice,
hold court; male dīcō, *w. dat.*:
slander; salūtem dīcō: send greeting

dictātūra, -ae, *f.* [dictātor (*dicta-*

tor)]: *the magistracy of a dictator*,
dictatorship

dictitō, -āre, -āvī, -ātus [2.dīcō]:
keep on saying, say often, declare

dictō, -āre, -āvī, -ātus [2.dīcō]: dic-
tate; suggest, remind

dictum, -ī, *n.* [2.dīcō]: something
said, saying, word; command

dī-dūcō, -dūcere, -dūxī, ductus [dī-,
dūcō]: draw apart, separate; disperse

diēs, diēī, *m.* (*often f. when denoting
a set date*): day, date; time

differō, differre, distulī, dīlātus [dis-,
ferō]: carry apart, separate; postpone; differ

difficilis, -e, *adj.* [dis-, facilis]: hard,
difficult

digitus, -ī, *m.*: finger; toe

dignitās, -ātis, *f.* [dignus]: worth,
merit; dignity, honor

dignus, -a, -um, *adj.* [decet]: worthy
(*w. abl.*); fit, proper

dī-gredior, -gredī, -gressus sum
[dī-, gradior]: walk away, go
away, depart

diī: *see* deus

dīlacerō, -āre, -āvī, -ātus [dī-, la-
cerō]: tear to pieces

dīligēns, *gen.* dīligentis, *adj.* [dīligō]:
diligent, industrious, careful

dīligentia, -ae, *f.* [dīligēns]: dili-
gence, earnestness, industry

dī-ligō, -ligere, -lēxī, -lēctus [dī-,
legō]: single out, value, cherish,
love

dī-lūcēscō, -lūcēscere, -lūxī [dī-,
lūcēscō (*begin to shine*): lūceō
(*shine*): lūx]: begin to shine; *impers.*, it grows light, the day
dawns

dīlūcidus, -a, -um, *adj.* [dīlūceō (*be
clear*): dī-, lūceō (*shine*): lūx]:
clear, distinct, plain

dīmicō, -āre, -āvī, -ātus [dī-, micō]:
fight, struggle

dīmidium, dīmidiī, *n.* [dī-, medius]:
half, one-half

dī-mittō, -mittere, -mīsī, -missus

[dī-, mittō]: send different ways, dismiss, disband; release, discharge; lose
dī-rigō, -rigere, -rēxī, -rēctus [dī-, regō]: arrange, lay out; direct, drive, steer
dir-imō, -imere, -ēmī, -ēmptus [dis-, emō]: take apart, separate; break up, destroy
dī-ripiō, -ripere, -ripuī, -reptus [dī-, rapiō]: tear asunder; ravage, plunder; snatch away
Dīs, Dītis, *m.: god of the lower world* (dīs)
dis-, dī-, *prefix:* apart, away, asunder, in different directions; not, un-
dis-cēdō, -cēdere, -cessī, -cessūrus [dis-, cēdō]: go apart, go away, depart
dis-cernō, -cernere, -crēvī, -crētus [dis-, cernō]: separate; distinguish, discern
dī-scindō, -scindere, -scidī, -scissus [dī-, scindō (*cut*)]: cut apart, tear asunder
disciplīna, -ae, *f.* [discipulus]: instruction, education; learning, knowledge; science, subject of instruction
discipulus, -ī, *m.* [discō]: pupil, student; follower
discō, discere, didicī: learn
disertus, -a, -um, *adj.:* eloquent; clever
dī-spergō, -spergere, -spersī, -spersus [dī-, spargō]: scatter, disperse
disputō, -āre, -āvī, -ātus [dis-, putō]: examine; argue, discuss
dissēnsiō, -iōnis, *f.* [dissentiō (*disagree*): dis-, sentiō]: disagreement
dis-sideō, -sidere, -sēdī [dis-, sedeō]: disagree
dissimulanter, *adv.* [dissimulō (*dissemble*): dis-, simulō]: with pretence, hiding the truth, dissemblingly
dissolūtus, -a, -um, *adj.* [dissolvō]: lax, dissolute

dis-solvō, -solvere, -solvī, -solūtus [dis-, solvō]: take apart, disunite; dissolve, destroy
diū, *adv.:* long, for a long time
diurnus, -a, -um, *adj.* [diēs]: of the day, by day, day-
diūturnitās, -ātis, *f.* [diūturnus (*lengthy*): diū]: length of time, long duration
dī-vellō, -vellere, -vellī, -vulsus [dī-, vellō (*tear*)]: tear apart, rend asunder
dīversus, -a, -um, *adj.* [dīverto (*turn away*): dī-, vertō]: turned different ways, opposite, contrary; different, diverse
dīves, *gen.* dīvitis, *adj.:* rich, wealthy
Dīviciācus, -ī, *m.: a Gallic nobleman* (dīvīshlā'cŭs)
dīvido, dīvidere, dīvīsī, dīvīsus: divide, separate
dīvīnitus, *adv.* [dīvīnus]: from heaven, by divine influence, from a deity
dīvīnus, -a, -um, *adj.* [*cp.* deus]: of a deity, divine; godlike, superhuman
dīvus, -a, -um, *adj.* [*cp.* deus]: divine; *of a deceased emperor,* deified
dō, dare, dedī, datus: give, grant; assign; place; lītem dō: decide a case; poenās dō: suffer penalty
doctrīna, -ae, *f.* [doceō]: teaching, instruction; science, learning
doceō, docēre, docuī, doctus: teach; *p.p.p.* doctus, -a, -um: learned, trained
documentum, -ī, *n.* [doceō]: lesson, example, proof
doleō, dolēre, doluī, dolitūrus: feel pain, suffer; grieve, be sorry
dolor, dolōris, *m.* [doleō]: pain, suffering; grief
dolōsus, -a, -um, *adj.* [dolus]: crafty, deceitful
dolus, -ī, *m.:* deceit, trickery
domicilium, domiciliī, *n.* [*cp.* domus]: habitation, dwelling
dominātiō, -iōnis, *f.* [dominor (*rule*):

dominus]: rule, dominion, lordship

dominus, -ī, m. [domus]: master, ruler; lord, owner

domus, -ūs, f.: house, home; household, family

dōnec, conj.: as long as, while; until

dōnō, -āre, -āvī, -ātus [dōnum]: present, give

dōnum, -ī, n. [dō]: gift, present

dorsum, -ī, n.: back

dōs, dōtis, f. [dō]: marriage-portion, dowry

druidēs, druidum, m. pl.: Gallic priests, druids

Dūbis, Dūbis, m.: a river in Gaul, the modern Doubs (dū'bǐs)

dubitō, -āre, -āvī, -ātus [cp. duo]: doubt; hesitate, delay

dubius, -a, -um, adj. [cp. duo]: wavering, uncertain; dubious, undetermined; subst. n., doubt

ducentī, -ae, -a, num. adj. [duo, centum]: two hundred

dūcō, dūcere, dūxī, ductus: lead, conduct; protract, drag out; consider, judge, reckon; in mātrimōnium dūcō: marry

dulcis, -e, adj.: sweet, gentle, pleasant

dum, conj.: as long as, while; until; provided that

duo, duae, duo, num. adj.: two

duodecim, indecl. num. adj. [duo, decem]: twelve

dūritia, -ae, f. [dūrus]: hardness; harshness, strictness

dūrus, -a, -um, adj.: hard, harsh; severe, toilsome

dux, ducis, m. and f. [cp. dūcō]: leader, guide; commander, ruler

ē: see ex

ecquis, ecquid, interrog. pron.: (is there) anyone, anything?; whether anyone, anything; n. as conj., whether

ē-discō, -discere, -didicī [ē, discō]: learn thoroughly, learn by heart

1. ē-dō, -dere, -didī, -ditus [ē, dō]: give out, give forth; lift up; build up, construct; produce, give birth to; utter; inflict

2. edō, ēsse, ēdī, ēsus: eat

ē-dormiō, -dormīre, -dormīvī [ē, dormiō (sleep)]: sleep off

1. ēducō, -āre, -āvī, -ātus [ē, cp. dūcō]: bring up, train, educate

2. ē-dūcō, -dūcere, -dūxī, -ductus [ē, dūcō]: lead forth, draw out; educate, rear

effēminō, -āre, -āvī, -ātus [ex, fēmina]: make womanish, weaken, effeminate

efferō, efferre, extulī, ēlātus [ex, ferō]: carry out, bring forth, remove; extol, praise

ef-ficiō, -ficere, -fēcī, fectus [ex, faciō]: work out, bring about, cause, accomplish, produce

effigiēs, acc. effigiem, f. [effingō (fashion)]: ex, fingō]: copy, likeness; image, statue

ef-fugiō, -fugere, -fūgī [ex, fugiō]: get away, escape

effugium, effugiī, n. [ex, cp. fugiō]: flight, escape

egeō, egēre, eguī, w. gen. or abl.: be in want, be without, lack

egestās, -ātis, f. [egeō]: want, poverty, lack

ego, meī, pers. pron.: I, me

egomet: see ego and -met

ē-gredior, -gredī, -gressus sum [ē, gradior]: go out, come forth, leave

ēgregius, -a, -um, adj. [ē, grex]: select, extraordinary, excellent

Ēlectra, -ae, f.: a princess of Mycenae (ēlěc'trà, mīsē'nē)

elegāns, gen. elegantis, adj. [ē, cp. legō]: fastidious; select, choice, elegant

elephantus, -ī, m.: elephant

ēlevō, -āre, -āvī, -ātus [ē, levō]: raise; make light of, belittle

ē-ligō, -ligere, -lēgī, -lēctus [ē, legō]: choose, select

ēlīmō, -āre, -āvī, -ātus [ē, līmō

(*file*): līma (*file*)]: file off, polish,
finish
ēloquentia, -ae, *f.* [ēloquor]: eloquence
ē-loquor, -loquī, -locūtus sum [ē,
loquor]: speak out, speak plainly,
pronounce
ē-lūdō, -lūdere, -lūsī, -lūsus [ē,
lūdō]: escape; delude, deceive;
mock, jeer, make sport of
ēmigrō, -āre, -āvī, -ātus [ē, migrō]:
move, depart, emigrate
ē-mineō, -minēre, -minuī [ē, mineō
(*project*)]: project; be prominent
ē-mittō, -mittere, -mīsī, -missus [ē,
mittō]: send out; hurl, cast; let
loose, let fall; utter
emō, emere, ēmī, ēmptus: buy, purchase; *in compounds*, take
ē-morior, -morī, -mortuus sum [ē,
morior]: die off, die
ēmptiō, -iōnis, *f.* [emō]: purchase
ēn, *interj.*: behold!, lo!, there!
enim, *conj.* (*regularly comes after
first word in its clause*): for; indeed, truly
Q. Ennius: *a Roman poet* (quĭn'tŭs
ĕn'ĭŭs)
ēnūntiō, -āre, -āvī, -ātus [ē, nūntiō]:
divulge, reveal
1. eō, *adv.* [is]: to that place, thither; to that end; to such a degree,
so far
2. eō, īre, iī, itūrus: go, come
eōdem, *adv.* [īdem]: to the same
place, in the same direction
Epamīnōndās, Epamīnōndae, *m.*: *a
Theban general* (ĕpămĭnŏn'dăs)
ephippiātus, -a, -um, *adj.* [ephip-
pium]: riding with a saddle
ephippium, ephippiī, *n.*: saddle
ephorus, -ī, *m.*: *Spartan magistrate*,
ephor
epigramma, epigrammatis, *n.*: inscription
epistula, -ae, *f.*: letter, epistle
epulae, epulārum, *f. pl.*: banquet,
feast
eques, equitis, *m.* [equus]: horse-

man, rider; cavalryman; knight
equester, equestris, equestre, *adj.*
[eques]: of a horseman, eques-
trian; of cavalry, cavalry-
equidem, *adv.*: indeed, truly; for my
part, as far as I am concerned
equitātus, -ūs, *m.* [equitō (*ride*):
eques]: cavalry
equus, -ī, *m.*: horse, steed
Eratosthenēs, Eratosthenis, *m.*: *a
Greek geographer* (ĕrătŏs'thĕnēş)
ergā, *prep. w. acc.*: towards, in relation to
ergō, *adv.*: therefore, so then, accordingly
ē-ripiō, -ripere, -ripuī, -reptus [ē,
rapiō]: tear out, snatch away, remove
error, errōris, *m.* [errō (*wander*)]:
error, delusion
ē-rubēscō, -rubēscere, -rubuī [ē,
rubēscō (*grow red*): rubeō (*be
red*)]: blush with shame, feel
ashamed
ē-rudiō, -rudīre, -rudīvī, -rudītus
[ē, rudis]: educate, instruct; *p.p.p.*
ērudītus, -a, -um: educated,
learned
ē-rumpō, -rumpere, -rūpī, -ruptus
[ē, rumpō]: break out, burst
forth
ēsca, -ae, *f.* [*cp.* 2.edō]: food
et, *conj. and adv.*: and; also, too
etiam, *adv.* [et, iam]: even, also
etiamsī, *conj.* [etiam, sī]: even if,
although
etsī, *conj.* [et, sī]: although
Euander, Euandrī, *m.*: Evander, *an
early settler on the site of Rome*
(ĕvăn'dēr)
Euāthlus, -ī, *m.*: *a Greek youth*
(ūăth'lŭs)
Euclīdēs, Euclīdis, *m.*: *a follower of
Socrates* (ūclī'dēş)
Eudosiī, Eudosiōrum, *m. pl.*: *a
Germanic people* (ūdō'sĭī)
ē-vādō, -vādere, -vāsī, -vāsūrus [ē,
vādō (*go*)]: go out, come out;
escape

ēvagor, -ārī, -ātus sum [ē, vagor]: wander forth

ē-vertō, -vertere, -vertī, -versus [ē, vertō]: overturn, upset, throw down

ēvocō, -āre, -āvī, -ātus [ē, vocō]: call out, summon

ex, ē, *prep. w. abl.*: out of, from; from among; in consequence of, by reason of; according to, in conformity with; ē rē pūblicā: to the advantage of the state; ex ūsū: advantageous

exanimō, -āre, -āvī, -ātus [exanimus (*lifeless*): ex, anima]: deprive of life, kill; terrify, stun, dishearten

excellēns, *gen.* excellentis, *adj.* [excellō]: superior, surpassing, excellent

ex-cellō, -cellere [ex, cellō (*tower*)]: be eminent, be superior, excel

ex-cīdō, -cīdere, -cīdī, -cīsus [ex, caedō]: cut out, cut down; destroy

ex-cipiō, -cipere, -cēpī, -ceptus [ex, capiō]: take out; take up, catch, receive, withstand; come next to, succeed

excitō, -āre, -āvī, -ātus [ex, citō]: call out; wake, arouse; excite, stimulate

exclāmō, -āre, -āvī, -ātus [ex, clāmō]: call out, cry aloud, exclaim

excruciō, -āre, -āvī, -ātus [ex, cruciō (*torture*): crux (*gallows, cross*)]: torment, torture

excursiō, -iōnis, *f.* [excurrō (*rush out*): ex, currō]: inroad, invasion

exemplum, -ī, *n.*: sample, copy; example; warning, penalty

ex-eō, -īre, -iī, -itūrus [ex, 2.eō]: go out, go forth

ex-erceō, -ercēre, -ercuī, -ercitus [ex, arceō]: keep busy; train, exercise; follow out, practise

exercitātiō, -iōnis, *f.* [exercitō]: exercise, training

exercitō, -āre, -āvī, -ātus [exerceō]: train, exercise

exercitus, -ūs, *m.* [exerceō]: army

ex-igō, -igere, -ēgī, -āctus [ex, agō]: drive out, expel; require, enforce

exiguitās, -ātis, *f.* [exiguus (*scanty*): exigō]: scantiness, shortness

eximius, -a, -um, *adj.* [eximō]: select, extraordinary, excellent

ex-imō, -imere, -ēmī, -ēmptus [ex, emō]: take out, take away, remove, release; consume

exīstimō, -āre, -āvī, -ātus [ex, aestimō]: think, suppose

exitium, exitiī, *n.* [exeō]: destruction, ruin

exitus, -ūs, *m.* [exeō]: going out, departure; way out, exit

ex-ōrdior, -ōrdīrī, -ōrsus sum [ex-, ōrdior (*begin*)]: begin, commence

exōrnō, -āre, -āvī, -ātus [ex, ōrnō]: deck out, adorn, embellish

expediō, expedīre, expedīvī, expedītus [ex, pēs]: extricate; procure, prepare; arrange; *p.p.p.* expedītus, -a, -um: unencumbered, free; light-armed

ex-pellō, -pellere, -pulī, -pulsus [ex, pellō]: drive out, expel

experior, experīrī, expertus sum [*cp.* perīculum]: try, test, experience

expers, *gen.* expertis, *adj.* [ex, pars], *w. gen.*: having no part in, not sharing; devoid of

ex-petō, -petere, -petīvī (*or* -petiī), -petītus [ex, petō]: seek after, strive for; desire

explōrātor, explōrātōris, *m.* [explōrō]: scout, spy

explōrō, -āre, -āvī, -ātus: search out, examine, explore; make an investigation

ex-pōnō, -pōnere, -posuī, -positus [ex, pōnō]: put out, set forth; explain

ex-primō, -primere, -pressī, -pressus [ex, premō]: press out, force out; portray, express; render, translate

ex-prōmō, -prōmere, -prōmpsī,

-prŏmptus [ex, prōmō (*give out*): prō, emō]: utter

ex-quīrō, -quīrere, -quīsīvī, -quīsītus [ex, quaerō]: search out, seek diligently, ascertain

exsanguis, -e, *adj.* [ex, sanguis (*blood*)]: bloodless, lifeless

ex-scrībō, -scrībere, -scrīpsī, -scrīptus [ex, scrībō]: write out, copy

exsertŏ, -āre [exserō (*stretch out*): ex, serō (*bind*)]: thrust out, stick out

exsilium, exsiliī, *n.* [exsul (*exile*)]: banishment, exile

ex-sistō, -sistere, -stitī [ex, sistō]: step out, come forth, emerge; turn out, become; exist

exspectŏ, -āre, -āvī, -ātus [ex, spectō]: look out for, await, expect

exspīrō, -āre, -āvī, -ātus [ex, spīrō]: breathe out; breathe one's last, expire

exstŏ, -āre [ex, stō]: stand out, extend; be extant, exist

ex-struŏ, -struere, -strūxī, -strūctus [ex, struō]: pile up, accumulate; build

ex-surgŏ, -surgere, -surrēxī [ex, surgō (*rise*)]: rise up, stand up

extemplŏ, *adv.* [ex, cp. tempus]: immediately, without delay

extrā, *adv. and prep. w. acc.* [exter (*outside*): ex]: outside, without; beyond, outside of; except

ex-trahŏ, -trahere, -trāxī, -tractus [ex, trahō]: draw out, pull out

extrēmus, -a, -um [exter (*outside*): ex]: outermost, utmost, farthest, extreme, last; *subst. n.,* last part, end

ex-tundŏ, -tundere, -tudī [ex, tundō (*beat*)]: beat out, crush

ex-ūrō, -ūrere, -ussī, -ustus [ex, ūrō]: burn out, burn up

fābella, -ae, *f.* [fābula]: short fable, fable

Q. Fabius Maximus: *a Roman consul* (quĭn'tŭs fā'bĭŭs mă̆c'sĭmŭs)

C. Fabricius Luscīnus: *a Roman general* (gā'yŭs fā̆brĭsh'ĭŭs lūsī'nŭs)

fābula, -ae, *f.* [*for]: story; play, drama; plot; fable

facētus, -a, -um, *adj.:* merry, facetious

faciēs, faciēī, *f.* [faciō]: appearance, shape; face, look

facilis, -e, *adj.* [faciō]: easy; ready, good-natured, willing

facinus, facinoris, *n.* [faciō]: deed; bad deed, crime

faciŏ, facere, fēcī, factus: make, build; do, perform; cause; bestow, give; serve, side; *pass.,* be done, become, happen; satis faciŏ: make amends

factiŏ, -iōnis, *f.* [faciō]: faction, party

factitŏ, -āre, -āvī, -ātus [faciō]: do frequently, practise

factum, -ī, *n.* [faciō]: deed, act, event

facultās, -ātis, *f.* [facilis]: capability, possibility, opportunity; abundance, supply

fallācia, -ae, *f.* [fallāx (*deceitful*): fallō]: deceit, artifice, craft

fallŏ, fallere, fefellī, falsus: deceive, trick; *pass.,* be deceived, err

falsus, -a, -um, *adj.* [fallō]: feigned, false

falx, falcis, *f.:* curved blade; sickle, scythe

fāma, -ae, *f.* [*for]: rumor, report; reputation; fame

famēs, famis, *abl.* famē, *f.:* hunger

familia, -ae, *f.* [famulus (*servant*)]: the slaves in a household, household establishment; household, family

familiāris, -e, *adj.* [familia]: familiar, intimate, friendly; *subst. m.,* intimate acquaintance, friend

fās (*only nom. and acc. s.*), *n.* [*for]: divine law; justice, equity; fās est: it is lawful, it is proper, it is fated

fastīdiō, fastīdīre, fastīdīvī, fastīdītus [fastĭdium (*disgust*)]: feel disgust, loathe, dislike

fātum, -ĭ, *n.* [*for]: fate, destiny

*faux, *faucis, *f.*: throat; voracity, greed

Favorīnus, -ī, *m.: a Roman philosopher* (făvŏrī'nŭs)

fēcundus, -a, -um, *adj.*: fertile

fēlēs, fēlis, *f.*: cat

fēlīcitās, -ātis, *f.* [fēlīx]: good fortune, luck

fēlīx, *gen.* fēlīcis, *adj.*: fertile; lucky, fortunate

fēmĭna, -ae, *f.*: woman

fenestra, -ae, *f.*: window

fera, -ae, *f.* [ferus]: wild beast, wild animal

ferē, *adv.*: in general, usually; nearly, almost

ferīnus, -a, -um, *adj.* [fera]: of a wild animal

fermē, *adv.*]ferē]: in general, usually, for the most part; nearly, almost

ferō, ferre, tulī, lātus: bear, carry; circulate; report, say; legem ferō: pass a law; sententiam ferō: pass judgment; signa ferō: proceed; suffrāgium ferō: cast a vote

ferōx, *gen.* ferōcis, *adj.* [ferus]: bold, fierce, savage

ferrum, -ī, *n.*: iron; iron implement, knife, sword

fertilis, -e, *adj.* [ferō]: fruitful, fertile

ferus, -a, -um, *adj.*: wild; *subst. m.*, wild animal

fervō, fervere: glow, blaze

fessus, -a, -um, *adj.*: wearied, tired, exhausted

fēstīnātiō, -iōnis, *f.* [fēstīnō]: haste, hurry

fēstīnō, -āre, -āvī, -ātus: hasten, make haste

fēstīvus, -a, -um, *adj.* [fēstus (*joyful*)]: agreeable, pleasing; jocose, jolly, merry

fētus, -ūs, *m.*: young, offspring, progeny

fictus: *see* fingō

fidēlis, -e, *adj.* [1.fidēs]: trusty, trustworthy, faithful

1. fidēs, fideī, *f.*: trust, faith, confidence; trustworthiness; assurance, promise

2. fidēs, fidis, *f.*: chord, string (*of a musical instrument*); *pl.*, stringed instrument, lyre, lute, harp

fidicen, fidicinis, *m.* [2.fidēs, canō]: lyre-player, harper

fīdūcia, -ae, *f.* [*cp.* fīdō (*trust*)]: trust, confidence

fīlia, -ae, *f.*: daughter

fīlius, fīliī, *m.*: son

fingō, fingere, fīnxī, fictus: form, shape; compose; feign, contrive, devise; *p.p.p.* fictus, -a, -um: feigned, fallacious, false

fīniō, fīnīre, fīnīvī, fīnītus [fīnis]: limit, determine, reckon; finish; cease

fīnis, fīnis, *m.*: end; purpose, aim; boundary, *pl.* borders, territory

fīnitimus, -a, -um, *adj.* [fīnis]: bordering upon, neighboring; *subst. m.*, neighbor

fīō, fierī (*used as passive of* faciō *in pres. system*): be made, become; be done, happen

firmō, -āre, -āvī, -ātus [firmus]: strengthen, fortify; confirm, establish

firmus, -a, -um, *adj.*: strong, stable; firm, faithful

fiscus, -ī, *m.*: wicker basket; money-basket

flāgitium, flāgitiī, *n.* [flāgitō]: shameful act, outrage; disgrace

flāgitō, -āre, -āvī, -ātus: demand urgently, require

flagrō, -āre, -āvī, -ātūrus: flame, blaze, burn

Flāminīnus: *see* Quīnctius

flamma, -ae, *f.*: blaze, flame

flāvēscō, flāvēscere [flāveō (*be golden yellow*): flāvus (*golden yellow*)]: become golden yellow, turn light yellow flectō, flectere, flexī, flexus: bend, curve, turn

fleō, flēre, flēvī, flētus: weep, cry; lament, bewail

flētus, -ūs, m. [fleō]: weeping, wailing, lament

flōreō, flōrēre, flōruī [flōs]: bloom; flourish, be eminent

flōs, flōris, m.: flower

flūctus, -ūs, m. [fluō (flow)]: wave

fluitō, -āre, -āvī [fluō (flow)]: float

flūmen, flūminis, n. [fluō (flow)]: river

foculus, -ī, m. [focus (hearth)]: fire-pan, brazier

fodiō, fodere, fōdī, fossus: dig, dig up

foedus, foederis, n. [cp. fīdō (trust)]: treaty, compact

fōns, fontis, m.: spring, well

*for, fārī, fātus sum: speak, say

forās, adv. [cp. 2.foris]: out of doors, out (denoting end of motion)

fore, forem: see sum

1. forīs, adv. [cp. 2.foris]: out of doors, abroad (denoting position)

2. foris, foris, f.: door; pl., folding-door, entrance

fōrma, -ae, f.: form, shape; fine form, beauty, handsomeness

formīdō, formīdinis, f.: fear, terror

fōrmōsus, -a, -um, adj. [fōrma]: beautiful, handsome

forsan, adv. [fors (chance), 1.an]: perchance, perhaps

forte, adv. [fors (chance)]: by chance, accidentally

fortis, -e, adj.: strong, powerful; brave

fortuītus, -a, -um, adj. [cp. fors (chance)]: happening by chance, accidental, fortuitous; adv. fortuītō: by chance

fortūna, -ae, f. [cp. fors (chance)]: chance, fortune; property, possessions

forum, -ī, n.: market-place, public square, forum

frangō, frangere, frēgī, frāctus: break

frāter, frātris, m.: brother

frāternus, -a, -um, adj. [frāter]: of a brother, brotherly

fraudātor, fraudātōris, m. [fraudō (cheat): fraus]: cheat, deceiver

fraudulentus, -a, -um, adj. [fraus]: cheating, deceitful, fraudulent

fraus, fraudis, f.: cheating, deceit, fraud

fremitūs, -ūs, m. [fremō (roar)]: roar

frēnum, -ī, n.; pl. frēnī, frēnōrum, m. or frēna, frēnōrum, n. [frendō (gnash)]: bridle, curb, bit; restraint

frequentia, -ae, f. [frequēns (numerous)]: great number; multitude, crowd

frīgidus, -a, -um, adj. [frīgus]: cold

frīgus, frīgoris, n.: cold, frost

1.frōns, frondis, f.: foliage; fodder

2.frōns, frontis, f.: forehead; front

frūctuōsus, -a, -um, adj. [frūctus]: fruitful, productive

frūctus, ūs, m. [fruor]: fruit, crops; profit, income; reward

frūmentārius, -a, -um, adj. [frūmentum]: of grain; rēs frūmentāria: grain supply

frūmentum, -ī, n. [fruor]: grain, harvested grain; pl., growing grain, standing grain

fruor, fruī, fructus sum, w. abl.: enjoy, delight in

frūstrā, adv.: in vain, uselessly

frūstror, -ārī, -ātus sum [frūstrā]: deceive, disappoint

frūstum, -ī, n.: piece, bit

frutex, fruticis, m.: foliage; shrub, bush

fuga, -ae, f. [fugiō]: flight, escape

fugiō, fugere, fūgī, fugitūrus: flee, run away; avoid, shun

fugitō, -āre, -āvī, -ātus [fugiō]: flee eagerly; avoid, shun

fugō, -āre, -āvī, -ātus [fuga]: put to flight, drive off, rout, defeat fulgeō, fulgēre, fulsī: flash, lighten; glitter, gleam

fulmineus, -a, -um, adj. [fulmen (*lightning-flash*): fulgeō]: lightning-like, destructive

fundō, fundere, fūdī, fūsus: pour, shed; scatter, throw into confusion

fundus, -ī, m.: bottom; farm, estate

fūnebris, -e, adj. [fūnus]: funereal, dismal

fungor, fungī, fūnctus sum, w. abl.: perform, administer, discharge

fūniculus, -ī, m. [fūnis (*rope*)]: cord

fūnus, fūneris, n.: funeral

fūr, fūris, m.: thief

fūrāx, gen. fūrācis, adj. [fūr]: given to thieving, thievish, dishonest

furor, furōris, m. [furō (*rage*)]: raving, rage, madness, fury

fūrtim, adv. [fūr]: by stealth, secretly

fūrtum, -ī, n. [fūr]: theft, robbery

futtilis, -e, adj. [fundō]: that easily pours out, weak; untrustworthy, worthless, futile

galea, -ae, f.: helmet

Gallia, -ae, f.: Gaul (gąl)

Gallicus, -a, -um, adj.: Gallic (găl'-ĭc)

Gallus, -a, -um, adj.: Gallic; subst. m., a Gaul, pl., the Gauls (găl'ĭc, gąl)

gaudeō, gaudēre, gāvīsus sum: rejoice

gaudium, gaudiī, n. [gaudeō]: joy

gemitus, -ūs, m. [gemō (*groan*)]: groan, lamentation

generātim, adv. [genus]: by nations, by tribes

gēns, gentis, f. [gignō]: race, clan; tribe, nation

gentīlis, -e, adj. [gēns]: of a clan; subst. m., one of the same clan, a fellow-clansman

genus, generis, n. [gignō]: race, clan, nation; birth; kind, division

geōmetria, -ae, f.: geometry

geōmetricus, -a, -um, adj.: of geometry, geometric

Germānia, -ae, f.: Germany

Germānus, -a, -um, adj.: German; subst. m., a German, pl., the Germans

gerō, gerere, gessī, gestus: carry, bear, wear; carry on, wage; rēs gestae: exploits

gestō, -āre, -āvī, -ātus [gerō]: bear, carry

gestus, -ūs, m. [gerō]: bearing, posture; gesture

gignō, gignere, genuī, genitus: produce, bear, bring forth; beget

gladius, gladiī, m.: sword

glōria, -ae, f.: glory, fame, honor

glōrior, -ārī, -ātus sum [glōria]: boast, vaunt, pride oneself

gnōmonica, -ae, f.: gnomonics, the art of the sundial

Gortyniī, Gortyniōrum, m. pl.: inhabitants of Gortyna *in Crete*, Gortynians (gôrtĭ'nå, gôrtĭn'-ĭåns)

grāculus, -ī, m.: jackdaw

gradior, gradī, gressus sum [gradus]: walk

gradus, -ūs, m.: step, pace

Graecia, -ae, f.: Greece

Graecus, -a, -um, adj.: Greek; adv. Graecē: in Greek

grandis, -e, adj.: large, great, abundant; nātū grandis: aged, old

grātia, -ae, f. [grātus]: thanks, gratitude; influence, prestige; abl. governing a preceding gen., grātiā: for the sake of, by reason of

grātulātiō, -iōnis, f. [grātulor]: rejoicing, thanksgiving, congratulation

grātulor, -ārī, -ātus sum [grātus]: rejoice; give thanks

grātus, -a, -um, adj.: pleasing, agreeable, dear; thankful, grateful

gravis, -e, adj.: heavy; serious, severe; hard to bear, grievous; eminent, venerable

gravitās, -ātis, f. [gravis]: weight;
severity; dignity, gravity

gravō, -āre, -āvī, -ātus [gravis]:
load, burden

gravor, -ārī, -ātus sum (gravō): be
loath, refuse

grex, gregis, m.: flock, herd

gruis, gruis, m. and f.: crane

gula, -ae, f.: gullet, throat; appetite

habeō, habēre, habuī, habitus:
have, hold; own, possess; believe,
consider; place; ōrātiōnem habeō:
deliver an oration; satis habeō:
be satisfied

habitō, -āre, -āvī, -ātus [habeō]:
dwell, live

habitus, -ūs, m. [habeō]: condition,
state; dress, attire, garb

hāctenus, adv. [2.hic, tenus (up to)]:
as far as this, thus far, hitherto

haereō, haerēre, haesī, haesūrus:
stick, cling, adhere

Hamilcar, Hamilcaris, m.: a Carthaginian general (hămĭl'cär)

Hannibal, Hannibalis, m.: a Carthaginian general (hăn'ĭbăl)

harēna, -ae, f.: sand; arena, amphitheatre

Harūdēs, Harūdum, m. pl.: a Germanic people (hărụ'dēg)

haud, adv.: not, not at all, by no
means

haudquāquam, adv. [haud, quis-
quam]: by no means whatever,
not at all

hauriō, haurīre, hausī, haustus:
drain, drink up; wound

haustus, -ūs, m. [hauriō]: drinking,
draught

Helvetiī, Helvetiōrum, m. pl.: the
Helvetians, a Gallic people (hĕl-
vē'shĭăns)

hercle, interj. [Herculēs]: by Hercules, by heaven, assuredly, indeed

Hercynius, -a, -um, adj.: Hercynian, the name of a forest in Germany (hẽrsĭn'ĭăn)

hērēditās, -ātis, f. [hērēs (heir)]: in-
heritance

hīberna, hībernōrum, n. pl. [hiber-
nus (of winter)]: winter-quarters

1.hīc, adv. [2.hic]: here; hereupon,
now, at this time, at this juncture

2.hĭc, haec, hŏc, demonstr. adj.: this
. . . here, this; the latter; subst.,
he, she, it, they

hilaris, -e, adj.: cheerful, joyful,
jolly

hilaritās, -ātis, f. [hilaris]: cheerfulness, gaiety, hilarity

hinc, adv. [2.hic]: from this place,
hence; from this

hiō, -āre, -āvī, -ātūrus: stand open,
gape, yawn

hircus, -ī, m.: he-goat, buck

Hispānia, -ae, f.: Spain

Hispānicus, -a, -um, adj.: Spanish

historia, -ae, f.: history; narrative,
story

histriō, -iōnis, m.: actor

hodiē, adv. [cp. 2.hic, diēs]: today

hodiernus, -a, -um, adj. [hodiē]: of
this day, today's; hodiernus diēs:
today

homō (in verse sometimes homŏ),
hominis, m. and f.: human being,
man, person

honestus, -a, -um, adj. [honōs]:
honorable, respectable; decent,
becoming

honor (or honōs), honōris m.: honor,
esteem; public honor, official
dignity, public office

honōrificus, -a, -um, adj. [honor,
faciō]: honorable, honorary, hon-
orific

honōs: see honor

Horātiī, Horatiōrum, m pl · the
name of three brothers (hōrā'shĭĭ)

hordeum, -ī, n.: barley

horreō, horrēre, horruī: shudder at,
tremble at, dread

horrendus, -a, -um, adj. [horreō]:
dreadful, fearful, terrible

hortor, -ārī, -ātus sum: urge, encourage, exhort

hospes, hospitis, *m.*: host; guest; *one bound by ties of hospitality,* guest-friend

hospita, -ae, *f.* [*cp.* hospes]: (female) visitor, (female) stranger

hospitium, hospitiī, *n.* [hospes]: hospitality; *the relation of host and guest,* guest-friendship

hostia, -ae, *f.*: sacrificial animal, victim

hostīlis, -e, *adj.* [hostis]: of an enemy, enemy's, hostile

hostis, hostis, *m. and f.*: foe, public enemy; *often pl.,* the enemy

hūc, *adv.* [2.hic]: to this place, hither; to this point, so far

huiuscemodī: *see* modus

hūmānitās, -ātis, *f.* [hūmānus]: humanity, kindliness; civilization, culture, refinement

hūmānus, -a, -um, *adj.* [homō]: human; humane, kind

humilis, -e, *adj.* [humus (*ground*)]: lowly, humble

hydrus, -ī, *m.*: water-serpent, serpent, snake

iaceō, iacēre, iacuī: lie

iaciō, iacere, iēcī, iactus: throw, cast, hurl

iactō, -āre, -āvī, -ātus [iaciō]: hurl, toss about; boast of, vaunt; boast

iam, *adv.*: now, already; soon, immediately; iam iam: just; nōn iam: no longer

iānua, -ae, *f.*: door, house-door

ibi, *adv.* [*cp.* is]: there; thereupon, then

ibīdem, *adv.*: in the same place, just there; at that very moment

*īcō, *īcere, īcī, ictus: strike, smite; foedus īcō: strike a treaty, make a covenant

ictus, -ūs, *m.* [*īcō]: blow, stroke, thrust, wound

idcircō, *adv.* [is, *cp.* circus]: for that reason, therefore

īdem, eadem, idem, *adj.*: the same; *subst. in apposition w. subject,* also, besides

ideō, *adv.* [is, id]: for that reason, therefore

idōneus, -a, -um, *adj.*: proper, suitable, apt

igitur, *conj.*: then, therefore; as I was saying

ignāvia, -ae, *f.* [ignāvus]: inactivity, laziness, sloth

ignāvus, -a, -um, *adj.* [2.in-, (g)nāvus (*diligent*)]: inactive, lazy, slothful

ignis, ignis, *m.*: fire

ignōminia, -ae, *f.* [2.in-, nōmen; *cp.* cognōmen]: disgrace, dishonor; degradation, infamy

ignōrō, -āre, -āvī, -ātus: not know, be ignorant

ignōscō, ignōscere, ignōvī, ignōtus, *w. dat.*: pardon, forgive

ignōtus, -a, -um, *adj.* [2.in-, (g)nōtus]: unknown, strange; unacquainted with, ignorant of

īlicō, *adv.* [1.in, locus]: on the spot, there; immediately

ille, illa, illud, *demonstr. adj.*: that, yon; the famous, the well-known; the former; *subst.,* he, she, it, they

illic, *adv.* [ille]: in that place, yonder

illō, *adv.* [ille]: to that place, thither

imbellis, -e, *adj.* [2.in-, bellum]: unwarlike, unfit for war

imber, imbris, *m.*: rain

imitor, -ārī, -ātus sum: imitate, copy

immānis, -e, *adj.*: monstrous, enormous, immense; frightful, fierce, savage

immēnsus, -a, -um, *adj.* [2.in-, mēnsus (*measured*)]: immeasurable, vast, immense

immeritō, *adv.* [2.in-, meritō]: undeservedly

im-misceō, -miscēre, -miscuī, -mixtus [1.in, misceō]: mix in, join

immītis, -e, *adj.* [2.in-, mītis]: harsh, severe

im-mittō, -mittere, -mīsī, -missus [1.in, mittō]: send in, drive in; put in, thrust in; let in; incite, instigate

immōbilis, -e, adj. [2.in-, mōbilis]: immovable, motionless

immolō, -āre, -āvī, -ātus [1.in, mola (sacrificial meal)]: sprinkle with sacrificial meal; sacrifice, offer as a sacrifice

immortālis, -e, adj. [2.in-, mortālis]: deathless, immortal

impediō, impedīre, impedīvī, impedītus [1.in, pēs]: entangle, ensnare; hinder, prevent; p.p.p. impedītus, -a, -um: clumsy, awkward

im-pellō, -pellere, -pulī, -pulsus [1.in, pellō]: drive forward, urge on, impel

impēnsus, -a, -um, adj. [impendō (weigh out): 1.in, pendō]: ample, great, considerable; adv. impensē: earnestly, eagerly

imperātor, imperātōris, m. [imperō]: commander-in-chief, general

imperfectus, -a, -um, adj. [2.in-, perfectus (perfect): perficiō]: unfinished, incomplete, imperfect

imperiōsus, -a, -um, adj. [imperium]: arbitrary, domineering, tyrannical

imperītus, -a, -um, adj. [2.in-, perītus], w. gen.: inexperienced, unskilled

imperium, imperiī, n. [imperō]: command, order; authority, power; sovereignty; command-in-chief, supreme command; empire

imperō, -āre, -āvī, -ātūrus [1.in, parō], w. dat.: command, order; rule, govern

impetrō, -āre, -āvī, -ātus [1.in, patrō (achieve)]: gain one's end, obtain what one requests

impetus, -ūs, m. [impetō (attack): 1.in, petō]: attack, assault; force, vehemence

impius, -a, -um, adj. [2.in-, pius]: ungodly, wicked, impious

im-pleō, -plēre, -plēvī, -plētus [1.in,

*pleō (fill)]: fill up, make full, fill

implōrō, -āre, -āvī, -ātus [1.in, plōrō (bewail)]: call for help, appeal to, entreat, implore

implūmis, -e, adj. [2.in-, plūma (feather)]: without feathers, unfledged

im-pōnō, -pōnere, -posuī, -positus [1.in, pōnō]: place upon, set on; impose

importō, -āre, -āvī, -ātus [1.in, portō]: bring in, import

improbitās, -ātis, f. [improbus]: wickedness

improbus, -a, -um, adj. [2.in-, probus (good)]: wicked, dishonest

imprōvīsus, -a, -um, adj. [2.in-, prōvīsus (foreseen): prōvideō]: unforeseen, unexpected

imprūdēns, gen. imprūdentis, adj. [2.in-, prūdēns]: not foreseeing, unaware, imprudent

imprūdentia, -ae, f. [imprūdēns]: want of foresight, imprudence

impudēns, gen. impudentis, adj. [2.in-, pudēns (shamefast): pudeō (be ashamed)]: shameless, impudent

impūne, adv. [impūnis (unpunished): 2.in-, poena]: without punishment, with impunity; unavenged, without revenge

imputō, -āre, -āvī, -ātus [1.in, putō]: ascribe, charge

īmus, -a, -um, adj.: lowest, deepest

1.in, prep. w. acc. or abl.: w. acc., into, to, upon; for; towards; over; against; w. abl., in, within, among; on; in the case of, in relation to

2.in-, prefix: not, un-

inānis, -e, adj.: empty, worthless, vain, useless

inaudītus, -a, -um, adj. [2.in-, audītus (heard): audiō]: unheard-of, unusual, new, strange

in-cēdō, -cēdere, -cessī, -cessūrus [1.in, cēdō]: advance, march, proceed incendium, incendiī, n. [incendō]: fire, conflagration

incendō, incendere, incendī, incēnsus: set fire to, burn; kindle, inflame

1.in-cidō, -cidere, -cidī [1.in, cadō]: fall in, fall upon; come upon, meet; occur

2.in-cīdō, -cīdere, -cīdī, -cīsus [1.in, caedō]: cut into, wound; inscribe

in-cipiō, -cipere, -cēpī, -ceptus [1.in, capiō]: take in hand, begin

incitō, -āre, -āvī, -ātus [1.in, citō]: urge on, hurry; incite, encourage

in-clūdō, -clūdere, -clūsī, -clūsus [1.in, claudō]: shut in, shut off, hinder

inclutus, -a, -um, adj.: celebrated, renowned, famous

incognitus, -a, -um, adj. [2.in-, cognitus (known): cognōscō]: unknown

incola, -ae, f. [incolō]: inhabitant, resident

in-colō, -colere, -coluī [1.in, colō]: dwell, inhabit

incolumis, -e, adj.: safe, unharmed; sound, entire

incommodus, -a, -um, adj. [2.in-, commodus]: inconvenient, unfit, disagreeable; subst. n.: inconvenience, annoyance, harm

incrēdibilis, -e, adj. [2.in, crēdibilis (believable): crēdō]: unbelievable, incredible

in-currō, -currere, -currī (or -cucurrī), -cursūrus [1.in, currō]: run into, run against, rush at; meet

incursiō, -iōnis, f. [incurrō]: inroad, incursion, attack

incūsō, -āre, -āvī, -ātus [1.in, cp. causa]: accuse, blame

inde, adv.: from that place, thence; from that time, since; then

1.indicō, -āre, -āvī, -ātus [1.in, 1. dicō]: point out, indicate, show

2.in-dīcō, -dīcere, -dīxī, -dictus [1.in, 2.dīcō]: summon, convoke

Indicus, -a, -um, adj.: of India, Indian

indigeō, indigēre, indiguī [indu (old form of 1.in), egeō], w. gen. or abl.: need, want, be without

indignor, -ārī, -ātus sum [indignus]: deem unworthy, despise; be indignant

indignus, -a, -um, adj. [2.in-, dignus], w. abl.: unworthy

in-dūcō, -dūcere, -dūxī, -ductus [1.in, dūcō]: lead in, bring in; exhibit, display

indulgeō, indulgēre, indulsī, indultus, w. dat.: favor, indulge

indūmentum, -ī, n. [induō]: clothing, garb

induō, induere, induī, indūtus: put on; dress, clothe

inedia, -ae, f. [2.in-, cp. 2. edō]: fasting, hunger

ineptus, -a, -um, adj. [2.in-, aptus]: absurd, silly; unsuitable, unfit

inermis, -e, adj. [2.in-, arma]: unarmed, defenseless

iners, gen. inertis, adj. [2.in-, ars]: unskillful, helpless

inexplicābilis, -e, adj. [2.in-, explicābilis (able to be uncoiled): explicō (uncoil)]: insoluble

infāmia, -ae, f. [īnfāmis (infamous): 2.in-, fāma]: ill fame, disgrace, infamy

īnfāns, gen. īnfantis, adj. [2.in-, fāns (speaking): *for]: speechless, mute

īnfēlīx, gen. īnfēlīcis, adj. [2.in-, fēlīx]: unfortunate, ill-fated, unhappy

īnferior, īnferius, adj. [īnferus (lower)]: lower, further down

in-ferō, -ferre, -tulī, -lātus [1.in, ferō]: bring in, introduce; carry in, bring against, inflict, wage; allege

īnfestus, -a, -um, adj.: hostile, inimical, dangerous

īnfirmus, -a, -um, adj. [2.in-, firmus]: weak, feeble, infirm

īnfitiae, īnfitiārum, f. pl.: denial; in-

ĭtĭăs eŏ: take refuge in denial, deny

ĭnflŏ, -āre, -āvī, -ātus [1.in, flō (*blow*)]: blow into, blow upon; blow up, inflate

ĭnfŏrmis, -e, *adj.* [2.in-, fōrma]: unformed, shapeless; misshapen, distorted

ĭnfrā, *adv. and prep. w. acc.* [ĭnferus (*lower*)]: below, beneath

ĭn-frĭngŏ, -frĭngere, -frēgī, -frāctus [1.in, frangō]: break off, break to pieces; subdue, overcome

ĭn-gemŏ, -gemere, -gemuī [1.in, gemō (*groan*)]: groan, lament, wail

ĭngenĭum, ĭngenĭī, *n.* [1.in, gignō]: innate quality; natural talent, cleverness, genius

ĭngēns, *gen.* **ĭngentis,** *adj.:* huge, vast, enormous

ĭngrātus, -a, -um, *adj.* [2.in-, grātus]: unpleasant; ungrateful; thankless

ĭn-gredĭor, -gredī, -gressus sum [1.in, gradior]: enter; advance

ĭn-icĭŏ, -icere, -iēcī, -iectus [1.in, iaciō]: throw in; bring into, impress, infuse

ĭnimĭcus, -a, -um, *adj.* [2.in-, amīcus]: unfriendly, hostile; *subst. m.*, personal enemy, enemy, foe

ĭnĭquus, -a, -um, *adj.* [2.in-, aequus]: uneven; unfavorable; unfair, unjust

ĭnĭtĭum, ĭnĭtĭī, *n.* [ineō (*enter*): 1.in, 2.eō]: beginning

ĭnĭūdicātus, -a, -um, *adj.* [2.in-, iūdicātus (*judged*): iūdicō]: unadjudged, undecided

ĭnĭūrātus, -a, -um, *adj.* [2.in-, iūrātus (*sworn*): iūrō]: unsworn, not under oath

ĭnĭūria, -ae, *f.* [iniūrius (*unjust*): 2.in-, iūs]: injustice, wrong, injury; *abl.:* unjustly, causelessly

ĭnĭūstus, -a, -um, *adj.* [2.in-, iūstus]: unjust, oppressive, wrongful

ĭnlecebra, -ae, *f.* [*cp.* inliciō]: enticement, lure; delight

ĭnlicĭŏ, ĭnlicere, ĭnlexī, ĭnlectus: allure, entice

ĭnlūstris, -e, *adj.* [1.in, *cp.* lūx]: bright, brilliant; famous, illustrious

ĭnnocēns, *gen.* **ĭnnocentis,** *adj.* [2.in-, nocēns (*harmful*): noceō (*harm*)]: harmless, inoffensive; guiltless, innocent

ĭnnocentĭa, -ae, *f.* [ĭnnocēns]: guiltlessness, innocence, integrity

ĭn-nŏtēscŏ, -nŏtēscere, -nŏtuī [1.in, nŏtēscō (*become known*): nōtus]: become known

ĭnnumerus, -a, -um, *adj.* [2.in-, numerus]: countless, innumerable

ĭnopĭa, -ae, *f.* [inops]: want, lack, scarcity, poverty

ĭnopīnāns, *gen.* **ĭnopīnantis,** *adj.* [2.in-, opīnāns (*expecting*): opīnor]: not expecting, taken by surprise

ĭnopīnātus, -a, -um, *adj.* [2.in-, opīnātus (*expected*): opīnor]: unexpected, surprising

ĭnops, *gen.* **ĭnopis,** *adj.* [2.in-, *ops]: without resources, weak, poor

ĭnquam, *defect.:* say (*after one or more words of a direct quotation*)

ĭnquĭnŏ, -āre, -āvī, -ātus: befoul, defile

ĭn-quīrŏ, -quīrere, -quīsīvī, -quīsītus [1.in, quaerō]: search for; examine, investigate, inquire

ĭn-rīdeŏ, -rīdēre, -rīsī, -rīsus [1.in, rīdeō]: laugh at, jeer, ridicule

ĭnrīdiculē, *adv.* [inrīdiculus (*not laughablo*): 2.in-, rīdiculus (*laughable*): rīdeō]: without wit, unwittily

ĭnsānĭa, -ae, *f.* [īnsānus (*insane*): 2.in-, sānus (*sane*)]: madness, insanity

ĭn-scendŏ, -scendere, -scendī [1.in, scandō]: climb up, ascend; mount

ĭnscĭēns, *gen.* **ĭnscientis,** *adj.* [2.in-,

sciēns (*knowing*): sciō]: unknowing, unaware

īnscītia, -ae, *f.* [īnscītus (*ignorant*): 2.in-, scītus]: ignorance, inexperience

īnscius, -a, -um, *adj.* [2.in-, scius (*knowing*): sciō]: unknowing, ignorant, unaware

īn-scrībō, -scrībere, -scrīpsī, -scrīptus [1.in, scrībō]: write upon, inscribe

īn-sequor, -sequī, -secūtus sum [1. in, sequor]: follow, pursue

īn-sideō, -sidēre, -sēdī [1.in, sedeō]: sit upon; settle; take possession

īnsidiae, īnsidiārum, *f. pl.* [īnsideō]: snare, ambuscade; plot, trick

īnsidiōsus, -a, -um, *adj.* [īnsidiae]: deceitful, treacherous, crafty

īnsigne, īnsignis, *n.* [īnsignis]: badge, ornament

īnsignis, -e, *adj.* [1.in, signum]: remarkable, extraordinary

īn-siliō, -silīre, -siluī [1.in, saliō]: leap in, leap upon

īn-sistō, -sistere, -stitī [1.in, sistō]: take a stand, settle, perch; pause, halt; insist; *w. inf.*, insist upon

īnsolēns, *gen.* īnsolentis, *adj.* [2.in-, solēns (*being accustomed*): soleō]: unaccustomed, unusual; haughty, insolent

īnspectō, -āre, -āvī, -ātus [1.in, spectō]: look at, look on

īn-spiciō, -spicere, -spexī, -spectus [1.in, speciō]: look into, look upon, examine

īnstīnctus, -a, -um, *adj.*: inspired, impelled

īn-stituō, -stituere, -stituī, -stitūtus [1.in, statuō]: establish; determine, resolve; begin; teach, instruct

īnstitūtum, -ī, *n.* [īnstituō]: purpose, intention; practice, custom

īn-stō, -stāre, -stetī, -statūrus [1.in, stō]: stand upon; approach, impend; urge, demand; pursue

īn-struō, -struere, -strūxī, -strūctus

[1.in, struō]: draw up, array; prepare, equip

īn-suēscō, -suēscere, -suēvī, -suētus [1.in, suēscō (*become accustomed*)]: become accustomed; *p.p. p.* īnsuētus, -a, -um: accustomed

1.īnsuētus, -a, -um, *adj.* [2.in-, suētus (*accustomed*): suēscō (*become accustomed*)]: unaccustomed; unusual, strange

2.īnsuētus, -a, -um: *see* īnsuēscō

īnsula, -ae, *f.*: island; tenement

īnsultō, -āre, -āvī, -ātus [1.in, saltō (*leap*): saliō]: leap upon; abuse, insult

integer, integra, integrum, *adj.* [2.in-, *cp.* tangō]: untouched, entire, unimpaired

intellegentia, -ae, *f.* [intellegēns (*understanding*): intellegō]: understanding, intelligence, knowledge

intel-legō, -legere, -lēxī, -lēctus [intęr, legō]: perceive, understand

in-tendō, -tendere, -tendī, -tentus [1.in, tendō (*stretch*)]: stretch out, extend; aim, direct; endeavor, intend

inter, *prep. w. acc.*: between, among, in the midst of; within, in the course of; *in compounds*, under; inter sē: among themselves, with one another

inter-cēdō, -cēdere, -cessī, -cessūrus [inter, cēdō]: come between, lie between; intervene; exist between

inter-clūdō, -clūdere, -clūsī, -clūsus [inter, claudō]: shut out, shut off; prevent, hinder

inter-dīcō, -dīcere, -dīxī, -dictus [inter, 2.dīcō]: forbid, prohibit (*w. dat. of person and abl. of thing*)

interdiū, *adv.* [inter, diū (*by day*)]: during the day, in the daytime

interdum, *adv.* [inter, dum]: sometimes, occasionally, now and then

VOCABULARY 229

inter-eā, adv.: meanwhile, in the meantime

inter-eō, -īre, -iī, -itūrus [inter, 2. eō]: die, perish

inter-ficiō, -ficere, -fēcī, -fectus [inter, faciō]: kill, slay, murder

interim, adv. [cp. inter]: meanwhile, in the meantime

interior, interius, adj. [cp. inter]: inner, interior, middle; intimate, secret

interitus, -ūs, m. [intereō]: death, destruction

interminor, -ārī, -ātus sum [inter, minor (threaten)], w. dat.: threaten, forbid with threats

inter-mittō, -mittere, -mīsī, -missus [inter, mittō]: leave off, neglect; cease, pause

interpellō, -āre, -āvī, -ātus [inter, cp. pellō]: interrupt; disturb, hinder, obstruct

inter-pōnō, -pōnere, -posuī, -positus [inter, pōnō]: put between, insert, interpose; allege, use as a pretext

interpres, interpretis, m. and f.: interpreter

interpretor, -ārī, -ātus sum [interpres]: explain, interpret; understand

interrogō, -āre, -āvī, -ātus [inter, rogō]: ask, question; inquire

inter-sum, -esse, -fuī, -futūrus [inter, sum]: be between; differ; be present; w. dat., take part in, be engaged in

intervallum, -ī, n. [inter, vallum (wall)]: interval, distance

intimus, -a, -um, adj. [cp. interior]: inmost, innermost

intrā, adv. and prep. w. acc. [cp. inter]: within

intrepidus, -a, -um, adj. [2.in-, trepidus (alarmed)]: unafraid, intrepid

intrō, adv. [cp. inter]: within, in

intrō-dūcō, -dūcere, -dūxī, -ductus [intrō, dūcō]: lead in; introduce

intro-eō, -īre, -iī [intrō, 2.eō]: go in, enter

intrō-gredior, -gredī, -gressus sum [intrō, gradior]: step in, enter

intrō-rumpō, -rumpere, -rūpī, -ruptus [intrō, rumpō]: break in, enter by force

in-tueor, -tuērī, -tuitus sum [1.in, tueor]: look upon, gaze at; consider

inūtilis, -e, adj. [2.in-, ūtilis]: useless; hurtful, injurious

in-vādō, -vādere, -vāsī, -vāsūrus [1.in, vadō (go)]: go into, enter; attack, assault

in-veniō, -venīre, -vēnī, -ventus [1.in, veniō]: come upon, find; invent, discover

inventor, inventōris, m. [inveniō]: discoverer, inventor

invicem, adv. [1.in, *vicis]: by turns, in turn

invictus, -a, -um, adj. [2.in-, victus (conquered)]: unconquered

invidia, -ae, f. [invidus (envious)]: invideō (envy): 1.in, videō]: envy, grudge; ill-will, unpopularity

invīsus, -a, -um, adj. [invideō (hate): 1.in, videō]: hated, detested

invītō, -āre, -āvī, -ātus: invite, summon

invītus, -a, -um, adj.: unwilling, reluctant

iocus, -ī, m.: jest, joke

ipse, ipsa, ipsum, intensive adj.: self, in person; very

īra, -ae, f.: anger, wrath

īrācundus, -a, -um, adj. [īra]: angry, irritable

īrāscor, īrāscī, īrātus sum [īra]: be angry; perf. part. īrātus, -a, -um: angry

is, ea, id, demonstr. adj.: this, that; such; subst. he, she, it, they

iste, ista, istud, demonstr. adj.: that . . . of yours, that

istic, istaec, istuc, demonstr. adj.: that . . . of yours, that

ita, adv. [cp. is]: in this manner,

thus, so; as follows; to such an extent

Italia, -ae, *f.*: Italy

item, *adv.* [*cp.* ita]: also, likewise

iter, itineris, *n.* [2.eō]: journey; road; **itinera magna** (*or* **maxima**): forced marches

iterum, *adv.*: again, a second time, once more

itidem, *adv.* [*cp.* ita]: in like manner, so, in the same way

iuba, -ae, *f.*: mane

iubeō, iubēre, iussī, iussus: order, bid, command

iūcundus, -a, -um, *adj.* [*cp.* iuvō]: pleasant, agreeable, delightful

iūdex, iūdicis, *m. and f.* [iūs, 2.dīcō]: judge; juror

iūdicium, iūdiciī, *n.* [iūdicō]: judgment, decision; trial, court

iūdicō, -āre, -āvī, -ātus [iūdex]: judge, decide

C. Iūlius Caesar: *a Roman statesman, general, and author* (gā'yŭs jū'lĭŭs sē'går)

iūmentum, -ī, *n.* [*cp.* iungō]: draught-animal; horse

iūnctūra, -ae, *f.* [iungō]: joining, manner of joining

iungō, iungere, iūnxi, iūnctus: join, unite, connect

Iuppiter, Iovis, *m.*: Jupiter, *the chief god of the Romans* (jṳ'pĭtĕr)

iūrgium, iūrgiī, *n.* [iūrgō (*quarrel*)]: quarrel, dispute

iūrō, -āre, -āvī, -ātus [iūs]: swear, take an oath; bind by an oath

iūs, iūris, *n.*: right, justice; law; court; **iūs dīcō:** administer justice, hold court

iūsiūrandum, iūrisiūrandī, *n.* [iūs, iūrō]: oath

iūstitia, -ae, *f.* [iūstus]: justice

iūstus, -a, -um, *adj.* [iūs]: just, righteous; proper, perfect; regular

iuvenis, *gen.* **iuvenis,** *adj.*: young, youthful; *subst.*, young person, youth

iuventūs, iuventūtis, *f.* [iuvenis]: age of youth, youth

iuvō, iuvāre, -iūvī, iūtus: aid, help; delight

L.: Lūcius (lū'shĭŭs)

T. Labiēnus: *Caesar's second-in-command* (tī'tŭs lābĭē'nŭs)

labor, labōris, *m.*: labor, toil

labōrō, -āre, -āvī, -ātus [labor]: work, labor; be in distress, be hard-pressed, suffer

lac, lactis, *n.*: milk

Lacedaemōn, Lacedaemonis, *f.*: *a city in Greece, also called* Sparta (lăsĕdē'mŏn)

Lacedaemonius, -a, -um, *adj.*: Lacedaemonian, Spartan (lăsĕdēmō'nĭàn)

lacerō, -āre, -āvī, -ātus: tear to pieces

lacessō, lacessere, lacessīvī, lacessītus: excite, provoke; exasperate, irritate

Lacōnia, -ae, *f.*: *a country in Greece* (làcō'nĭà)

lacrima, -ae, *f.*: tear

lacrimō, -āre, -āvī, -ātus [lacrima]: weep, cry

lacus, -ūs, *m.*: lake, pool

laedō, laedere, laesī, laesus: hurt, injure

laetitia, -ae, *f.* [laetus]: joy, rejoicing, delight

laetor, -ārī, -ātus sum [laetus]: rejoice, be glad

laetus, -a, -um, *adj.*: joyful, cheerful, glad

lambō, lambere: lick, lap

lāmenta, lāmentōrum, *n. pl.*: wailing, lamentation

lāna, -ae, *f.*: wool; woolen bandage

lāniger, lānigera, lānigerum, *adj.* [lāna, gerō]: wool-bearing; *subst. m.*, wool-bearing creature, sheep, lamb

laniō, -āre, -āvī, -ātus: tear in pieces, mangle

lapis, lapidis, *m.*: stone

largior, largīrī, largītus sum [largus]:

give bountifully, lavish, bestow
largus, -a, -um, *adj.*: abundant,
plentiful, copious
latebra, -ae, *f.* [lateō]: hiding-place
latēbrōsus, -a, -um, *adj.* [latēbra]:
full of hiding-places
lateō, latēre, latuī: lie hidden, be
concealed
latibulum, -ī, *n.* [lateō]: hiding-place
Latīnus, -a, -um, *adj.* Latin; *subst.*
m. pl., the Latins; *adv.* Latīnē: in
Latin
1.lātrō, -āre, -āvī, -ātus: bark
2.latrō, latrōnis, *m.*: robber, thief,
brigand
latrōcinium, latrōciniī, *n.* [2.latrō]:
robbery
1.lātus, -a, -um, *adj.*: broad, wide
2.latus, lateris, *n.*: side, flank
laudō, -āre, -āvī, -ātus [laus]:
praise
laus, laudis, *f.*: praise, glory, fame
lavō, lavāre, lāvī, lautus: wash;
pass., wash oneself, bathe
laxō, -āre, -āvī, -ātus [laxus (*loose*)]:
loosen, relax
lēgatiō, -iōnis, *f.* [lēgō (*delegate*)]:
embassy, legation
lēgātus, -ī, *m.* [lēgō (*delegate*)]:
ambassador, legate; lieutenant-
general, second-in-command
legiō, -iōnis, *f.* [legō]: body of soldiers, legion
legiōnārius, -a, -um, *adj.* [legiō]: of
a legion; *subst. m.*, legionary
soldier
lēgitimus, -a, -um, *adj.* [lēx]: fixed
by law, legal; regular
legō, legere, lēgī, lēctus: gather,
collect; choose, pick; read
lēnis, -e, *adj.*: soft, mild, gentle
lentus, -a, -um, *adj.*: slow, sluggish;
indifferent, unconcerned
leō (*in verse sometimes* leō), leōnis,
m.: lion
lepidus, -a, -um, *adj.* [lepōs
(*charm*)]: charming, agreeable;
witty
lepus, leporis, *m.*: hare

Lesbius, -a, -um, *adj.*: of Lesbos,
Lesbian (lĕs'bŏs, lĕs'bĭán)
lētum, -ī, *n.*: death
Leucae, Leucārum, *f. pl.*: *a city in*
Asia Minor (lū'sē)
Leucī, Leucōrum, *m. pl.*: *a Gallic*
people (lū'sī)
Leuctra, Leuctrōrum, *n. pl.*: *a city*
in Greece (lūc'trá)
levis, -e, *adj.*: light, nimble; slight,
small, trivial
levō, -āre, -āvī, -ātus [levis] lift up,
elevate; make lighter, relieve
lēx, lēgis, *f.*: law
libēns, *gen.* libentis, *adj.* [libet]:
willing, with pleasure, glad
1.līber, lībera, līberum: free, unre-
stricted; frank; *subst. m. pl.*,
children
2.liber, librī, *m.*: book
līberālis, -e, *adj.* [1.līber]: befitting
a freeman, dignified; liberal
līberālitās, -ātis, *f.* [līberālis]: in-
genuousness; generosity, liber-
ality
līberī, līberōrum, *m. pl.*: *see* 1.līber
līberō, -āre, -āvī, -ātus [1.līber]: set
free, liberate
lībertās, -ātis, *f.* [1.liber]: freedom,
liberty; frankness, boldness
libet, lībēre, libuit (*or* libitum est),
impers., w. dat.: it pleases
lībra, -ae, *f.*: pound; scale
librārius, -a, -um, *adj.* [2.liber]: of
books; *subst. m.*, copyist, scribe,
secretary
lībrō, -āre, -āvī, -ātus [lībra]: bal-
ance, poise
licentia, -ae, *f.* [licet]: unrestrained
liberty, license; permission
licet, licēre, licuit (*or* licitum est),
impers., w. dat.: it is permitted;
per mē licet: it is permitted as far
as I am concerned, I have no
objection
P. Licinius Crassus: *a Roman offi-*
cer (pŭb'lĭŭs lĭsĭn'ĭŭs crăs'ŭs)
P. Licinius Crassus Dīves Mūciānus: *a Roman governor* (pŭb'lĭŭs

līsīn'ī̆ŭs crās'ŭs dī'vĕg mŭshlă'-nŭs)

ligneus, -a, -um, *adj.* [lignum]: wooden

lignum, -ī, *n.:* wood, timber

līmen, līminis, *n.:* threshold, sill

līmus, -ī, *m.:* mud, mire

lineāmentum, -ī, *n.* [lineō (*draw a line*): linea (*line*)]: feature, lineament

Lingonēs, Lingonum, *m.* *pl.:* a *Gallic people* (līn'gŏnēg)

lingua, -ae, *f.:* tongue, language

linquō, linquere, līquī: leave, abandon

linter, lintris, *f.:* boat, skiff

liqueō, liquēre, licuī: be fluid; be clear, be apparent

liquor, liquōris, *m.* [liqueō]: fluid, liquid

līs, lītis, *f.:* dispute; law-suit; lītem dō: decide a case

lītigiōsus, -a, -um, *adj.* [lītigium (*law-suit*): lītigō (*sue*): līs, *cp.* agō]: full of disputes, quarrelsome

littera, -ae, *f.:* letter *of the alphabet*; *pl.*, epistle, letter; literature, letters

locus, -ī, *m.; pl.* loca, locōrum, *n.:* place, spot; station, rank; room, opportunity

longē, *adv.* [longus]: a long way off, far; by far

longinquus, -a, -um, *adj.* [longē]: far removed, remote; lasting, long

longitūdō, longitūdinis, *f.* [longus]: length; long duration

longus, -a, -um, *adj.:* long, extended; lasting, prolonged; distant

loquor, loquī, locūtus sum: speak, talk

lōrum, -ī, *n.:* thong, strap, leash

luctātor, luctātōris, *m.* [luctor (*wrestle*)]: wrestler

lūctŭs, -ūs, *m.* [lūgeō]: grief, sorrow

lūdō, lūdere, lūsī, lūsus [lūdus]: play, sport; mock, ridicule; deceive, delude

lūdus, -ī, *m.:* play, game; sport, fun

lūgeō, lūgēre, lūxī, lūctus: mourn, lament

lūgubris, -e, *adj.* [lūgeō]: mournful

lūna, -ae, *f.* [*cp.* lūx]: the moon

lupus, -ī, *m.:* wolf

Lūsitānus, -a, -um, *adj.:* of Lusitania *in Spain,* Lusitanian (lūsī-tā'nĭá, lūsītā'nĭàn)

lūx, lūcis, *f.:* light; daylight; prīma lūx: dawn

lūxuria, -ae, *f.:* luxury, profusion; excess

lympha, -ae, *f.:* water

Lȳsander, Lȳsandrī, *m.:* a *Spartan general* (lĭsăn'dĕr)

Lȳsimachus, -ī, *m.:* an *Athenian* (lĭsĭm'ácŭs)

M.:Mārcus (mär'cŭs)

M'.: Manius (mā'nĭŭs)

T. Maccius Plautus: a *Roman playwright* (tī'tŭs măc'sĭŭs plạ'tŭs)

Macedonia, -ae, *f.:* a *region of Europe north of Greece* (măsĕdō'-nĭá)

maciēs, *abl.* maciē, *f.* [macer (*thin*)]: leanness, thinness; privation

M. Maecius: a *Gaul* (mär'cŭs mē'-shĭŭs)

maereō, maerēre: be sad, be mournful

maeror, maerōris, *m.* [maereō]: sadness, grief

maestus, -a, -um, *adj.* [maereō]: sad, sorrowful

Magetobriga, -ae, *f.:* a *Gallic town* (măgĕtŏb'rĭgá)

magis: *see* magnus

magister, magistrī, *m.* [magis]: master, chief; teacher

magistrātus, -ūs, *m.* [magister]: magistracy; magistrate; body of magistrates

magnificus, -a, -um, *adj.* [magnus, faciō]: great, noble; splendid, fine

magnitūdō, magnitūdinis, *f.* [magnus]: greatness, size; abundance

magnus, -a, -um, *adj.:* great, large,

hig; important, considerable; strong, mighty; *comp.* maior, maius: greater, larger; rather important; *superl.* maximus, -a, -um: greatest, largest; *adv.* magnopere: greatly; *comp. adv.* magis: more greatly, more, rather maior, maius: *see* magnus

malitia, -ae, *f.* [1. malus]: ill-will, spite, malice

1.malus, -a, -um, *adj.:* bad, wicked; *subst. n.,* evil, calamity; fault; *comp.* peior, peius: worse; *superl.* pessimus, -a, -um: worst, very bad; male dīcō, *w. dat.:* slander

2.mālus, -ī, *m.:* mast, pole

mandātum, -ī, *n.* [mandō]: charge, commission; command, order; *pl.,* message

mandō, -āre, -āvī, -ātus, *w. dat.:* commit, entrust; order, command

maneō, manēre, mānsī, mānsūrus: stay, remain; abide; await, expect

Mānliānus, -a, -um, *adj.:* Manlian (măn'lĭản)

T. Mānlius Imperiōsus Torquātus: *a Roman consul* (tī'tŭs măn'lĭŭs ĭmpērĭō'sŭs tôrquā'tŭs)

mānsuētus, -a, -um, *adj.* [manus, suēscō (*become accustomed*)]: tame, gentle

manus, -ūs, *f.:* hand; band, troop; *pl.,* labor

Marathōnius, -a, -um, *adj.:* of Marathon *in Greece* (măr'áthŏn)

Marcomannī, Marcomannōrum, *m. pl.: a Germanic people* (märcŏ-măn'ĭ)

mare, maris, *n.:* the sea

margō, marginis, *m.:* well-curb, curb

C. Marius: *a Roman general* (gā'yŭs măr'ĭŭs)

marītus, -a, -um, *adj.:* of marriage; *subst. m.,* husband

Marō, Marōnis, *m.: see* Vergilius

Mārs, Mārtis, *m.: god of war* (märz)

māter, mātris, *f.:* mother

mātrimōnium, mātrimōnii, *n.* [māter]: marriage, matrimony

mātrōna, -ae, *f.* [māter]: married woman, matron

mātūrēscō, mātūrēscere, mātūrui [mātūrus]: become ripe, ripen

mātūrō, -āre, -āvī, -ātus [mātūrus]: make haste, hasten

mātūrus, -a, -um, *adj.:* ripe, mature; early, speedy

maximus, -a, -um: *see* magnus

medeor, medērī, *w. dat.:* heal, cure; remedy, relieve

medicīna, -ae, *f.* [medicīnus]: medicine; remedy, cure

medicīnus, -a, -um, *adj.* [medicus]: of a physician; medicīna rēs: medicine

medicus, -ī, *m.* [medeor]: physician, doctor

mediocris, -e, *adj.* [medius]: moderate, ordinary; mediocre, inferior

meditor, -ārī, -ātus sum [medeor]: reflect, consider; meditate upon, study

medius, -a, -um, *adj.:* in the middle, middle, half-way between; *subst. n.,* middle; common fund, treasury

Megara, Megarōrum, *n. pl.: a Greek city* (měg'árà)

Megarēnsis, -e, *adj.:* of Megara, Megarian; *subst. m. pl.,* the Megarians (mēgā'rĭăn)

meherculēs, *interj.* [ego, Herculēs]: by Hercules, by heaven, assuredly, indeed

melior, melius: *see* bonus

membrum, -ī, *n.:* part of the body, limb

memor, *gen.* memoris, *adj.:* mindful, heedful

memoria, -ae, *f.* [memor]: memory; story

memorō, -āre, -āvī, -ātus [memor]: bring to remembrance, mention

Menander, Menandrī, *m.: a Greek playwright* (měnăn'dĕr)

mendācium, mendāciī, *n.* [mendāx

(*false*): menda (*fault*)]: lie, untruth

mēns, mentis, *f.:* mind; plan, purpose

mēnsa, -ae, *f.:* table

mēnsis, mēnsis, *m.:* month

mentiō, -iōnis, *f.:* mention

mentior, mentīrī, mentītus sum [mēns]: lie, assert falsely

mercātor, mercātōris, *m.* [mercor]: merchant, trader

mercātūra, -ae, *f.* [mercor]: trade, commerce

mercēs, mercēdis, *f.* [merx (*merchandise*)]: price; wages, pay

mercor, -ārī, -ātus sum [merx (*merchandise*)]: buy

Mercurius, Mercuriī, *m.:* Mercury, *god of commerce* (mĕr′cûrў)

mereor, merērī, meritus sum [mereō (*deserve*)]: deserve, merit

mergō, mergere, mersī, mersus: dip, immerse, plunge

merīdiānus, -a, -um, *adj.* [merīdiēs]: of midday, noonday-

merīdiēs, merīdiēī, *m.* [medius, diēs]: midday, noon

meritō, *adv.* [meritum]: deservedly, justly

meritum, -ī, *n.* [mereō (*deserve*)]: service, benefit, favor

M. Messāla: *a Roman consul* (mär′-cŭs mĕsä′lȧ)

Messēnē, Messēnēs, *abl.* Messēnē, *f.:* *a Greek city* (mĕsē′nē)

messis, messis, *f.* [metō]: harvest

-met, *enclitic added to pers. pronouns for emphasis:* self

Metellus: *see* Caecilius

Mēthymnaeus, -a, -um, *adj.:* of Methymna *on the island of Lesbos,* Methymnian (mĕthĭm′nȧ, mĕthĭm′nĭȧn)

metō, metere, messuī, messus: reap, harvest

metuō, metuere, metuī [metus]: fear, be afraid

metus, -ūs, *m.:* fear, dread; anxiety

meus, -a, -um, *poss. adj.* [ego]: my, mine

micō, micāre, micuī: gleam, glitter, shine

migrō, -āre, -āvī, -ātus: move, depart, migrate

mīles, mīlitis, *m.:* soldier

Mīlēsius, -a, -um, *adj.:* of Miletus, Milesian; *subst. m. pl.,* the Milesians (mĭlē′zĭȧn)

Mīlētus, -ī, *f.:* *a city in Asia Minor* (mĭlē′tŭs)

mīlitāris, -e, *adj.* [mīles]: of a soldier, military

mīlitia, -ae, *f.* [mīles]: military service, warfare, war

mīlle, *num. adj., indecl. in s.; pl.* mīlia, mīlium, *n.:* a thousand; mīlle passūs: a thousand paces, a mile

Mīlō, Mīlōnis, *m.:* *a Greek athlete* (mĭ′lō)

mīluus, -ī, *m.:* kite, *a bird of prey*

Minerva, -ae, *f.:* *goddess of wisdom* (mĭnĕr′vȧ)

minimus, -a, -um: *see* parvus

ministrō, -āre, -āvī, -ātus [minister (*servant*)]: attend, wait upon; serve

minor, minus: *see* parvus

minuō, minuere, minuī, minūtus [*cp.* minor]: make small, diminish; reduce, abate

minus: *see* parvus

mīrāculum, -ī, *n.* [mīror]: marvel, miracle

mīrificus, -a, -um, *adj.* [mīrus, faciō]: wonderful, marvelous, strange

mīror, -ārī, -ātus sum [mīrus]: wonder, marvel; wonder at, admire

mīrus, -a, -um, *adj.:* wonderful, marvelous, astonishing

misceō, miscēre, miscuī, mixtus: mix, mingle; throw into confusion, disturb

miser, misera, miserum, *adj.:* wretched, unfortunate, miserable

misereor, miséréri, miseritus sum
[miser], w. gen.: feel pity, have
compassion, pity
miseror, -ārī, -ātus sum [miser]:
lament, deplore, pity
Mithridātēs, Mithridātī, m.: a king
of Pontus (mǐthrǐdā'tēg)
mītis, -e, adj.: mild, gentle, kind
mittō, mittere, mīsī, missus: send,
despatch; hurl, cast; release, dismiss
mōbilis, -e, adv. [moveō]: easy to
move, movable; inconstant, fickle
moderor, -ārī, -ātus sum [modus]:
moderate, restrain; act moder-
ately
modestus, -a, -um, adj. [modus]:
moderate, temperate
modius, modiī, m. [modus]: peck,
a measure of grain
modo, adv. and conj. [modus]: only,
merely, simply; nōn modo . . .
sed (or vērum): not only . . .
but; just now, just; if but, if
only, provided that
modus, -ī, m.: measure, proper
measure, amount; bound, limit;
way, manner, method; kind,
sort; huiuscemodī: of this very
kind, of the following kind
moenia, moenium, n. pl.: defensive
walls, ramparts, bulwarks
molestia, -ae, f. [molestus]: trouble,
vexation, annoyance
molestus, -a, -um, adj. [mōlēs
(mass)]: troublesome, irksome,
annoying
mōlimentum, -ī, n. [mōlior]: exertion, trouble, effort
mōlior, mōlīrī, mōlītus sum [mōlēs
(mass)]: exert oneself, endeavor;
attempt, contrive, plot
mollis, -e, adj.: tender, gentle; mild,
easy; weak, unmanly
moneō, monēre, monuī, monitus:
remind; admonish, warn, teach
monīle, monīlis, n.: necklace, collar
monimentum, -ī, n. [moneō]: me-
morial, reminder
mōns, montis, m.: mountain, hill

morbus, -ī, m.: sickness, disease
moribundus, -a, -um, adj. [morior]:
dying, moribund
morior, morī, mortuus sum [cp.
mors]: die
moror, -ārī, -ātus sum [mora (delay)]: delay, wait
mōrōsus, -a, -um, adj. [mōs]: cross,
cranky
mors, mortis, f.: death
morsus, -ūs, m. [mordeō (bite)]: bite
mortālis, -e, adj. [mors]: mortal
mōs, mōris, m.: habit, manner, custom
mōtus, -ūs, m. [moveō]: motion,
movement
moveō, movēre, mōvī, mōtus: move,
stir, set in motion; wag; disturb,
affect, remove, expel
mox, adv.: soon, directly, presently
mulcō, -āre, -āvī, -ātus: beat,
handle roughly
muliebris, -e, adj. [mulier]: of a
woman, of women, feminine
mulier, mulieris, f.: woman
multitūdō, multitūdinis, f. [multus]:
great number, multitude, crowd
multō, -āre, -āvī, -ātus [multa
(penalty)]: punish
multus, -a, -um, adj.: much, abundant, large; fluent; pl. many;
comp. plūs, gen. plūris: more;
superl. plūrimus, -a, -um: most,
very much, very many
mūlus, -ī, m.: mule
munditia, -ae, f. [mundus (neat)]:
neatness, elegance
mundus, -ī, m.: universe, world
mūniō, mūnīre, mūnīvī, mūnītus
[moenia]: fortify, strengthen
mūnītiō, -iōnis, f. [mūniō]: fortifying, fortification
mūnus, mūneris, n.: service, function; duty; present, gift
murmur, murmuris, n.: low roar,
growl, grumbling
mūrus, -ī, m.: city-wall, wall
mūs, mūris, m. and f.: mouse
mūsa, -ae, f.: muse, goddess of the
arts

musica, -ae, *f.*: music

mustēla, -ae, *f.*: weasel

mūtō, -āre, -āvī, -ātus: change, alter; exchange

mūtus, -a, -um, *adj.*: dumb, mute, speechless

mūtuus, -a, -um, *adj.* [mūtō]: borrowed, lent; reciprocal, mutual; opera mūtua: assistance

Mȳlasēnsis, -e, *adj.*: of Mylasa *in Asia Minor*, Mylasian; *subst. m. pl.*, the Mylasians (mī'lȧsà, mĭlā'-zĭän)

Cn. Naevius: *a Roman playwright* (nē'ŭs nē'vĭŭs)

M. Naevius: *a Roman tribune* (mär'cŭs nē'vĭŭs)

nam, *conj.*: for; *enclitic with interrog.*, . . . in the world?

namque, *conj.* [nam]: for, for in fact

nancīscor, nancīscī, nanctus [*or* nactus) sum: get, obtain, find

nāris, nāris, *f.*: nostril

nārrātiō, -iōnis, *f.* [nārrō]: narrative, story

nārrō, -āre, -āvī, -ātus: relate, tell, narrate

nāscor, nāscī, nātus sum: be born; *perf. part.* nātus, -a, -um: born; *w. expressions of time*, old, of the age of

Nasua, -ae, *f.*: *a German leader* (năsh'ŭȧ)

nātālis, -e, *adj.* [1.nātus]: of birth, birth-, natal

nātiō, -iōnis, *f.* [nāscor]: race, nation, people

natō, -āre, -āvī, -ātūrus [nō (*swim*)]: swim

nātūra, -ae, *f.* [nāscor]: origin, birth; nature; the world, universe

1.nātus, -a, -um: *see* nāscor

2.*nātus, *nātūs, *m.* [nāscor]: birth, age, years; nātū grandis: old, aged

naufragium, naufragiī, *n.* [nāvis, *cp.* frangō]: shipwreck; naufragium faciō: meet destruction, be wrecked

nauta, -ae, *m.* [*cp.* nāvis]: sailor

nāvicula, -ae, *f.* [nāvis]: small vessel, boat, skiff

nāvis, nāvis, *f.*: ship

1.ne-, *prefix*: not, no, un-

2.nĕ, *adv. and conj.*: no, not; lest, that . . . not, in order that . . . not, to prevent; nĕ . . . quidem: not even

3.-ne, *enclitic interrog. particle and conj.*: sign of a direct question; in indirect questions, whether

nebulō, nebulōnis, *m.* [nebula (*mist*)]: worthless fellow, good-for-nothing

nec: *see* neque; nec *in compounds is another word, an old negative*, not, no, un-

necessārius, -a, -um, *adj.* [necesse]: necessary; *adv.* necessāriō: of necessity, unavoidably

necesse, *indecl. adj.*: necessary

necessitūdō, necessitūdinis, *f.* [necesse]: close connection, friendship

necne, *adv.* [nec, 3.-ne]: or not

necō, -āre, -āvī, -ātus [nex]: kill, slay

necopīnus, -a, -um, *adj.* [nec, *cp.* opīnor]: unexpected; not expecting, unsuspecting

nefās, *indecl. n.* [1.ne-, fās]: impious deed, sin, crime

neg-legō, -legere, -lēxī, -lēctus [nec, legō]: disregard, neglect

negō, -āre, -āvī, -ātus: say no, say . . . not; deny; refuse

negōtium, negōtiī, *n.* [nec, ōtium]: business; task; difficulty, trouble, labor

Nemētēs, Nemētum, *m. pl.*: *a Germanic people* (nĕmē'tēş)

nēmō, *dat.* nēminī, *m. and f.* [1.ne-, homō]: no one, nobody

nemorōsus, -a, -um, *adj.* [nemus]: full of woods, woody

nemus, nemoris, *n.*: woods, grove, forest

Nepōs, Nepōtis, *m.*: *see* Cornēlius

nēquāquam, *adv.* [2.nē, quisquam]: by no means, not at all

neque (*or* nec), *conj.* [1.ne-, -que]: and not, nor; neque . . . neque: neither . . . nor

nē . . . quidem: *see* 2.nē

nēquitia, -ae, *f.* [nēquam (*worthless*)]: worthlessness, wickedness

nescius, -a, -um, *adj.* [nesciō (*not know*): 1.ne-, sciō]: unknowing, unaware

nēve, *conj.* [2.nē, -ve]: and not, nor, and that . . . not, and lest

nex, necis, *f.:* violent death, murder, slaughter

Nīcānōr, Nicānoris, *m.: acc* Seleucus

Niciās, Niciae, *m.: a Greek* (nĭsh'ĭăs)

nīdulus, -e, *m.* [nīdus]: little nest, nest

nīdus, -ī, *m.:* nest

nihil (*or* nīl), *indecl. n.* [nihilum]: nothing; not at all, in no wise

nihilum, -ī, *n.* [1.ne-, hilum (*trifle*)]: nothing

nīl: *see* nihil

Nīlus, -ī, *m.:* the Nile

nimis, *adv.:* too, too much

nimium, *adv.* [nimius]: too, too much

nimius, -a, -um, *adj.* [nimis]: excessive, too great

nisi, *conj.* [1.ne-, sī]: if not, unless; except

nīsus, *abl.* nīsū, *m.* [1.nītor]: exertion, effort

niteō, nitēre, nituī: shine, glisten

1.nītor, nītī, nīxus (*or* nīsus) sum: bear upon, support oneself; strive, labor; *w. abl.*, depend upon

2.nitor, nitōris, *m.* [niteō]: brightness, lustre, sheen

nix, nivis, *f.:* snow

nōbilis, -e, *adj.* [nōscō]: well-known, famous; noteworthy; high-born, noble

nōbilitās, -ātis, *f.* [nōbilis]: fame, renown; aristocracy, nobility

noctū, *adv.* [nox]: at night, by night

nocturnus, -a, -um, *adj.* [nox]: of night, by night, nocturnal

nōdus, -ī, *m.:* knot; impediment

nōlō, nōlle, nōluī [1.ne-, 1.volō]: wish . . . not, not wish, be unwilling, refuse

nōmen, nōminis, *n.:* name; account, behalf

nōminō, -āre, -āvī, -ātus [nōmen]: call by name, name, call

nōn, *adv.* [1.ne-, ūnus]: not, by no means

nōndum, *adv.* [nōn, dum]: not yet

nōnne, *interrog. adv.* [nōn, 3.-ne]: *sign of a question with expectation of an affirmative answer,* . . . not?

nōnnūllus, -a, -um, *adj.* [nōn, nūllus]: some, *pl.,* several

nōnnumquam, *adv.* [nōn, numquam]: sometimes, a few times

Nōricus, -a, -um, *adj.:* Norican, of the Norici, *an Alpine people* (nôr'ĭcăn, nôr'ĭsī)

nōs, nostrum (*or* nostrī), *pers. pron.:* we, us

nōscō, nōscere, nōvī, nōtus: get knowledge of, learn; *in perf. system,* know, understand; *p.p.p.* nōtus, -a, -um: known, renowned

nōsmet: *see* nōs *and* -met

noster, nostra, nostrum, *poss. adj.* [nōs]: our, ours; *subst. m. pl.,* our men, our soldiers

nota, -ae, *f.:* mark, sign; censure, reproach, disgrace

nōtitia, -ae, *f.* [nōscō]: fame; acquaintance, familiarity; knowledge

nōtus, -a, -um: *see* nōscō

nōvī: *see* nōscō

novem, *indecl. num. adj.,* nine

novissimē, *adv.* [novus]: finally, at last

novus, -a, -um, *adj.:* new, fresh, recent; novel, strange

nox, noctis, *f.:* night

noxa, -ae, *f.* [*cp.* nex]: hurt, harm, injury

noxia, -ae, *f.* [noxius (*harmful*): noxa]: hurt, injury; crime, offense

nūbō, nūbere, nūpsī, nūptus, *w. dat.:* marry (*said of a woman*); *p.p.p.* nūpta: married; *subst. f.,* married woman, wife, bride

nūdus, -a, -um, *adj.:* naked, unclothed

nūllus, -a, -um, *adj.* [1.ne-, ūllus]: not any, none, no

nūmen, nūminis, *n.* [nuō (*nod*)]: divine will, divine power, divinity

numerus, -ī, *m.:* number; collection, quantity; rank, position, estimation; rhythm, metre

nummus, -ī, *m.:* coin, money

numquam, *adv.* [1.ne-, umquam]: at no time, never

nunc, *adv.:* now, at present, at this time; as a matter of fact, as matters are

nūntiō, -āre, -āvī, -ātus [nūntius]: announce, declare, report

nūntius, nūntiī, *m.:* messenger; message, news

nūper, *adv.* [novus]: newly, recently, lately, just

nūptiae, nūptiārum, *f. pl.* [nūbō]: wedding, marriage

nusquam, *adv.* [1.ne-, usquam]: nowhere, in no place; in no way, in nothing

nūtus, *abl.* nūtū, *m.* [nuō (*nod*)]: nod, beck; command

ob (*in compounds, sometimes* obs), *prep. w. acc.:* towards, to; before, in front of, over against, facing; because of, on account of

ob-iciō, -icere, -iēcī, -iectus [ob, iaciō]: throw before; throw up to, reproach with, taunt with; place at the mercy of

obiūrgō, -āre, -āvī, -ātus [ob, iūrgō (*quarrel*)]: scold, rebuke, taunt

oblātus, -a, -um: *see* offerō

ob-linō, -linere, -lēvī, -litus [ob,

linō (*smear*)]: smear over, daub over

oblīvīscor, oblīvīscī, oblītus sum, *w. gen.:* forget

obnoxius, -a, -um, *adj.* [ob, noxius (*guilty*): noxa]: liable, exposed

oboediō, oboedīre, oboedīvī, oboedītūrus, *w. dat.:* obey

obs: *see* ob

obsecrō, -āre, -āvī, -ātus [ob, sacrō (*hallow*): sacer]: beseech, entreat

obsequium, obsequiī, *n.* [obsequor (*yield*): ob, sequor]: compliance, obedience

observō, -āre, -āvī, -ātus [ob, servō (*watch*)]: watch, observe; guard, keep; respect, regard

obses, obsidis, *m. and f.:* hostage

ob-sideō, -sidēre, -sēdī, -sessus [ob, sedeō]: besiege, blockade

obsidiō, -iōnis, *f.* [obsideo]: siege, blockade

obsignō, -āre, -āvī, -ātus [ob, signō]: seal up, attest under seal

ob-stringō, -stringere, -strīnxī, -strictus [ob, stringō (*bind*)]: bind, obligate, lay under obligation

ob-terō, -terere, -trīvī, -trītus [ob, terō (*rub*)]: bruise, crush

ob-tineō, -tinēre, -tinuī, -tentus [ob, teneō]: occupy, maintain; govern, rule; gain, acquire

obtrectō, -āre, -āvī, -ātus [ob, tractō]: belittle, disparage; *inter sē* obtrectant: they belittle each other, they are bitter enemies

obtulī: *see* offerō

obviam, *adv.* [ob, via]: in the way, to meet; obviam fīō, *w. dat.:* meet, happen upon

obvius, -a, -um, *adj.* [obviam]: in the way, to meet; *subst. m. pl.* passers-by, bystanders

occāsiō, -iōnis, *f.* [occidō (*fall*): ob, cadō]: opportunity

occāsus, -ūs, *m.* [occidō (*fall*): ob, cadō]: setting, -set ŏc-cĭdŏ, -cĭdere, -cĭdī, -cīsus [ob, caedō]: cut down, kill, slay

occultŏ, -āre, -āvī, -ātus [occultus]: hide, conceal

occultus, -a, -um, adj. [occulō (hide): ob, cp. cēlō]: hidden, secret; subst. n., hidden place

occupŏ, -āre, -āvī, -ātus [ob, cp. capiŏ] take possession of, seize, occupy

oc-currŏ, -currere, -currī [or -cucurrī), -cursūrus [ob, currō]: run up, run to meet, meet; attend to, remedy; occur

octŏ, indecl. num. adj.: eight

oculus, -ī, m.: eye

ŏdī, ŏdisse, ōsūrus, defect.: hate

odium, odiī, n. [ŏdī]: hatred, enmity

offerŏ, offerre, obtulī, oblātus [ob, ferō]: offer, present; show, exhibit

officium, officiī, n.: service, favor; function, duty; obligation, sense of duty

of-fundŏ, -fundere, -fūdī, -fūsus [ob, fundō]: pour out upon, spread over; spread, disseminate

Olympia, -ae, f.: a sacred region in Greece (ŏlĭm'pĭă)

o-mittŏ, -mittere, -mīsī, -missus [ob, mittō]: neglect, disregard; pass over, omit

omninŏ, adv. [omnis]: altogether, entirely; at all; by all means; generally, universally

omnis, -e, adj.: all, every; of every kind, all sorts

onus, oneris, n.: load, burden

opera, -ae, f. [opus]: effort, labor, work; fault; operam dŏ: make efforts, make it one's business; opera mutua: assistance

operiŏ, operīre, operuī, opertus: cover; shut, close

opīmus, -a, -um, adj.: rich, fat, choice

opīniŏ, -iōnis, f. [opīnor]: opinion, belief; expectation; reputation

opīnor, -ārī, -ātus sum: be of opinion, suppose, believe

oportet, oportēre, oportuit, impers.: it is necessary, it is proper

opperior, opperīrī, oppertus sum: wait for, expect, await

op-petŏ, -petere, -petīvī, -petītus [ob, petō]: encounter, meet

oppidum, -ī, n.: town, city

op-pleŏ, -plēre, -plēvī, -plētus [ob, *pleō (fill)]: fill completely, fill

op-pōnŏ, -pōnere, -posuī, -positus [ob, pōnō]: set against, oppose

opportūnus, -a, -um, adj.: seasonable, opportune, advantageous

op-primŏ, -primere, -pressī, -pressus [ob, premō]: press against, press down; pounce upon; crush; oppress, overwhelm, overcome

opprobrātiŏ, -iōnis, f. [opprobrō (reproach): ob, probrō (censure): probrum (reproach)]: censure, reproach

oppugnŏ, -āre, -āvī, -ātus [ob, pugnō]: attack, assail, storm

*ops, opis, f.: aid, help, support; pl., riches, resources; power, might

optimus, -a, -um: see bonus

opus, operis, n.: work, labor; art; structure, fortification; opus est: there is need, it is necessary

ōrāculum, -ī, n. [ōrō]: divine announcement, oracle

ōrātiŏ, -iōnis, f. [ōrō]: speech, oration

orbis, orbis, m.: ring, circle

Orcus (or Orchus), -ī, m.: the lower world (ôr'cŭs)

Orcynius, -a, -um, adj.: Orcynian, the Greek name for the Hercynian Forest (ôrsĭn'ĭăn)

ōrdŏ, ōrdinis, m.: order; rank; company, century

Orestēs, Orestī (or Orestis), m.: a prince of Mycenae (ŏrĕs'tēş, mĭsē'nē)

orior, orīrī, ortus sum: arise, get up

ōrnāmentum, -ī, n. [ōrnō]: decoration, ornament

ōrnātus, -ūs, m. [ōrnō]: fine attire; decoration, ornament

ŏrnŏ, -āre, -āvī, -ātus: fit out, equip; adorn, decorate

ŏrŏ, -āre, -āvī, -ātus: speak; pray, beg, plead; causam ŏrŏ: plead a case

orthius, -a, -um, adj.: orthian, i.e. high-pitched, shrill (a term of Greek music)

ortus, -ūs, m. [orior]: rising, -rise

1.ŏs, ŏris, n.: mouth; face

2.os, ossis, n.: bone

Oscē, adv.: in Oscan (an Italic dialect), in the Oscan tongue (ŏs'cán)

ŏsculum, -ī, n. [1.ŏs]: kiss

os-tendŏ, -tendere, -tendī, -tentus [obs, tendŏ]: spread before, show, display; make clear

ostentŏ, -āre, -āvī, -ātus [ostendŏ]: show; show off, vaunt, boast

ōtiŏsus, -a, -um, adj. [ōtium]: at leisure, leisurely; peaceful, unconcerned

ōtium, ōtiī, n.: leisure, peace, repose

ovis, ovis, f.: sheep

P.: Pūblius (pŭb'lĭŭs)

pābulum, -ī, n. [pāscŏ]: food, fodder

paciscor, paciscī, pactus sum [cp. pāx]: agree, contract; perf. part. pactus, -a, -um: agreed, settled

pactum, -ī, n. [pactus]: agreement, pact; in abl., manner, way, means

pactus, -a, -um: see paciscor

M. Pācuvius: a Roman playwright (mär'cŭs pācу'vĭŭs)

paene, adv.: nearly, almost

paenitentia, -ae, f. [paenitet (it repents)]: repentance, penitence

pāgus, -ī, m.: district, canton

palam, adv.: openly, publicly

Palātium, Palātiī, n.: the Palatine Hill, in Rome (pāl'átīn)

pallium, palliī, n.: Greek cloak, mantle

palūs, palūdis, f.: swamp, marsh

pancratiastēs, acc. pancratiastēn, m.: pancratiast, contestant in the pancratium, a contest involving

boxing and wrestling (păncrā'-shĭăst, păncrā'shĭŭm)

pandŏ, pandere, pandī, passus: spread out, extend, hold out

pangŏ, pangere, pepigī, pāctus: settle, determine; agree, contract

pānis, pānis, m.: bread

Papīrius Praetextātus: a Roman boy (păpĭr'ĭŭs prētĕxtā'tŭs)

par, gen. paris, adj.: equal; equivalent, same

parcŏ, parcere, pepercī (or parsī), parsūrus, w. dat.: spare

parēns, parentis, m. and f. [cp. pariŏ]: parent

pareŏ, parēre, paruī: appear; w. dat., obey

pariŏ, parere, peperī, partus: bring forth, give birth to; produce, accomplish

parŏ, -āre, -āvī, -ātus: prepare, furnish; intend, resolve

pars, partis, f.: part, portion; direction, way

particeps, gen. participis, adj. [pars, cp. capiŏ], w. gen.: sharing, partaking; subst. m.: partner

partior, partirī, partītus sum [pars]: share, distribute

partus, -ūs, m. [pariŏ]: birth; offspring, young

parum: see parvus

parvus, -a, -um, adj.: small, little; comp. minor, minus: smaller, less; superl. minimus, -a, -um: smallest, least, very small; adv. parum: too little, not enough, insufficiently; comp. adv. minus: less

pāscŏ, pāscere, pāvī, pāstus: feed, pasture

passer, passeris, m.: sparrow

1.passus, -a, -um: see pandŏ and patior

2.passus, -ūs, m. [pandŏ]: step, pace; mīlle passūs: mile

pāstum: see pāscor

pāstus, -ūs, m. [pāscor]: pasture, fodder, food

pateō, patēre, patuī: lie open, be
open; extend

pater, patris, *m.*: father; *pl.*, senators

paternus, -a, -um, *adj.* [pater]: of a father, paternal

patiēns, *gen.* patientis, *adj.* [patior]: suffering, enduring, patient

patientia, -ae, *f.* [patiēns]: patience, endurance

patior, patī, passus sum: bear, suffer, endure; allow, permit; aegrē patior: bear with difficulty, be indignant

patria, -ae, *f.* [patrius (*of a father*): pater]: native land, father-land, own country

paucī, -ae, -a, *adj.*: few

paulātim, *adv.* [paulum]: little by little, gradually

paululus, -a, -um, *adj.* [paulus]: very little, very small

paulus, -a, -um, *adj.*: small, little; *subst. n.*, a little, a trifle; *adv.* paulum: a little, somewhat

pauper, *gen.* pauperis, *adj.* [*cp.* paucī]: poor; *subst. m.*, poor man

pave-faciō, -facere, -fēcī, -factus [paveō, faciō]: dismay, terrify

paveō, pavēre, pāvī: be terrified

pavidus, -a, -um, *adj.* [paveō]: timid, fearful

pāvō, pāvōnis, *m.*: peacock

pavor, pavōris, *m.* [paveō]: terror, dread, panic

pāx, pācis, *f.*: peace

peccō, -āre, -āvī, -ātus: commit a fault, do wrong; act unjustly

pectus, pectoris, *n.*: breast, chest; soul, spirit, mind

pecūnia, -ae, *f.* [pecu (*herd*)]: money

pecus, pecoris, *n.*: cattle; flock, herd

pedes, peditis, *m.* [pēs]: foot-soldier, infantryman

pedester, pedestris, pedestre, *adj.* [pedes]: of a foot-soldier, infantryman's, infantry-

Pelasgī, Pelasgōrum, *m. pl.*: *a very ancient people* (pĕlăs'gī)

pellis, pellis, *f.*: skin, hide, leather

pellō, pellere, pepulī, pulsus: beat, strike; drive, impel; defeat; drive out, expel

Pelopidās, Pelopidae, *m.*: *a Greek general* (pĕlŏp'ĭdăs)

Peloponnēsiacus, -a, -um, *adj.*: Peloponnesian (pĕlŏpŏnē'shĭán)

Peloponnēsus, -ī, *f.*: *the southern peninsula of Greece* (pĕlŏpŏnē'sŭs)

penātēs, penātium, *m. pl.* [penus (*larder*)]: household gods, penates (pĕnā'tēş)

pendō, .pendere, pependī, pēnsus: hang; weigh; pay

penes, *prep. w. acc.*: with, in the power of

penitus, *adv.* [penes]: inwardly, deeply, thoroughly

penna, -ae, *f.*: feather; *pl.*, wing

per, *prep. w. acc.*: through, across, along, among; throughout, during, for; by the agency of, by the hands of; by means of; *in compounds, with intensive force*, thoroughly, completely, very

pēra, -ae, *f.*: bag, sack, wallet

percontātiō, -iōnis, *f.* [percontor]: questioning, inquiry

percontor, -ārī, -ātus sum [per, contus (*sounding-pole*)]: sound out; inquire, ask

per-crēbēscō, -crēbēscere, -crēbuī [per, crēbēscō (*become frequent*): crēber (*frequent*)]: be spread abroad, become generally known

per-cutiō, -cutere, -cussī, -cussus [per, quatiō]: strike hard, smite, beat; slay, kill

per-discō, -discere, -didicī [per, discō]: learn thoroughly, learn by heart

per-dō, -dere, -didī, -ditus [per, dō]: destroy, ruin, squander; lose

per-dūcō, -dūcere, -dūxī, -ductus [per, dūcō]: lead through, conduct; draw out, lengthen

perendiē, *adv.*: on the day after the morrow

per-eō, -īre, -iī, -itūrus [per, 2.eō]:
perish, die
per-ferō, -ferre, -tulī, -lātus [per,
ferō]: bear through, carry, convey; bring news; suffer through,
serve out
per-ficiō, -ficere, -fēcī, -fectus [per,
faciō]: achieve, perform, accomplish
perfidia, -ae, f. [perfidus (faithless)]:
faithlessness, treachery
per-fodiō, -fodere, -fōdī, -fossus
[per, fodiō]: pierce through, trans-
fix
Periander, Periandrī, m.: a tyrant
of Corinth (pĕrĭăn'dĕr)
Periclēs, Periclis, m.: an Athenian
statesman (pĕr'ĭclēş)
perīclum = perīculum
perīculōsus, -a, -um, adj. [perīcu-
lum]: dangerous
perīculum, -ī, n.: trial, test; danger,
peril
perītus, -a, -um, adj., w. gen.: experienced, practised, skilled
per-maneō, -manēre, -mānsī, -mān-
sūrus [per, maneō]: remain, per-
sist, persevere
per-mētior, -mētīrī, -mēnsus sum
[per, mētior (measure)]: traverse,
travel
per-mittō, -mittere, -mīsī, -missus
[per, mittō]: entrust, commit; w.
dat., allow, permit
per-moveō, -movēre, -mōvī, -mōtus
[per, moveō]: move deeply, disturb; influence, prevail upon
permūtātiō, -iōnis, f. [permūtō]:
exchange
permūtō, -āre, -āvī, -ātus [per,
mūtō]: interchange, exchange
perniciēs, acc, perniciem, f. [per, cp.
nex]: destruction, ruin, disaster
pernīcitās, -ātis, f. [pernīx (nimble)]:
nimbleness, quickness
perōrō, -āre, -āvī, -ātus [per, ōrō]:
finish pleading, conclude
perpāstus, -a, -um, adj. [per, pāstus
(fed): pāscō]: well-fed

perpaucī, -ae, -a, adj. [per, paucī]:
very few
perperam, adv.: wrongly, incorrectly
per-petior, -petī, -pessus sum [per,
patior]: bear steadfastly, endure
perpetuus, -a, -um, adj.: continuous, perpetual; adv. perpetuō:
uninterruptedly, forever
Persae, Persārum, m. pl.: the Persians
Persicus, -a, -um, adj.: Persian
persōna, -ae, f.: mask
per-spiciō, -spicere, -spexī, -spectus
[per, speciō]: look through, examine; perceive clearly, discern
per-suādeō, -suādere, -suāsī, -suā-
sus [per, suādeō], w. dat.: persuade, convince
per-taedet, -taedēre, -taesum est,
impers. [per, taedet (it wearies)]:
it wearies, it disgusts
per-terreō, -terrēre, -terruī, -terri-
tus [per, terreō]: frighten thoroughly, terrify
per-timēscō, -timēscere, -timuī
[per, timēscō (become frightened):
timeō]: be frightened, fear greatly
pertinācia, -ae, f. [pertināx (perse-
vering): per, tenāx (tenacious):
teneō]: persistence, stubbornness
per-tineō, -tinēre, -tinuī [per, te-
neō]: stretch out, extend; belong
to, pertain to; tend
perturbō, -āre, -āvī, -ātus [per,
turbō]: confuse, disturb, alarm
per-veniō, -venīre, -vēnī, -ventūrus
[per, veniō]: arrive, reach, come;
accrue, fall
pēs, pedis, m.: foot
pestilentia, -ae, f. [pestilentus (in-
fected): pestis (plague)]: plague,
pestilence
Petīlius: the nōmen gentīle of certain
Roman tribunes (pĕtĭl'ĭŭs)
petō, petere, petīvī (or petiī), petī-
tus: strive for, seek, aim at; make
for, travel to; attack; demand,
beg, ask
petulāns, gen. petulantis, adj. [cp.

petō]: impudent, wanton, petulant

petulantia, -ae, f. [petulāns]: impudence, wantonness, petulance

phalanx, phalangis, f.: compact body of heavy-armed men, battalion, phalanx

phalerae, phalerārum, f. pl.: metal breast-plate, studs, bosses

Phalēricus, -a, -um, adj.: of Phalerum in Attica, Phaleric (fále'rŭm, fálē'rĭc)

Pharnabāzus, -ī, m.: a Persian governor (färnábā'zŭs)

Philēmōn (or Philēmō), Philēmonis, m.: a Greek playwright (fĭlē'mŏn)

Philippus, -ī, m.: Philip, the name of several kings of Macedonia

philosophia, -ae, f.: philosophy

philosophus, -ī, m.: philosopher

piget, pigēre, piguit (or pigitum est), impers.: it irks, it is displeasing

pīlum, -ī, n.: javelin

Pīraeus, -ī, m.: the sea-port of Athens (pīrē'ŭs)

Pīsistratus, -ī, m.: a tyrant of Athens (pĭsĭs'trátŭs)

M. Pīsō (gen. Pīsōnis, m.): a Roman consul (mär'cŭs pī'sō)

pius, -a, -um, adj.: dutiful, pious; devoted, filial; kindly, benevolent, good

placeō, placēre, placuī, placitūrus, w. dat.: please, be pleasing; impers., it is resolved, it is decided

placidus, -a, -um, adj. [placeō]: quiet, calm

placō, -āre, -āvī, -ātus [cp. placeō]: quiet, soothe, appease

plānitiēs, plānitiēī, f. [plānus]: flat surface, plain

plānus, -a, -um, adj.: even, level, flat, plane; adv. plānē: plainly, clearly, distinctly; wholly, entirely, quite

Platō, Platōnis, m.: a Greek philosopher (plā'tō)

Platōnicus, -a, -um, adj.: of Plato, Platonic (plátŏn'ĭc)

Plautus: see Maccius

plēbs, plēbis (or plēbēs, plēbeī), f.: the common people, the commons, the plebeians

*plectō, *plectere: punish

plēnus, -a, -um, adj. [*pleō (fill)]: full

plērusque, plēraque, plērumque, adj. [cp. plēnus]: a very great part, the majority, most; pl., many; adv. plērumque: for the most part, mostly, generally

plumbum, -ī, n.: lead

plūmō, -āre, -āvī, -ātus [cp. plūma (feather)]: grow feathers, become feathered

plūrimus and plūs: see multus

pōculum, -ī, n. [pōtus (having drunk)]: drinking-vessel, cup, goblet

poena, -ae, f.: punishment, penalty; poenam dō: suffer punishment, pay a penalty

Poenicus, -a, -um: see Pūnicus

Poenus, -a, -um, adj.: Punic, Carthaginian (pū'nĭc, cärthágĭn'ĭan)

poēta, -ae, m.: poet

polliceor, pollicērī, pollicitus sum: promise

Polus, -ī, m.: a Greek actor (pō'lŭs)

Pomptīnus, -a, -um, adj.: Pomptine, the name applied to a region between Rome and Naples (pŏmp'tĭn)

pondō, adv. [pendō]: by weight, in weight

pondus, ponderis, n. [pendō]: weight; heavy body, mass

pōnō, pōnere, posuī, positus: put, place; lay aside, put away

pōns, pontis, m.: bridge

Pontus, -ī, m.: a region in Asia Minor (pŏn'tŭs)

populor, -ārī, -ātus sum: lay waste, ravage, devastate

populus, -ī, m.: people, nation; body of citizens, popular assembly

porcellus, -ī, *m.* [porcus *(pig)*]: little pig

M. Porcius Catō Cēnsōrius: *a Roman statesman of the second century B. C.* (mär'cŭs pôr'shĭŭs cā'tō sĕnsō'rĭŭs)

M. Porcius Catō Uticēnsis: *a Roman statesman of the first century B.C.* (mär'cŭs pôr'shĭŭs cā'tō ūtĭsĕn'sĭs)

por-rigō, -rigere, -rēxī, -rēctus [prō, regō]: stretch out, extend

porrō, *adv.* [*cp.* prō]: forward, onward; far; hereafter, afterwards; next, in turn

portō, -āre, -āvī, -ātus [*cp.* portus]: carry, bear, take, bring

portus, -ūs, *m.:* harbor, haven, port

poscō, poscere, poposcī: ask urgently, beg, demand

possessiō, -iōnis, *f.* [possīdō]: possession

pos-sideō, -sidēre, -sēdī, -sessus [potis *(powerful)*, sedeō]: own, possess

pos-sīdō, -sīdere, -sēdī, -sessus [potis *(powerful)*, *cp.* sedeō]: seize, occupy

possum, posse, potuī [potis *(powerful)*, sum]: be able; be powerful

post, *adv. and prep. w. acc.:* behind; after; afterwards, later

posteā, *adv.:* afterwards, hereafter, thereafter

posteāquam, *conj.* [posteā, quam]: after

posterus, -a, -um, *adj.* [post]: coming after, following, next; *subst. m. pl.,* descendants, posterity; *superl.* **postrēmus, -a, -um:** last; *subst. n. s. and pl.,* the last part, the end

posthāc, *adv.* [post, 2.hic]: after this, hereafter; thereafter, in the future

postlīminium, postlīminiī, *n.* [post, līmen]: *right of return to one's native land with complete restoration of citizenship,* postliminium

postquam, *conj.* [post, quam]: after

postremus, -a, -um: *see* posterus

postridiē, *adv.* [*cp.* post, diēs]: on the next day, on the morrow; **postrīdiē eius diēī:** on the following day

postulātiō, -iōnis, *f.* [postulō]: demand, request

postulātum, -ī, *n.* [postulō]: demand, request

postulō, -āre, -āvī, -ātus [poscō]: ask, demand, request; require, call for

potēns, *gen.* **potentis,** *adj.* [potis *(powerful)*]: mighty, strong, powerful

potentātus, -ūs, *m.* [potēns]: power, government

potentia, -ae, *f.* [potēns]: might, power

potestās, -ātis, *f.* [potis *(powerful)*]: ability, capability; power, might; possibility, opportunity

potior, potīrī, potītus sum [potis *(powerful)*]: *w. abl. or gen.:* gain possession of, get, obtain

potius, *adv.* [potis *(powerful)*]: rather

prae, *adv. and prep. w. abl.:* before, in front of; *in compounds,* very

praebeō, praebēre, praebuī, praebitus [prae, habeō]: hold forth, offer, give; furnish, supply; render

prae-caveō, -cavēre, -cāvī, -cautūrus [prae, caveō]: take care, be on one's guard; guard against, provide against

praeceps, *gen.* **praecipitis,** *adj.* [prae, caput]: headforemost, headlong

praeceptum, -ī, *n.* [praecipiō]: maxim, rule, precept

prae-cīdō, -cīdere, -cīdī, -cīsus [prae, caedō]: cut off in front, cut off

prae-cipiō, -cipere, -cēpī, -ceptus [prae, capiō], *w. dat.:* instruct, teach; direct, order

praecipuus, -a, -um, *adj.* [prae, *cp.* capiō]: particular, especial; excellent, distinguished

praeclārus, -a, -um, *adj.* [prae,

VOCABULARY 245

clārus]: very bright, brilliant; magnificent, splendid, famous

prae-clūdō, -clūdere, -clūsī, -clūsus [prae, claudō]: shut off, close; hinder, impede

praeda, -ae, f.: booty, plunder, spoil

1.praedicō, -āre, -āvī, -ātus [prae, 1.dicō]: proclaim, announce; state, declare; vaunt, boast

2.prae-dīcō, -dīcere, -dīxī, -dictus [prae, 2.dīcō]: say before; foretell, predict; admonish, command

praedium, praediī, n.: farm; estate, property

praeditus, -a, -um, adj. [prae, datus (given): dō]: furnished, provided; surrounded

praefātus: see *praefor

praefectus, -ī, m. [praeficiō]: commander of troops, prefect; admiral

prae-ficiō, -ficere, -fēcī, -fectus [prae, faciō]: place at the head, appoint to command

prae-fīniō, -fīnīre, -fīnīvī, -fīnītus [prae, fīniō]: ordain, prescribe

*prae-for, -fārī, -fātus sum [prae, *for]: say beforehand, say by way of preface

prae-fulgeō, -fulgēre [prae, fulgeō]: shine forth, gleam, glitter

prae-metuō, -metuere [prae, metuō]: fear beforehand, be apprehensive of

praemium, praemiī, n.: reward, recompense; prize

prae-moneō, -monēre, -monuī, -monitus [prae, moneō]: forewarn, admonish beforehand, admonish

prae-pōnō, -pōnere, -posuī, -positus [prae, pōnō]: place in front; make commander, place in charge; set before, prefer

praesaepe, praesaepis, n. [prae, saepēs (enclosure)]: stable, stall

prae-scrībō, -scrībere, -scrīpsī, -scrīptus [prae, scrībō]: ordain, direct, prescribe

praescrīptum, -ī, n. [praescrībō]: precept, rule, regulation

praesēns, gen. praesentis, adj. [prae, cp. sum]: at hand, present; present-day, modern; subst. n., the present

praesertim, adv.: especially, chiefly, particularly

praeses, praesidis, m. [prae, sedeō]: protector; governor

praesidium, praesidiī, n. [praeses]: defense, protection; help, aid; guard, garrison

prae-stō, -stāre, -stitī, -statūrus [prae, stō]: be superior, excel; keep, preserve; show, exhibit; furnish

prae-sum, -esse, -fuī [prae, sum]: be in charge of, rule, command

praeter, prep. w. acc. [prae]: past, by; beyond, contrary to; besides, in addition to; except, except for

praetereā, adv.: in addition, further, besides, moreover

praeter-eō, -īre, -iī, -itūrus [praeter, 2.eō]: go by, go past; pass over, disregard

praeteritus, -a, -um, adj. [praetereō]: gone by, past

praetextātus, -a, -um, adj. [praetexta (bordered toga)]: wearing the toga praetexta; minor, under the age of discretion

praetor, praetōris, m. [praeeō (go before): prae, 2.eō]: judge, praetor; commander, general

praetōrius, -a, -um, adj. [praetor]: of a general, of a commander, praetorian

prātum, -ī, n.: meadow

prāvus, -a, -um, adj.: improper, bad, wicked

prehendō, prehendere, prehendī, prehēnsus (or prēndō, prēndere, prēndī, prēnsus): lay hold of, seize; grasp; arrest

premō, premere, pressī, pressus: press; close, shut; check, restrain; oppress, overwhelm

prēndō, prēnsus: see **prehendō**

pretiōsē, *adv.* [pretiōsus (*costly*): pretium]: expensively, richly, splendidly

pretium, pretiī, *n.*: price, value; recompense, reward

***prex, *precis,** *f.*: prayer, entreaty

prīdiē, *adv.* [prī- (*before*), diēs]: on the day before, the previous day; **prīdiē eius diēī:** on the day before

prīmus, -a, -um, *adj.* [prī- (*before*)]: first, foremost; *adv.* **prīmō:** at first, in the first place; *adv.* **prīmum:** at first; for the first time; **ubi prīmum:** as soon as

prīnceps, *gen.* **prīncipis,** *adj.* [prīmus, *cp.* capiō]: first, foremost; *subst. m.*, chief, leader, leading citizen; ruler, prince

prīncipātus, -ūs, *m.* [prīnceps]: leadership, supremacy

prīncipium, prīncipiī, *n.* [prīnceps]: beginning, early stage; *pl.* principles, elements

prior, prius, *adj.* [prī- (*before*)]: former, previous; superior

prīscus, -a, -um, *adj.* [*cp.* prīmus]: of former times, olden, ancient; old-fashioned

pristinus, -a, -um, *adj.* [*cp.* prīscus]: former, early, original

prius, *adv.* [prior]: before, sooner; rather

priusquam, *conj.* [prius, quam]: earlier than, sooner than, before

prīvātus, -a, -um, *adj.* [prīvō (*deprive*)]: personal, private; *subst. m.*, private citizen; private soldier, private

prō (*in compounds, sometimes* prō- *or* prōd-), *prep. w. abl.*: before, in front of; for, in behalf of, in favor of; as, instead of, in exchange for; in proportion to, in comparison with; because of; **prō eō:** because of the fact

probō, -āre, -āvī, -ātus [probus (*good*)]: approve; prove, show; test, try

procāx, *gen.* **procācis,** *adj.* [procus (*suitor*)]: bold, insolent, wanton

prō-cēdō, -cēdere, -cessī [prō, cēdō]: go forward, advance

prōcēritās, -ātis, *f.* [prōcērus]: height, tallness

prōcērus, -a, -um, *adj.*: high, tall

prōcōnsulāris, -e, *adj.* [prōcōnsul (*provincial governor*): prō cōnsule]: of a proconsul, proconsular

procul, *adv. and prep. w. abl.*: in the distance, far, away; far from, apart from; **procul dubiō:** without doubt

prōculcō, -āre, -āvī, -ātus [prō, calcō (*trample*): calx]: tread down, trample upon

prōcurō, -āre, -āvī, -ātus [prō, cūrō]: take care of, attend to

prō-currō, -currere, -currī, -cursūrus [prō, currō]: run forth, rush forward

prōd-: see **prō**

prōd-eō, -īre, -iī, -itūrus [prōd-, 2.eō]: come forward

prōditor, prōditōris, *m.* [prōdō]: betrayer, traitor

prō-dō, -dere, -didī, -ditus [prō, dō]: relate, record, hand down, transmit; reveal, make known; betray; surrender, give up

prō-dūcō, -dūcere, -dūxī, ductus [prō, dūcō]: lead forth; stretch out, lengthen; bring forth, produce

proelior, -ārī, -ātus sum [proelium]: battle, fight

proelium, proeliī, *n.*: battle, combat

profectō, *adv.* [prō factō]: actually, indeed, really, truly, certainly

prō-ferō, -ferre, -tulī, -lātus [prō, ferō]: bring forth, produce; put off, postpone

proficīscor, proficīscī, profectus sum [prōficiō (*make progress*): prō, faciō]: set out, start, depart

pro-fiteor, -fitērī, -fessus sum [prō, fateor (*acknowledge*)]: declare openly, confess, profess; volunteer prŏ-fugiŏ, -fugere, -fūgī, -fugitūrus [prō, fugiō]: flee, run away, escape

profundus, -a, -um, adj. [prō, fundus (depth)]: deep, profound; subst. n., the deep, the sea

prŏgeniĕs, acc. prŏgeniem, f. [prō, gignō]: offspring, progeny

prŏgnātus, -a, -um, adj. [prō, (g)nātus]: born, descended, sprung; subst. m., offspring, descendant

prŏ-gredior, -gredī, -gressus sum [prō, gradior]: come forward; advance, proceed

pro-hibeō, -hibēre, -hibuī, -hibitus [prō, habeō]: keep away, keep from, hinder, prevent; forbid, prohibit

prŏ-iciō, -icere, -iēcī, -iectus [prō, iaciō]: cast forth, throw; thrust forward, hold out, extend

proinde, adv. [prō, inde]: hence, therefore; accordingly; just so, in like manner, just; proinde ac, proinde quasi: just as; proinde . . . quam: so much . . . as

prōlātus: see prōferō

prōlēs, prōlis, f. [prō, alō]: offspring, progeny, children

prŏ-loquor, -loquī, -locūtus sum [prō, loquor]: speak out, declare

prŏ-mittō, -mittere, -mīsī, -missus [prō, mittō]: promise, assure

prŏ-moveō, -movēre, -mōvī, -mōtus [prō, moveō]: move forward, cause to advance, advance

*prōmptus, *prōmptūs, m. [prōmō (bring forth): prō, emō]: in prōmptū: manifest, before the eyes, at hand

prōnūntiō, -āre, -āvī, -ātus [prō, nūntiō]: proclaim, announce; pronounce, decide

prōpatulus, -a, -um, adj. [prō, patulus (open): pateō]: open, uncovered; subst. n., open place, open court

prope, adv. and prep. w. acc.: near; nearly; comp. propius: nearer; see proximē, under proximus

properē, adv. [properus (quick)]: hastily, speedily

properō, -āre, -āvī, -ātūrus [properus (quick)]: make haste, be quick

propinquitās, -ātis, f. [propinquus]: nearness, proximity; relationship, kindred

propinquus, -a, -um, adj. [prope]: neighboring; subst. m. and f., relation, relative, kinsman

prŏ-pōnō, -pōnere, -posuī, -positus [prō, pōnō]: put forth, display; set forth, declare, relate; resolve, determine

prŏpositum, -ī, n. [prōpōnō]: point, theme, proposition

proprius, -a, -um, adj.: one's own; appropriate; subst. n., characteristic

propter, prep. w. acc. [prope]: because of, on account of

proptereā, adv.: therefore, on that account; proptereā quod: because of the fact that, because

prŏpugnāculum, -ī, n. [prōpugnō]: bulwark, rampart

prŏpugnō, -āre, -āvī, -ātus [prō, pugnō]: fight in defense, resist

prŏpulsō, -āre, -āvī, -ātus [prō, pulsō (drive): pellō]: drive back, repel

prŏ-ripiō, -ripere, -ripuī, -reptus [prō, rapiō]: drag forth; drive out; impel; w. reflex. pron., rush forth

prōrsum or prōrsus, adv. [prō, versus (turned): vertō]: forward, right onward; straightway; by all means, entirely

prŏ-sequor, -sequī, -secūtus sum [prō, sequor]: follow, accompany, escort

prōspectus, -ūs, m. [prōspiciō]: distant view, prospect; sight, view

prōsperē, adv. [prōsperus (prosperous)]: fortunately, successfully

prŏ-spiciŏ, -spicere, -spexī, -spectus [prō, speciō]: look out, look, see; look out for, provide for

prŏsum, prŏdesse, prŏfuī [prō, sum]: be useful, benefit, profit

Prŏtagorăs, Prŏtagorae, *m.:* a Greek philosopher and sophist (prŏtăg'-ŏrăs)

prŏ-tendō, -tendere, -tendī, -tentus [prō, tendō (*stretch*)]: stretch forth, stretch out

prōtinus, *adv.* [prō, tenus (*toward*)]: right onward, forward; continuously; immediately

prŏ-vehŏ, -vehere, -vexī, -vectus [prō, vehō]: carry forward, propel; *pass.*, be moved forward, sail

prŏ-videŏ, -vidēre, -vīdī, -vīsus [prō, videō]: act with foresight, take precautions, be careful; see to, provide

prōvincia, -ae, *f.:* province

prŏvŏcŏ, -āre, -āvī, -ātus [prō, vocō]: call forth, summon, challenge

proximus, -a, -um, *adj.* [prope]: nearest, next; *subst. m. pl.*, those nearest; previous, last, most recent; following, ensuing, coming, next; *adv. and prep. w. acc.*, proximē: very near, next to

prūdēns, *gen.* prūdentis, *adj.* [prōvidēns (*foreseeing*): prōvideō]: foreseeing; wise, sensible, prudent

prūdentia, -ae, *f.* [prūdēns]: discretion, judgment, prudence

Prūsiăs, Prūsiae, *m.:* a king of Bithynia (prụ'sĭăs)

Ptolmaeī, Ptolmaeōrum, *m. pl.:* the Ptolemies, kings of Egypt (tŏl'-ĕmēẓ)

pūblicus, -a, -um, *adj.:* of the people, of the state, public, official; *adv.* pūblicē: on behalf of the state, officially, publicly

pudor, pudōris, *m.* [pudet (*it shames*)]: shame, modesty, decency; honor, propriety

puer, puerī, *m.:* boy, lad; slave

puerīlis, -e, *adj.* [puer]: of a boy, boy's; boyish, childish

puerulus, -ī, *m.* [puer]: little boy

pugil, pugilis, *m.* [*cp.* pugnus (*fist*)]: fist-fighter, boxer, pugilist

pugna, -ae, *f.* [pugnō]: battle, combat

pugnŏ, -āre, -āvī, -ātus [pugnus (*fist*)]: fight, combat, contend

pulcher, pulchra, pulchrum, *adj.:* beautiful, handsome

pulchritūdŏ, pulchritūdinis, *f.* [pulcher]: beauty, handsomeness

pullus, -ī, *m.:* young creature, offspring; chick

pulmentārium, pulmentāriī, *n.:* relish, appetizer

Pūnicus, -a, -um, *adj.:* Punic, Carthaginian (pū'nĭc, cärthăgĭn'ĭan)

puppis, puppis, *f.:* hinder part of a ship, stern, poop

pūrgŏ, -āre, -āvī, -ātus [pūrus, *cp.* agō]: clean, cleanse, purify

pūrus, -a, -um, *adj.:* clean, pure

puteus, -ī, *m.:* well

putŏ, -āre, -āvī, -ātus: think, suppose, believe

Pyrrhus, -ī, *m.:* a king of Epirus in Greece (pĭr'ŭs, epĭ'rŭs)

Pythagorăs, Pythagorae, *m.:* a Greek philosopher (pĭthăg'orăs)

Q.: Quīntus (quĭn'tŭs)

quā, *rel. adv.* [2.quī]: where

quadrātus, -a, -um, *adj.* [quadrō (*square*): quadrus (*square*): quattuor]: squared, square

Quadrīgārius: *see* Claudius

quadringentī, -ae, -a, *num. adj.* [quattuor, centum]: four hundred

quaepiam: *see* quispiam

quaerŏ, quaerere, quaesīvī, quaesītus: seek, look for; ask, demand; inquire

quaesŏ, quaesere: beg, pray; *parenthetical,* quaesō: I beg, I pray, prithee, please

quaestiŏ, -iōnis, *f.* [quaerō]: inquiry, investigation

quaestor, quaestōris, *m.* [quaerō]:

financial officer, paymaster-general, quartermaster-general, quaestor

quaestus, -ūs, *m.* [quaerō]: pursuit; gain, profit; occupation, employment

quālis, -e, *adj.: interrog.,* of what sort, of what nature, what kind of a; *rel.,* such as, as (*see* **tālis**)

quam, *adv.* and *conj.: rel.,* how, how much (*see* **tam**); *interrog.,* how; *w. superl.,* as . . . as possible; than, rather than

quamlibet, *adv.* [quam, libet]: as much as one will, however much, to any extent

quamobrem, *conj.* [quam ob rem]: *interrog.,* for what reason, on what account, wherefore, why; *rel.,* on account of which, wherefore, why; and for this reason, and therefore

quamquam, *conj.* [quam]: though, although; yet, however

quamvīs, *adv.* [quam, vīs: volō]: as you will, however much

quantus, -a, -um, *adj.* [quam]: *rel.,* of what size, how much, as (*see* **tantus**); as great as, as much as; *interrog.,* how great, how much

quārē, *conj.* [quā rē]: *interrog.,* how; for what reason, wherefore, why; *rel.,* because of which, wherefore, and therefore

quārtus, -a, -um, *adj.* [quattuor]: fourth

quasi, *adv.:* as if, as though; just as; nearly, almost, so to speak

quatiō, quatere, ————, quassus: shake, shatter; demolish

quattuor, *indecl. num. adj.:* four

-que, *enclitic conj.:* and; *in compounds, with generalizing force,* -ever

quemadmodum, *conj.* [quem ad modum]: *interrog.,* in what manner, how; *rel.,* in what way, how, as, just as

queō, quīre, quīvī, quitūrus: be able, can

quercus, -ūs, *f.:* oak-tree, oak

querēla, -ae, *f.* [queror]: lamentation; complaint, reproach

queror, querī, questus sum: lament, bewail; complain

questus, -ūs, *m.* [queror]: plaint, complaint

1.**quī,** *adv.* [2.quī]: how, in what manner

2.**quī, quae** (*as adj. also* qua), **quod,** *rel. pron., interrog. adj., and indef. adj.: rel. pron.,* who, which, what; *interrog. adj.,* which, what; *indef. adj.,* some, any

quia, *conj.:* because

quīcumque, quaecumque, quodcumque, *rel. pron.* [2.quī, -cumque (-ever)]: whoever, whatever

quīdam, quaedam, quoddam (*subst. n.* quiddam), *indef. adj.* [*cp.* 2. quī]: a certain, certain; a kind of, as one might say

quidem, *adv.:* assuredly, certainly, in fact, indeed; even (*see* 2. nē)

quiēs, quiētis, *f.:* rest, repose, quiet; sleep

quiēscō, quiēscere, quiēvī [quiēs]: rest, repose, sleep; cease, stop

quiētus, -a, -um, *adj.* [quiēscō]: quiet, undisturbed, peaceful

quīn, *conj.* [1.quī, 3.-ne]: why not; nay, in fact; **quīn etiam:** nay . . . even; but that, that

T. Quīnctius Flāminīnus: a Roman general (tī'tŭs quĭnc'shĭŭs flā-mĭnī'nŭs)

quīndecimvir, quīndecimvirī, *m.* [quīndecim (*fifteen*), vir]: member of a board of fifteen; *pl.,* board of fifteen

quīnquāgintā, *indecl. num. adj.* [quīnque]: fifty

quīnque, *indecl. num. adj.:* five

quīntus, -a, -um, *adj.* [quīnque]: fifth

quippe, *adv.:* of course, obviously, as one might expect

Quirītēs, Quirītium, *m. pl.: the official name used to address the Romans in their civil capacity,* Romans, Quirites (quĭrī'tēş)

quis, quid, *interrog. and indef. pron.: interrog.,* who, which one, what; *indef.* someone, something; anyone, anything

quisnam, quidnam, *interrog. pron.* [quis, nam]: who in the world, what in the world

quispiam, quaepiam, quodpiam (*subst. n.* quidpiam), *indef. adj.* [*cp.* quis]: some, any; a certain; *subst.,* someone, something; anyone, anything

quisquam, quicquam, *indef. pron.* [*cp.* quis]: anyone, anything

quisque, quaeque, quodque [*subst. n.* quidque), *indef. adj.* [*cp.* quis]: each, every; *subst.,* each one, each thing

quisquis, quicquid, *indef. pron.* [*cp.* quis]: whoever, whatever

quīvīs, quaevīs, quodvīs, *indef. adj.* [2.quī, vīs: volō]: whomever you please, whatever you please; any, any . . . whatever

quŏ, *adv. and conj.* [2.quī]: *of place,* whither, to what place, to the place to which; to any place, anywhere; *of manner,* how, in what way; because; *in purpose clauses,* in order that, so that

quoad, *adv. and conj.* [quŏ, ad]: as far as; until; while, as long as

quod, *conj.* [2.quī]: the fact that, that; because; **quod sī:** but if

quŏminus, *conj.* [2.quī, minus]: so that . . . not, that . . . not

quondam, *adv.:* once upon a time, once, formerly

quoniam, *conj.:* since, because, whereas

quoque, *adv.:* also, too

quotannīs, *adv.* [quot (*as many as*), annus]: every year, annually

quotiēns, *adv.* [quot (*how many*)]: *interrog.,* how many times, how

often; *rel.,* as many times as, as often as

rādix, rādīcis, *f.:* root; *of a mountain,* lowest part, foot

raeda, -ae, *f.:* four-wheeled carriage, carriage

rāmōsus, -a, -um, *adj.* [rāmus]: full of branches; branching

rāmus, -ī, *m.:* branch, bough

rāna, -ae, *f.:* frog

rapidus, -a, -um, *adj.* [rapiō]: swift, quick, rapid

rapīna, -ae, *f.* [rapiō]: robbery, plunder

rapiŏ, rapere, rapuī, raptus: snatch, hurry away; plunder, ravage; steal

raptor, raptōris, *m.* [rapiō]: robber, plunderer

ratiō, -iōnis, *f.* [reor]: reckoning, account; reasoning, reasoned plan, plan; manner, method, procedure; motive, reason; transaction, business

ratus: *see* reor

re- (*or* red-), *prefix:* again, anew; back; against

re-cēdŏ, -cēdere, -cessī, -cessūrus [re-, cēdō]: go back, withdraw, retreat

recēns, *gen.* recentis, *adj.:* fresh, young, recent

re-cipiŏ, -cipere, -cēpī, -ceptus [re-, capiō]: take back, regain; receive, welcome; take upon oneself, undertake, take on; *w. reflex. pron.,* draw back, withdraw, retire

recitŏ, -āre, -āvī, -ātus [re-, citō]: read aloud

recognitiō, -iōnis, *f.* [recognōscō (*recall*): re-, cognōscō]: recognition

re-condŏ, -condere, -condidī, -conditus [re-, condō]: store up, store; *w. reflex. pron.,* betake oneself

rēctē, *adv.* [rēctus (*right*): regō]: rightly, correctly, properly

re-cumbŏ, -cumbere, -cubuī [re-, *cp.* cubō (*lie*)]: lie back, recline

recŭpĕrō, -âre, -âvī, -âtus [re-, *cp.* capiō]: get back, recover
recūsō, -âre, -âvī, -âtus [re-, *cp.* causa]: decline, refuse
red-: *see* re-
red-dō, -dere, -didī, -ditus [red-, dō]: give back, return, restore; render; give, bestow
red-eō, -īre, -iī, -itūrus [red-, 2.eō]: go back, return; be restored, revert
red-igō, -igere, -ēgī, -āctus [red-, agō]: drive back, force back; reduce
red-imō, -imere, -ēmī, -ēmptus [red-, emō]: buy, purchase, procure
reditus, -ūs, *m.* [redeō]: return; income, revenue
re-dūcō, -dūcere, -dūxī, -ductus [re-, dūcō]: lead back, bring back; draw back, replace, sheathe
referō, referre, rettulī, relātus [re-, ferō]: bear back, bring back, bend back; restore, pay back; gratiam referō: show gratitude, return thanks; report, announce, relate: enter to one's credit, credit
rēfert, rēferre, rētulit, *impers.* [rēs, ferō]: it is of advantage, it concerns
re-fugiō, -fugere, -fūgī [re-, fugiō]: run away, escape
regiō, -iōnis, *f.* [regō]: region, district, territory
rēgius, -a, -um, *adj.* [rēx]: of a king, royal, regal
rēgnō, -âre, -âvī, -âtus [rēgnum]: be king, rule, reign
rēgnum, -ī, *n.* [rēx]: royal power, kingship; kingdom
regō, regere, rēxī, rēctus: direct, guide; rule, govern
re-gredior, -gredī, -gressus sum [re-, gradior]: go back, turn back, return
re-iciō, -icere, -iēcī, -iectus [re-, iaciō]: throw back, hurl back; refer, turn over; refuse, reject

religiō, -iōnis, *f.*: religious scruple, fear of the gods; worship; cult, religion
re-linquō, -linquere, -līquī, -lictus [re-, linquō]: leave behind, abandon, leave
rēliquiae, rēliquiārum, *f. pl.* [reliquus]: remains
reliquus, -a, -um, *adj.* [relinquō]: left, left over, remaining; other
re-maneō, -manēre, -mānsī, -mānsūrus [re-, maneō]: stay behind, remain
remedium, remediī, *n.* [re-, medeor]: remedy, antidote, medicine; help, cure
re-mittō, -mittere, -mīsī, -missus [re-, mittō]: send back, return; loosen, relax; decrease, abate, remit
re-mollēscō, -mollēscere [re-, mollēscō (*soften*): mollis]: grow soft, soften; be enervated, lose strength
remōtus, -a, -um: *see* removeō
re-moveō, -movēre, -mōvī, -mōtus [re-, moveō]: move back, take away, remove; *p.p.p.* remōtus, -a, -um: removed; distant, remote
remūneror, -ārī, -ātus sum [re-, mūneror (*bestow*): mūnus]: repay, reward, remunerate
reor, rērī, ratus sum: reckon, calculate; think, suppose
repellō, repellere, reppulī, repulsus [re-, pellō]: drive back, repel
repente, *adv.* [repēns (*sudden*)]: suddenly, unexpectedly
repentīnus, -a, -um, *adj.* [repēns (*sudden*)]: sudden, unexpected
reperiō, reperīre, repperī, repertus [re , pariō]: find, discover
re-petō, -petere, -petīvī, -petītus [re-, petō]: seek again, demand back, seek as one's due; memoriā repetō: recall; poenās repetō: inflict penalty in revenge
re-pleō, -plēre, -plēvī, -plētus [re-, *pleō (*fill*)]: fill again; fill up
repraesentō, -âre, -âvī, -âtus [re-,

praesentō (*present*): praesēns]: make present, do immediately

re-primō, -primere, -pressī, pressus [re-, premō]: press back, check, restrain, repress

repudiō, -āre, -āvī, -ātus: reject, disdain, repudiate

repulsa, -ae, *f.* [repellō]: rejection, repulse, defeat

re-quīrō, -quīrere, -quīsīvī, -quīsītus [re-, quaerō]: seek again, search for; ask, inquire for; need, require

rēs, reī, *f.:* thing, object, matter, affair, circumstance, deed, event; wealth; **rēs cibāria:** food supply; **rēs frūmentāria:** grain supply; **rēs gestae:** exploits; **rēs pūblica:** commonwealth, state, republic; official business; the public interest, the common weal; **rēs uxōria:** matrimony

re-scindō, -scindere, -scidī, -scissus [re-, scindō (*cut*)]: tear open

re-scrībō, -scrībere, -scrīpsī, -scrīptus [re-, scrībō]: enroll anew, reenlist; **ad equum rescrībō:** *in military sense*, transfer to the cavalry; *in civil sense*, raise to the rank of knight

reservō, -āre, -āvī, -ātus [re-, servō (*save*)]: keep back, reserve

re-sideō, -sidēre, -sēdī, -sessūrus [re-, sedeō]: sit back, remain seated; rest

re-sistō, -sistere, -stitī [re-, sistō]: stand still, halt; *w. dat.*, resist, oppose

re-spondeō, -spondēre, -spondī, -spōnsūrus [re-, spondeō]: *w. dat.:* answer, reply

respōnsum, -ī, *n.* [respondeō]: answer, reply

rēs pūblica: *see* **rēs**

re-spuō, -spuere, -spuī, -spūtus [re-, spuō (*spit*)]: reject, spurn, refuse

re-stituō, -stituere, -stituī, -stitūtus [re-, statuō]: restore, renew

re-surgō, -surgere, -surrēxī, -sur-

rēctūrus [re-, surgō (*rise*)]: rise again, rise

re-tineō, -tinēre, -tinuī, -tentus [re-, teneō]: hold back, retain; hold in check, restrain

re-trahō, -trahere, -trāxī, -tractus [re-, trahō]: draw back, withdraw, remove; rescue

reus, -ī, *m.* [rēs]: defendant, accused, prisoner

re-vellō, -vellere, -vellī, -vulsus [re-, vellō (*tear*)]: pluck away, tear off; tear apart

re-vertō, -vertere, -vertī, -versus [re-, vertō]: turn back, turn about; *pass.*, return, come back

re-vinciō, -vincīre, -vīnxī, -vīnctus [re-, vinciō]: tie back, bind, fasten

revolō, -āre [rĕ-, 2.volō]: fly back

rēx, rēgis, *m.:* king

Rhēnus, -ī, *m.:* the Rhine

rhētor, rhētoris, *m.:* rhetorician; teacher of rhetoric

Rhodanus, -ī, *m.:* the Rhône

Rhodius, -a, -um, *adj.:* of Rhodes, Rhodian (rōds, rō'dĭán)

rīca, -ae, *f.:* veil

rīdeō, rīdēre, rīsī, rīsus: laugh; laugh at, deride

rīma, -ae, *f.:* cleft, crack

rīpa, -ae, *f.:* bank, shore

rīsus, -ūs, *m.* [rīdeō]: laughter

rīvus, -ī, *m.:* small stream, brook

rōdō, rōdere, rōsī, rōsus: gnaw

rogō, -āre, -āvī, -ātus: ask, question; request; request the loan of; invite; **sententiam rogō:** ask for one's vote

Rōma, -ae, *f.:* Rome

Rōmānus, -a, -um, *adj.:* Roman

rōstrum, -ī, *n.* [rōdō]: beak, bill

ruber, rubra, rubrum, *adj.:* red

rudis, -e, *adj.:* rough, rude

Rūfīnus: *see* **Cornēlius**

rūgōsus, -a, -um, *adj.* [rūga (*wrinkle*)]: wrinkled

ruīna, -ae, *f.* [ruō (*rush down*)]: downfall; avalanche; ruin, destruction rūmor, rūmōris, *m.*: common talk, report, rumor

rumpō, rumpere, rūpī, ruptus: break, burst, split; destroy, annul, cancel

rūrsum *or* rūrsus, *adv.* [re-, versus (*turned*): vertō]: turned back, backwards; again, anew, once more

rūs, rūris, *n.*: country (*as contrasted with city*)

rūsticus, -a, -um, *adj.* [rūs]: of the country, rural, rustic; *subst. m.*, countryman, peasant, farmhand

Rutēnī, Rutēnōrum, *m. pl.*: *a Gallic people* [rᵫtē'nī)

saccus, -ī, *m.*: sack, bag

sacellum, -ī, *n.* [sacrum (*temple*): sacer]: little sanctuary, chapel

sacer, sacra, sacrum, *adj.*: sacred

sacrārium, sacrāriī, *n.* [sacer]: shrine

sacrificium, sacrificiī, *n.* [sacrificus (*sacrificial*): sacer, faciō]: sacrifice

sacrificō, -āre, -āvī, -ātus [sacrificus (*sacrificial*): sacer, faciō]: sacrifice

saepe, *adv.*: often

saepenumerō, *adv.* [saepe, numerus]: oftentimes, often

saepiō, saepīre, saepsī, saeptus [saepēs (*enclosure*)]: enclose, surround

saetōsus, -a, -um, *adj.* [saeta (*bristle*)]: bristly, bristling

saeviō, saevīre, saeviī, saevītūrus [saevus (*fierce*)]: rage

Salamīnius, -a, -um, *adj.*: of Salamis, *an island near Attica* (săl'-ămĭs)

saliō, salīre, saluī: leap, jump

saltus, -ūs, *m.*: woodland, forest-pasture

salūbris, -e, *adj.* [salūs]: healthful, wholesome

salum, -ī, *n.*: open sea, high sea

salūs, salūtis, *f.* [*cp.* salvus]: health; safety, welfare; salūtem dīcō: send greeting

salūtō, -āre, -āvī, -ātus [salūs]: greet, hail

salvus, -a, -um, *adj.*: sound, safe, uninjured

Samnītēs, Samnītium, *m. pl.*: *an Italic people* (săm'nīts)

sanciō, sancīre, sānxī, sānctus [*cp.* sacer]: make sacred; establish, ordain

sānctitās, -ātis, *f.* [sānctus]: sanctity; virtue, integrity

sānctus, -a, -um, *adj.* [sanciō]: sacred, holy; venerable

sanguinolentus, -a, -um, *adj.* [sanguis (*blood*)]: blood-stained, bloody

saniēs, *acc.* saniem, *f.*: bloody matter, gore

sānitās, -ātis, *f.* [sānus (*sound*)]: soundness; discretion, sanity

sapiēns, *gen.* sapientis, *adj.* [sapiō (*be wise*)]: wise, sage; *subst. m.*, sage, wise man

sarcina, -ae, *f.*: pack, baggage

satiō, -āre, -āvī, -ātus [satis]: satisfy, satiate

satira, -ae, *f.*: poetic miscellany, satire

satis, *indecl. adj. and adv.*: enough, sufficient; sufficiently; satis faciō: make amends; satis habeō: be satisfied

satisfactiō, -iōnis, *f.* [satis, faciō]: excuse, apology, amends

sauciō, -āre, -āvī, -ātus [saucius (*wounded*)]: wound

saxulum, -ī, *n.* [saxum (*stone*)]: little stone

scaena, -ae, *f.*: stage, scene

scandō, scandere: climb, ascend

scateō, scatēre: bubble over, gush forth

scelerātus, -a, -um, *adj.* [scelerō (*desecrate*): scelus (*crime*)]: impious, wicked, vicious

scelestus, -a, -um, *adj.* [scelus (*crime*)]: impious, wicked, vicious

scientia, -ae, *f.* [sciēns (*knowing*): sciō]: knowledge, science

scīlicet, *adv.* [scīre, licet]: you may

know, evidently, of course, no doubt

sciō, scīre, scīvī, scītus: know, know how

Scīpiō, Scīpiōnis, m.: see Cornēlius

scītum, -ī, n. [scīscō (decree): sciō]: decree, statute

scītus, -a, -um, adj. [scīscō (learn): sciō]: knowing, clever, skillful

scopulus, -ī, m.: rock, crag

scrībō, scrībere, scrīpsī, scrīptus: write; report

scrīptor, scrīptōris, m. [scrībō]: writer

scrīptum, -ī, n. [scrībō]: writing, book

scrūtor, -ārī, -ātus sum: examine, investigate

scūtum, -ī, n.: shield, buckler

sē-, prefix: away, apart

sē and sēsē: see suī

sēcessus, -ūs, m. [sēcēdō (withdraw): sē-, cēdō]: separation, withdrawal

sēcrētus, -a, -um, adj. [sēcernō (separate): sē-, cernō]: separated; secret; adv. sēcrētō: in secret, secretly

secundum, prep. w. acc. [secundus]: following; according to; in favor of; in addition to

secundus, -a, -um, adj. [sequor]: following, next, second

secūris, secūris, f. [secō (cut)]: axe

sēcūrus, -a, -um, adj. [sē-, cūra]: free from care, relieved of anxiety

sed, conj. [cp. sē-]: but

sēdecim, indecl. num. adj. [sex, decem]: sixteen

sedeō, sedēre, sēdī, sessūrus: sit

sēdēs, sēdis, f. [sedeō]: seat; abode, habitation

sēdō, -āre, -āvī, -ātus [cp. sedeō]: settle, allay, appease

seges, segetis, f.: grain-field; standing grain, crop

sēgregō, -āre, -āvī, -ātus [sē-, grex]: set apart, separate

Seleucus Nicānōr: a king of Syria (sělū'cǔs nǐcā'nôr)

sēlībra, -ae, f. [sē- (for sēmi-, half), lībra]: half-pound

sēmanimus = sēmianimus

semel, adv.: once

sēmentis, sēmentis, f. [sēmen (seed): serō (sow)]: sowing; growing crops, young crops

sēmet: see suī and -met

sēmianimus, -a, -um, adj. [sēmi- (half), anima]: half-alive, half-dead

semper, adv. [cp. semel]: ever, always

senātor, senātōris, m. [senātus]: senator

senātus, -ūs, m. [senex]: senate

senex, senis, m.: old man

sēnsim, adv. [sentiō]: just perceptibly, gradually

sēnsus, -ūs, m. [sentiō]: perception, feeling; sense

sententia, -ae, f. [sentiō]: opinion, judgment; decision, vote; vein, tenor; sententiam ferō: pass judgment; sententiam rogō: ask for one's vote

sentiō, sentīre, sēnsī, sēnsus: feel, perceive; decide

sēparō, -āre, -āvī, -ātus [sē-, parō]: divide, separate

septimus, -a, -um, adj. [septem (seven)]: seventh

septingentī, -ae, -a, num. adj. [septem (seven), centum]: seven hundred

sepulcrum, -ī, n. [sepeliō (bury)]: tomb, sepulchre

Sēquanī, Sēquanōrum, m. pl.: a Gallic people (sěk'wànī)

sequor, sequī, secūtus sum: follow

sērius, -a, -um, adj.: grave, earnest, serious

sermō, sermōnis, m.: conversation, talk

Q. Sertōrius: an insurgent Roman general (quĭn'tǔs sěrtō'rǐǔs)

sērus, -a, -um, adj.: late

servīlis, -e, adj. [servus]: of a slave, of slaves, servile

servīo, servīre, servīvī, servītūrus [servus], w. dat.: be a slave, serve
servitūs, servitūtis, f. [servus]: slavery, servitude
servus, -ī, m.: slave
sēscentī, -ae, -a, num. adj. [sex, centum]: six hundred
sestertius, sestertiī, gen. pl. sestertium, m.: small coin, sesterce; sestertia, n. pl.: thousands of sesterces
sētius, adv.: less; nihilō sētius: nevertheless
sevērus, -a, -um, adj.: strict, austere, severe
sex, indecl. num. adj.: six
sī, conj.: if; quod sī: but if
Sibyllīnus, -a, -um, adj.: of the Sibyl, Sibylline (sĭb'ĭl, sĭb'ĭlīn)
sīc, adv.: thus, so
Sicānī, Sicānōrum, m. pl.: early inhabitants of Sicily (sĭcā'nī)
siccō, -āre, -āvī, -ātus [siccus (dry)]: dry
Sicilia, -ae, f.: Sicily
sīcut or sīcutī, adv. [sīc, ut]: so as, just as, as; like; for instance
sīdus, sīderis, n.: constellation, star
significō, -āre, -āvī, -ātus [signum, faciō]: make signs, show by signs; mean, signify
signō, -āre, -āvī, -ātus [signum]: affix a seal to, seal
signum, -ī, n.: mark, sign; signal; seal; standard, banner; signa ferō: proceed
silentium, silentiī, n. [silēns (silent): sileō (be silent)]: silence
silva, -ae, f.: woods, forest
silvestris, -e, adj. [silva]: of a forest; overgrown with forests, wooded
similis, -e, adj. [cp. semel]: like, similar; vērī similis: like the truth, plausible; adv. similiter: in like manner
similitūdō, similitūdinis, f. [similis]: likeness, resemblance
sīmius, sīmiī, m.: ape, monkey

simpliciter, adv. [simplex (simple)]: simply, plainly, frankly
simul, adv. [cp. similis]: at the same time, at once, together; likewise; simul atque: as soon as
simulācrum, -ī, n. [simulō]: likeness, image, statue
simulātiō, -iōnis, f. [simulō]: pretence, simulation; pretended concern
simulō, -āre, -āvī, -ātus [similis]: imitate, copy; feign, pretend
sīn, conj. [sī, 1.ne]: but if
sincērus, -a, -um, adj.: pure, whole; truthful, sincere
sine, prep. w. abl.: without
singulī, -ae, -a, distr. num. adj. [cp. semel]: one at a time, one each, single
sinister, sinistra, sinistrum, adj.: left (as opposed to right)
sinō, sinere, sivī, situs: put down, place, set; p.p.p. situs, -a, -um: placed, situated, located
sinus, -ūs, m.: fold
sistō, sistere, stitī, status [cp. stō]: cause to stand, place; w. reflex. pron., present oneself, appear
sitiō, sitīre, sitīvī [sitis]: thirst, be thirsty
sitis, sitis, f.: thirst
situs, -a, -um: see sinō
sīve, conj. [sī, -ve]: or if; sīve . . . sīve: whether . . . or
sōbrius, -a, -um, adj. [sē-, ēbrius (drunk)]: sober
societās, -ātis, f. [socius]: association, partnership
socius, sociī, m.: comrade, associate; ally
Sōcratēs, Sōcratis, m.: a Greek philosopher (sŏc'rātēş)
Sōcraticus, -a, -um, adj.: of Socrates, Socratic (sŏcrăt'ĭc)
sōl, sōlis, m.: the sun
sōlācium, sōlāciī, n. [sōlor (console)]: consolation
soleō, solēre, solitus sum: be accustomed

256 VOCABULARY

sōlitūdō, sōlitūdinis, *f.* [sōlus]: solitude, wilderness
sollemnis, -e, *adj.:* sacred, solemn
sollers, *gen.* sollertis, *adj.* [sollus (*all*), ars]: skilled, expert
sollertia, -ae, *f.* [sollers]: skill, expertness
sollicitus, -a, -um, *adj.* [sollus (*all*), citus (*disturbed*): cieō (*disturb*)]: agitated, disturbed
sōlum, *adv.* [sōlus]: only
sōlus, -a, -um, *adj.:* alone, only, sole
solvō, solvere, solvī, solūtus [sē-, luō (*loose*)]: unfasten, untie; dissolve, break up; set free, acquit, absolve; pay, discharge
somnium, somniī, *n.* [somnus (*sleep*)]: dream
sonipēs, *gen.* sonipedis, *adj.* [sonus, pēs]: with resounding hoof; *subst. m.*, horse, steed
sonōrus, -a, -um, *adj.* [sonor (*noise*): sonus]: loud, resounding
sonus, -ī, *m.:* sound, noise
Sophoclēs, Sophoclis, *m.:* a Greek playwright (sŏf'ŏclēs)
soror, sorōris, *f.:* sister
sors, sortis, *f.:* lot, drawing of lots
spargō, spargere, sparsī, sparsus: scatter, strew
Sparta, -ae, *f.:* a Greek city (spär'tà)
spatium, spatiī, *n.:* space, room
speciēs, *acc.* speciem, *f.* [speciō]: sight, look; appearance, semblance, show; splendor, beauty
speciō, specere, spexī, spectus: look, see (*in classical Latin found only in compounds*)
spectō, -āre, -āvī, -ātus [speciō]: look, at, behold; look on; look towards, be intended for; regard, consider
speculor, -ārī, -ātus sum [specula (*watch-tower*): speciō]: spy; observe, explore
speculum, -ī, *n.* [speciō]: mirror
specus, -ūs, *m.:* cave, cavern
spernō, spernere, sprēvī, sprētus: despise, reject, spurn

spērō, -āre, -āvī, -ātus [spēs]: hope
spēs, speī, *f.:* hope
spīritus, -ūs, *m.* [spīrō]: breath; life; high spirit, haughtiness
spīrō, -āre, -āvī, -ātus: breathe, live
splendor, splendōris, *m.* [splendeō (*shine*)]: magnificence, splendor
spoliō, -āre, -āvī, -ātus [spolium (*spoil*)]: rob, despoil, plunder; sully
spondeō, spondēre, spopondī, spōnsus: assume an obligation, become surety, vouch, promise
*spōns, *spontis, *f.:* free will, accord
spōnsor, spōnsōris, *m.* [spondeō]: surety, guarantor
stadium, stadiī, *n.:* race-course, stadium
stāgnum, -ī, *n.:* standing water, lake, pool, swamp
statim, *adv.* [stō]: on the spot, immediately, at once
statiō, -iōnis, *f.* [stō]: position, abode, residence
statua, -ae, *f.* [*cp.* stō]: statue
statuō, statuere, statuī, statūtus [status]: set up, erect, establish, ordain
status, -ūs, *m.* [stō]: standing; position, status
stimulō, -āre, -āvī, -ātus [stimulus (*spur*)]: spur on, incite, stimulate
stīpendiārius, -a, -um, *adj.* [stīpendium]: paying tribute, tributary
stīpendium, stīpendiī, *n.:* tribute, tax
stirps, stirpis, *f.:* stock, stem, root; race, family, lineage, origin, source
stō, stāre, stetī, statūrus: stand; *w. abl.*, abide by
strāmentum, -ī, *n.* [sternō (*strew*)]: straw, straw bedding
strēnuus, -a, -um, *adj.:* vigorous, strenuous
struō, struere, strūxī, strūctus: construct, build
studeō, studēre, studuī, *w. dat.:* be

eager, be zealous; apply oneself; endeavor, try; desire, wish
studiōsus, -a, -um, *adj.* [studium]: eager, zealous, desirous
studium, studiī, *n.* [studeō]: zeal, eagerness, enthusiasm; desire; pursuit; study
stultus, -a, -um, *adj.:* stupid
stupe-faciō, -facere, -fēcī, -factus [stupeō (*be stunned*), faciō]: stun, stupefy
stupor, stupōris, *m.* [stupeō (*be stunned*)]: dullness, stupidity
suadeō, suadēre, suāsī, suāsūrus, *w. dat.:* advise, recommend, urge, persuade
suāvior, -ārī [suavium (*kiss*): suavis (*sweet*)]: kiss
sub (*in compounds, sometimes* subs), *prep. w. acc. and abl.: w. acc.,* to a place under, under, beneath; towards, just before; *w. abl.,* under, below, beneath; in, during; *in compounds,* a little, somewhat
sub-dō, -dere, -didī, -ditus, [sub, dō]: put under, place below
subdolus, -a, -um, *adj.* [sub, dolus]: crafty, deceitful
sub-eō, -īre, -iī, -itūrus [sub, 2.eō]: go under, approach; undergo, submit to; enter
sub-iciō, -icere, -iēcī, -iectus [sub, iaciō]: throw under, place under; substitute
subinde, *adv.* [sub, inde]: repeatedly, often
subitus, -a, -um, *adj.* [subeō]: sudden; *adv.* subitō: suddenly, unexpectedly
sublātus: *see* tollō
sublevō, -āre, -āvī, -ātus [sub, levō]: lift from beneath, raise, support; help, assist
sublimis, -e, *adj.:* lofty, high
subministrō, -āre, -āvī, -ātus [sub, ministrō]: furnish, supply
subs-: *see* sub
sub-sequor, -sequī, -secūtus sum

[sub, sequor]: follow after, follow up
subsidium, subsidiī, *n.:* support, aid, protection
sub-trahō, -trahere, -trāxī, -tractus [sub, trahō]: draw from below, draw off; take away, remove
sub-vertō, -vertere, -vertī, -versus [sub, vertō]: overturn, overthrow
suc-cēdō, -cēdere, -cessī, -cessūrus [sub, cēdō]: go below, come under; get close to, draw near; succeed
succendō, succendere, succendī succēnsus: set on fire; inflame
Suebus, -a, -um, *adj.:* Suebian, of the Suebi; *subst. m. pl.,* the Suebi, a Germanic people (swē'bĭán, swē'-bĭ)
suffrāgium, suffrāgiī, *n.:* vote; suffrāgium ferō: cast a vote
suī, *dat.* sibi, *acc. and abl.* sē *or* sēsē, *reflex. pron.:* himself, herself, itself, themselves; inter sē: among themselves, with one another
Sulla: *see* Cornēlius
sum, esse, fuī, futūrus; *imperf. subjv. often* forem, forēs, *etc.; fut. infin. often* fore: be, exist
summa, -ae, *f.* [summus]: chief place, highest rank, supremacy, supreme control; sum, total, whole
sum-moveō, -movēre, -mōvī, -mō-tus [sub, moveō]: move out of the way, send away
summus, -a, -um, *adj.:* uppermost, highest, supreme
sūmō, sūmere, sūmpsī, sūmptus: take; take upon oneself, assume; exact, inflict
sūmptuōsus, -a, -um, *adj.* [sūmptus (*expense*): sūmō]: expensive, sumptuous
super, *adv. and prep. w. acc.:* above, over, upon; about, concerning; beyond, in addition
superbia, -ae, *f.* [superbus]: pride, arrogance

superbus, -a, -um, *adj.* [super]: proud, haughty, arrogant

superior, superius, *adj.* [superus (*higher*): super]: higher, upper; former

superō, -āre, -āvī, -ātus [superus (*higher*): super]: overcome, surpass, defeat; **vītā superō:** survive

superstes, *gen.* **superstitis,** *adj.* [superstō (*stand over*): super, stō]: surviving

super-sum, -esse, -fuī [super, sum]: be left, remain; survive

supplex, *gen.* **supplicis,** *adj.:* beseeching, suppliant

supplicium, supplicii, *n.* [supplex]: punishment, penalty; **supplicium sūmō:** inflict punishment

supportō, -āre, -āvī, -ātus [sub, portō]: convey, bring up; supply

suprā, *adv. and prep. w. acc.* [superus (*higher*): super]: above, over; before; on top of

sur-ripiō, -ripere, -ripuī, -reptus [sub, rapiō]: snatch away, steal

sūs, suis, *m. and f.:* swine; boar, sow

susceptiō, -iōnis, *f.* [suscipiō]: undertaking; taking over, assumption

sus-cipiō, -cipere, -cēpī, -ceptus [subs-, capiō]: undertake, assume

sus-pendō, -pendere, -pendī, -pēnsus [subs-, pendō]: hang up, suspend

1.suspiciō, suspicere, suspexī, suspectus [sub, speciō]: suspect

2.suspiciō, -iōnis, *f.* [*cp.* 1.suspiciō]: suspicion; **in suspiciōnem veniō:** fall under suspicion

suspicor, -ārī, -ātus sum [sub, *cp.* speciō]: suspect

sus-tineō, -tinēre, -tinuī, -tentus [subs-, teneō]: sustain, maintain; bear, endure, tolerate

sustulī: *see* **tollō**

suus, -a, -um, *reflex. poss. adj.* [suī]: his own, her own, its own, their own; his, her, its, their

synanchē, synanchēs, *f.:* constriction of the throat, sore throat

T.:Titus (tī'tŭs)

taberna, -ae, *f.:* shop, store; tavern, inn

tabernāculum, -ī, *n.* [taberna]: tent

tabula, -ae, *f.:* board, plank; writing-tablet, record; placard

tabulātum, -ī, *n.* [tabulātus (*made of planks*): tabula]: floor, story

taceō, tacēre, tacuī, tacitus: be silent, keep quiet

tacitus, -a, -um, *adj.* [taceō]: silent, quiet; secret

taedium, taediī [taedet (*it disgusts*)]: weariness, disgust

Taenarum, -ī, *n.:* a promontory and town in Laconia (tē'nărŭm)

talentum, ī, *n.:* talent, a Greek standard of weight

tālis, -e, *adj.:* such; **tālis . . . quālis:** such . . . as, in the same guise as

tam, *adv.:* so, in such a degree; **tam . . . quam:** as . . . as, so . . . as, so much as, as well as

tamen, *adv.* [tam]: nevertheless, however, yet

tametsī, *conj.* [tam, etsī]: although, though

tamquam, *adv.* [tam, quam]:as much as, just as; as if, so to speak

tandem, *adv.:* at length, at last, finally; *in impatient questions,* pray, . . . in the world

tangō, tangere, tetigī, tāctus: touch; affect, stir, move

tantopere, *adv.* [tantus, opus]: so greatly, to such an extent

tantus, -a, -um, *adj.:* so great, so large, such; **tantus . . . quantus:** as much . . . so much; as large . . . as

Tarquinius Superbus: Tarquin the Proud, *last king of Rome* (tär-quĭn'ĭŭs sŭpĕr'bŭs, tär'quĭn)

taurus, -ī, *m.:* bull

Taurus: *see* **Calvisius**

tēctum, -ī, *n.* [tēctus]: house, dwelling; roof

tēctus, -a, -um, *adj.* [tegō (cover)]: covered, roofed; hidden, concealed

tēlum, -ī, *n.:* missile weapon, spear, dart; **extrā tēla:** out of range

temerārius, -a, -um, *adj.* [temerē]: rash, inconsiderate, precipitate

temerē, *adv.:* at random, rashly, without good reason

temperantia, -ae, *f.* [temperāns (*temperate*): temperō]: moderation, self-control, temperance

temperō, -āre, -āvī, -ātus: be moderate, abstain; *w. dat. of reflex. pron.,* restrain oneself, keep from

tempestīvus, -a, -um, *adj.* [tempestus (*in time*): tempus]: timely, seasonable, opportune

templum, -ī, *n.:* temple, shrine

temptō, -āre, -āvī, -ātus: try, attempt

tempus, temporis, *n.:* time; appointment

teneō, tenēre, tenuī: hold, keep; keep back, restrain

tener, tenera, tenerum, *adj.:* tender, soft

tenuis, -e, *adj.:* thin, slender

tenuitās, -ātis, *f.* [tenuis]: slenderness, thinness, poverty

ter, *num. adv.* [trēs]: three times, thrice

M. **Terentius Varrō:** *a Roman scholar* (mär'cŭs tĕrĕn'shĭŭs vär'ō)

tergum, -ī, *n.:* the back; **terga vertō:** turn back, flee, retreat

terra, -ae, *f.:* the earth; ground, earth; land, country, region

terrēnus, -a, -um, *adj.* [terra]: of earth, earthen

terreō, terrēre, terruī, territus: frighten, terrify

terrificus, -a, -um, *adj.* [terreō, faciō]: frightful, terrible

terror, terrōris, *m.* [terreō]: dread, terror, panic

tertius, -a, -um, *adj.* [trēs]: third

testāmentum, -ī, *n.* [testor]: testament, will

testimōnium, testimōniī, *n.* [testis]: evidence, testimony

testis, testis, *m. and f.:* witness

testor, -ārī, -ātus sum [testis]: bear witness, prove

testula, -ae, *f.* [testa (*potshard*)]: bit of baked earthenware, potsherd, ostracon; ostracism

Teutonī, Teutonōrum, *m. pl.:* a Germanic people (tū'tŏnī)

Thēbae, Thēbārum, *f. pl.:* Thebes, a city in Greece (thēbȿ)

Thēbānus, -a, -um, *adj.:* of Thebes, Theban (thē'băn)

Themistoclēs, Themistoclis, *m.:* a Greek statesman (thĕmĭs'tōclēȿ)

thēsaurus, -ī, *m.:* store-house, treasure-chamber, treasury

Ti.: Tiberius (tībē'rĭŭs)

tībia, -ae, *f.:* pipe, flute

tībīcen, tībīcinis, *m.* [tībia, canō]: piper, flute-player

tigillum, -ī, *n.* [tignum (*timber*)]: bar of wood, log

timeō, timēre, timuī: fear

timidus, -a, -um, *adj.* [timeō]: fearful, afraid, timid

Tīmocharēs, Tīmocharis, *m.:* an Ambracian (tīmŏc'ȧrēȿ)

timor, timōris, *m.* [timeō]: fear, dread

tintinnābulum, -ī, *n.* [tintinnō (*jingle*)]: bell

toga, -ae, *f.* [*cp.* tegō]: Roman cloak, toga

tolerō, -āre, -āvī, -ātus: tolerate, bear

tollō, tollere, sustulī, sublātus: lift, raise; take away, remove; *p. p. p.* **sublātus, -a, -um:** raised, high, shrill

tormentum, -ī, *n.* [torqueō (*twist*)]: torture, torment

Torquātus: *see* **Mānlius**

torquis, torquis, *f.* [torqueō (*twist*)]: twisted neck-chain, necklace

torreō, torrēre, torruī, tostus: roast

totidem, *indecl. num. adj.:* just as many, the same number of

tōtus, -a, -um, *adj.:* all, whole, entire

trabs, trabis, *f.:* beam

tractō, -āre, -āvī, -ātus [trahō]: touch, handle, treat

trā-dō, -dere, -didī, -ditus [trāns, dō]: hand over, hand; surrender; hand down, transmit, relate; ordain

trā-dūcō, -dūcere, -dūxī, -ductus, [trāns, dūcō]: lead across, carry over

tragicus, -a, -um, *adj.:* of tragedy, tragic

trahō, trahere, trāxī, tractus: draw, drag, drag along

trānō, -āre, -āvī [trāns, nō (*swim*)]: swim across

trāns, *prep. w. acc.:* across, over, beyond

trāns-currō, -currere, -currī, -cursūrus [trāns, currō]: run across; pass, elapse

trāns-eō, -īre, -iī, -itūrus [trāns, 2.eō]: go across, cross; pass by

trāns-ferō, -ferre, -tulī, -lātus [trāns, ferō]: bear across, carry over; transfer

trāns-igō, -igere, -ēgī, -āctus [trāns, agō]: drive through, pierce through

trānsmarīnus, -a, -um, *adj.* [trāns, marīnus (*of the sea*): mare]: from over the sea

trānsportō, -āre, -āvī, -ātus [trāns, portō]: carry over, transport

trecentī, -ae, a, *num. adj.* [trēs, centum]: three hundred

tredecim, *indecl. num. adj.* [trēs, decem]: thirteen

tremibundus, -a, -um, *adj.* [tremō (*tremble*)]: trembling, all a-flutter

trepidō, -āre, -āvī, -ātūrus [trepidus (*alarmed*)]: be alarmed, be in confusion

trēs, tria, *num. adj.:* three

Trēverī, Trēverōrum, *m. pl.: a Gallic people* (trĕv'ĕrī)

Tribocī, Tribocōrum, *m. pl.: a Germanic people* (trĭb'ōsī)

tribūnus, -ī, *m.* [tribus (*tribe*)]: tribune

tribuō, tribuere, tribuī, tribūtus [tribus (*tribe*)]: assign, allot; give, render, bestow

tribūtum, -ī, *n.* [tribuō]: tribute, tax

trīduum, -ī, *n.* [trēs, diēs]: period of three days, three days

triennium, trienniī, *n.* [trēs, annus]: period of three years, three years

trigeminus, -a, -um, *adj.* [trēs, geminus (*twin*)]: born three at a birth; *subst. m. pl.,* triplet-brothers

trīnī, -ae, -a, *distr. num. adj.* [trēs]: three each, three

triplex, *gen.* **triplicis,** *adj.* [trēs, *cp.* plectō (*weave*)]: threefold, triple

trīstis, -e, *adj.:* sad, gloomy; grim, stern

trīstitia, -ae, *f.* [trīstis]: sadness, gloom

trīticum, -ī, *n.* [trītus (*threshed*): terō (*thresh*)]: wheat

tū, tuī, *pers. pron.:* thou, you; *emphatic form* tūte: you yourself

tueor, tuērī, tūtus sum: gaze upon, behold, watch over, protect

M. Tullius Cicerō: *a Roman orator* (mär'cŭs tŭl'lŭs sĭs'ĕrō)

tum, *adv.:* then, at that time; tum, cum: at a time when, just when

tumeō, tumēre: swell, be swollen

tumultus, -ūs, *m.:* uproar, bustle, tumult; uprising, insurrection

tumulus, -ī, *m.* [*cp.* tumeō]: mound

tunc, *adv.* [tum]: then, at that time

tunica, -ae, *f.:* tunic

turba, -ae, *f.:* turmoil, disturbance; crowd, throng

turbō, -āre, -āvī, -ātus [turba]: disturb, agitate

turbulentus, -a, -um, *adj.* [turba]: disturbed, troubled

turpis, -e, *adj.:* ugly, unsightly; shameful, disgraceful, base

turris, turris, *f.:* tower

tūte: *see* tū

tūtor, -ārī, -ātus sum [tueor]: watch, guard, protect

tūtus, -a, -um, adj. [tueor]: guarded; safe, secure

tuus, -a, -um, poss. adj. [tū]: thy, thine; your, yours

tyrannus, -ī, m.: autocrat, absolute monarch; tyrant

über, gen. überis, adj. [über (breast)] fertile, rich

ubi, adv. and conj.: where; when; ubi prīmum: as soon as; in which, by which

ubīque, adv. [ubi, -que]: everywhere

ūllus, -am -um, adj. [ūnus]: any, anyone, anything

ultimus, -a, -um, adj.: farthest, most distant; subst. n. pl., farthest part

ultrā, adv. and prep. w. acc.: beyond

ultrō, adv.: beyond, on the other side (see citrō); voluntarily, spontaneously, of one's own accord

umerus, -ī, m.: shoulder

umquam, adv.: at any time, ever

ūnā, adv. [ūnus]: together

unda, -ae, f.: wave, billow

unde, adv.: from which place, whence, from whom, from which

ūndēvīcēnsimus, -a, -um, adj. [ūndēvīgintī (nineteen): ūnus, dē, vīgintī]: nineteenth

undique, adv. [unde, -que]: from all directions; on all sides

unguis, unguis, m.: nail, claw, hoof

ūnicē, adv. [ūnicus (sole): ūnus]: uniquely, especially, particularly

ūniversus, -a, -um, adj. [ūnus, versus (turned): vertō]: all together, all in one, whole, entire

ūnus, -a, -um, num. adj.: one; only

urbānus, -a, -um, adj. [urbs]: of the city, city-, urban; cultivated, urbane

urbicus, -a, -um, adj. [urbs]: of the city, city-, urban

urbs, urbis, f.: city

urgeō, urgēre, ursī: press, urge

urna, -ae, f.: urn, jar

ūrō, ūrere, ussī, ustus: burn

ursīnus, -a, -um, adj. [ursus (bear)]: of a bear, bear-like

usquam, adv.: anywhere, in anything, at all

usque, adv.: all the way, right on; even

ūsus, -ūs, m. [ūtor]: use; experience; advantage; ūsus est: there is need, it is necessary; ūsū venit: it happens; ex ūsū: advantageous

ut or utī, adv. and conj.: when; as; how; that, in order that, so that; after verbs of fearing, that . . . not

uter, utra, utrum, adj.: which of two, which, whichever

uterque, utraque, utrumque, adj. [uter, -que]: each, either, both; subst. m. pl., those on both sides

Uticēnsis, -e, adj.: see Porcius

ūtilis, -e, adj. [ūtor]: useful, advantageous

ūtilitās, -ātis, f. [ūtilis]: use, usefulness, advantage

ūtor, ūtī, ūsus sum, w. abl.: use, enjoy, take advantage of

utpote, adv. [ut, pote (able)]: as is possible, as being, namely

utrimque, adv. [uterque]: on both sides, on either side

utrum, adv. [uter]: introduces the first member of a disjunctive direct question; in indirect questions, whether

ūva, -ae, f.: grape, bunch of grapes

uxor, uxōris, f.: wife

uxōrius, -a, -um, adj. [uxor]: of a wife; rēs uxōria: matrimony

vacca, -ae, f.: cow

vadimōnium, vadimōniī, n. [vas (bail)]: bail-bond, bail, security

vador, -ārī, -ātus sum [vas (bail)]: bind over for appearance, accept security

vadum, -ī, n.: shallow place, ford; body of water, pond

vagor, -ārī, -ātus sum [vagus (wandering)]: wander, roam, travel

valeō, valēre, valuī, valitūrus: be strong, be powerful, be able, be well

Valerius Antiās: *a Roman historian,* Valerius of Antium (*a town of Latium*) (vălē'rĭŭs, ăn'shĭŭm)

C. Valerius Caburus: *a Gaul* (gā'yŭs vălē'rĭŭs căb'ŭrŭs)

M. Valerius Corvīnus: *a Roman hero* (mär'cŭs vălē'rĭŭs côrvī'nŭs)

C. Valerius Flaccus: *a Roman governor of Gaul* (gā'yŭs vălē'rĭŭs flăc'ŭs)

C. Valerius Procillus: *a Gaul* (gā'yŭs vălē'rĭŭs prōsĭl'ŭs)

validus, -a, -um, *adj.* [valeō]: strong; effective; well-founded, valid

valītūdō, valītūdinis, *f.* [valeō]: health

Vangionēs, Vangionum, *m. pl.: a Germanic people* (vănĭ'ōnēş)

vānus, -a, -um, *adj.:* empty, void; fruitless, vain; false, deceptive

Varrō, Varrōnis, *m.: see* Terentius

vāstō, -āre, -āvī, -ātus [vāstus]: devastate, ravage

vāstus, -a, -um, *adj.:* empty, desolate; vast, immense, enormous

vāticinātiō, -iōnis, *f.* [vāticinor (*prophesy*): vātēs (*prophet*)]: soothsaying, prophesy

-ve, *enclitic conj.:* or

vectigal, vectigālis, *n.:* tax, tribute

vectō, -āre [vehō]: bear, carry

vehemēns, *gen.* vehementis, *adj.:* violent, eager, active, strong, vehement

vehō, vehere, vexī, vectus: carry, convey

vel, *adv.* [volō]: even

vēlō, -āre, -āvī, -ātus [vēlum (*veil*)]: enfold, wrap, conceal

vēlōx, *gen.* vēlōcis, *adj.:* swift

velut *or* velutī, *adv. and conj.* [vel, ut]: just as, like; as, for example

vēnātiō, -iōnis, *f.* [vēnor]: hunting; hunting spectacle, beast-fight

vēnātor, vēnātōris, *m.* [vēnor]: hunter

vēnātus, -ūs, *m.* [vēnor]: hunting, hunt

vēndō, vēndere, vēndidī [vēnum, dō]: sell

venēnum, -ī, *n.:* poison

veneror, -ārī, -ātus sum: reverence, revere, worship, honor

venia, -ae, *f.:* kindness, favor, pardon, forgiveness

veniō, venīre, vēnī, ventūrus: come; ūsū venit: it happens

vēnor, -ārī, -ātus sum: hunt

venter, ventris, *m.:* belly, stomach

ventitō, -āre, -āvī [veniō]: come often, keep coming

vēnum, *acc. n.:* sale (*only in such expressions as* vēnum dō: offer for sale, sell)

venustās, -ātis, *f.* [venus (*charm*)]: loveliness; charm, grace

venustus, -a, -um, *adj.:* [venus (*charm*)]: lovely, charming, graceful

*verber, verberis, *n.:* lashing, flogging, beating

verbum, -ī, *n.:* word; verba faciō: speak, talk

verēcundus, -a, -um, *adj.* [vereor]: bashful, shy, modest, diffident

vereor, verērī, veritus sum: revere, respect; fear, dread

P. Vergilius Marō: Vergil, *a Roman epic poet* (pŭb'lĭŭs vērgĭl'ĭŭs mā'rō, vēr'gĭl)

vēritās, -ātis, *f.* [vērus]: truth

vērō: *see* vērus

versicolor, *gen.* versicolōris, *adj.* [vertō, color]: of changeable color, of various colors

versor, -ārī, -ātus sum [vertō]: be situated, be engaged, be

versus, -ūs, *m.* [vertō]: verse, line

versūtus, -a, -um, *adj.* [vertō]: adroit, shrewd, clever

vertex, verticis, *m.* [vertō]: whirlpool, vortex; top, peak, summit

vertō, vertere, vertī, versus: turn; *pass.*, revolve, hinge, depend; be involved

vērus, -a, -um, *adj.:* true, real, actual; right, just; *subst. n.,* truth;

vērī similis: like the truth, plausible; adv. vērō: in truth, truly; adv. vērum: truly; but, but yet

vēscor, vēscī, w. abl.: use as food, live on, eat

Vesontiō, -iōnis, m.: a town in Gaul, the modern Besançon (vĕsŏn'shĭō)

vesper, vesperī, m.: evening

vester, vestra, vestrum, poss. adj. [vōs]: your, yours

vestīgium, vestīgiī, n.: bottom of the foot, sole; footprint, trace; place, spot

vestīmentum, -ī, n. [vestiō]: clothing, garment

vestiō, vestīre, vestīvī, vestītus [vestis]: clothe

vestis, vestis, f.: clothing, garment

vestītus, -ūs, m. [vestiō]: clothing, clothes, attire

vetō, vetāre, vetuī, vetitus: forbid, prohibit

vetus, gen. veteris, adj.: old, aged; of former times, ancient

via, -ae, f.: way, road; march, journey; method, manner

viātor, viātōris, m. [via]: magistrate's attendant, court-officer, bailiff

vibrō, -āre, -āvī, -ātus: shake, brandish

vīcēnī, -ae, -a, distr. num. adj. [vīgintī]: twenty each, twenty

vīciēns, num. adv. [vīgintī]: twenty times

vīcīnus, -a, -um, adj. [vīcus (neighborhood)]: neighboring, near, in the vicinity; subst. m., neighbor

*vicis, vicis, f.: change, turn, chance; place, stead

victima, -ae, f.: victim

victor, victōris, m. [vincō]: conqueror, victor; in apposition, victorious

victoria, -ae, f. [victor]: victory

victus, -ūs, m. [vīvō]: manner of life; means of living, food

videō, vidēre, vīdī, vīsus: see; pass.,

seem, appear; pass. impers., seem good

vigilia, -ae, f. [vigil (awake): vigeō (be lively)]: time of keeping watch, watch (one-fourth of the night)

vigilō, -āre, -āvī, -ātūrus [vigil (awake): vigeō (be lively)]: watch, keep awake

vīgintī, indecl. num. adj.: twenty

vigor, vigōris, m. [vigeō (be lively)]: force, vigor

vīlicus, -ī, m. [vīlla]: overseer of an estate, steward

vīlis, -e, adj.: cheap; poor, trifling, worthless

vīlla, -ae, f.: country-house, farmhouse

vīmen, vīminis, n.: pliant twig, withe, osier

vinciō, vincīre, vīnxī, vīnctus: bind, fetter

vincō, vincere, vīcī, victus: conquer, defeat; be victorious; overcome

vinculum, -ī, n. [vinciō]: bond, fetter; pl., prison

vindicō, -āre, -āvī, -ātus [vindex (maintainer)]: claim; in lībertātem vindicō: set free; avenge, revenge, punish

vindicta, -a, f. [vindex (maintainer)]: vengeance, revenge

vinea, -ae, f. [vīnum]: vine

vīnum, -ī, n.: wine

violentus, -a, -um, adj. [vīs]: impetuous, violent

violō, -āre, -āvī, -ātus [vīs]: dishonor, violate; mistreat

vir, virī, m.: man, male; husband; brave man, hero

vīrēs: see vīs

virga, -ae, f.: switch, rod, scourge; virgīs caedō: have beaten

virtūs, virtūtis, f. [vir]: manliness, courage; virtue, excellence; merit, value

vīs, acc. vim, f.: force, manifestation; pl. vīrēs, vīrium: strength, power

vīsō, vīsere, vīsī, vīsus [videō]: view, behold

vīta, -ae, f. [vīvus]: life; vītā superō: survive

vītis, vītis, f.: vine

vitium, vitiī, n.: fault, defect; offense, crime; vice

vītō, -āre, -āvī, -ātus: avoid, evade

vituperō, -āre, -āvī: censure, blame, disparage

vīvāx, gen. vīvācis, adj. [vīvō]: lively, vivacious

vīvō, vīvere, vīxī, vīctūrus: live

vīvus, -a, -um, adj. [vīvō]: alive

Vocciō, -iōnis, m.: a king of the Norici (vŏc'shĭō, nôr'ĭsĭ)

vocō, -āre, -āvī, -ātus [vŏx]: call, summon; name

Volcae Tectosagēs, Volcārum Tectosagum, f. pl.: a Gallic people (vŏl'sē tĕctŏs'ágēs)

1.volō, velle, voluī: wish, will, be willing

2.volō, -āre, -āvī, -ātūrus: fly

volucer, volucris, volucre, adj. [2.-volō]: flying, winged; subst. f., bird

volūmen, volūminis, n. [volvō (roll)]: roll, volume, book

voluntārius, -a, -um, adj. [voluntās]: willing, voluntary; subst. m., volunteer

voluntās, -ātis, f. [1.volō]: will, wish

voluptās, -ātis, f.: satisfaction, pleasure, delight

volūtō, -āre, -āvī, -ātus [volvō (roll)]: roll; w. reflex. pron., wallow

vōs, vestrum (or vestrī), pers. pron.: you

voveō, vovēre, vōvī, vōtus: vow, pledge, dedicate, consecrate

vōx, vōcis, f.: voice, sound; word, saying, speech

Vulcānus, -ī, m.: Vulcan, god of fire (vŭl'căn)

vulgō, adv. [vulgus]: among the multitude, generally, commonly, everywhere

vulgus, -ī, n. (acc. also vulgum, m.): multitude, common people, populace; crowd, mob

vulnerō, -āre, -āvī, -ātus [vulnus]: wound

vulnus, vulneris, n.: wound

vulpēcula, -ae, f. [vulpēs]: little fox, fox

vulpēs, vulpis, f.: fox

vultus, -ūs, m.: countenance, visage, features, mien, face

Xanthippē, Xanthippēs, f.: wife of Socrates (zăntĭp'ē)

Xerxēs, Xerxis, m.: a king of Persia (zērk'sēs)